America's Longest War

The United States and Vietnam, 1950–1975

FIFTH EDITION

George C. Herring
University of Kentucky

Mc
Graw
Hill
Education

AMERICA'S LONGEST WAR: THE UNITED STATES AND VIETNAM, 1950–1975, FIFTH EDITION

Published by McGraw-Hill Education, 2 Penn Plaza, New York, NY 10121. Copyright © 2014 by McGraw-Hill Education. All rights reserved. Printed in the United States of America. Previous editions © 2002, 1996, 1986, and 1979. No part of this publication may be reproduced or distributed in any form or by any means, or stored in a database or retrieval system, without the prior written consent of McGraw-Hill Education, including, but not limited to, in any network or other electronic storage or transmission, or broadcast for distance learning.

Some ancillaries, including electronic and print components, may not be available to customers outside the United States.

This book is printed on acid-free paper.

2 3 4 5 6 7 8 9 0 DOC/DOC 1 0 9 8 7 6 5 4

ISBN 978-0-07-351325-6
MHID 0-07-351325-3

Senior Vice President, Products & Markets: *Kurt L. Strand*
Vice President, General Manager: *Michael Ryan*
Vice President, Content Production & Technology Services: *Kimberly Meriwether David*
Executive Director of Development: *Lisa Pinto*
Managing Director: *Gina Boedeker*
Director: *Matthew Busbridge*
Marketing Specialist: *Alexandra Schultz*
Managing Development Editor: *Penina Braffman*
Brand Coordinator: *Adina Lonn*
Director, Content Production: *Terri Schiesl*
Senior Project Manager: *Joyce Watters*
Buyer: *Jennifer Pickel*
Cover Designer: *Studio Montage, St. Louis, MO*
Cover Image: *Top right: AP Images; Top left: Photographic collection of Wayne DeWitt Larabee; Bottom right: AP Images; Bottom left: John Filo*
Compositor: *Cenveo® Publisher Services*
Typeface: *10/12 Palatino LT Std*
Printer: *R. R. Donnelley*

All credits appearing on page or at the end of the book are considered to be an extension of the copyright page.

Library of Congress Cataloging-in-Publication Data

CIP data has been applied for.

www.mhhe.com

For
Christy, John, Andrew, Madeline, and Kennedy
and
Lisa, Peter, Caili, Jonathan, and Emma

Contents

Maps

To the Instructor

CHANGES TO THE FIFTH EDITION

The fifth edition of *America's Longest War* continues the tradition of explaining how the United States became involved in the Vietnam War and what the consequences of this involvement were for both the Vietnamese and the Americans. New features include:

- Extensive revision of chapters based on recent scholarship on North Vietnam, the origins of the Vietnamese revolution, the First Indochina War between the Viet Minh revolutionaries and France, and more.
- Additional material further characterizing Lyndon B. Johnson's and Richard Nixon's opinions and actions during wartime.
- Updates that take into account recent progress toward a United States–Vietnam strategic partnership and other major developments in the twenty-first century.

SUPPLEMENTS

Visit the Online Learning Center for a wealth of student and instructor resources. At www.mhhe.com/herring5e, you will find:

For the Student	For the Instructor
• Multiple Choice Quiz • Internet Exercise • Flash Cards • Review Questions • Additional Links	• Instructor's Manual • Powerpoint Lecture Slides

This edition of *America's Longest War* includes an exciting supplements package. Orders of new (versus used) textbooks help defray the cost of developing such supplements, which is substantial. Please consult your local McGraw-Hill representative for more information on any of the supplements.

CourseSmart
Learn Smart. Choose Smart.

This text is available as an eTextbook at www.CourseSmart.com. With CourseSmart, your students take advantage of significant savings off the cost of the print book, reduce their impact on the environment, and gain access to powerful Web tools for learning. CourseSmart eTextbooks can be viewed online or downloaded to a computer. The eTextbooks allow students to do full text searches, add highlighting and notes, and share notes with classmates.

 **create**

With McGraw-Hill Education's custom publishing platform Create, content from *America's Longest War* can be easily incorporated into a resource for any course. With Create you can **find** the content you want, **arrange** it in the way you teach your course, and **personalize** your book by selecting from various formats. Visit create.mcgraw-hill.com to get started!

About the Author

GEORGE C. HERRING has devoted much of his career to teaching and writing about the Vietnam War. He is widely recognized as the "dean" of American scholars of that conflict.

Dr. Herring taught his first class on the war in the spring of 1973 as the last U.S. troops were returning home from Vietnam. He began research on *America's Longest War* in 1975, shortly after the fall of Saigon. First published in 1979, the book quickly established itself as a standard work in the field and enjoyed extensive classroom use. Dr. Herring has published numerous articles and essays on the war and has lectured across the United States and abroad. His books include *The Secret Diplomacy of the Vietnam War: The Negotiating Volumes of the Pentagon Papers* (1983) and *LBJ and Vietnam: A Different Kind of War* (1994). At the University of Kentucky, he directed the work of scores of doctoral and M.A. students who have also contributed significantly to the history of the Vietnam War.

A native of Virginia, Dr. Herring graduated from Roanoke College. After service in the U.S. Navy, he earned M.A. and Ph.D. degrees at the University of Virginia. He taught at the University of Kentucky from 1969 until his retirement in 2005. In 1993–1994, he was a visiting professor at the U.S. Military Academy, West Point, and in 2001 Douglas Southall Freeman Professor of History at the University of Richmond. His most recent book is *From Colony to Superpower: U.S. Foreign Relations Since 1776* (2008), a volume in the Oxford History of the United States Series. He lives in Lexington, Kentucky.

Introduction

"Vietnam, Vietnam . . . there are no sure answers." So wrote the distinguished Southeast Asian correspondent Robert Shaplen in the midst of a long and traumatic war.[1]

More than four decades have passed since Shaplen penned those words. During that time, millions of pages of documents have been declassified and thousands of books and articles have been written. We now know a great deal more about the Vietnam War. New and exciting avenues of inquiry have been opened. It is possible to produce a much fuller, more nuanced, and multidimensional analysis.

One of the most important developments in Vietnam scholarship in recent years has been its internationalization. Studies based on European archives, for example, have shown how British and French pressures in the late 1940s contributed significantly to the first American commitment to Vietnam in 1950. New work drawing upon Soviet and Chinese archives has exposed with much greater clarity those nations' close ties with and massive aid to North Vietnam, giving some credence to the idea of a Communist monolith, a basic premise of the U.S. policy of global containment. These studies also confirm that at critical points in Soviet and Chinese relations with each other and North Vietnam, national interests generally prevailed over ideology, sometimes with significant consequences for the war.

[1]Robert Shaplen, *The Road from War: Vietnam: 1965–1970* (New York, 1970), p. 283.

The most important and exciting development in recent Vietnam War scholarship has been its Vietnamization (to borrow a word from the war itself). A new generation of scholars conversant in the Vietnamese language and trained in Vietnam's history and culture are now producing pathbreaking studies based on archival materials from both South and North Vietnam that fill out the story with rich detail and sometimes dramatically alter our interpretations. Vietnamese, who were largely invisible in the early American writing on the war, have moved to the forefront. This new Vietnam War history has given us a much fuller and more sophisticated view of South Vietnam in the era of Ngo Dinh Diem and the origins and evolution of the National Liberation Front insurgency. Although North Vietnam's major wartime archives remain tightly sealed, scholars have secured some very revealing documents, which, along with other sources, have enabled them to shed much light on policymaking in Hanoi, a topic once completely enshrouded in mystery. This new research makes answers to some of our questions more "sure," to use Shaplen's word, and answers to all of them more complex and still controversial.

I have attempted to integrate this new scholarship into the fifth edition of *America's Longest War*. I have extensively revised the first three chapters based on new information about the origins of the Vietnamese revolution, the First Indochina War between the Viet Minh revolutionaries and France, the coming to power of the Diem regime in South Vietnam and its increasingly tenuous and volatile relations with the United States. Chapters 4, 5, and 6 incorporate new scholarship clarifying North Vietnam's decision to launch an end-the-war offensive in 1964, its 1965–1966 response to U.S. escalation, and the 1968 Tet Offensive. Material has also been added from Lyndon Johnson's fascinating and often quite revealing telephone conversations elucidating his sometimes painful ambivalence about escalation of the war—and his fierce determination not to "lose" South Vietnam.

The last two chapters also incorporate important new material dealing with the climactic events leading up to the Easter Offensive of 1972, the abortive peace agreement of October 1972, the Paris Peace Accords of January 1973, and their implementation—and nonimplementation—in the two years leading to the fall of Saigon. In the last decade, vast new resources have also been made available for the Nixon presidency, including verbatim records of telephone

conversations and long, sometimes meandering, and always absorb-
ing White House policy discussions. They clarify—yet in some ways
render more murky—Nixon's handling of the war. They reveal a
great deal about his personality and mind-set while also making
clear the difficulties he labored under—some of his own making—
and the extent to which an extraordinarily complex war at times
reduced this sophisticated geopolitical thinker to improvisation.
After years of enmity, the United States and the Socialist Republic of
Vietnam are now discussing a strategic partnership. The last chapter
has been updated to take into account this and other major developments since the turn of the twenty-first century.

    This book seeks to place U.S. intervention in Vietnam in his-
torical perspective. I have given the most detailed treatment to the
years 1963–1973, the decade of heaviest American involvement. But
I have also devoted considerable attention to the period 1950–1963.
The assumptions that led to the crucial commitments took form
during those years. In addition, as CIA operative Edward Lansdale,
himself a key player in these events, once observed, without an
understanding of this formative period, "one is a spectator arriving
in the middle of a complex drama, without true knowledge of the
plot or of the identity and motivation of those in the drama."[2]

    This is not primarily a military history. Rather, in keeping with the
original purpose of the "America in Crisis" series, it attempts to integrate military, diplomatic, and political factors to explain America's
involvement and ultimate failure in Vietnam. My focus is on the
United States, but I have sought to provide sufficient discussion of
other nations to permit a rounded account of these major events.

    The questions I raised in the first edition of this book remain
central today. Why did the United States make such a vast commitment of blood and treasure in an area seemingly of so little importance to it, a place where before 1945 it had scarcely been involved?
What did it attempt to do during the quarter century of its involvement there? Why, despite the expenditure of more than $150 billion,
the loss of more than 58,000 lives, application of the most up-to-date
technology and a vast arsenal of destructive force did the world's
most powerful nation fail to achieve its objectives and suffer its first
defeat in war, a humiliating and deeply frustrating experience for a

---

[2]Quoted in W. Scott Thompson and Donaldson D. Frizzell, *The Lessons of Vietnam*
(New York, 1977), p. 43.

people accustomed to success. What have been the consequences for Americans, Vietnamese, and others of the nation's longest and most divisive war?

The U.S. war in Vietnam was a logical, if by no means inevitable, outgrowth of its Cold War world view and the policy of containment that Americans in and out of government accepted without serious question for more than two decades. The concept of containment of Communist expansion provided the broad parameters in which the Vietnam commitment took shape. Some writers have argued that the dictates of the Cold War consensus were so compelling that policymakers had little choice but to follow where they led. Recent scholarship has challenged this view. At each step on the long road to war alternatives were presented and discussed; choices were available. That presidents chose escalation was not primarily a result of blind obeisance to the dictates of ideology.

Why *were* such commitments made? It was not a case of overzealous advisers leading busy presidents blindly into a quagmire, as some early writers contended. The dangers and pitfalls were apparent. Nor was it a matter of hubris, of leaders plunging ahead certain of the efficacy of American power, confident that the United States would prevail, as it always had. Each president did take office believing that he could succeed where his predecessor had failed, a conviction that influenced early decisions in each administration. Even after they became more aware of the problems, some presidents may have clung to the belief that things would somehow work out in the end. In time, the commitment took on a life of its own, as important in and of itself as the aims it was originally designed to achieve. Presidents repeatedly held on in Vietnam in the belief that success or at least not failing was vital to maintaining America's credibility and world position.

Domestic politics was a crucial part of this calculation. Especially after Harry S. Truman's "loss" of China in 1949 and the huge political consequences that seemed to follow it, no president wanted to "lose" Vietnam. Policymakers repeatedly warned in the 1950s and 1960s that the fall of South Vietnam would set off the collapse of "dominoes" throughout Southeast Asia. Pointing to domestic political exigencies, Leslie Gelb argued many years ago that the White House was the "essential domino."[3]

---

[3]Leslie Gelb, "The Essential Domino: American Politics and Vietnam," *Foreign Affairs* 50 (April 1972): 459–475.

Personality also played a major role in the decision-making process. A strange sequence of events conspired to place Lyndon Baines Johnson and Richard Milhous Nixon in office at crucial points in the history of U.S. involvement in Vietnam. The personalities and leadership styles of these powerful and driven but deeply insecure individuals exerted crucial influence on the decisions to go to war, the manner in which the war was fought and ultimately ended, and especially the ways in which dissent at home was handled.

I still believe that U.S. intervention in Vietnam was misguided. It can be argued that the containment policy worked in Europe, contributing significantly, maybe even decisively, to the outcome of the Cold War. That said, I am persuaded that containment was misapplied in Vietnam. Obsessed with their determination to stop the advance of communism, and abysmally ignorant of the Vietnamese people and their history, Americans profoundly misread the nature of the struggle in Vietnam, its significance for their vital interests, and its susceptibility to their influence.

Defeat came hard, and in its aftermath it has been fashionable for many Americans to argue that victory could have been attained if the United States had only fought the war more decisively or in a different way. Such views are perhaps comforting for a people spoiled by success. They accord with what the English scholar D. W. Brogan once called "the illusion of American omnipotence," the belief, almost an article of faith among Americans, that this nation can do anything it sets its mind to. The enduring "lesson" of the Vietnam War is that power, no matter how great, has limits. American power in Vietnam was constrained by the Cold War, in whose name, ironically, it was fought. It was limited by the weakness of America's client, South Vietnam, and by the determination and willingness of its foes—North Vietnam and the National Liberation Front of South Vietnam—to pay any price. Given these circumstances, I do not believe that the war could have been won in any meaningful sense or at a moral or a material price Americans would—or should—have been willing to pay.

The costs of these mistakes—crimes, some would say—still stagger the imagination: 58,000 Americans dead, a deep wound to the national psyche, deep-seated and still lingering domestic divisions. For the Vietnamese, the cost was much, much higher, as many as 3 to 4 million dead, an estimated 300,000 North Vietnamese and NLF missing in action, the devastation of a beautiful country, and enormous ecological costs. These costs, many of which are still being paid today on both sides, make it urgent, especially in the wake of failed interventions in Iraq and Afghanistan, that Americans better understand one of the most traumatic events in their history and what it can tell them about themselves and how they deal with other peoples.

It has become conventional wisdom that the war in Afghanistan already has or will soon become the longest war in which the United States has been engaged. In an age when wars rarely begin with formal declarations and end with ceremonial surrenders, it can be very difficult to pinpoint exactly when they start and conclude. Former Secretary of Defense Robert Gates has suggested, for example, that the United States has fought two wars in Afghanistan, one in 2001–2002, a smashing success, the other beginning in 2006 with the resurgence of the Taliban.[4] Similarly, the wars in Vietnam lasted for almost three decades, beginning with Ho Chi Minh's declaration of independence from France on September 2, 1945, and ending with the fall of Saigon on April 30, 1975. During much of this time, the United States was deeply involved. By 1950, the assumptions upon which subsequent escalation was based were firmly set. By 1954, the United States was paying close to 80 percent of France's war against the Viet Minh. The Second Indochina War—what the Vietnamese call the American War— began in 1959–1960; the first Americans were killed in July 1959. In 1961–1962, John F. Kennedy "initiated the process through which the United States assumed a combat role," as Defense Department historian John Carland has put it, a process completed by Lyndon Johnson.[5] Because of its quarter century involvement in the wars in Indochina, the devastating impact of those wars at home and abroad, and consequences that lingered long after, Vietnam can still lay strong claim to the dubious distinction of being America's longest war.

[4]Terry H. Anderson, *Bush's Wars* (New York, 2011), p. 211.
[5]John Carland, "When Did the Vietnam War Start for the United States?" June 17, 2012, copy in author's possession.

Acknowledgments

Numerous people and institutions have assisted me in the preparation of this fifth edition. Lori Bradshaw of the S4 Carlisle Publishing Services, Penina Braffman and Joyce Watters of McGraw-Hill Education, and Harleen Chopra of Cenveo Publisher Services skillfully guided me through the process of revision.

From the time I began writing the first edition in 1976, I have relied heavily on the excellent resources of the University of Kentucky Libraries. I would like to thank Dr. Terry Birdwhistell, Dean of Libraries, and his capable librarians for their invaluable assistance over many years.

My former UK colleague Dr. John Carland has made major contributions to Vietnam War history with his work at the Army's Center of Military History, his compilation of the splendid *Foreign Relations of the United States* volumes for the Nixon–Ford years, and a most stimulating conference at the Department of State in September 2010. I have enjoyed and profited immensely from our lengthy discussions during get-togethers in Washington and via email and telephone. John has provided me with important information and helped me work through a number of difficult issues.

Steve Wrinn, the Director of the University Press of Kentucky, has offered encouragement and applied his formidable editorial skills to my writing.

I would especially like to thank those scholars who have so dramatically rewritten the history of the Vietnam War in recent years. Their work has made this revision far and away the most exciting—and challenging—of the four. I would like to make special mention of my colleague Hang Nguyen, whose prize-winning scholarship has forced us to rethink so much about the war and whose presence at UK keeps alive a tradition of interest in Southeast Asia going back before my time. We treasure the friendship of Hang and her spouse Paul Chamberlin, himself an accomplished historian of U.S. foreign relations.

I am grateful to reviewers of the fifth edition, who offered helpful suggestions for revision:

Anthony Edmonds, Ball State University
Robert Lee, STLCC–Meramec
Kyle Longley, Arizona State University
Gregory Olson, University of Wisconsin–Oshkosh
Patricia Richard, Metropolitan State College of Denver
Thomas Zeiler, University of Colorado–Boulder

Dottie Leathers typed the manuscript for the first edition of this book. The wonders of word-processing have spared her repeat performances on subsequent editions, but as my wife of the last eighteen years, she has been a source of constant encouragement and support. She has also been very tolerant of me for continuing to work long after I officially retired. I am grateful daily for her love and companionship.

My students have contributed far more to my work on the Vietnam War than they can ever realize or I can properly acknowledge. At Ohio University, in my first academic position, their insistent questioning sparked my interest in Vietnam. My students at the University of Kentucky, my academic home from 1969 to 2005, were quite simply an essential part of my life. Their research added immeasurably to my knowledge of the war. Their curiosity helped me keep learning; their questions prevented me from becoming complacent with my own answers. It was a joy to learn with them and from them. Their friendship made work fun. Their influence is present in these pages far more than the footnotes can indicate. My last class was a week-long Alumni College at Washington and Lee University in my native Virginia in 2009. Most of the "students" were from the Vietnam generation. Many had served in the war or protested it. During that exciting and often intense week, I was reminded many times of the powerful and varied influence the war exerted on individuals.

I have dedicated this book, with all my love, to my son, John; my daughter, Lisa; their spouses Christy and Peter; and to my very special grandchildren, Andrew, Madeline, and Kennedy; Caili, Jonathan, and Emma.

George C. Herring

America's Longest War

The United States and Vietnam, 1950–1975

Ho Chi Minh, March 1946
The charismatic and indefatigable Ho Chi Minh
(the name means "he who enlightens") led the
Vietnamese revolution from its inception until
his death in 1969, and his organizational genius
and indomitable will were instrumental to
Vietnamese victories over France and the
United States.
Photographic collection of Wayne DeWitt Larabee

CHAPTER 1

A Dead-End Alley

The United States, France, and the First Indochina War, 1950–1954

When Ho Chi Minh proclaimed the independence of Vietnam from French rule on September 2, 1945, he borrowed liberally from Thomas Jefferson, opening with the words "We hold these truths to be self-evident. That all men are created equal." During celebrations in Hanoi later in the day, sleek U.S. fighter planes swooped down over the city, U.S. Army officers stood near the reviewing stand, and a Vietnamese band played the "Star-Spangled Banner." Toward the end of the festivities, Vo Nguyen Giap spoke warmly of Vietnam's "particularly intimate relations" with the United States— something, he noted, "which it is a pleasant duty to dwell upon." The prominent role played by Americans at the birth of Vietnam appears in retrospect one of history's most bitter ironies. Despite the glowing professions of friendship on September 2, the United States in 1945 acquiesced in the return of France to Vietnam and from 1950 to 1954 actively supported its efforts to suppress Ho's revolution, the first phase of a quarter-century American struggle to control the destiny of Vietnam.[1]

HO CHI MINH AND THE AUGUST REVOLUTION

Ho Chi Minh's declaration of independence struck one of the first blows for a major phenomenon of the post–World War II era—what would be called *decolonization*, the breakup of colonial empires that

---

[1]David Marr, *Vietnam 1945: The Quest for Power* (Berkeley, Calif., 1995), pp. 532–545.

had been a standard feature of world politics for centuries. The war and Allied rhetoric vaguely supporting self-determination gave a huge boost to nationalism among peoples in the colonial areas. It also drastically weakened the European colonial powers and Japan, enormously hampering their ability to hang on to their imperial holdings. A global transformation of this magnitude did not occur smoothly. It sparked turmoil, conflict, and, in the case of Vietnam, war.

One of the most celebrated events in modern Vietnamese history, the August Revolution of 1945, also marked another milestone in that nation's centuries' old struggle against foreign domination. From 111 BC to 939 AD the land of Nam Viet, centered in the Red River Delta, had been a protectorate or outright colony of China. The Vietnamese absorbed from their larger northern neighbor their language and much of their culture. The Chinese introduced a system of building dikes, methods to reclaim the land from the sea, and advanced agricultural practices. The Vietnamese adopted Chinese legal codes, forms of taxation, and local government. As in China, the tenets of Confucianism provided for the Vietnamese a system of governance, a means of selecting public officials, and indeed an ethos for life.

While borrowing extensively from China, the Vietnamese also fiercely resisted its rule. Perhaps the most famous of their heroes, the Trung sisters, led a major first century AD rebellion against superior Chinese forces. When defeated, they drowned themselves in a lake in Hanoi. Another woman, Trieu Au, usually depicted wearing armor and riding an elephant, led yet another unsuccessful revolt in 248 AD. In the tenth century, the Vietnamese finally won their independence by luring an attacking Chinese fleet into a river bed planted with iron-tipped spikes. They stubbornly resisted Chinese efforts at reconquest. Three times in the thirteenth century, they repulsed the legendary Mongol warrior Kublai Khan, in the process pioneering methods of guerrilla warfare later used against the French and Americans. In 1426, another legendary hero, Le Loi, drove out the Chinese after a two-decade occupation, finally securing Vietnamese independence.

Expansion to the south forms as important a part of Vietnamese history as resistance to outside invaders. Following their defeat of the Mongols, the Viets moved south against the Muslim kingdom of Champa. After nearly two centuries of fighting, they destroyed its capital of Indrapura.

National unity remained elusive, however. Geography, religion, and ethnicity produced sharp regional differences. Buddhism was more pronounced in the South than Confucianism. The climate was more salubrious, land more plentiful, and the people more prosperous; the result was a much more easygoing lifestyle than that of the more intense and restive northerners. Civil war between two ruling families continued into the nineteenth century.

In the last third of that century, France took China's place as Vietnam's imperial overlord. In colonizing Vietnam, the French hoped to find wealth in the form of vital minerals. They also sought an outpost from which to exploit China and compete with British and Dutch colonies in South and Southeast Asia. They established protectorates with nominal Vietnamese rule in Tonkin (the North) and Annam (the center) and imposed outright colonial rule on Cochin China (the South). Protectorates in Laos and Cambodia filled out what became known as French Indochina. The French brought Western-style modernity to their new colonies in the form of major cities: Saigon (later called the Pearl of the Orient) and Hanoi, with their broad tree-lined avenues and gleaming buildings. They imposed a capitalist economy and in time Romanized the Vietnamese language. They modernized agriculture. They perpetrated massive change with no intention of promoting self-government and eventual independence. Rather, their colonial ideal was what they called the *mission civilisatrice,* which aimed to make the colonial areas and their people integral parts of France. The result for many Vietnamese was disruption of traditional village society, political oppression, economic exploitation, high taxes, and atrocious working conditions in the mines and on the railroads and rubber plantations.

The Vietnamese resisted French imperialism as persistently as they had resisted the Chinese. A late nineteenth-century scholars' movement sought unsuccessfully to remove the French and restore the old imperial order. Emulating Japanese and Chinese models, early twentieth-century nationalists attempted to mold traditional opposition to outside domination into modern, pro-Western republicanism. French colonialism created an urban middle class and proletariat, and the exploitation of the country sparked increasingly radical revolutionary activity. In 1930, a nationalist party headed by urban intellectuals launched the abortive Yen Bay revolt in northern Vietnam, while peasant and worker rebellions backed by the

Communists erupted throughout the central part of the country. The French brutally suppressed the latter, jailing as many as ten thousand dissidents and even using aircraft to drop bombs on demonstrators. "The French have mercilessly slain our patriots," Ho affirmed in his September 2 declaration. "They have drowned our uprisings in rivers of blood."[2]

The revolution of 1945 was in many ways the personal creation of the charismatic patriot and revolutionary agitator who took the name Ho Chi Minh ("He Who Enlightens"). Born in the central province of Nghe An, the cradle of Vietnamese revolutionaries, Ho inherited from his father a sturdy patriotism and adventurous spirit. Departing Vietnam in 1911 as a cook aboard a French merchant steamer, he spent time in the United States and England before settling in France with a cohort of Vietnamese nationalists. When the Paris Peace Conference ending World War I ignored his petition for democratic reforms for Vietnam, he found "our path to liberty" in Russian revolutionary leader Vladimir Lenin's treatise on imperialism. He became a founding member of the French Communist Party. Then known as Nguyen Ai Quoc ("Nguyen the Patriot"), he worked for more than two decades as a party functionary and revolutionary organizer in the Soviet Union, China, Thailand, and Vietnam, hiding behind aliases, eluding French, Chinese, and British police, doing time in prison, and once even being reported dead. In 1930, he organized the Indochinese Communist Party (ICP). Frail in appearance, a gentle man who radiated warmth and serenity, he was also willing to sanction the most cold-blooded methods to achieve his aims. He was a tireless worker, master organizer, and determined revolutionary—a "fiery stallion" in the words of an associate. His dark, piercing eyes revealed the intensity of his commitment to the cause to which he dedicated his life.[3]

The onset of World War II in Europe and Asia would have profound implications for Vietnam. Hitler's conquest of France in June 1940 vastly complicated French efforts to manage their overseas

---

[2]Quoted in Dennis Merrill and Thomas G. Paterson, *Major Problems in American Foreign Relations*, Vol. 2, *Since 1914*, 5th ed. (Boston, 2000), pp. 444–445.
[3]Two excellent up-to-date biographies are William J. Duiker, *Ho Chi Minh: A Life* (New York, 2000), and Pierre Brocheux, *Ho Chi Minh: A Biography*, trans. Claire Duiker (New York, 2007).

holdings. Exploiting French vulnerability to improve their strategic position in their stalemated war against China and to secure vitally needed oil and rubber from Southeast Asia, the Japanese established a protectorate over Vietnam in 1940–1941, leaving French officials nominally in charge but themselves exercising control. France's defeat in Europe and its humiliation by an Asian power further discredited it in Vietnamese eyes and set off a surge of nationalism. Initially welcomed by the Vietnamese, the Japanese proved cruel masters, strengthening the urge for freedom.

Seeking to capitalize on these momentous events, Ho returned to his homeland in 1940. Establishing headquarters in caves near the Chinese border by a mountain he named Karl Marx and a river he called Lenin, he founded the Independence League of Vietnam (Viet Minh) and conceived the strategy that would eventually drive the French from Vietnam. He and the other Communists who constituted the Viet Minh leadership skillfully tapped the deep reservoir of Vietnamese nationalism, muting their commitment to social revolution and adopting a broad platform stressing independence and "democratic" reforms. Displaying an organization and discipline far superior to competing nationalist groups, many of which spent as much time fighting each other as fighting the French, the Viet Minh gradually established itself as a preeminent voice of Vietnamese nationalism.

The Viet Minh also skillfully exploited the chaos that marked the end of the Pacific War. Fearing an Allied invasion of Indochina and distrustful of the French, the Japanese in March 1945 overthrew Vietnam's puppet government, disbanding its army and jailing officials. The coup further damaged French authority and encouraged Vietnamese resistance. Japan's inability or unwillingness to address a devastating famine that killed an estimated two million people in the winter–spring of 1945 added to Vietnamese anger. By the spring of 1945, Ho had mobilized a base of mass support in northern Vietnam and, with the assistance of Giap, a former professor of history and admirer of Napoleon, he had raised an army of five thousand soldiers. With limited help from the U.S. Office of Strategic Services (OSS) intelligence unit (hence the American presence on September 2), the Viet Minh began the systematic harassment of their former and new masters. When the atomic bomb brought the unexpectedly quick surrender of Japan on August 14, the Viet Minh opportunistically filled the vacuum by moving into government headquarters in Hanoi. Wearing the faded khaki suit and rubber sandals that would become his trademark, Ho Chi Minh stood before cheering throngs on September 2 and proclaimed the independence of his country.

Independence would not come without a struggle. Looking backward rather than forward, French leaders were determined to regain the empire they had ruled for more than a half century. Businesses such as the Michelin rubber company claimed that economic recovery demanded retention of the Indochina colony. Some French officials continued to preach its strategic importance. The main concern was restoration of France's status as a world power. Humiliated by their defeat at the hands of Germany, their subsequent occupation, and the fact that their country had to be liberated by its allies, French leaders acquired what philosopher Jean-Paul Sartre called a "formidable inferiority complex."[4] They looked upon colonies as a sure path to regaining their nation's greatness. Recognizing that their present weakness prevented them from achieving their goals immediately, they spoke vaguely of new arrangements in which reforms would be instituted and, rather than colonies, the colonial areas would be "associated states"—or independent.

For the Vietnamese, independence and unification represented fulfillment of centuries-old nationalist dreams and therefore comprised their essential goals. Keenly aware of his fledgling government's vulnerability, Ho scrambled desperately to advance its interests. Ever the pragmatist, he continued to seek aid from the United States as well as the Soviet Union. He negotiated the withdrawal of Nationalist Chinese forces, which had been designated by the Allies to occupy northern Vietnam upon the Japanese surrender. While eliminating internal rivals wherever possible, the Viet Minh also sought to coopt competing nationalist groups, even to the point of officially disbanding (in fact, sending underground) the ICP. To the disgruntlement of some of his compatriots, Ho was willing to forgo immediate independence and unity for future promises. In March 1946, the French recognized his government as a "free state"; he granted them the right to station fifteen thousand troops in the North.

[4]Fredrik Logevall, *Embers of War: The Fall of an Empire and the Making of America's Vietnam* (New York, 2012), p. 74.

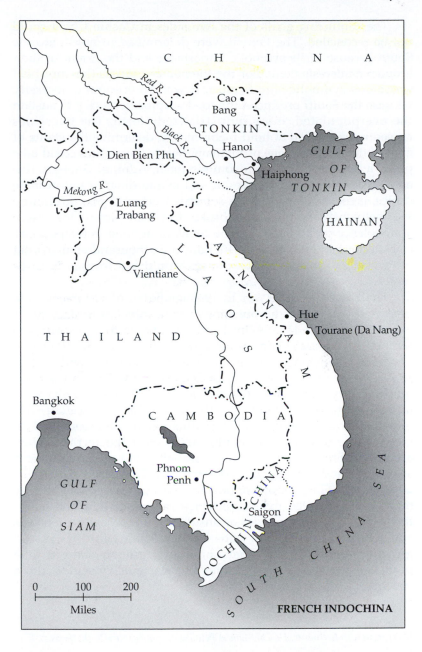

C H I N A

Red R.

Cao
Bang

TONKIN

Black R.

Hanoi

Dien Bien Phu

GULF
OF
TONKIN

Haiphong

Mekong R.

HAINAN

Luang
Prabang

L
A
O
S

A
N
N
A
M

Vientiane

Hue

Tourane (Da Nang)

T H A I L A N D

Bangkok

C A M B O D I A

Phnom
Penh

COCHIN CHINA

S O U T H   C H I N A   S E A

GULF
OF
SIAM

Saigon

0   100   200

Miles

FRENCH INDOCHINA

The conflicting goals of the two sides in Cochin China could not be reconciled. The French were determined to hold onto the South because of its symbolic importance and the extent of their economic interests there. For the Vietnamese, unification also held enormous symbolic significance. It was an economic necessity because the South produced the food surplus necessary to sustain the overpopulated, more industrialized North. The two sides agreed in early 1946 to hold plebiscites to determine the status of each of the three sections of Vietnam. Before these votes could take place, a new hard-line high commissioner, Admiral Georges Thierry d'Argenlieu, a former Jesuit and extraordinarily unfortunate choice, launched a move for a separate Cochin China, infuriating the Vietnamese. Negotiations broke down, suspicions increased, and violence proliferated. The outbreak of fighting in the port city of Haiphong in November 1946, killing six thousand civilians, set off a war that in its various phases would last for nearly three decades.

The French went to war in 1946 confident of victory, but Ho predicted the nature and outcome of the conflict more accurately. "If ever the tiger [Viet Minh] pauses," he said, "the elephant [France] will impale him on his mighty tusks. But the tiger will not pause, and the elephant will die of exhaustion and loss of blood."[5] Certain of their superior firepower, the French sought a quick victory. Employing the classical dictates of guerrilla warfare, Giap hoped to deny it to them. The Viet Minh guerrillas retreated to safe areas, avoided conflict where the French had an edge, and exploited their familiarity with the terrain. They ambushed French convoys where possible and employed terror selectively and with deadly effectiveness. They used nationalist appeals to build support among the Vietnamese people and by mid-1947 controlled extensive territory. France held the major towns and cities, but a series of unsuccessful and costly offensives and relentless hit-and-run raids by Viet Minh guerrillas placed growing strain on French personnel and resources and in time produced war-weariness at home. The war quickly settled into a stalemate.

---

[5]Quoted in Jean Lacouture, *Ho Chi Minh: A Political Biography* (New York, 1968), p. 171.

THE UNITED STATES AND
THE FIRST INDOCHINA WAR

For a time during World War II, the United States actively opposed the return of Indochina to France. Before 1940, Vietnam had been of little concern to Americans, but the Japanese takeover made clear its importance as a gateway to China, Southeast Asia, and the U.S. colony in the Philippines. Japan's conquest of Southeast Asia shortly after its December 7, 1941, attack on Pearl Harbor further underscored the importance of that region's sea lanes and essential raw materials, such as oil, tin, and rubber. Some U.S. officials feared that a French attempt to reimpose colonial rule might provoke war and instability in an area of strategic importance. President Franklin D. Roosevelt seems instinctively to have perceived that colonialism was doomed and that the United States should identify with peoples seeking freedom. Something of a Francophobe, FDR especially disliked the French leader Gen. Charles de Gaulle and he often expressed outrage with France's handling of its imperial responsibilities. The French were "poor colonizers," he declaimed, who had "badly mismanaged" Indochina and brutally exploited its people. At the same time, Roosevelt viewed the "Annamites" [Vietnamese] as an inferior people, backward, politically immature, and unready to govern themselves without tutelage from an "advanced" Western nation. Throughout the war, he repeatedly advocated placing French Indochina under international trustee-ship in preparation for independence.[6]

The United States also contributed in a small way to the success of the Vietnamese revolution. The OSS agents who journeyed to Ho Chi Minh's remote base in 1945 furnished the Viet Minh small arms and provided rudimentary military training in return for informa-tion on Japanese troop movements and aid in locating downed U.S. pilots. The Americans formed close ties with Ho (code-named "Lucius" and "Agent 19"). They even provided him with possibly life-saving quinine and sulfa drugs when he was gravely ill with malaria. Eager for U.S. support, Ho carefully cultivated his American guests. The conspicuous and by no means coincidental

[6]Mark Philip Bradley, *Imagining Vietnam and America: The Making of Postcolonial Vietnam, 1919–1950* (Chapel Hill, N.C., 2000), pp. 76–80.

United States presence at the independence ceremonies gave the Viet Minh legitimacy with other Vietnamese and conveyed the appearance of international support.[7]

In fact, as early as the spring and summer of 1945, official U.S. policy was shifting in other directions. Concerned for their own vast imperial holdings and hoping to restore France as a power in Europe, the British, and especially Prime Minister Winston Churchill, vigorously objected to FDR's trusteeship scheme. Some of the president's top advisers also warned him not to antagonize a crucial ally by opposing its colonial aspirations. Roosevelt's hatred for French colonialism never seems to have wavered and he continued to prefer a trusteeship for Indochina. Amidst the vast array of problems he faced in 1945, Vietnam did not loom large. In the face of opposition from allies and his own advisers, Roosevelt did not push ahead on the trusteeship issue or spell out a clear policy for Vietnam.[8]

After FDR's death in April 1945, U.S. policy moved sharply toward France. Harry S. Truman did not share his predecessor's keen personal interest in Indochina or his opposition to colonialism. More important, American thinking about the postwar world underwent a major reorientation in the spring of 1945. Military and civilian strategists perceived that the war had left the Soviet Union the most powerful nation in Europe. The sometimes brutal Soviet takeover of Eastern Europe raised growing fears that dictator Joseph Stalin had broader, perhaps even global, expansionist designs. Assigning top priority to the promotion of stable, friendly governments in Western Europe that could stand as bulwarks against Soviet expansionism, the Truman administration concluded that the United States had "no interest" in "championing schemes of international trusteeship" that would weaken or alienate those "European states whose help we need to balance Soviet power in Europe." France assumed a special place in this new scheme of things. The State Department insisted that the United States must repair the rift that had opened under Roosevelt by cooperating "wholeheartedly" with France and allaying "her apprehensions

[7]Dixee R. Bartholomew-Feis, *The OSS and Ho Chi Minh: Unexpected Allies in the War against Japan* (Lawrence, Kans., 2006), pp. 208–209, 213, 243.
[8]Stein Tønnesson, "Franklin Roosevelt, Trusteeship, and Indochina: A Reassessment," in Mark Atwood Lawrence and Fredrik Logevall (eds.), *The First Vietnam War: Colonial Conflict and Cold War Crisis* (Cambridge, Mass., 2007), pp. 56, 63–64.

that we are going to propose that territory be taken away from her."[9] The administration scrapped FDR's trusteeship plan. In May, Truman privately assured de Gaulle that the United States would not oppose the restoration of French sovereignty in Indochina.

U.S. officials viewed the outbreak of war in Vietnam with alarm. Along with anticolonial revolutions in Burma, Malaya, and Indonesia, the Indochinese war highlighted the explosiveness of nationalism in Southeast Asia. France's stubborn pursuit of out-moded colonial goals seemed to preclude anything except a military solution. But the U.S. State Department's Asian experts doubted that France could subdue the revolution and feared that its defeat would eliminate Western influence from an important area. These diplomats further warned of the dangers of identifying with French colonialism and pressed the administration to compel France to come to terms with Vietnamese nationalism.

Skepticism about French policy in Asia continued to be out-weighed by European concerns.[10] In the spring of 1947, through what came to be called the Truman Doctrine, the United States formally committed itself to blunt a perceived Soviet threat to Greece and Turkey. The following year, to further this new policy of containing communism, the Marshall Plan committed massive funds to the reconstruction of Western Europe. U.S. attention was riveted on France, where economic stagnation and political volatility aroused fears of a Communist takeover. Warned by moderate French politicians that outside interference in colonial matters would play into the hands of the French Communist Party, the United States left France to handle Indochina its own way. An "immediate and vital interest" in retaining a "friendly government to assist in the furtherance of our aims in Europe," the State Department concluded, must "take precedence over active steps looking toward the realization of our objectives in Indochina."[11]

[9]Office of Strategic Services, "Problems and Objectives of United States Policy," April 2, 1945, Harry S. Truman Papers, Harry S. Truman Library, Independence, Mo., Rose Conway File, Box 15.

[10]James Dunn memorandum, April 23, 1945, 851G.00/4-2345, Department of State Records, National Archives, Washington, D.C.; George C. Herring, "The Truman Administration and the Restoration of French Sovereignty in Indochina," *Diplomatic History* 1 (Spring, 1977): 97–117.

[11]Department of State, "Policy Statement on Indochina," September 27, 1948, in Department of State, *Foreign Relations of the United States, 1948* (Washington, D.C., 1974), 6: 48. Hereafter cited as *FR* with date and volume number.

By early 1947, U.S. officials had also drawn conclusions about the Vietnamese revolution that would shape American policy for the next two decades. From the outset, the Viet Minh and the United States viewed each other through badly distorted lenses. Isolated in the northern mountains of Vietnam and cut off from the outside world, Ho Chi Minh clung to hopes that the friendly demeanor of OSS agents reflected official American views. On numerous occasions between 1945 and 1949, he appealed for U.S. support, even suggesting that Vietnam would be a "fertile field for American capital and enterprise" and raising the possibility of an American naval base at Cam Ranh Bay. Ho emphatically denied that he was a "Moscow puppet," noting, correctly, that he had received more aid from the United States than from the Soviet Union. To those who questioned the Viet Minh's capacity to defeat France, he referred back to the revolution of 1776. "You Americans ought to remember," he observed, "that a ragged band of barefoot farmers defeated the pride of Europe's best armed professionals."[12] In April 1947, the Viet Minh dispatched an emissary to Bangkok to persuade the United States of its moderation and seek political and economic aid. He stressed to Americans that his people sought mainly independence from France. Speaking a language he thought might appeal to capitalists, he offered tax-free monopolies for U.S. imports and the rice trade.

Such incentives had no impact in Washington. American political reporting about Vietnam was devoid of expertise and based on racial prejudices and stereotypes that reflected deep-seated convictions about the superiority of Western culture. In U.S. eyes, the Vietnamese were a passive and uninformed people, totally unready for self-government. The "Annamites" were not "particularly industrious," one diplomat sneered, nor were they noted for "honesty, loyalty, or veracity."[13] U.S. officials thus concluded that even if the Vietnamese were to secure independence from France, they would be susceptible to the establishment of a Communist police state and vulnerable to external control.

---

[12]Duiker, *Ho Chi Minh*, pp. 342–343, 379.
[13]Quoted in Mark Bradley, "An Improbable Opportunity: America and the Democratic Republic of Vietnam's 1947 Initiative," in Jayne S. Werner and Luu Doan Huynh (eds.), *The Vietnam War: Vietnamese and American Perspectives* (New York, 1993), pp. 13–14.

Ho's long-standing Communist ties reinforced such fears. In fact, between 1945 and 1949 Stalin was no more supportive of the Viet Minh than the United States had been. He doubted that southern Asian nations were ripe for revolution. Like the United States, he assigned top priority to Europe and feared that helping the Viet Minh might jeopardize the French Communist Party's chances of taking power. Stalin distrusted Ho from earlier ideological spats. He was angered by the Viet Minh revolution's having been launched without his approval, and by its seeming ties with the United States. He refused to recognize the Viet Minh government or to take the Vietnam issue to the United Nations. The Kremlin declined even to answer Ho's letters.[14] U.S. officials, of course, could not have been aware of these differences among Communists. In any event, the Cold War mentality that was already gripping Washington left little room for nuance. U.S. diplomats in Vietnam correctly reported they could find no evidence of direct ties between the USSR and the Viet Minh and stressed that, regardless of ideology, Ho had established himself as the "symbol of nationalism and the struggle for freedom to the overwhelming majority of the population."[15] Intelligence assessments countered that Ho had remained loyal to Moscow throughout his career. The lack of close ties with the USSR simply meant that he was trusted to carry out Stalin's plans without supervision. In the absence of irrefutable evidence to the contrary, the State Department concluded, the United States could not "afford to assume that Ho is anything but Moscow-directed." Unwilling to see "colonial empires and administrations supplanted by philosophies and political organizations emanating from the Kremlin," the administration refused to do anything to facilitate a "Communist" triumph in Indochina.[16]

During the first three years of the war in Indochina, the United States maintained a distinctly pro-French "neutrality." Fearful of

[14]Ilya V. Gaiduk, "Soviet Cold War Strategy and Prospects for Revolution in South and Southeast Asia," in Christopher E. Goscha and Christian Ostermann (eds.), *Connecting Histories: Decolonization and the Cold War in Asia, 1945–1962* (Stanford, Calif., 2010), pp. 123–126; Christopher E. Goscha, "Courting Diplomatic Disaster? The Difficult Integration of Vietnam into the International Communist Movement (1945–1950)," *Journal of Vietnamese Studies* 1 (Nos. 1–2): 62–65.

[15]"Policy and Information Statement on Indochina," July 1947, Philippine and Southeast Asia Branch File, Department of State Records, Box 10.

[16]George C. Marshall to U.S. Embassy Paris, February 3, 1947, *FR, 1947,* 6: 67–68.

antagonizing a key European ally and of assisting the Viet Minh even indirectly, it refused—like Moscow—to acknowledge Ho's numerous letters appealing for support or to use its leverage to end the fighting. The contact in Thailand was quietly terminated. Unwilling to support colonialism openly, the administration provided indirect assistance. Ships turned over to France during World War II were used to transport French troops to Indochina. The United States extended credits for the purchase of additional transports. It provided weapons for use in Europe that were, in fact, employed in Vietnam. Marshall Plan funds enabled France to divert its own resources to the Indochina war.

INTERNATIONALIZATION OF THE WAR, 1949–1950

The landscape of international politics changed almost beyond recognition in 1949–1950, making the world a more confusing and much more dangerous place for large nations and small. The Cold War heated up in Europe, sparking a war scare and the beginnings of rearmament on both sides. The culmination of China's epic civil war in a Communist triumph brought Cold War conflict to East Asia, with implications extending far beyond. Much of the globe was increasingly divided into two hostile camps. World leaders were compelled to make difficult choices. After years of trying to play all sides, Ho Chi Minh's Viet Minh officially joined the emerging Communist "bloc." The diplomatic upheaval of 1949–1950 brought fear and alarm to the United States. Following a sweeping reassessment of national security strategy, a nation that had spurned international commitments during much of its history redefined its global interests in a remarkably broad fashion and began to assume an array of obligations. In early 1950, the United States signed on as an active partner of France in Vietnam despite grave doubts about French policies there. Through an extremely complex sequence of events, the Vietnam War was internationalized. What had been a regional anticolonial war in Indochina was transformed into an integral part of the Cold War. This expansion of the war ensured its prolongation and also made it much more destructive, with horrendous long-term consequences for the Vietnamese.

Internationalization of the war actually began in 1947, when France launched a systematic campaign to wean the United States from its neutrality. Failing to win a quick military victory, French leaders formulated a parallel political strategy to rally non-Communist Vietnamese behind an ostensibly independent national government. By changing an anticolonial conflict into a war against communism, French leaders sought to win greater support at home. More important, they hoped to use anticommunism to neutralize U.S. anticolonialism and secure aid for the war in Vietnam. [17] They selected the former emperor of Annam, Bao Dai, to head the "free" Vietnamese government. Properly skeptical of French intentions, the so-called playboy emperor at first refused to go along. But the growing likelihood of a Communist victory in China heightened pressure on both sides to reach an agreement. In March 1949, a new government headed by Bao Dai was formed. The French redoubled their efforts to gain U.S. support.

For its own reasons, Britain energetically backed the French campaign to draw the United States into the war. British officials increasingly saw France as the key to a stable Southeast Asia and the protection of their colonies in Singapore and Malaya. With their nation overcommitted globally and perilously short of resources, they viewed U.S. aid as essential for French military success in Indochina. Greater American involvement would also allow Britain to avoid the taint of supporting French colonialism, Labour government officials reasoned, thus pacifying their party's anticolonial left wing and the newly independent and fiercely anticolonial government of India. British officials repeatedly appealed to the United States to help France and enlisted the support of sympathetic Americans to plead their case. Speaking in Washington in April 1949, Foreign Minister Ernest Bevin called for a "Great Combination" of Britain, Europe, and the United States, to prevent the Communist conquest of Southeast Asia.[18]

Escalation of the Cold War in Europe made the United States more susceptible to Franco-British appeals. Fearing for its sphere of influence in Eastern Europe, in 1948 the Soviet Union overthrew a

[17]Logevall, *Embers of War*, p. 198; Mark Atwood Lawrence, *Assuming the Burden: Europe and the American Commitment to War in Vietnam* (Berkeley, Calif., 2005), pp. 187–232.
[18]Mark Atwood Lawrence, "Forging the 'Great Combination': Britain and the Indochina Problem, 1945–1950," in Lawrence and Logevall, eds., *First Vietnam War*, pp. 48–50.

neutralist government in Czechoslovakia, installed Stalinist regimes throughout the region, and shored up its control through exclusive economic agreements and eventually a military alliance. Stalin's bold—and risky—blockade of West Berlin in the summer of 1948 brought the two Cold War antagonists dangerously close to a hot war. The United States and the Western European nations expedited plans for a defensive alliance, culminating in the formation of the North Atlantic Treaty Organization (NATO) in April 1949. U.S. officials viewed France as the linchpin of the new pact. They recognized that the so-called Bao Dai Solution was a smoke screen for continued French domination of Vietnam and doubted it would work. But it seemed the only alternative to "Commie domination of Indochina,"[19] and they felt compelled to back France in Indochina to keep it closely allied in Europe. In June 1949, the United States issued a statement of support for the Bao Dai government, a hugely significant first step toward active involvement in the war.

The Chinese Communist victory in the summer of 1949 provided the major catalyst for internationalization of the Indochina war. After a brief period of hesitancy, during which accommodation with the United States seemed at least remotely possible, Communist leader Mao Zedong publicly declared that his government would "lean to one side" in an increasingly divided world: It would align with the Soviet Union. Viewing their revolution as a model for other Asian peoples, the Chinese saw assistance for the Viet Minh as part of their "glorious international duty" and also as a means to secure their southern border. For the dangerously isolated Viet Minh, the Chinese success raised the possibility of external aid that might make possible expanded military operations, breaking the stalemate with France, and perhaps even military victory.[20] In late 1949, the two sides proclaimed their mutual allegiance. During a year-end trip to Moscow, Mao urged Soviet assistance for the Viet Minh. Still wary of Ho Chi Minh, Stalin would do no more than promise to recognize his government. In what he

---

[19]Acheson to U.S. Embassy Manila, January 7, 1950, *FR, 1950*, 6: 692; Gary R. Hess, "The First American Commitment in Indochina: Acceptance of the Bao Dai Solution," *Diplomatic History* 2 (Fall 1978): 331–350.

[20]Chen Jian, "Bridging Revolution and Decolonization: The 'Bandung Discourse' in China's Early Cold War Experience," in Goscha and Ostermann, eds., *Connecting Histories*, pp. 137–143.

called a "division of labor," he also cleverly assigned China responsibility for promoting the revolution in Asia and aiding the Vietnamese. In January 1950, China and the USSR formally recognized the Democratic Republic of Vietnam (DRV). China immediately began preparations for sending military aid and advisers and providing sanctuary for training Vietnamese troops. Long impatient with Ho's pragmatic approach, many Viet Minh Communists enthusiastically embraced their new role as a "fortress on the anti-imperialist defense perimeter in Southeast Asia." The DRV made clear its zeal by publicly praising Stalin and denouncing the United States, purging the leadership of moderates, pushing land reform, and instigating revolution in Laos and Cambodia.[21]

Soviet and Chinese recognition of Ho's government seemed to confirm what most U.S. officials had long believed: that the revolution in Vietnam was part of a broader Communist drive for world domination spearheaded by Moscow. According to Secretary of State Dean Acheson, the establishment of close ties among these three Communist parties revealed Ho Chi Minh in his "true colors as the mortal enemy of native independence in Indochina." Acheson thus sought to impugn Ho's nationalist credentials while boosting the legitimacy of the Bao Dai government.[22]

The stunning events of 1949 sent shock waves across the United States. Soviet explosion of an atomic bomb in the summer came much sooner than Americans had expected. It eliminated the U.S. nuclear monopoly and aroused fears that an already aggressive Stalin might take even greater risks. The fall of China to the Communists had an especially profound impact. For years, many Americans had clung to the belief that China was a special protégé that, with their guidance, would become a close friend and reliable ally. The collapse of Chiang Kai-shek's government and the "loss" of China to communism at this seemingly pivotal moment in the Cold War had profoundly unsettling consequences. With one stroke, it appeared to tilt the global balance of power against the United States and its allies. It left frustrated and fearful Americans

---

[21]Tuong Vu, "From Cheering to Volunteering: Vietnamese Communists and the Coming of the Cold War, 1950–1951," in ibid., pp. 189–192; Goscha, "Diplomatic Disaster," pp. 87–90.

[22]*Department of State Bulletin* (February 13, 1950): 244; Charles Yost memorandum, January 31, 1950, *FR, 1950*, 6: 710–711.

asking the portentous—and pretentious—question: Who lost China? Sensationalist revelations of Communist espionage in the United States seemed to provide the answer. Soviet spies had allegedly speeded Stalin's nuclear timetable by stealing U.S. secrets. Communist sympathizers within the U.S. government had sabotaged the Kuomintang government, thus ensuring a Communist takeover.

Shaken from their complacency, a people who, through much of their history, had enjoyed maximum security at minimal cost reacted to these seemingly sinister and ominous threats with near panic. They sought scapegoats for their newfound predicament and political retribution against those deemed responsible. A Cold War culture of near-hysterical fear, paranoiac suspiciousness, and stifling conformity began to take shape. Militant anticommunism came to dominate both foreign policy and domestic politics. In February 1950, a heretofore obscure Wisconsin senator by the name of Joseph R. McCarthy claimed to have the names of more than 200 Communists working in the State Department, setting off the Red Scare/witch hunt that would bear his name. "McCarthyism" would poison the nation's politics and cripple its diplomacy for years to come.[23]

The fall of China set loose in the United States powerful domestic political pressures to prevent the loss of additional Asian real estate to communism. Already under fire from Republicans—and some Democrats—for "losing" China, the Truman administration felt compelled to hold the line elsewhere. It attempted to divert attention from China and demonstrate its resolve by focusing on Southeast Asia. Significantly, the first aid committed to France for Vietnam came from a fund originally appropriated for Nationalist China.[24] The year 1950 initiated an almost ritualistic process in which each major political party tried to outdo the other in demonstrating toughness against the Communist onslaught and labeling the adversary as weak.

The crisis of 1949–1950 also produced a sweeping reassessment of U.S. national security policy that assigned major significance to previously peripheral areas. This universalist worldview was best expressed in National Security Council (NSC) document 68 (NSC 68),

[23]Stephen J. Whitfield, *The Culture of the Cold War* (Baltimore, Md., 1991).
[24]Robert M. Blum, *Drawing the Line: The Origins of the American Containment Policy in East Asia* (New York, 1982).

one of the most significant statements of American Cold War policy. Drafted in early 1950, NSC 68 set as its fundamental premise that the USSR, "animated by a new fanatical faith," was seeking to "impose its absolute authority on the rest of the world." In this emotionally supercharged atmosphere, U.S. policymakers also concluded that Soviet expansion had reached a point beyond which it must not be permitted to go. "Any substantial further extension of the area under the control of the Kremlin," NSC 68 warned, "would raise the possibility that no coalition adequate to confront the Kremlin with greater strength could be assembled." In this context of a world divided into two hostile power blocs, a fragile balance of power, a zero-sum situation in which any gain for communism was automatically a loss for the United States, and the frightening possibility of global war, the Truman administration initiated plans to increase American military capabilities, shore up the defense of Western Europe, and extend the containment policy to East Asia.[25]

In the dramatically altered strategic context of 1950, Southeast Asia assumed special importance. The raging conflict in Indochina and insurgencies in Burma, Malaya, and Indonesia all sprang from indigenous roots, but in a seemingly polarized world, their mere existence and leftist orientation persuaded anxious American officials—mistakenly—that Southeast Asia was "the target of a coordinated offensive directed by the Kremlin." Should the region be swept by communism, the NSC warned, "we shall have suffered a major political rout the consequences of which will be felt throughout the world."[26]

The loss of an area so large and populous would tip the balance of power against the United States and might tempt European nations to come to terms with communism. America's European allies desperately needed dollars to rebuild their devastated economies. The United States thus purchased raw materials from former colonial areas in Southeast Asia, which then bought finished products from Western Europe, thus making up the "dollar gap" and permitting Europeans to buy U.S. goods.[27] If Southeast Asia joined

---

[25]The document is printed in its entirety in *FR, 1950*, 1: 237–290.

[26]U.S. Congress, Senate Subcommittee on Public Buildings and Grounds, *The Pentagon Papers, Senator Gravel Edition*, 4 vols. (1971), 1: 37–38. Hereafter cited as *Pentagon Papers (Gravel)*.

[27]Andrew J. Rotter, *The Path to Vietnam: Origins of the American Commitment to Southeast Asia* (Ithaca, N.Y., 1987), pp. 141–164.

the Communist bloc, the United States and its allies would be denied access to important markets. Southeast Asia was the world's largest producer of natural rubber and a vital source of oil, tin, tungsten, and other strategic commodities. Its loss would threaten control of the air and sea routes between Australia and the Middle East, thus imperiling nations such as Japan, India, and Australia, in which the West retained predominant influence.

The impact on Japan, America's recent enemy and now its most important Asian ally, as well as the richest economic prize in the area, was viewed as potentially disastrous. Even before the fall of China, the United States was pushing for the reintegration of Japan with Southeast Asia, a region that had served as Japan's rice bowl and bread basket and an essential source of raw materials and markets. With China already lost, U.S. officials feared that the loss of Southeast Asia would compel Japan to shift toward communism. The United States therefore set out to defend a "vital segment" of the "great crescent" of containment extending from Japan to India.[28]

By early 1950, American policymakers had come to view Vietnam as the key to keeping Southeast Asia out of Communist hands, an importance it would retain for nearly a quarter of a century. The Viet Minh's increasingly well-organized and well-equipped military forces had already scored major gains against France and, with increased Chinese aid, might force a French withdrawal, removing the last obstacle between China and Southeast Asia. Indochina was in "the most immediate danger," the State Department warned and was therefore "the most strategically important area of Southeast Asia."[29]

Indochina was considered intrinsically important for its raw materials, rice, and naval bases, but it was deemed far more significant for the presumed effect its loss would have on other areas. By early 1950, U.S. policymakers had firmly embraced what would become known as the *domino theory,* the firmly rooted conviction that the fall of Indochina would cause the collapse of the rest of Southeast Asia, like a row of dominoes falling. Acceptance of this concept reflected the perceived fragility of the region in 1950 as

[28]Michael Schaller, "Securing the Great Crescent: Occupied Japan and the Origins of Containment in Southeast Asia," *Journal of American History* 69 (September 1982): 392–413.
[29]Dean Rusk to James H. Burns, March 7, 1950, *Pentagon Papers (Gravel)*, 1: 363.

From By Sea, Air and Land: An Illustrated History of the U.S. Navy and the War in Southeast Asia *by Edward J. Marolda, 1994, p. 2. Naval Historical Center.*

well as memories from 1940–1942 when Germany and Japan over-ran vast regions in very short spaces of time. First employed to jus-tify aid to Greece in 1947, the idea, once it was applied to Southeast Asia, became an article of faith.[30]

This strategic reassessment of 1950 ended American "neutral-ity" in the war in Indochina. In February, the United States for-mally recognized the Bao Dai government. In early March, it committed itself to furnish France military and economic aid for the war against the Viet Minh. The principles upon which these decisions were based would form the basis for U.S. policy in Vietnam for years and, in time, would lead to large-scale U.S. involvement.

The assumptions on which U.S. policymakers acted were flawed in numerous ways. The Southeast Asian revolutions were not inspired by Moscow. Although the Soviet Union and especially China would at times seek to control them, their capacity to do so was limited by their lack of military and especially naval power and mainly by the force of local nationalism. The U.S. assessment of the situation in Vietnam was off the mark. Although a dedicated Communist, Ho Chi Minh was no tool of the Kremlin. He was will-ing to accept help from the major Communist powers, but he was not prepared to subordinate Vietnamese independence to them. Vietnam's historic fears of its larger northern neighbor made sub-mission to China especially unlikely. "It is better to sniff French shit for a while than eat China's all our life," Ho once said, graphically expressing a traditional principle of Vietnamese foreign policy.[31] Perhaps most important, regardless of his ideology Ho had cap-tured the standard of Vietnamese nationalism by 1950. By support-ing France, even under the guise of the Bao Dai solution, the United States attached itself to a dubious cause.

American policymakers were not unaware of the pitfalls. Should the United States commit itself to Bao Dai and he turn out to be a French puppet, a State Department Asian specialist warned, "we must then follow blindly down a dead-end alley, expending our limited resources . . . in a fight that would be hopeless."[32]

---

[30]Frank Ninkovich, *Modernity and Power: A History of the Domino Theory in the Twentieth Century* (Chicago, 1994), traces it back to Woodrow Wilson.
[31]Quoted in Lacouture, *Ho Chi Minh*, p. 119.
[32]Charles Reed to C. Walton Butterworth, April 14, 1949, 851G.00/4–1449, Depart-ment of State Records.

Some officials even dimly perceived that the United States might get sucked into direct involvement in Vietnam. But the initial commitments seemed limited and the risks smaller than those of inaction. Caught up in a perilous global struggle and with memories of the first years of World War II fresh in their minds, U.S. officials were certain that if they did not back Bao Dai and France, Southeast Asia might be lost, leaving the more frightful choice of a "staggering investment" to recover the losses or a "much contracted" line of defense in the western Pacific.[33]

THE FRANCO-AMERICAN
PARTNERSHIP IN VIETNAM

By the time the United States began to assist France, the Viet Minh had gained the military initiative in Indochina. Its regulars and guerrillas numbered in the hundreds of thousands, and it controlled an estimated two-thirds of the countryside. By early 1950, and with Chinese encouragement, Giap felt sufficiently confident to take the offensive. The French maintained tenuous control of the major cities and production centers, but at very high cost, suffering a thousand casualties per month and in 1949 alone spending 167 million francs on the war. Even in areas under nominal French control, the Viet Minh spread terror after dark, sabotaging power plants and factories, tossing grenades into cafés and theaters, and brutally assassinating French officials. "Anyone with white skin caught outside protected areas after dark is courting horrible death," an American journalist reported.[34]

The Bao Dai Solution, Bao Dai himself ruefully conceded, was "just a French solution."[35] The much-maligned emperor was in fact a tragic figure. An intelligent man, genuinely concerned for the future of his nation, he had spent much of his life as a puppet of France and then Japan, whiling away the years by indulging an apparently insatiable taste for sports cars, women, and gambling. Under the February 1950 agreement, the French retained control of

---

[33]Acheson to Truman, May 14, 1950, Truman Papers, Confidential File.
[34]Tilman Durdin, "War 'Not for Land but for People,'" *New York Times Magazine*, May 28, 1950, 48.
[35]Robert Shaplen, *The Lost Revolution: The U.S. in Vietnam, 1946–1966* (New York, 1966), p. 64.

Vietnam's treasury, commerce, and foreign and military policies. They refused even to turn over Saigon's Norodom Palace. The government was composed mainly of wealthy southern landowners, in no way representative of the people. Nationalists of stature refused to support Bao Dai; the masses backed the resistance or remained aloof. The emperor lacked the temperament for leadership. Introverted and given to depression and indolence, he isolated himself in one of his palaces or aboard his six-hundred-ton air-conditioned yacht or fled to the French Riviera, all the while salting away large sums of money in Swiss bank accounts. Not "the stuff of which Churchills are made," U.S. ambassador Donald Heath lamented with marvelous understatement.[36]

The outbreak of war in Korea in June 1950 brought new perils. Communist North Korea's invasion of South Korea confirmed deeply embedded U.S. suspicions that the Soviet Union sought to conquer all of Asia, even at the risk of war, and Indochina assumed even greater importance. The United States responded by sending its own military forces to help defend South Korea, placing the Seventh Fleet between Taiwan and the Chinese mainland to protect Chiang Kai-shek's exile government, and stepping up aid to the French in Indochina. These crucial decisions would shape U.S. policies in Asia for years to come.

By the end of the year, the United States and France had suffered devastating defeats. Massive Chinese intervention in Korea forced Gen. Douglas MacArthur's troops into headlong retreat from the Yalu River. In the meantime, Giap had inflicted upon France its "greatest colonial defeat since Montcalm had died at Quebec," trapping an entire army in Cao Bang in northeastern Vietnam and costing the French more than six thousand troops and enough equipment to stock an entire enemy division.[37] Chinese intervention in Korea raised fears of a similar thrust into Vietnam. U.S. policymakers increasingly feared that growing defeatism and war-weariness in France would raise demands for withdrawal from Indochina.

Against this background of stunning defeat, the Truman administration struggled to devise workable policies. With large

---

[36]Heath to John Foster Dulles, April 28, 1953, *FR, 1952–1954*, 13: 523; Ellen Hammer, "The Bao Dai Experiment," *Pacific Affairs* 23 (March 1950): 58.

[37]Bernard Fall, *Street without Joy* (New York, 1972), p. 33.

numbers of U.S. troops committed to Korea and Europe seemingly vulnerable to a Soviet invasion, military officials insisted that even if China invaded Vietnam, the United States could not send military forces. France must hold the line; the United States could do no more than provide military assistance. In late 1950, the administration committed more than $133 million and ordered large quantities of arms, ammunition, ships, aircraft, and military vehicles. Americans appreciated, of course, that such aid might not be enough. As early as May, Acheson complained that the French seemed "paralyzed, in a state of moving neither forward or backward."[38] A fact-finding mission dispatched to Vietnam *before* the Cao Bang disaster reported that the French state of mind was "fatuous, even dangerous," and warned that unless France prosecuted the war more determinedly, used Vietnamese personnel more effectively, and offered generous political concessions, the United States and its ally might be "moving into a debacle which neither of us can afford."[39] Some U.S. officials proposed that aid be conditioned on French pledges to take drastic measures, including the promise of eventual independence.

The administration demurred. Acheson conceded that if the United States supported France's "old-fashioned colonial attitudes," it might "lose out." But the French presence was essential to defend Indochina, and the United States could not push France to the point where it would say, "All right, take over the damned country. We don't want it." Admitting the inconsistency of U.S. policy, he saw no choice but to encourage the French to remain until the crisis had eased but at the same time to try to persuade them to "play with the nationalist movement and give Bao Dai a chance really to get the nationalists on his side."[40] The administration would go no further than to gently urge France to make symbolic concessions and build a Vietnamese army, while holding Bao Dai's "feet to the fire" to get him to assert effective leadership under French tutelage.[41]

[38]Minutes of meeting, NSC, May 4, 1950, Truman Papers, President's Secretary's File.
[39]Melby Mission Report, August 6, 1950, *FR, 1950*, 6: 843–844; Policy Planning Staff memorandum, August 16, 1950, ibid., 857–858.
[40]U.S. Congress, Senate, *Reviews of the World Situation, 1949–1950 Hearings Held in Executive Session before the Committee on Foreign Relations* (Washington, D.C., 1974), pp. 266–268, 292–293.
[41]Livingston Merchant to Dean Rusk, October 19, 1950, *FR, 1950*, 6: 901–902.

To strengthen the "free states" and increase their popular appeal, the United States spent more than $50 million between 1950 and 1952 for economic and technical assistance. American experts provided fertilizer and seeds for agricultural production, constructed dispensaries, developed malaria control programs, and distributed food and clothing to refugees. To ensure achievement of its objectives, the United States insisted that the aid go directly to the local governments. To secure maximum propaganda advantage, zealous U.S. officials tacked posters on pagoda walls and airdropped pamphlets into villages indicating that the programs were gifts of the United States and contrasting the "real gains" with "Communism's empty promises." The U.S. Information Service even prepared a Vietnamese-language *History of the United States* with an introduction by President Truman, expressing hope that an "account of the progress of the American people toward a just and happy society can be an inspiration to those Vietnamese who today knowing something of the same difficulties as they build a new nation."[42]

These initiatives brought limited results. Their hopes of victory revived by increased U.S. assistance, in late 1950 the French appointed the flamboyant Gen. Jean de Lattre de Tassigny to command the armed forces in Indochina and instructed him to prosecute the war vigorously. A born crusader and practitioner of what he called *dynamisme*, de Lattre vowed upon arriving in Vietnam that he would win the war in fifteen months. Under his inspired leadership French forces repulsed a major Viet Minh offensive in the Red River Delta in early 1951, inflicting enormous losses. But when de Lattre followed up by attacking enemy strongholds just south of Hanoi, France suffered its worst defeat of the war. De Lattre himself would die of cancer in 1952. The French military position was more precarious than when he had arrived.

In other areas, also, there was little progress. Desperately short of personnel, de Lattre made determined efforts to create a Vietnamese National Army (VNA), a process the French called *jaunissement*

---

[42]Mutual Security Agency, *Dateline Saigon: Our Quiet War in Indochina* (Washington, D.C., 1952). Roger Tubby to Joseph Short, March 8, 1951, Truman Papers, Official File 203-F. The French dismissed as the "height of national egotism" the fact that this first book translated by Americans into Vietnamese was a history of the United States. Heath to Secretary of State, June 14, 1951, *FR, 1951*, 6: 425–427.

("yellowing"). But the Vietnamese were understandably reluctant to fight for a French cause, and by the end of 1951 the VNA numbered only thirty-eight thousand soldiers, far short of its projected strength of one hundred fifteen thousand. Responding to U.S. entreaties, the French vaguely promised to "perfect" the independence of the Associated States, but the massive infusion of American supplies and de Lattre's early victories seemed to eliminate any need for concessions. The French refused to fight for Vietnamese independence and never seriously considered the only sort of concession that would have satisfied the aspirations of Vietnamese nationalism. The "free states" remained shadow governments lacking authority and popular support.

By 1952, the United States was bearing roughly one-third of the cost of the war, but it found itself powerless to influence French policy. A small Military Assistance and Advisory Group (MAAG) had been sent to Vietnam in 1950 to screen French requests for aid, assist in training Vietnamese soldiers, and advise on strategy. By going directly to Washington to get what he wanted, de Lattre reduced the MAAG to virtual impotence. Proud, sensitive, and highly nationalistic, he ignored the Americans in formulating strategy, denied them any role in training the Vietnamese, and refused even to tell them what he was doing.[43]

Deeply suspicious of American intrusion into their domain, the French expressed open resentment against and obstructed the civilian aid program. De Lattre bitterly complained that there were too many Americans in Vietnam, spending too much money, and making France "look like a poor cousin in Vietnamese eyes." The Americans were "fanning the flames of extreme [Vietnamese] nationalism," he declaimed. At a dinner for the U.S. consul in Hanoi in the spring of 1951, the general launched an anti-American tirade that lasted until 1:00 a.m., raving like a "madman," according to a British diplomat, and accusing the United States of trying to replace France in Vietnam. French officials attempted to block projects they felt did not contribute directly to the war and encouraged Vietnamese suspicions by warning that U.S. aid contained "hidden traps" to subvert their independence. Largely as a result of French obstruction, the aid program touched only a few people.

[43]Ronald H. Spector, *Advice and Support: The Early Years, 1941–1960* (Washington, D.C., 1983), pp. 115–121.

U.S. officials conceded that its "beneficial psychological results" effects were largely negated because the United States at the same time was pursuing a "program of [military] support to the French." America was looked upon "more as a supporter of colonialism than as a friend of the new nation."[44]

France continued to demand additional military assistance; the United States could do little but comply. The Truman administration in June 1952 approved $150 million in new aid. Although thoroughly dissatisfied with France's military performance and deeply annoyed by its secretiveness and obstructionism, Truman and Acheson continued to reject proposals to use military aid to compel France to adopt a more aggressive strategy and make political concessions. The State Department feared that if it "pressed the French too hard they would withdraw and leave us holding the baby."[45]

America's Indochina policy continued to be a hostage to its preeminent interests in Europe. Since 1951, the United States had pushed for a European Defense Community (EDC) that would integrate French and German forces into a multinational army, a plan originally put forward by France to delay German rearmament. The French repeatedly warned that they could not furnish troops for European defense without generous U.S. support in Southeast Asia, a ploy Acheson accurately described as "blackmail." The EDC had become a volatile political issue in France, where there was strong resistance to surrendering the identity of the French army and collaborating with a recent and still despised enemy. With the question awaiting approval by the French parliament, Acheson later recalled, no one "seriously advised" that it would be "wise to end, or threaten to end, aid to [France in] Indochina unless an American plan of military and political reform was carried out."[46]

Despite a substantial investment in Indochina, Truman and Acheson left to their successors a problem infinitely more complex and dangerous than the one they had taken on in 1950. A localized rebellion against French colonialism had expanded into an

[44]Shaplen, *Lost Revolution*, pp. 86–89; Embassy Saigon to Secretary of State, May 15, 1951, *FR, 1951*, 6: 419; Frank Gibbs to R. H. Scott, April 28, 1951, FO 371/92420, Foreign Office Records, Public Records Office, London.

[45]Quoted in John M. Allison, *Ambassador from the Prairie, or Allison Wonderland* (New York, 1976), pp. 191, 194.

[46]Dean G. Acheson, *Present at the Creation* (New York, 1969), p. 676.

international conflict of major proportions. The United States was now bearing more than 40 percent of the cost of the war and had a huge stake in its outcome. Chinese aid to the Viet Minh had increased more than sevenfold. The war had spilled over into neighboring Laos and Thailand, where China and the Viet Minh backed insurgencies against governments supported by the United States and France. In Vietnam itself, France controlled enclaves around Hanoi, Haiphong, and Saigon, and a narrow strip along the Cambodian border. It now faced a new and much more ominous military threat. "The enemy, once painted as a bomb-throwing terrorist or hill sniper lurking in night ambush," journalist Theodore White observed, "has become a modern army, increasingly skillful, armed with artillery, organized into divisional groups."[47]

Both sides had suffered horrendous losses, and yet, to each, victory seemed no closer. Driven relentlessly by Viet Minh leaders, Vietnamese peasants were showing distinct signs of war-weariness and disaffection. The French had naively hoped that U.S. aid might be a substitute for increased French sacrifices but had come to realize that it only required more of them. Fearful of their growing dependence on the United States and painfully aware of the possible costs of victory, in late 1952 some French political leaders outside the Communist Party for the first time began to call for withdrawal from Indochina. The "real" problem, Acheson warned the incoming administration was the "French will to carry on the . . . war."[48]

EISENHOWER, DULLES, AND VIETNAM

The Republican administration of former U.S. Army general and World War II hero Dwight D. Eisenhower accepted without major modification the principles of Indochina policy bequeathed by the Democrats. The new president and his secretary of state, John Foster Dulles, a corporate lawyer and long-time Republican foreign policy expert, agreed that the Vietnamese revolution was part of a larger Communist drive for world domination. They further

---

[47]Theodore H. White, "France Holds on to the Indo-China Tiger," *New York Times Magazine*, June 8, 1952, 9.
[48]Henry Cabot Lodge, Jr., *As It Was* (New York, 1976), p. 36.

concurred that defeat in Indochina could have consequences more disastrous even than in Korea, where the United States was then seeking to negotiate a settlement. Korea was a peninsula and the impact could be isolated, they reasoned, but the fall of Indochina might cause the loss of all Southeast Asia, with potentially devastating political, strategic, and economic repercussions for the United States and its allies. France must not be permitted to negotiate. In the campaign, the Republicans had attacked the Democrats for failing to halt the advance of communism, and they were even more determined to win the war in Indochina. While vowing to wage the Cold War vigorously, Eisenhower and Dulles also promised cuts in defense spending. Their "New Look" defense policy called for sharp reductions in U.S. ground forces. They were even more reluctant than their predecessors to commit ground forces to Southeast Asia. France must hold the line.

The Republicans introduced changes more of mood and tactics than of substance. As would happen so often in the long history of U.S. involvement in Vietnam, a new administration came into office confident that new methods or the more persistent application of old ones could reverse a deteriorating situation. Eisenhower branded the French generals in Indochina a "poor lot" and insisted that new leadership was essential. The Joint Chiefs of Staff (JCS) opined that France could win the war within a year if it made better use of Vietnamese forces, as the United States had done with the Koreans. Most U.S. observers also agreed that France had not done enough to win nationalist support by making timely and substantive political concessions. The Republicans were certain that it was time to get tough with France. Diplomat Rob McClintock averred that the United States should refuse to pay the bill until the French stopped "sitting in their Beau Geste forts on champagne cases" and aggressively took the war to the enemy. Eisenhower and Dulles agreed with Gen. J. Lawton "Lightning Joe" Collins that it was time to "put the squeeze on the French to get them off their fannies."[49]

The new administration set out zealously to correct the perceived mistakes of its predecessor. Alarmed by evidence of French war-weariness, Eisenhower and Dulles gave firm assurances of continued assistance and promised that French "tiredness" would

[49]British Embassy, Saigon, to Foreign Office, April 24, 1953, PREM 11/645, Public Record Office; JCS meeting, April 24, 1953, *FR, 1952–1954*, 13: 500.

"evaporate in the face of a positive and constructive program."[50] They also made clear that continued aid would depend on detailed and specific information about French plans and military operations and on firm pledges to expand the VNA and develop an aggressive strategy with an explicit timetable for victory. Eisenhower himself impressed on the French the urgency of appointing a "forceful and inspirational leader, empowered with the means and authority to win victory" and of making "clear and unequivocal public announcements, repeated as often as may be desirable," that complete independence would be granted when the war was won.[51]

Although they refused to admit it to their American allies, the French by this time had all but abandoned hope of victory. They had also come to deeply regret their dependence on the United States, a "catastrophe," President Vincent Auriol called it. However, they saw little choice but to comply with U.S. demands. In early May 1953, the government appointed Gen. Henri Navarre to command its forces in Indochina. Two months later, a new cabinet headed by Joseph Laniel, promised (again!) to "perfect" the independence of the Associated States by giving them additional responsibilities. Shortly after, the French presented for U.S. approval a new strategic concept, the so-called Navarre Plan. Tailored to specifications set forth by the United States, the plan proposed a vast augmentation of the VNA, along with the commitment to Indochina of an additional nine battalions of French regulars. Navarre proposed to withdraw his scattered forces from their isolated garrisons, combine them with the new troops available to him, and initiate a major offensive in the Red River Delta. In a secret report to Paris, he admitted that the war could not be won in a strictly military sense. The best that could be hoped for was a draw. The Laniel government apparently adopted the plan as a last-ditch measure to salvage some return on an already huge investment and to ensure continued U.S. support. It also attached a high

---

[50]Dulles to U.S. Embassy Paris, March 27, 1953, U.S. Congress, House Committee on Armed Services, *United States–Vietnam Relations, 1945–1967: A Study Prepared by the Department of Defense* (Washington, D.C., 1971), Book 9: 20. Hereafter cited as *USVN* with book number.

[51]Eisenhower to C. Douglas Dillon, May 6, 1953, Dwight D. Eisenhower Papers, Dwight D. Eisenhower Library, Abilene, Kans., International File: France, 1953(3), Box 10.

price tag, sending Washington the by-now-ritualistic warning that without an additional $400 million in aid it would have to consider withdrawal from Indochina.

Although deeply skeptical of French intentions and capabilities, Washington felt compelled to go along. Eisenhower privately complained that Laniel's promise of independence had been made "in an obscure and roundabout fashion—instead of boldly, forthrightly, and repeatedly."[52] The JCS doubted France's willingness and ability to pursue the Navarre Plan vigorously. By this time, however, the two nations were caught in a tangle of conflicting aims, mutual distrust and dependence, and spiraling commitments. The Navarre Plan seemed to offer a chance of success. Laniel's fall might bring in a government committed to negotiations resulting in the "eventual loss to Communism not only of Indochina but of the whole of Southeast Asia."[53] After extracting a French promise to pursue the plan determinedly, in September 1953 the U.S. administration agreed to provide an additional $385 million in military aid. With characteristic bravado, Dulles proclaimed that the new French strategy would "break the organized body of Communist aggression by the end of the 1955 fighting season."[54]

THE DIEN BIEN PHU CRISIS

In fact, within six months, France's position in Vietnam was in peril. An outburst of Vietnamese nationalism later in 1953 further undermined its already tenuous political authority. When the French opened negotiations to "perfect" Vietnamese independence, non-Communist nationalists, including some of Bao Dai's associates, demanded not only complete independence but severance of all ties with France. The United States faced a dilemma. Although it had taken a firm stand for eventual independence, it feared that Vietnamese demands might provoke a French withdrawal, and it was certain that Bao Dai's government could not stand alone. Ambassador Heath charged the Vietnamese with "childlike" and

---

[52]Eisenhower to Ralph Flanders, July 7, 1953, Eisenhower Papers, Diary Series, Box 2.
[53]State Department report to NSC, August 5, 1953, *USVN*, Book 9: 128.
[54]Quoted in Bernard Fall, *The Two Vietnams: A Political and Military Analysis* (New York, 1967), p. 122.

"irresponsible" behavior. Dulles denounced their "ill-considered" actions and dangled before them promises of large-scale aid if they behaved.[55] The U.S. embassy in Saigon pressed the Vietnamese to tone down their demands; "We are the last French colonialists in Indochina," an American diplomat remarked with wry humor.[56] Despite U.S. attempts to mediate, the two sides could not agree on the status of an independent Vietnam.

The political crisis of late 1953, an increasingly costly military stalemate, and a major shift in Soviet and Chinese foreign policies created irresistible pressures for negotiations. Despairing of military victory, many French politicians had already concluded that Vietnamese association with the French Union, if only symbolic, was all that could be salvaged. The leaders who took power in the Kremlin after Stalin's death in February 1953 wanted a respite from Cold War tensions to solidify their grasp on power and address critical domestic problems. They had taken a conciliatory stance on numerous Cold War issues, Indochina included, and the French government hoped that Soviet influence might make possible an acceptable settlement. Following the Korean peace agreement, China also sought a breather to boost its international status, complete the revolution at home, and focus on essential issues such as liberating Taiwan.[57] Over Dulles's vigorous objections, in early 1954 France agreed to place Indochina on the agenda of an East-West conference scheduled to meet in Geneva to consider Asian problems.

Eisenhower and Dulles could only acquiesce. Distrustful of Soviet overtures and skeptical of French wisdom, they could not openly oppose the peaceful settlement of a major international issue. The French still refused to ratify the EDC, and the new Kremlin line complicated the prospect by easing European fears of the USSR. Like Acheson before him, Dulles hesitated to press France too hard on Indochina lest it reject the EDC altogether, splitting the Western alliance and playing into the hands of the Soviets.

[55]Heath to State Department, October 18, 1953, *FR, 1952–1954*, 13:836; Dulles to U.S. Embassy Saigon, October 21, 1953, *USVN*, Book 9: 169–170.
[56]Quoted in Hammer, *Struggle for Indochina*, p. 319.
[57]Chen Jian, "Bridging Revolution and Decolonization: The 'Bandung Discourse' in China's Early Cold War Experience," in Goscha and Ostermann, *Connecting Histories*, pp. 148–149.

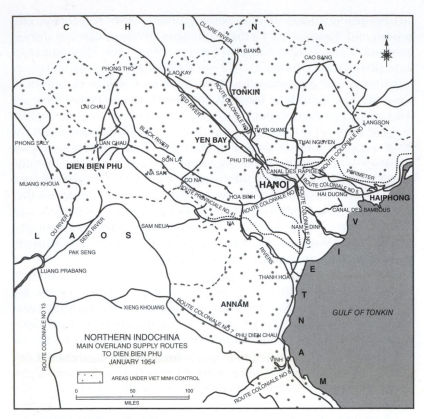

The Battle of Dien Bien Phu
UAGS

With negotiations now pending, France and the Viet Minh prepared for battle near the remote village of Dien Bien Phu in the
northwestern corner of Vietnam. Called the "Arena of the Gods" by
local peoples, the eleven-mile-long valley was one of the few open
spaces in a region of rugged mountains. It was strategically placed
at the crossroads of Vietnam, Laos, and China. It produced ample
rice and enough opium to help fund both the French and the Viet
Minh war efforts. By establishing a major base there, Navarre
hoped to draw Viet Minh forces away from the Red River Delta and
Annam. He sought to protect Laos, whose loss could have

disastrous political consequences, and to defend the Tai and Hmong hill people who had fiercely resisted Viet Minh domination. Drawing upon French success at the battle of Na San in late 1952, Navarre planned to use Dien Bien Phu as a base from which to mount air–land operations against Viet Minh forces in the area and even to draw the enemy into a pitched battle where French artillery and air power might prevail. He counted upon logistical difficulties to limit the enemy's ability to get large numbers of troops into the area and sustain them. Victory at Dien Bien Phu would give France an edge in the upcoming negotiations. In late 1953, Navarre dispatched twelve battalions of regulars supported by aircraft and heavy artillery. His base commander, the flamboyant aristocrat Col. Christian Marie Ferdinand de la Croix de Castries, constructed an airfield and a garrison ringed with barbed wire and bunkers and protected by a series of artillery bases in the outlying hills, each, according to legend, named for one of his mistresses.[58]

Giap took the "bait." Although keenly aware of the difficulties of fighting in such a distant area and on such difficult terrain, he, too, saw an opportunity to strike a decisive blow at a critical point in the war. Following defeat at Na San, he determined never again to fight at a disadvantage. He set out to get to Dien Bien Phu sufficient forces and equipment to overwhelm the French garrison. Giap drove his soldiers and civilian workers mercilessly, day and night, for weeks. In one of the most spectacular logistical feats in the history of warfare, the Viet Minh moved an army of fifty thousand men into the hills around the French garrison. Coolies devoted hours of grueling labor to repairing existing roads and building new ones. Thousands of porters, including a "long-haired army" of women, used trucks, twenty thousand bicycles, and sheer human exertion to move tons of equipment and supplies over the hundreds of miles from southern China and the delta. U.S. and French "experts" had predicted that it would be impossible to get heavy artillery up to the high ground surrounding the garrison. The Viet Minh formed "human anthills," carrying disassembled weapons up piece by piece, putting them back together, placing them in underground casements, and camouflaging them so effectively that they

---

[58]Logevall, *Embers of War*, pp. 383–384; Martin Windrow, *The Last Valley: Dien Bien Phu and the French Defeat in Vietnam* (Cambridge, Mass., 2004), pp. 56–62, 211, 218–223.

were impervious to French artillery and air attacks. By January 1954, the two sides were girded for the decisive battle of the First Indochina War.[59]

At this point, for the first time, the United States faced the prospect of military intervention in Vietnam. Eisenhower expressed strong opposition to putting U.S. troops into the jungles of Indochina. But he went on to insist that the United States could not forget its vital interests there. Comparing the region to a "leaky dike," he warned that it was "sometimes better to put a finger in than to let the whole structure wash away."[60] A special committee reviewing Indochina policy recommended in mid-March that the United States should discourage defeatist tendencies in France. If, despite its efforts, the French negotiated an unsatisfactory agreement, the United States might have to join the Associated States and other nations to fight without France.[61]

While the United States pondered intervention, Giap tightened the noose around Dien Bien Phu. After two months of painstaking preparation, on March 13 the Viet Minh unleashed a withering artillery assault on the furthest hill outposts of Gabrielle and Beatrice. The severity of the fire stunned the French defenders. The Viet Minh's 75 mm and 105 mm guns shredded French defenses, destroyed weapons, collapsed trenches, and killed and maimed the outgunned defenders. The attackers seized the outposts within twenty-four hours and knocked out the airfield, making resupply impossible except by parachute drop and leaving the garrison isolated and vulnerable. The French had gone into battle confident of the outcome. By upsetting the calculations upon which their confidence had been based, the Viet Minh artillery assault by itself sent their morale plummeting. Top leaders recognized that they must stay, but they were no longer hopeful of the outcome.[62]

The spectacular initial Viet Minh success at Dien Bien Phu raised the prospect of immediate U.S. intervention. During a visit to Washington in late March, French chief of staff Gen. Paul Ely still estimated a "50-50 chance of success" and merely requested the transfer of additional U.S. aircraft to be used for attacks on Viet

---

[59]Logevall, *Embers of War*, pp. 412–417; Windrow, *Last Valley*, pp. 258–259.
[60]Record of NSC meeting, January 8, 1954, *FR, 1952–1954*, 13: 949, 952.
[61]*Pentagon Papers (Gravel)*, 1: 90–92.
[62]Windrow, *Last Valley*, pp. 370–371, 374–379.

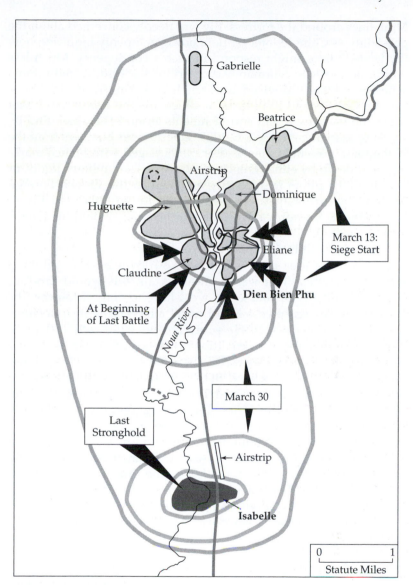

Gabrielle

Beatrice

Airstrip

Dominique

Huguette

Eliane

Claudine

March 13:
Siege Start

Dien Bien Phu

At Beginning
of Last Battle

Noua River

March 30

Last
Stronghold

Airstrip

Isabelle

0   1
Statute Miles

Progress of the Battle

Minh lines around the fortress. Ely was deeply concerned about the possibility of Chinese intervention, however, openly inquiring how the United States might respond in such a contingency. Much less optimistic, the JCS chairman, Adm. Arthur Radford, seized upon a scheme originally devised by French and American officers in Saigon. Code-named VULTURE, it called for the bombing of Viet Minh supply lines to and entrenchments around Dien Bien Phu by a fleet of as many as sixty U.S. B-29 Superfortress bombers from the Philippines, possibly unmarked or camouflaged with French markings and flown by either French crews, American military pilots, or U.S. military pilots temporarily assigned to the French Foreign Legion. Radford's apparent enthusiasm for the plan led Ely to believe that U.S. approval would be forthcoming should the French formally request it.[63]

VULTURE won little support in Washington. Eisenhower briefly toyed with the idea of a "single strike [flown by U.S. pilots in unmarked planes], if it were almost certain this would produce decisive results." "Of course . . . we'd have to deny it forever," he added.[64] Dulles accepted air and naval intervention in Indochina, but only as a last resort. He preferred what he called "United Action," the formation of a coalition composed of the United States, Great Britain, France, Australia, New Zealand, the Philippines, Thailand, and the Associated States, to guarantee the security of Southeast Asia. By its very existence, such a grouping might deter Chinese intervention in Indochina and aggression elsewhere in Asia. United Action, as some scholars have argued, may have been primarily a bluff. Or, if military intervention became necessary, it would remove the stigma of a war for French colonialism and ensure that the burden did not fall upon the United States. In keeping with the New Look defense policy, local and regional forces could bear the brunt of ground fighting while the United States provided air and naval support and money and supplies and trained indigenous forces.

[63]Laurent Cesari and Jacques de Folin, "Military Necessity, Political Impossibility: The French Point of View on Operation *Vautour*," in Lawrence S. Kaplan et al. (eds.), *Dien Bien Phu and the Crisis of Franco-American Relations, 1954–1955* (Wilmington, Del., 1990), pp. 105–120.

[64]Memorandum of conversation, Eisenhower and Dulles, March 24, 1954, Lot 64D199, Box 22, Department of State Records; James Hagerty Diary, April 1, 1954, James Hagerty Papers, Dwight D. Eisenhower Library, Abilene, Kans.

Most top military advisers opposed air intervention at Dien Bien Phu. Some questioned whether an air strike could relieve the siege without destroying the French garrison itself. Others wondered whether intervention could be kept limited; "One cannot go over Niagara Falls in a barrel only slightly," one military analyst warned.[65] Among the JCS, only U.S. Air Force Gen. Nathan F. Twining approved the proposal, and he insisted on conditions the French would never have accepted. The other chiefs advised that air intervention would not decisively affect the outcome of the war. Army Chief of Staff Matthew Ridgway was particularly outspoken, warning Eisenhower that airpower alone could not ensure victory and ground forces would have to fight under the most difficult logistic circumstances and on singularly inhospitable terrain.[66]

Although profoundly skeptical about an air strike, the administration was sufficiently alarmed by the emerging crisis to seek congressional support for possible military intervention. The fall of Dien Bien Phu seemed likely by early April. Eisenhower and Dulles preferred to act in concert with other nations, but they feared that a defeat might produce a French collapse before plans for United Action could be implemented, leaving U.S. naval and airpower the only means to save Indochina. Sensitive to Truman's fate in Korea, they were unwilling to act without congressional backing. Thus on April 3, Dulles met with legislative leaders to seek discretionary authority to employ U.S. naval and air forces— with allies if possible, without them if necessary—should the fall of Dien Bien Phu threaten the loss of Indochina. The secretary met stubborn resistance. No one questioned his assessment of the gravity of the situation, but the members of Congress insisted that there must be "no more Koreas with the United States furnishing 90% of the manpower." They also made clear that the United States could not go to war in defense of French colonialism. They would agree to support a resolution authorizing U.S. intervention only if "satisfactory commitments" could be secured from Great Britain and other allies to support military intervention and from France to "internationalize" the war and speed the move toward Vietnamese independence. Congressional insistence on prior allied

[65]*Pentagon Papers (Gravel)*, 1: 89.
[66]Ridgway memorandum to Joint Chiefs, April 2, 1954, Matthew B. Ridgway Papers, U.S. Army Military History Institute, Carlisle Barracks, Pa.

commitments eliminated the option of unilateral intervention and placed major obstacles in the way of United Action.[67]

The April 3 session also doomed an air strike at Dien Bien Phu. Although wary of U.S. intervention in any form, the French government eventually concluded that an air strike offered the only hope of saving the beleaguered fortress and two days later requested its implementation. Eisenhower promptly rejected the French request. On April 6, the NSC agreed to initiate planning for possible later intervention while attempting to meet the essential preconditions for United Action.[68]

With the fate of Dien Bien Phu hanging in the balance, the United States frantically promoted United Action. Dulles hustled off to London and Paris to consult with allied leaders. Eisenhower penned a long personal letter to Prime Minister Winston Churchill urging British support for a coalition that would be "willing to fight" to check Communist expansion in Southeast Asia. At a much publicized news conference on April 7, he laid the foundation for possible U.S. intervention. Outlining in simple language the principles that had shaped U.S. policy for years, he emphasized that Indochina was a vital source of tin, tungsten, and rubber and that having lost China to "Communist dictatorship," the United States "simply can't afford greater losses." More important, he added, should Indochina fall, the rest of Southeast Asia would "go over very quickly," like a "row of dominoes" when the first one is knocked down, causing much greater losses of raw materials and people, jeopardizing America's strategic position in the region, and driving Japan into the Communist camp. "So the possible consequences of the loss," he concluded, "are just incalculable to the free world."[69]

The U.S. initiative exposed fundamental cleavages with major allies. Churchill and Foreign Secretary Anthony Eden did not agree that the loss of Indochina would bring the fall of Southeast Asia. They believed that France could salvage a reasonable settlement at Geneva. They feared that outside intervention would undermine a negotiated settlement and perhaps provoke war with China.

[67]Dulles memorandum, April 5, 1954, John Foster Dulles Papers, Dwight D. Eisenhower Library, Abilene, Kans.
[68]Record of telephone conversation, Eisenhower and Dulles, April 5, 1954, Eisenhower Papers, Diary Series, Box 3; record of NSC meeting, April 6, 1954, *FR, 1952–1954*, 13: 1253.
[69]Dwight D. Eisenhower, *Public Papers, 1954* (Washington, D.C., 1955), pp. 382–384.

Most important, they had no desire to entangle Britain in a war they were certain could not be won. The French insisted that Vietnam must retain ties with the French Union. They wanted nothing more than an air strike to help relieve the siege of Dien Bien Phu. They opposed internationalization of the war, which would undermine their prestige in Indochina and take control from their hands.

The administration was deeply annoyed with the European response. U.S. officials privately complained that the British were "weak-kneed" and showed a "woeful unawareness" of the risks of inaction. Eisenhower accused the French of using "weasel words" in their promises to the Vietnamese.[70] They "want us to come in as junior partners and provide materials, etc., while they themselves retain authority in that region." He would "not go along with them on any such notion."[71]

Congressional opposition reinforced the administration's determination to avoid unilateral intervention. In a speech that won praise from members of both parties, Senator John F. Kennedy, a Massachusetts Democrat, warned that no amount of military aid could conquer "an enemy of the people which has the support and covert appeal of the people." There could be no victory as long as France remained. When a "high administration source," subsequently identified as Vice President Richard M. Nixon, remarked "off the record" that if United Action failed, the United States might have to send troops to Indochina, the reaction was immediate and strong.

Continued British opposition sealed the fate of United Action. In late April, French Foreign Minister Georges Bidault made a last desperate appeal for U.S. support, warning that only a "massive" air attack would save Dien Bien Phu and that France was prepared to internationalize the war. Dulles frantically sought to sway Eden, urgently warning that without allied support France would give up the fight. The British would have none of it. Eisenhower informed congressional leaders on April 26 that it would be a "tragic error to go in alone as a partner of France" and reaffirmed that the United States would intervene only as a "grouping of interested nations."

[70]Hagerty Diary, April 25, 1954, Hagerty Papers; Eisenhower Diary, April 27, 1954, Eisenhower Papers, Diary Series, Box 3.
[71]Eisenhower to E. E. Hazlett, April 27, 1954, Eisenhower Papers, Diary Series, Box 4; record of telephone conversation, Eisenhower and Walter Bedell Smith, April 24, 1954, ibid., Box 3.

Three days later, the NSC formally decided to "hold up for the time any military action in Indo China until we see how Geneva is coming along."[72] Eisenhower and Dulles may have conceived of United Action mainly as a bluff designed to neutralize "hawks" in Congress and the country. More likely, they were prepared to intervene but were thwarted by legislative leaders and allies.

The decision ensured the fall of Dien Bien Phu. Giap's army had suffered horrendous losses in the capture of Beatrice and Gabrielle, threatening morale in the ranks. While resting and rebuilding his forces, he shifted to what he called "nibbling away," building a veritable spider web of assault trenches, picking off the remaining French outposts a few at a time, and eventually closing in on the main camp. Old-timers among the French troops compared the battlefield to Verdun. After six weeks of siege warfare, the Viet Minh launched their final assault in early May. Isolated, badly bloodied, hopelessly outmanned, without adequate food, water, and medicine, the French surrendered on May 7 after fifty-five days of courageous but futile resistance.[73]

Dien Bien Phu is generally considered one of the most important battles of the twentieth century. For much of the nine-week siege, the world's attention was focused on that remote and beleaguered French outpost. The battle was enormously costly for both sides. The French lost an estimated 1,500 killed, 4,000 wounded, and as many as 10,000 missing or captured, the latter subjected to horrific treatment by their captors. The Viet Minh suffered an estimated 25,000 casualties, 10,000 of them killed, requiring weeks to recover. The French lost a much smaller proportion of their active forces, still controlled the major cities of Vietnam, and were in a position to fight on. But the defeat at Dien Bien Phu was a devastating blow to already shaky morale at home. The mood of "shocked despair" in France was compared to that of 1940. A day of mourning was declared in Paris; theaters and eating places were closed.[74]

Dien Bien Phu thus brought about the end of the First Indochina War, the first time in the postwar era that anticolonial forces

[72]Dulles to State Department, April 22, 23, 1954, Eisenhower Papers, Ann Whitman File; summary of meeting, April 26, 1954, Eisenhower Papers, "Cleanup" File, Box 16; Hagerty Diary, April 29, 1954, Hagerty Papers.
[73]Windrow, *Last Valley*, pp. 499–566.
[74]Ibid., pp. 628–633; see also John Prados, "Assessing Dien Bien Phu," in Lawrence and Logevall, *First Vietnam War*, pp. 215–239.

had defeated a Western power. The battle left deep marks on those involved. The French felt betrayed by a United States that had pushed them to fight and then left them to die. Americans attributed the debacle to the French Army's "bunker psychosis," ignoring what the war might teach them about Viet Minh tactics and reinforcing their confidence in their own aggressive way of war. For the Viet Minh, the battle vindicated "peoples' war" and became a celebrated part of their larger historical record of exploiting human resources to expel powerful outside invaders. They would seek a similar battle with similar results to defeat the United States in the war that would soon follow.[75]

THE GENEVA CONFERENCE

With the fall of Dien Bien Phu, the attention of belligerents and outside parties immediately shifted to Geneva, where consideration of Indochina was to begin the following day. The British, Soviets, and Chinese took the lead in the conference and sought mainly to end the war and thereby avert U.S. intervention. For China, Geneva was a sort of coming out party, its first appearance on the world stage, and it hoped by participating and promoting a settlement to advance its stature as a great power. Reeling from Dien Bien Phu, France came to Geneva, Bidault lamented, holding a "two of clubs and a three of diamonds."[76] Resigned to getting out of Vietnam, it sought the best settlement it could obtain. Buoyed by its victory, the DRV savored the prize for which it had been fighting for seven years. Its leaders perceived, however, that Dien Bien Phu had not significantly altered the balance of forces in its favor and that, exhausted from their recent sacrifices, its own armies desperately needed a respite. Like their allies, Viet Minh leaders also saw that U.S. intervention must be avoided and that they might have to compromise to forestall that eventuality.[77]

[75]Dennis Showalter, "Dien Bien Phu in Three Cultures," *War and Society* 16 (October 1998): 93–98.

[76]Quoted in Chester Cooper, *The Lost Crusade: America in Vietnam* (New York, 1970), p. 79.

[77]Jian, "China," pp. 242–245; Pierre Asselin, "The Democratic Republic of Vietnam and the 1954 Geneva Conference: A Revisionist Critique," *Cold War History* 11 (May 2011): 158–159.

The United States was a reluctant participant at Geneva. In these tension-ridden days of the early Cold War, negotiation with any Communist nation was anathema, but the presence of Communist China, which the United States had refused to recognize and was seeking to isolate diplomatically, was especially unpalatable. Dulles remained in Geneva only briefly and, in the words of a biographer, conducted himself with the "pinched distaste of a puritan in a house of ill repute."[78] He once remarked that the only way he and Chinese delegate Zhou En-lai would meet was if their cars collided. When they actually met face-to-face and Zhou extended his hand, the secretary, according to some accounts, turned his back. The administration faced a dilemma. For reasons of international and domestic politics, it did not want to "lose" all or even part of Indochina to the Communists. But it was also keenly aware that there was little public support for military intervention. Eisenhower and Dulles had long feared that Geneva might provide a fig leaf of respectability for a French surrender, and the fall of Dien Bien Phu increased its concern. After departing Geneva, Dulles instructed his delegation to participate in the conference only as an "interested nation," not as a "belligerent or a principal in the negotiations" and not to endorse an agreement that in any way impaired the territorial integrity of the Associated States.[79] Given the military position of the Viet Minh when the conference opened, he was saying that the United States would endorse no settlement at all.

During the first five weeks of the conference, the United States also kept alive the possibility of military intervention. When Laniel requested U.S. help if the Chinese stalled the talks while the Viet Minh pressed on for military victory, the administration resumed planning for possible intervention. The JCS drew up detailed contingency plans for deploying U.S. forces, even agreeing that nuclear weapons might be used if militarily advantageous. Officials also drafted a congressional resolution authorizing the president to employ U.S. military forces in Indochina. They hoped to develop a new scheme for United Action that did not require British backing.

As before, the talks foundered. The administration demanded of France an unequivocal advance commitment to internationalize the war and a guarantee that the Associated States could withdraw

---

[78]Townsend Hoopes, *The Devil and John Foster Dulles* (Boston, 1973), p. 222.
[79]Dulles to Smith, May 12, 1954, *USVN*, Book 9: 457–459.

from the French Union. The French indicated a willingness only to discuss the U.S. conditions and insisted on at least a token commitment of American ground forces and a prior commitment to employ airpower if the Chinese intervened. France eventually concluded that it must exhaust every possibility of a negotiated settlement before prolonging the war. Eisenhower and Dulles surmised that Paris was keeping alive the possibility of U.S. intervention primarily as a "card to play at Geneva." In any event, the refusal of Australia and New Zealand to go along effectively ditched United Action. The discussions all but ended by mid-June.[80] They may have reinforced Communist concerns about U.S. intervention, thereby encouraging compromise and a settlement.

After more than a month of deadlock, the conferees at Geneva began to inch toward an agreement based on the temporary partition of Vietnam, to be followed by national elections. Laniel had promised Bao Dai he would reject partition, but his cabinet fell on June 12 and he was replaced by Pierre Mendès-France. The new prime minister was flexible on partition and upon taking power also promised to resign if a settlement was not reached by July 21. From the outset, the Soviets and the Chinese had pressed the DRV to accept partition. The DRV had itself concluded that such a settlement might be all it could obtain. Its willingness to compromise was spurred in June when France recognized the independence of the State of Vietnam and Bao Dai named Ngo Dinh Diem prime minister. The DRV viewed the fiercely anti-Communist Diem as an "American lackey" and increasingly feared that the United States would seek to replace France in Vietnam. Following conversations with Chou En-lai in early July, Ho Chi Minh agreed to partition while hoping for a dividing line at the sixteenth parallel.[81]

In mid-June, the United States also adopted a change of policy with momentous long-range implications. Recognizing that the war could not be prolonged without grave risks and that part of Vietnam would likely be lost at Geneva, the administration began to plan for the defense of what was left in Indochina and the rest of Southeast Asia. Dulles told congressional leaders on June 24 that whatever emerged from Geneva would be "something we would have to gag about," but he expressed optimism that the United

[80]Dulles to American Consulate Geneva, June 8, 1954, ibid., p. 541.
[81]Asselin, "Geneva Conference," pp. 168–169; Jian, "China," pp. 253–262.

States could still "salvage something" in Southeast Asia "free of the taint of French colonialism." The United States would have to assume responsibility for defending Laos, Cambodia, and non-Communist Vietnam. The first step would be to draw a line that the Communists would not cross and then "hold this area and fight subversion within it with all the strength we have" by providing economic aid and building a strong military force. The United States must also take the lead in forming a regional defense grouping "to keep alive freedom" in Southeast Asia.[82]

Over the next three weeks, Dulles worked relentlessly to ensure this outcome. He secured British commitment to an agreement that would include freedom for Laos, Cambodia, and southern Vietnam to maintain "stable, non-communist regimes" and accept foreign arms and advisers. To the point of threatening to disassociate the United States from Geneva, he pushed Mendès-France to go along. Even then, Dulles approached the last stages of Geneva determined to retain complete freedom of action. The United States must play no role in the negotiations, he instructed chief delegate Walter Bedell Smith. If the agreement lived up to its standards, the United States would issue a unilateral statement of endorsement. Otherwise, it would reserve the freedom to "publicly disassociate itself." Under no circumstances would it be a "cosignatory with the Communists" and "it would not guarantee the results."[83]

By mid-July pressures for a settlement had mounted. Mendès-France's July 21 deadline was approaching and Anglo-American backing improved his bargaining position. The Russians and Chinese continued to press for a compromise agreement. Taking seriously Dulles's bluster and increasingly fearing that a breakdown of negotiations might provoke U.S. intervention, the DRV agreed to remove its forces from and to accept neutrality for Laos and Cambodia and the partition of Vietnam at the seventeenth parallel. "After French withdrawal, the whole of Vietnam will be yours," Zhou assured DRV leaders.[84]

The Geneva Agreements (Geneva Accords) provided that Vietnam would be partitioned along the seventeenth parallel to permit

---

[82]Hagerty Diary, June 23, 24, 28, Hagerty Papers.
[83]*Pentagon Papers (Gravel)*, 1: 152.
[84]Quoted in Qiang Zhai, *China and the Vietnam Wars, 1950–1975* (Chapel Hill, N.C., 2000), p. 58; see also Asselin, "Geneva Conference," pp. 169–170.

regrouping of military forces from both sides. The division was to be temporary and should not be "interpreted as constituting a political or territorial boundary." The country was to be reunified by elections scheduled for the summer of 1956 and supervised by an international commission composed of Canada, Poland, and India. To insulate Vietnam against a renewal of conflict during the transitional period, troops were to be withdrawn from the partition zones within three hundred days. The introduction of new forces and equipment and the establishment of foreign military bases were prohibited. Neither part of Vietnam was to join a military alliance. Cease-fire arrangements for Laos and Cambodia explicitly recognized the two nations' right to self-defense, but to ease Chinese fears of U.S. intervention, they were not to enter military alliances or permit foreign bases on their soil except in cases where their security was endangered.

The Geneva Agreements, in the words of a Canadian diplomat, constituted a "nasty bargain accepted by all parties as the only way to avoid a dangerous confrontation."[85] The major issues over which the war had been fought were not settled. The terms were vague in crucial places; different people viewed their meaning quite differently. The manner in which the accords were handled was unusual if not unique and reflected the tenuous nature of the understandings themselves. The United States and the State of Vietnam refused to associate themselves with the formal agreements. Other nations signed only the cease-fire agreement, merely listing their names on the political "instruments."

For the members of the DRV leadership, Geneva represented at best a bittersweet victory. They found partition difficult to accept, even temporarily, and they had hoped that the line would be drawn further south and the elections held sooner. They appreciated, however, that they could not get better terms. They had committed huge resources to Dien Bien Phu, suffered enormous losses, and were in no position to follow up with major campaigns elsewhere. Even without U.S. involvement, Giap estimated that it would take at least two more years to defeat the French. Prolonging the war risked American intervention. Ever the pragmatist, Ho cautioned those "intoxicated with victories" that the "struggle for

[85]Quoted in James Eayrs, *In Defence of Canada: Indochina and the Roots of Complicity* (Toronto, 1983), p. 225.

peace is a hard and complex one." The Viet Minh must work within the framework of Geneva to attain its goals of independence and unity.[86]

The United States also took a mixed view toward Geneva. The settlement produced some domestic political backlash. California Republican senator and hard-core anti-Communist William Knowland hyperbolically called it "the greatest victory the communists have won in twenty years." The Eisenhower administration itself viewed with concern the loss of northern Vietnam—"the keystone to the arch of Southeast Asia"—but Eisenhower and Dulles realized, as Smith put it, that "diplomacy has rarely been able to gain at the conference table what cannot be held on the battlefield." The administration protected itself against domestic attacks and retained its freedom of action by refusing to associate itself with the agreements. In a unilateral statement, Smith simply "took note" of the Geneva Accords and vowed that the United States would not "disturb them" by the "threat or the use of force."[87]

In truth, the administration was not displeased. The agreements were better than had been anticipated when the conference opened, and they allowed sufficient latitude to proceed along the path Dulles had outlined. Partition at least gave the United States the chance to build up non-Communist forces in southern Vietnam, a challenge the administration took up eagerly. The accords placed some limits on outside intervention, to be sure, but they were not viewed as prohibitive. And some of the terms seemed advantageous. Eisenhower and Dulles agreed, for example, that if the elections were held immediately, Ho Chi Minh would be an easy victor. But the two-year delay gave the United States "fairly good time" to get ready. Canada's presence on the commission would enable it to "block things."[88]

Eisenhower and Dulles viewed the apparent demise of French colonialism with equanimity if not outright enthusiasm. The Franco-American partnership in Indochina had been marked by profound mutual suspicion and deep-seated tensions. The United States had provided France more than $2.6 billion in military aid,

[86]Quoted in Duiker, *Ho Chi Minh*, pp. 460–461; Logevall, *Embers of War*, pp. 747–749.
[87]*Pentagon Papers (Gravel)*, 1: 571–572.
[88]Record of telephone conversation, Eisenhower and Dulles, July 20, 1954, Eisenhower Papers, Diary Series, Box 4.

but its efforts to influence French policies by friendly persuasion and attaching strings had failed. The commitment to France had indeed turned out to be a "dead-end alley." Americans attributed France's failure mainly to its misguided attempts to perpetuate colonialism in Indochina. They were confident that without France they could find a viable non-Communist alternative to the Viet Minh. "We must work with these people, and then they themselves will soon find out that we are their friends and they can't live without us," Eisenhower observed.[89] Conceding that the Geneva Accords included "many features he did not like," Dulles still insisted that they contained many "good aspects," most important, the "truly independent status" of Laos, Cambodia, and southern Vietnam. The "important thing," he concluded, was "not to mourn the past but to seize the future opportunity to prevent the loss in Northern Vietnam from leading to the extension of communism throughout Southeast Asia and the Southwest Pacific."[90]

[89]Hagerty Diary, July 23, 1954, Hagerty Papers.
[90]Dulles news conference, July 23, 1954, John Foster Dulles Papers, Seely G. Mudd Manuscript Library, Princeton, N.J.

The Ngo Family
With American assistance, Ngo Dinh Diem played a major role in the
founding of South Vietnam, but his increasing isolation and reliance on his
family ultimately contributed to his undoing.
© *Bettmann/CORBIS*

CHAPTER 2

Our Offspring

Nation Building in South Vietnam, 1954–1961

"The fundamental tenets of this nation's foreign policy . . . depend in considerable measure upon a strong and free Vietnamese nation," Senator John F. Kennedy proclaimed in 1956. "Vietnam represents the cornerstone of the Free World in Southeast Asia, the keystone in the arch, the finger in the dike." Should the "red tide of Communism" pour into it, Kennedy warned, much of Asia would be threatened. Vietnam's economy was essential to the prosperity of Southeast Asia, the senator went on to say, its "political liberty" an "inspiration to those seeking to obtain or maintain their liberty in all parts of Asia—and indeed of the world." The United States had special obligations to Vietnam that extended beyond mere considerations of the national interest, he stressed in conclusion: "It is our offspring, we cannot abandon it, we cannot ignore its needs."[1]

Kennedy was addressing the American Friends of Vietnam (AFV), and he may have been indulging in after-dinner hyperbole, but his words spoke volumes about the way Americans viewed Vietnam in the 1950s. His reference to South Vietnam as "our offspring" betrayed the sort of paternalism that typified U.S. dealings with Asians. His speech summed up the rationale for American policy in South Vietnam, touched on the pivotal role played by the United States at its birth, and highlighted the importance it came to assume. Certain that its fall to Communism would cause the "loss" of all Southeast Asia, after Geneva the Eisenhower

[1]John F. Kennedy, "America's Stake in Vietnam," *Vital Speeches* 22 (August 1, 1956): 617–619.

administration set out to create a nation that could stand as a bulwark against Communist expansion and serve as a proving ground for democracy in Asia. Originating from the exigencies of the Cold War, the experiment in nation building also tapped the wellsprings of American idealism and took on the trappings of a crusade. Begun as a high-risk gamble, it appeared for a time one of the great success stories of postwar U.S. foreign policy. But Americans' certainty that they knew what was best for their "offspring" inevitably clashed with the views of a proud people who had their own vision for an independent South Vietnam. Their neocolonial approach produced a dependent society whose weaknesses in time became evident. Only at the end of the decade, when South Vietnam was swept by revolution and its government increasingly threatened did Americans begin to perceive the magnitude and complexity of the problem they had taken on.

A GOOD STOUT EFFORT

Warning that Geneva had been a "disaster" that had made possible a "major forward stride of Communism," the National Security Council (NSC) in the summer of 1954 called for a "new initiative" to shore up the U.S. position in Southeast Asia. The NSC recommended the use of "all available means" to undermine the infant Democratic Republic of Vietnam (DRV) regime in northern Vietnam.[2] Throughout the rest of the year, a CIA team stationed in Saigon and headed by Col. Edward Lansdale devised numerous clandestine methods to harass the Hanoi government. Paramilitary groups infiltrated across the demilitarized zone on sabotage missions, attempting to destroy the government's printing presses and pouring contaminants into the engines of buses to demobilize the transportation system. The teams also carried out "psywar" operations to embarrass the DRV and encourage emigration to the south. They distributed fake leaflets announcing the harsh methods the

---

[2]NSC, "Review of U.S. Policy in the Far East," August 1954, U.S. Congress, House Committee on Armed Services, *United States–Vietnam Relations, 1945–1967: A Study Prepared by the Department of Defense* (Washington, D.C., 1971), Book 10, 731–741. Hereafter cited as *USVN* with book number.

government was prepared to take and even hired astrologers to predict hard times in the north and good times in the south.[3]

In the meantime, Dulles hastened off to Manila and negotiated the Southeast Asian security pact he had promoted so vigorously during the Dien Bien Phu crisis. The Southeast Asian Treaty Organization (SEATO) had obvious weaknesses. The major neutralist nations of the region—Burma, India, and Indonesia—declined to join. Because of restrictions imposed by the Geneva Accords, Laos, Cambodia, and southern Vietnam could not formally participate. Eisenhower and Dulles admitted that the "western colorization" of the alliance was "unfortunate," but they conceded that it was necessary because of the weakness of the countries in the area. The member nations bound themselves only to "meet common danger" in accordance with their own "constitutional processes" and to "consult" with each other.

From Dulles's standpoint, SEATO was more than satisfactory. The mere existence of the alliance might deter Communist aggression in the region. More important, a separate protocol specifically designated Laos, Cambodia, and southern Vietnam as areas that, if threatened, would "endanger" the "peace and security" of the signatories. During the Dien Bien Phu crisis, Dulles had felt hampered by the lack of a legal basis for intervention in Indochina. The SEATO protocol not only remedied this defect but also established the foundation, should United Action become necessary in the future, and gave South Vietnam a semblance of international status as a "free" nation.[4]

The key to the new American "initiative" was South Vietnam. The NSC recommended that the United States "make every possible effort, not openly inconsistent with the U.S. position as to the armistice agreements . . . to maintain a friendly non-Communist South Vietnam and to prevent a Communist victory through all-Vietnam elections."[5] Violating the spirit and sometimes the letter of the Geneva Accords, the Eisenhower administration in 1954 and after firmly committed itself to the fragile government of Ngo Dinh

---

[3]Neil Sheehan et al., *The Pentagon Papers as Published by the New York Times* (New York, 1971), pp. 16–18. Hereafter cited as *Pentagon Papers (NYT)*.

[4]SEATO included the United States, the United Kingdom, France, Australia, New Zealand, Thailand, the Philippines, and Pakistan.

[5]NSC, "Review of U.S. Policy in the Far East," August 1954, *USVN*, Book 10, 731–741.

Diem, eased the French out of Vietnam, and used its resources unsparingly to construct in southern Vietnam a viable, non-Communist nation that would stand as the "cornerstone of the Free World in Southeast Asia."

Had it looked all over the world, the United States might not have chosen a less promising place for an experiment in nation building. The partition settlement left an estimated 14 of 25 million Vietnamese above the seventeenth parallel. The DRV regime was not without internal opposition. It faced an enormous challenge of postwar reconstruction. At the same time, it had a large, reasonably well-equipped army and a tightly organized government. Ho Chi Minh was the best-known nationalist leader in all of Vietnam. The Viet Minh had won broad popular respect for leading the struggle against France. Ho and his cohorts remained deeply committed to unification and left between 10,000 and 15,000 operatives in the south to promote that goal.

In southern Vietnam, chaos reigned. The colonial economy depended entirely on exports of rice and rubber to finance essential imports. It had been devastated by nearly fourteen years of war and was held together by enormous French military expenditures that would soon cease. The French had finally granted unqualified independence to the State of Vietnam in June 1954, but the government, still nominally presided over by Bao Dai, was a fiction. Assuming the premiership in the summer of 1954, the staunchly anti-French Ngo Dinh Diem inherited antiquated institutions patterned on French practices and ill-suited to the needs of an independent nation—an "oriental despotism with a French accent," one American scornfully labeled it. Diem's government lacked experienced civil servants. Tainted by its long association with France, it had no base of support in the countryside or among the non-Communist nationalists in Saigon. Its army had been created by the French out of desperation in the last stages of the war and was accurately dismissed by General Navarre as a "rabble."[6]

The French had employed the classical imperialist device of divide and conquer to rule their Indochinese colonies, and political fragmentation was the fundamental fact of life in post-Geneva South

---

[6]Robert McClintock to State Department, May 20, 1953, and May 8, 1954, in Department of State, *Foreign Relations of the United States, 1952–1954* (Washington, D.C., 1981), 13: 575, 1519. Hereafter cited as *FR* with date and volume number.

Vietnam. The French army remained, and the French government persisted in trying to exert influence in its former colony. The Viet Minh retained pockets of control, even on the doorstep of Saigon. The so-called sects, politico-religious organizations with their own governments and armies, ruled the Mekong Delta and the suburbs of Saigon as fiefdoms. Viewing a mass emigration from North Vietnam as a possible means of tipping the political balance toward the south and perhaps even winning the 1956 elections, the French and Americans actively encouraged northerners to cross the seventeenth parallel. Within weeks after Geneva, northern Catholics began pouring into predominantly Buddhist South Vietnam at the rate of 7,000 a day, adding new religious and ethnic tensions to an already volatile mix.

Some U.S. officials issued stern warnings about the pitfalls of nation building in South Vietnam. A National Intelligence Estimate of August 1954 admonished that even with solid support from the United States, the chances of establishing a strong, stable government were "poor."[7] When asked to formulate a program for training a South Vietnamese army, the Joint Chiefs of Staff (JCS) responded that it would be "hopeless" to build an army without a "reasonably strong, stable civil government in control."[8] Agreeing that the situation in South Vietnam was "utterly hopeless," Secretary of Defense Charles E. Wilson urged the United States to get out as "completely and as soon as possible." In words that would take on the ring of prophecy, he warned that he could "see nothing but grief in store for us if we remained in that area."[9]

Eisenhower and Dulles were not deterred by these gloomy forecasts. Dulles admitted that the chances of success might not exceed 1 in 10. On the other hand, he and the president agreed that to do nothing risked the probable loss to Communism of a vital area. The administration could not afford to act only when success was assured, the secretary explained to the Senate Foreign Relations Committee. Vietnam was one of those places where it was necessary to "put up a good stout effort even though it is by no

[7]National Intelligence Estimate 63-5-54, "Post-Geneva Outlook in Indochina," August 3, 1954, *USVN,* Book 10, 692.
[8]Joint Chiefs of Staff to Secretary of Defense, August 4, 12, 1954, ibid., 701–702, 759–760.
[9]Record of National Security Council meeting, October 26, 1954, *FR, 1952–1954,* 13: 2184–2186.

means certain that we will succeed." They seem also to have felt that because of the purity of its motives and the superiority of its methods, the United States might succeed where the French had failed. In its first two years in office, moreover, the administration had, with limited effort, toppled unfriendly governments in Iran and Guatemala, and Eisenhower and Dulles may have concluded that they could beat the odds in Vietnam as well. Admitting that he was indulging in the "familiar hen-and-egg argument as to which comes first," Dulles flatly informed the JCS that a strong army would do more than anything else to stabilize the government of South Vietnam.[10]

His arguments eventually prevailed. At an NSC meeting on October 22, 1954, Eisenhower affirmed with "great conviction" that "in the lands of the blind, one-eyed men are kings," by which he presumably meant that despite the obstacles, the United States had the resources and ingenuity to succeed.[11] Shortly after, the administration committed itself to a major aid program for South Vietnam. The commitment was carefully limited and conditioned on Diem's instituting major reforms, but its significance was unmistakable: the experiment in nation building was under way.

NGO DINH DIEM

The man to whom Eisenhower made the fateful commitment had impeccable credentials as a nationalist and, from the U.S. standpoint, more important, as an anti-Communist. One of nine children of Ngo Dinh Kha, an official at the imperial court of Hue, Ngo Dinh Diem attended French Catholic schools in Hue and the school of public administration in Hanoi, where, after finishing at the top of his class, he was given an appointment in the bureaucracy of the protectorate of Annam. A devout Catholic, he became a staunch opponent of communism before he became a nationalist. As a village supervisor in central Vietnam, he unearthed a Communist-inspired uprising in 1929 and severely punished its leaders. The French rewarded him with an appointment as minister of the

[10]Dulles to Charles E. Wilson, August 18, 1954, *USVN*, Book 10, 728–729.
[11]Record of National Security Council meeting, October 22, 1954, *FR, 1952–1954*, 13: 2157.

interior, the highest position in the government, but when they refused to enact the reforms he had proposed, he resigned and would not return to his post even when threatened with deportation.

During the next two decades, Diem remained active in politics. He was deeply involved in the frantic maneuvering that took place at the end of World War II, rejecting offers of a post from the Japanese, the Viet Minh, and Bao Dai, but only after they refused to meet his terms. When the formation of Bao Dai's government in 1949 and the Viet Minh shift toward the Communist bloc seemed to foreclose all his options, he journeyed to Rome and then settled at a Maryknoll seminary in Lakewood, New Jersey. In the United States, he lectured widely, and his impassioned appeals for an independent, non-Communist Vietnam attracted him to such luminaries as Catholic prelate Francis Cardinal Spellman, Democratic senators John F. Kennedy and Mike Mansfield, and Supreme Court justice William O. Douglas. He also kept in close touch with people in Vietnam who were plotting his return to power.[12]

Diem's fervent nationalism and administrative experience made him an obvious choice for the premiership of an independent Vietnam. He brought to the office personal traits that would prove both assets and liabilities in governing and would in time provoke conflict with his patron, the United States. Among his most noteworthy qualities was a determination to persist in the face of severe challenge and even threats to his person. He had a remarkable penchant for survival. He was a man of principle, but he also inclined toward an all-or-nothing integrity that limited his ability to deal with the intractable problems and deep-seated conflicts he faced. In many ways a skilled politician, he was also an introverted and self-absorbed elitist who did not relate easily to the people he served. A compulsive talker—"a single question was likely to provoke a dissertation for an hour or more," journalist Robert Shaplen observed—he was a poor listener who seemed almost indifferent to

[12]Edward Miller, "Vision, Power, and Agency: The Ascent of Ngo Dinh Diem," in Mark Philip Bradley and Marilyn Young, (eds.), *Making Sense of the Vietnam Wars: Local, National, and Transnational Perspectives* (New York, 2008), pp. 137–143. See also Seth Jacobs, *America's Miracle Man in Vietnam: Ngo Dinh Diem, Religion, Race, and U.S. Intervention in Southeast Asia* (Durham, N.C., 2004), pp. 27–29.

the reaction he evoked in others.[13] He lacked the charisma of Ho Chi Minh. Dismissed by Americans at that time and later as a man who sought to restore South Vietnam to its old ways, he was in fact a dedicated modernizer with his own vision for his country. Although accepting U.S. aid, he often staunchly resisted American ways of doing things.

The United States has often—mistakenly—been accused of conspiring to put Diem in power. In fact, he deserves far more credit for his own fate than he has usually been given. While in exile, he lobbied hard for U.S. backing. Eisenhower and Dulles came to favor him because of his Catholicism and apparent religiosity but mainly because he seemed the only alternative to communism and French colonialism. Despite his notorious Francophobia, he also gained the endorsement of some French officials. But the crucial events took place in Vietnam. His brother and alter ego Ngo Dinh Nhu and other political operatives worked feverishly on his behalf. Rising non-Communist Vietnamese demands for full independence, a position he had long supported, made him an increasingly attractive candidate for high office. Outflanked by Diem and Nhu, Bao Dai saw little choice in June 1954 but to play the "Ngo Dinh Diem" card by choosing him prime minister of the State of Vietnam and giving him full powers.[14]

Many top U.S. officials found little encouragement in Diem's assumption of power. Indeed, what is striking in retrospect is the extent to which early on-the-scene estimates of the prime minister's leadership potential anticipated the problems that would develop later. From Geneva, Walter Bedell Smith did express hope that Diem might be a "modern political Joan of Arc" who could "rally the country behind him." In Paris, however, Ambassador Douglas Dillon was reassured by the emergence of this "Yogi-like mystic" only because the standard set by his predecessors had been so low. Within weeks after Diem took office, Chargé Robert McClintock in Saigon characterized him as a "messiah without a message," complained

[13]Robert Shaplen, *The Lost Revolution: The U.S. in Vietnam, 1946–1966* (New York, 1966), p. 104.
[14]Miller, "Vision, Power, and Agency," pp. 143–158; Jacobs, *Miracle Man*, p. 54; Kathryn C. Statler, *Replacing France: The Origins of American Intervention in Vietnam* (Lexington, Ky., 2007), pp. 118–119; Philip E. Catton, *Diem's Final Failure: Prelude to America's War in Vietnam* (Lawrence, Kans., 2002), p. 7.

of his "narrowness of view," and commented scornfully that his only "formulated policy is to ask immediate American assistance in every form."[15]

Throughout the fall and winter of 1954–1955, Diem was the focal point of a bitter and protracted conflict between the United States and France. Controversy was probably inevitable given the accumulated tensions of four years of uneasy partnership. It was sharpened by profound mutual suspicions that extended from top policy levels in Paris and Washington down to the operational level in Saigon. The French doubted Diem's capacity to lead, viewed him as a threat to implementation of the Geneva Accords, and actively sought to get rid of him. The Americans feared, with justification, that Paris was playing a double game, seeking to maintain its position in the south while attempting to build bridges to Hanoi. U.S. officials also feared that the French inclination to let the best man win the upcoming election would bring about a Ho Chi Minh victory. The French had always resented American intrusion in Vietnam. They suspected that the United States was using Diem to supplant them. Diem has that "one rare quality, so precious in Asia," a French journalist snarled, "he is pro-American."[16] Differences over Vietnam were exacerbated by French rejection of the European Defense Community, which strained Franco-American relations to the breaking point and, at least momentarily, left the Western alliance in disarray.

In Vietnam, the United States now held most of the cards, and it eventually imposed its will on a recalcitrant France. The French still depended on American aid to support their army in Vietnam, and Washington used this leverage in the fall of 1954 to extract a commitment to support Diem. The Eisenhower administration also insisted on giving its economic and military aid directly to the Diem government rather than funneling it through the French mission in Saigon, as Paris had proposed. Throughout the winter of 1954–1955, French officials insisted that Diem was incapable of running the government and proposed that he be replaced by Bao Dai or some other reputable nationalist figure. Dulles would have

---

[15]T. B. Miller (ed.), *Australian Foreign Minister: The Diaries of R. G. Casey, 1951–1960* (London, 1972), p. 159; Dillon to State Department, May 24, 1954, *FR, 1952–1954*, 13: 1608–1609; McClintock to State Department, July 4, 1954, ibid., 1783–1784.

[16]Quoted in *FR, 1952–1954*, 13: 2333; Statler, *Replacing France*, pp. 120–130.

none of it. If Bao Dai was the only person who could save Vietnam, the secretary concluded, "then indeed we must be desperate." He conceded Diem's shortcomings but accepted Ambassador Donald Heath's argument "that there is no one to take his place who would serve US interests better."[17] The unstinting support provided by Dulles and the United States enabled Diem to remain in power against strong French opposition.

Timely American backing also helped Diem thwart a series of military plots against his government. The U.S. embassy foiled a coup attempt in the fall of 1954 by making it known that a change of government would result in termination of American aid. Lansdale helped abort another coup in November. A former advertising executive, he had served in the Office of Strategic Services during World War II and afterward had assisted Philippine President Ramon Magsaysay in suppressing the Huk rebellion. A flamboyant and imaginative operator, he had quickly ingratiated himself with Diem and became one of the prime minister's most trusted advisers and vocal supporters. Learning that a group of army officers was plotting to overthrow the government, he lured several of the ringleaders out of the country with an expense-paid trip to Manila, and the scheme quickly collapsed.[18]

Working closely with France, the United States also helped Diem cope with one of the most urgent problems he confronted during his first year in office. Responding more to their own clergy than to U.S. propaganda, thousands of northern Catholics sought to "regroup" to South Vietnam after the Geneva cease-fire. They were joined by Vietnamese who had worked with the French government in the north or had served in the Vietnamese National Army and feared DRV reprisals if they remained. In all, more than 800,000 regroups braved North Vietnamese harassment and obstructionism, crammed ships, and an arduous sea passage to Saigon or other southern ports. French and American personnel collaborated to ensure the success of what was dubbed Passage to Freedom. Along with private charitable organizations, they established reception centers and offered emergency food, clothing, and medical care to the newcomers. Himself a northerner and Catholic, Diem was

---

[17]Embassy Paris to State Department, December 19, 1954, *USVN*, Book 10, 826–834; Heath to Walter Robertson, December 17, 1954, ibid., 824–825.
[18]Sheehan et al., *Pentagon Papers (NYT)*, p. 20; Statler, *Replacing France*, pp. 128–129.

sympathetic to the refugees, and his government gave them funds to build new dwellings and purchase clothing and food. Passage to Freedom was one of the most successful refugee operations in history, for which both French and American publicists claimed credit. The dramatic story of the diaspora linked Americans to South Vietnam in a very personal way. Diem's effective handling of the short-term problems created by the refugees was cited as early evidence of his ability to govern South Vietnam under U.S. tutelage. The long-term problem of resettlement and integration proved much more difficult. The prime minister's favoritism for the northern Catholics was one of the major articles in the later indictment against him.[19]

THE SECTS CRISIS

Diem barely survived the sects crisis of 1955. The Cao Dai and Hoa Hao represented the most potent political forces in the fragmented society of post-Geneva Vietnam. Organized along the lines of the Catholic Church with a pope as head, the Cao Dai claimed two million adherents, maintained an army of 20,000, and exercised political control over much of the Mekong Delta. Also centered in the delta, the Hoa Hao had as many as one million followers and an army of 15,000. The Binh Xuyen, a mafia-like organization headed by a colorful brigand named Bay Vien, had an army of 25,000 men, earned huge revenues from gambling, an opium factory, and prostitution in Saigon, and actually ran the city's police force. Unable to subdue the sects while fighting the Viet Minh, the French had given them virtual autonomy. Accustomed to running their own affairs, they refused to surrender their power or fortunes to the new national government.[20]

Diem's divide-and-conquer tactics at first united the sects against him. To win their support, he offered the Cao Dai and Hoa Hao cabinet posts. Lansdale journeyed deep into the jungles near the Cambodian border and bribed the most important Cao Dai

[19]Ronald B. Frankum, Jr., *Operation Passage to Freedom: The United States Navy in Vietnam, 1954–1965* (Lubbock, Tex., 2007), pp. 14, 28, 36, 100–112, 138; Jacobs, *Miracle Man*, pp. 140–171.

[20]Mark Philip Bradley, *Vietnam at War* (New York, 2009), p. 80.

leaders to work with the government. The U.S. embassy backed Diem by warning that if the sects overthrew the president, American aid would be withdrawn, leaving South Vietnam at the mercy of the Viet Minh. Diem stubbornly refused to negotiate with the Binh Xuyen, however, and his rapprochement with the Cao Dai and Hoa Hao broke down when he rejected their demands for autonomy within their own territories. In the spring of 1955, the sects joined the Binh Xuyen in an all-out assault against the government. By March, government forces and sect armies were waging open warfare in the streets of Saigon.

Diem's mishandling of the sects persuaded top French and U.S. officials in Saigon that he must be removed. Gen. Paul Ely, the French high commissioner for Vietnam, advised the American Embassy that Diem verged on megalomania and probably could not be saved, and if he were, "we shall have spared for Vietnam the worst Prime Minister it ever had." Eisenhower had appointed Gen. J. Lawton Collins (called "Lightning Joe" for his bold and decisive military leadership) as his Special Representative to Vietnam with the rank of ambassador. The general had expressed misgivings about Diem from the time he arrived in Saigon. The sects crisis persuaded him that Ely was right.

Collins's repeated calls for Diem's ouster in the spring of 1955 spurred week-to-week reassessments in Washington and rampant political maneuvering. Either to confirm his own views or to cover the administration's political flank, Dulles consulted Senator Mansfield, widely known as that body's Asian expert (and also a close acquaintance of Diem). The senator threatened to cut off aid to South Vietnam if Diem was deposed. Eisenhower and Dulles acquiesced. Soon after, in response to another Collins plea for Diem's removal, Eisenhower and Dulles appeared ready to go along. But Mansfield forced a compromise by which Diem would be retained as president, a largely titular position, while the power to govern was given to someone else. When Collins strenuously objected, the administration brought him home for consultation. He could not budge Mansfield, but this time he appears to have won over the president and even a more reluctant Dulles.[21]

While Collins was en route to Vietnam to implement the change, a sudden turn of events gave Diem's American backers

[21]Jacobs, *Miracle Man*, pp. 175–216.

another chance. When the Binh Xuyen launched a mortar attack on the presidential palace, Diem ordered his army into battle. To the surprise of everyone, it drove the opposition back into the Cho Lon district of Saigon. Although ordered to remain neutral, many Americans openly sided with Diem. General John W. O'Daniel, chief of the U.S. military mission, "rode past the Vietnamese troops in his sedan, flying the American flag . . . and gave them the thumbs-up sign, shouting 'Give em' hell, boys.'"[22] Lansdale convinced a skeptical embassy that the successful counterattack demonstrated the loyalty of the army and Diem's strength as a leader. At a critical moment in the struggle, moreover, the ubiquitous CIA agent persuaded Diem to ignore a cable from Bao Dai demanding Diem's resignation.

Diem's success against the Binh Xuyen produced a U.S. policy reversal of momentous significance. Senate leaders, including Mansfield and California Republican William Knowland, lobbied furiously for Diem's retention. Having lost the first round to Collins, Dulles, with the support of his brother, CIA director Allen Dulles, ably exploited the developments in Saigon. Arguing that Diem was the only means to "save South Vietnam and counteract revolution" and that he must be supported "wholeheartedly," the secretary persuaded the president to stick by a man whose political career had appeared doomed just days before.[23]

The American commitment to Diem provoked a final—and, not unwelcome—crisis with France. In a dramatic confrontation in Paris in mid-May, Prime Minister Edgar Faure argued heatedly that Diem was "not only incapable but mad" and that France could "no longer take risks with him": If the United States persisted in its support, France would have to withdraw from Vietnam.[24] Dulles perceived that the French presence had permitted the United States to avoid major commitments in the region and to blame failures on its ally. He also recognized, as the Joint Chiefs warned, that a French withdrawal, although desirable from a long-term standpoint, would leave the new nation highly vulnerable for the short term.

By the spring of 1955, however, Dulles concluded that the French had outlived their usefulness in the region, and resolution

---

[22]Edward G. Lansdale, *In the Midst of Wars* (New York, 1972), p. 288.
[23]Dulles to State Department, May 8, 1955, *USVN*, Book 10, 962–963.
[24]Ibid.

of the German problem permitted the United States for the first time to deal with Indochina issues on their own merits. Dulles thus persuaded the French to remain and support Diem until the Vietnamese could settle the future of their country through elections. He also let it be known that the United States would frame its policies independently and would not feel bound to consult France before acting. In all, it was a bravura performance. This "gentleman's agreement" ensured French support for the short run but separated the United States from France and opened the way for bilateral relations with South Vietnam. Frustrated by Dulles and Diem and faced with rebellion in their North African colonies, the French abandoned what remained of their dreams of influence and began a phased withdrawal from what had been the most glittering jewel in the French Union. The United States had already begun to replace France by assuming primary responsibility for the survival of the Saigon regime.[25]

Buoyed by his successes and by assurances of U.S. support, Diem set out to consolidate his power. His army drove the Binh Xuyen deep into the swamps east of Saigon—where it eventually surrendered—and routed Hoa Hao forces in the Mekong Delta. Now isolated, the Cao Dai saw no choice but to come over to Diem's side.

Spurning U.S. advice and North Vietnamese protests, the premier also blocked the national elections called for by the Geneva Accords. This issue was especially awkward for the United States, given its traditional support for self-determination and its Cold War advocacy of elections for divided nations such as Germany and Korea. U.S. officials saw quite clearly, however, that Ho Chi Minh's reputation as a nationalist leader made elections risky and that the more populous North, operating under iron Communist discipline, was "mathematically certain" to win. Not eager for elections but not wanting to appear to obstruct them, Americans encouraged Diem to agree in principle while delaying and insisting on conditions that North Vietnam would not accept. They also urged him to discuss with the DRV the modalities for elections. Ignoring his American advisers, the premier refused even to talk with the North and

---

[25]Kathryn Statler, "The Diem Experiment: Franco-American Conflict over South Vietnam, July 1954–May 1955," *Journal of American–East Asian Relations* 6 (Summer–Fall 1997): 168–173.

ignored the July 1955 deadline for consultations. He adamantly insisted that because South Vietnam had not signed the Geneva Accords it would not be "tied down" by them. In any event, there could be no free elections where Communists were involved.[26]

Diem shrewdly used a hastily called "referendum" as a substitute for the national elections called for by Geneva, a "legal" means to get rid of Bao Dai, and a way to establish claims of legitimacy for his newly created Republic of Vietnam. He ordered the vote in July 1955 about the time he announced his nonparticipation in talks with the DRV. He and his supporters skillfully managed the referendum, portraying Bao Dai as the "Master Keeper of the Gambling Dens," corrupt, debauched, incompetent, and above all a traitor who had collaborated with the French and the Viet Minh, and putting forth Diem as the "Savior of the People" who was leading South Vietnam toward modernization and democracy. Diem hailed his overwhelming victory as a sign that South Vietnam had joined the Free World. The obvious contradiction between his claims of democracy and his 98.2 percent electoral majority raised concerns about corruption, frustrated the hopes of those who had put faith in him, and sparked an opposition that would grow steadily in coming years.[27]

The Geneva conferees had assumed that national elections would take place and were caught off guard by Diem's maneuvers. Preoccupied with other matters, they acquiesced. Soviet leader Nikita Khrushchev refused to permit a dispute over elections in faraway Vietnam to interfere with his newly proclaimed policy of "peaceful coexistence." He was happy not to set a dangerous precedent for elections in Germany or Korea. In 1957, the USSR even backed the admission of both Vietnams to the United Nations. Absorbed with domestic problems and not inclined at this point to challenge Moscow, China contented itself with perfunctory protests. France preferred that the elections be held but was powerless to achieve that result.[28] As a cosponsor of the Geneva Conference, the British at first sought to implement the accords. They shared France's low estimate of Diem and feared that with American

[26]Statler, *Replacing France*, pp. 156–170.
[27]Jessica M. Chapman, "Saving Democracy: South Vietnam's 1955 Referendum to Depose Bao Dai," *Diplomatic History* 30 (September 2006): 671–703.
[28]Statler, *Replacing France*, pp. 170–172.

backing he might destroy the precarious peace in Vietnam. Privately, they scoffed at U.S. willingness to support free elections only when they seemed likely to produce the "desired result." At the same time, they conceded their inability to influence their more powerful ally. "We are treated like Australia," Prime Minister Anthony Eden moaned in April 1955. Unwilling to jeopardize their "special relationship" with America for no more than marginal interests in Vietnam, the British abdicated. "If the U.S. takes the responsibility," Eden affirmed, "they will have to shoulder it before the world."[29] Shocked by Diem's unexpected moves and disappointed in the lack of help provided by the major powers, North Vietnam could do nothing more than condemn the United States for "sabotaging" the elections.[30] Through luck, political savvy, and sheer force of will, by the end of 1955 Diem had established unchallenged control over a separate South Vietnam.

Diem's refusal to participate in the elections ended, at least temporarily, any chance for the reunification of Vietnam, and the division of the country increasingly took on permanent form. Diem would not permit any traffic with the North, including even a postal arrangement. The seventeenth parallel became one of the most restricted boundaries in the world. The breakdown of the Geneva Accords all but assured the resumption of war in Vietnam at some future point.

NATION BUILDING IN SOUTH VIETNAM

Having assisted the survival of the Diem regime through its tumultuous first years, the United States supported it lavishly for the rest of the decade. The preservation of an independent South Vietnam as a bulwark against further Communist penetration of Southeast Asia remained the goal of U.S. policy. During the mid-1950s, the major battleground of the Cold War shifted from Europe to the newly emerging nations of Asia and Africa, where the United States and the Soviet Union vied for influence and sought to demonstrate the superiority of their respective systems. In this context,

---

[29] Quoted in Arthur Combs, "The Path Not Taken: The British Alternative to U.S. Policy in Vietnam, 1954–1956," *Diplomatic History* 19 (Winter 1995): 51.
[30] Statler, *Replacing France*, pp. 170–175.

South Vietnam assumed even greater importance as a testing ground for the viability of American ideology and institutions in underdeveloped nations.

The experiment in nation building, launched on a crash basis, quickly assumed the form of a crusade. Private charitable agencies distributed food, soap, toothbrushes, and emergency medical supplies and worked zealously to improve amenities in refugee camps. Nongovernmental organizations such as CARE and Catholic Relief Services (CRS) set out to teach villagers modern methods of farming, fishing, and forestry, created health and sanitation programs to curb disease, and initiated self-help projects to promote economic development, in the process seeking to educate the South Vietnamese in the values of democratic capitalism. The International Rescue Committee (IRC) went further. Originally established to assist refugees from Nazi Germany, the IRC had since shifted its efforts to the Cold War. In Vietnam, it professed to stand as a "lighthouse of inspiration" for those eager to preserve and broaden "concepts of democratic culture." It staged anti-Communist plays in the villages and, in the cities, sponsored recitals and art exhibitions built around democratic themes. It also established Freedom Centers in Saigon, Hue, and Dalat to win over disaffected Vietnamese intellectuals and students through such diverse and apparently contradictory efforts as research into "pure Vietnamese culture" and English-language courses.[31]

Meanwhile, in the United States, liberals and conservatives joined hands to form the American Friends of Vietnam (AFV), a group created to enlighten Americans about the "realities" in Vietnam and to lobby the U.S. government to support Diem. "A free Vietnam means a greater guarantee of freedom in the world," the AFV affirmed in its statement of purpose. "There is a little bit of all of us in that faraway country," Gen. O'Daniel, a charter member, would write in 1960.[32]

Already deeply committed to South Vietnam, the Eisenhower administration needed little urging from private lobby groups.

[31]Robert McAlister reports to IRC, May–October 1955, document #4084, William J., Donovan Papers, U.S. Army Military Institute, Carlisle Barracks, Pa. For CARE and CRS, see Delia Pergande, "Private Voluntary Aid in Vietnam: The Humanitarian Politics of Catholic Relief Services and CARE, 1954–1965" (Ph.D. diss., University of Kentucky, 1999), especially pp. 43–157.
[32]American Friends of Vietnam, "Statement of Purpose," n.d., copy in Hans Morgenthau Papers, Library of Congress, Washington, D.C.; John W. O'Daniel, *The Nation That Refused to Starve* (New York, 1960), p. 11.

From 1955 to 1960, the United States poured more than $1.5 billion in economic and military assistance into South Vietnam. By 1961, Diem's government ranked fifth among all recipients of U.S. foreign aid. More than 1,500 Americans assisted South Vietnam in various ways; the U.S. mission in Saigon was the largest in the world. Certain of the superiority of their own methods, institutions, and values, and of South Vietnam's need for their help, Americans firmly believed that they knew what was best for their client state. They set out to create a modern nation based on their own model that would be invulnerable to communism and would demonstrate the magic of the American way. However well intentioned, the visitors' cultural arrogance and determination to impose their own ways could not but come across to many South Vietnamese as yet another form of colonialism. As the U.S. presence mushroomed and spread into many areas of society, it increasingly butted up against Vietnamese nationalism, provoking tensions that would grow throughout the decade.[33]

The U.S. aid program accorded top priority to building a South Vietnamese army. Dulles had insisted from the outset that the development of a strong, modern army was an essential first step in promoting stable government. The withdrawal of French military forces; the presence of large, experienced armies in the north; and continued instability in the south all underscored the necessity of providing South Vietnam with a strong military force. Between 1955 and 1961, military assistance constituted more than 78 percent of the total American foreign aid program.

In early 1956, the United States assumed from France full responsibility for training the South Vietnamese Army. The Military Assistance and Advisory Group (MAAG) in Saigon undertook a crash program to build it into an effective force. Limited by the Geneva Accords to a strength of 342 men, the MAAG was augmented by various subterfuges to 692. From 1955 to 1960, it was headed by Lt. Gen. Samuel Williams, a spit-and-polish veteran of the two world wars and Korea whose insistence on rigid discipline and vicious tongue-lashings earned him the nickname "Hanging Sam."

---

[33] Catton, *Final Failure*, pp. 19-21; Statler, *Replacing France*, p. 217; James M. Carter, *Inventing Vietnam: The United States and State Building, 1954–1968* (New York, 2008), p. 111.

The MAAG faced truly formidable obstacles. The United States inherited from France an army of more than 250,000 soldiers, poorly organized, trained, and equipped; lacking in national spirit; suffering from low morale; and deficient in officers and trained specialists such as engineers and artillerymen. The army's supply problems were compounded by the French, who took most of the best equipment with them and left behind tons of useless and antiquated matériel. The U.S. advisers had to bridge profound language and cultural gaps. Despite good intentions, they often patronized the Vietnamese, some-times even referring to them as "natives." "Probably the greatest single problem encountered by the MAAG," one of its officers wrote at the time, "is the continual task of assuring the Vietnamese that the United States is not a colonial power—an assurance that must be renewed on an individual basis by each new adviser."[34] From this weak foundation and in the face of serious practical difficulties, the MAAG was assigned the challenging mission of building an army capable of maintaining internal security and holding the line against an invasion from the north until outside forces could be brought in.

Under the MAAG's direction, the United States reorganized, equipped, and trained the South Vietnamese Army. It provided roughly $85 million per year in military equipment, including uni-forms, small arms, vehicles, tanks, and helicopters. It paid the sala-ries of officers and enlisted personnel, financed the construction of military installations, and underwrote the cost of training pro-grams. The MAAG scaled down the army to a strength of 150,000 and organized it into mobile divisions capable of a dual mission. It launched an ambitious training program, based on American models, including a Command and General Staff College for senior officers, officer candidate schools, and specialized schools for non-coms. In 1960 alone, more than 1,600 Vietnamese soldiers partici-pated in the Off-Shore Program, studying in the United States and other Free World countries. Official publicists proclaimed by 1960 that the United States had achieved a "minor miracle," transform-ing what had been "little more than a marginal collection of armed men" into an efficient, modern army.[35]

---

[34]Judson J. Conner, "Teeth for the Free World Dragon," *Army Information Digest*, (November 1960): 41; Ronald H. Spector, *Advice and Support: The Early Years, 1941–1960* (Washington, D.C., 1983), pp. 278–282.

[35]Conner, "Teeth for the Free World Dragon," p. 33.

As would happen so often in Vietnam, official rhetoric bore little resemblance to reality. The army still lacked sufficient officers in 1960, and General Williams later conceded that many of the officers holding key positions were of "marginal quality." As one of Williams's top assistants put it, "No one can make good . . . commanders by sending uneducated, poorly trained, and poorly equipped and motivated boys to Benning or Knox or Leavenworth or Quantico."[36] Diem's determination to maintain tight control over the army frustrated the MAAG's efforts to establish a smoothly functioning command system. The president personally ordered units into action, bypassing the Ministry of Defense and the General Staff. He chose safe rather than competent officers for critical posts. He promoted them on the basis of loyalty rather than merit and constantly shuffled the high command—"generals and colonels, it was said jokingly in Saigon, were the only first-class travelers in Vietnam."[37]

The basic problem was that the army was trained for the wrong mission. The MAAG would be sharply criticized for failing to prepare the South Vietnamese Army for dealing with guerrillas, but from the perspective of the mid-1950s its emphasis appears quite logical. Confronting the near-impossible task of building from scratch an army capable of performing two quite diverse missions, the MAAG naturally leaned toward the conventional warfare with which it was most familiar. At least until 1958, moreover, the countryside was quiet and Diem appeared firmly entrenched. Williams and most of his staff had served in Korea, and the seeming resemblance between the two situations inclined them to focus on the threat of invasion from the north. Also learning from experiences in Greece and the Philippines, they doubted that North Vietnam could mount an insurgency capable of threatening the South. The army was therefore trained, organized, and equipped to fight a conventional war. Its inadequacies were obvious only after South Vietnam was enveloped by a rural insurgency.

A paramilitary force, the Civil Guard, was to assist the army in maintaining internal security, but it was hampered from the outset by conflicts over organization and training. Advisers from Michigan State University sought a small group trained and equipped for

---

[36]Robert H. Whitlow, "The United States Military in South Vietnam, 1954–1960" (Master's thesis, University of Kentucky, 1972), p. 87.
[37]Jean Lacouture, *Vietnam between Two Truces* (New York, 1966), p. 117.

police duties at the province and village level. Diem, supported by the MAAG, preferred an auxiliary military force equipped with helicopters, armored cars, and bazookas and capable of small-scale military operations. Washington backed the Michigan State group and refused to furnish assistance for the Civil Guard until Diem acquiesced, but the guard never developed into an effective force. Diem used it as a dumping ground for inferior officers and in general gave it little support. The training provided by the Michigan State police experts, in Lansdale's words, left the guard "pathetically unready for the realities of the Vietnamese countryside. A squad of Civil Guard policemen, armed with whistles, nightsticks and 38 caliber revolvers, could hardly be expected to arrest a squad of guerrillas armed with submachine guns, rifles, grenades and mortars."[38]

The United States also pumped millions of dollars in foreign aid into the South Vietnamese economy. Academic theorists of modernization and political operatives viewed economic development as the solution to the problems of poverty, political instability, and internal conflict that wracked many of the new nations. Much of U.S. assistance came through what was called the Commodity Import Program (CIP). Described by one zealous U.S. official as the "greatest invention since the wheel," this program was designed to make up South Vietnam's huge foreign exchange deficit while preventing the runaway inflation that might be set loose by a massive infusion of dollars into a vulnerable economy. The idea was that in time economic growth would enable South Vietnam to wean itself from American assistance.[39]

Through the CIP, Vietnamese importers ordered from foreign export firms goods ranging from foodstuffs to automobiles, with Washington footing the bill. The importers paid for the goods in piasters, which then went into a "counterpart fund" held by the National Bank of Vietnam and were used by the government to cover operating expenses and finance development projects. From 1955 to 1959, the import program generated almost $1 billion in counterpart funds. The United States also furnished South Vietnam more than $127 million in direct economic assistance and more than $16 million in technical aid.

---

[38]Lansdale, *Midst of Wars*, p. 353.
[39]Carter, *Inventing Vietnam*, pp. 35–36.

American aid brought significant results. The CIP covered South
Vietnam's foreign exchange deficit and, by making available large
quantities of consumer goods, held inflation in check. U.S. money
and technology helped repair the vast destruction from more than a
decade of war, rebuilding highways, railroads, and canals and spurring a modest increase in agricultural productivity. Specialists from
American land-grant colleges promoted new crops and established
credit facilities for small farmers. U.S. educators supervised the
founding of schools and furnished textbooks. U.S. public health
experts provided drugs and medical supplies and assisted in training nurses and paramedics. A group of public administration specialists from Michigan State University (MSU) instructed
Vietnamese civil servants in skills ranging from typing to personnel
management. Experts from MSU's school of law enforcement established a police academy to train what one brochure described as
"Vietnam's finest," reorganized and updated the methods of the
Vietnam Bureau of Investigation, and even helped the Saigon police
install traffic lights and paint street lines to better handle growing
traffic problems in the burgeoning metropolis.[40]

American aid helped South Vietnam survive the first few critical
years after independence. Indeed, by the late 1950s the new nation
appeared to be flourishing. In Saigon, one visitor reported, "the
stores and market places are filled with consumer goods; the streets
are filled with new motor scooters and expensive automobiles; and in
the upper-income residential areas new and pretentious housing is
being built."[41] After conducting an investigation of the uses of
American economic assistance, Democratic senator Gale McGee of
Wyoming proposed that South Vietnam be made a "showcase" for
the foreign aid program, a place to which people from other countries could be brought to observe firsthand the "wholesome effects
of our efforts to help other peoples help themselves."[42]

Appearances were again deceptive. The recipients were
undoubtedly grateful for U.S. generosity, but they could not help but
be suspicious as well. "After eighty years of ruthless exploitation

[40]U.S. Operations Mission, *Building Economic Strength* (Washington, D.C., 1958),
p. 75; John Ernst, *Forging a Fateful Alliance* (East Lansing, Mich., 1998), pp. 41–84.
[41]Milton C. Taylor, "South Vietnam: Lavish Aid, Limited Progress," *Pacific Affairs* 34
(1961): 242.
[42]Senate, *Hearings, 1959,* p. 369.

by the French," one American observed, "many Vietnamese wonder why America is suddenly spending so much money in Vietnam." U.S. officials working at the village level sought to promote their own values and culture, and they sometimes met indifference or even hostility among the Vietnamese. The villagers' reluctance to adopt their ways, in turn, frustrated the Americans and led them to question the Vietnamese work ethic.[43]

More important, although U.S. aid prevented an economic collapse and supported a high standard of living in Saigon, it did little to promote economic development or improve conditions in the villages where more than 90 percent of South Vietnam's population lived. From 1955 to 1959, military aid was four times greater than economic and technical assistance. Of the nearly $1 billion in counterpart funds, more than 78 percent went for military purposes. Such was the preoccupation with "security" among Vietnamese and Americans alike that those interested in other projects found it expedient to justify them in terms of defense. Saigon and Washington insisted that the continuing presence of serious external and internal threats allowed them no choice, but the heavy emphasis on military aid left little money for long-range economic development. The military program was the "tail that wags the dog," a Senate committee pointed out in 1960.[44]

The CIP also contained built-in weaknesses. It was enormously wasteful, importers frequently ordered far more than could be consumed, and it created abundant opportunities for fast profits. The most serious weakness was that it financed an artificially high standard of living while contributing little to development. As late as 1957, about two-thirds of the imports consisted of consumer goods. Much of the wealth was drained off in conspicuous consumption rather than going into industry or agriculture. Diem stubbornly resisted American attempts to reduce the proportion of consumer goods, arguing that a lowering of living standards would create domestic unrest. The United States made some changes on its own, dropping from the list such obvious luxury items as record players and water skis and reducing consumer goods to about one-third of

[43]MacAlister Report to International Rescue Committee, n.d., document #4084, Donovan Papers; Pergande, "Private Voluntary Aid," p. 152.
[44]U.S. Senate, Committee on Foreign Relations, *United States Aid Program in Vietnam, Report, February 26, 1960* (Washington, D.C., 1960), p. 8.

the total, but with little effect. Robert Scigliano concluded in 1963 that the CIP had been a "large-scale relief project" that had not promoted "significant economic development in Vietnam."[45]

The massive infusion of U.S. aid thus kept South Vietnam alive, but it fostered dependency rather than laying the foundation for a genuine independence. Rice production doubled between 1955 and 1960, but much of the increase was taken up in increased domestic consumption. Gains in industrial productivity were insignificant. South Vietnam relied on a high level of imports to maintain its standard of living and on U.S. money to pay for them. Vietnamese and Americans agreed that a cutback or termination of American assistance would bring economic and political collapse. Vietnam was the "prototype of the dependent economy," Milton Taylor wrote in 1961, "its level of national income as dependent on outside forces as was the case when the country was a French colony. . . . American aid has built a castle on sand."[46]

The basic problem of nation building was political. There was much talk about assisting the Vietnamese to construct an American-style democracy. U.S. advisers helped draft a constitution that contained many of the trappings of Western democracies, including a president and legislature elected by popular vote and guarantees of basic political rights. In fact, the United States devoted little attention to political matters and, despite its massive foreign aid program, exerted very little influence. Some Americans naively assumed that Diem shared their political values; others were preoccupied with the security problems that seemed most urgent. Most probably shared Dulles's view that it was enough for Diem to be "competent, anti-Communist and vigorous" and that although representative government was a desirable long-range objective, it could not be accomplished overnight.[47] For whatever reason, the United States did little to promote democracy or even political reform until South Vietnam was swept by revolution.

In both the economic and political realms, Americans met increasingly stubborn resistance from their protégé Ngo Dinh Diem. Often dismissed as backward looking, Diem in truth held

---

[45]Robert Scigliano, *South Vietnam: Nation under Stress* (Boston, 1964), p. 125.
[46]Taylor, "South Vietnam," p. 256.
[47]Dulles news conference, May 7, 1955, Dulles Papers, Princeton, N.J., Box 99; Frederick Reinhardt oral history interview, ibid.

very strong views about the direction Vietnamese society should take. His beliefs were influenced by his own country's history and also by the philosophy of French Catholic humanists who had pondered at length the problems of industrial society. He was critical of Marxism, which he believed to be too materialistic and devoid of spirituality, and also of liberal capitalism, whose stress on individualism could produce chaos. Through a philosophy called *personalism*, he sought a middle way by which individuals could balance the fulfillment of their own aspirations with the broader concerns of the community, especially the need for order. He and his chief theorist, Nhu, in the president's words, sought to "adapt the best of our heritage to the modern heritage."[48] Their personalism was notably vague and indeed impenetrable to most Westerners. They never really developed from it tangible political or economic programs. But it set their view of a modernized Vietnam and they clung to it doggedly in the face of American intrusion.[49]

Given the strong views and personalities of Diem and Nhu, it is not surprising that they would run afoul of the United States as its presence mushroomed. Diem protested the small amount of aid provided and the purposes for which it was given. The United States required that industrial development be based on private enterprise. Diem and his entourage shared the mandarin's contempt for business and the nationalist's distrust of foreign capital. They denounced U.S. attitudes as "medieval and retrograde." They insisted that South Vietnam must have government ownership of major industries, at least at the start. Diem sought the kind of aid that would help his country be strong and independent. He feared and was angered by its growing reliance on the United States. He resented the way U.S. advisers told Vietnamese what to do. He complained that Americans were politically naive and did not understand his country and people. Nhu spoke bluntly of a "clash of civilizations."[50]

---

[48]Catton, *Final Failure*, p. 35.

[49]Ibid., pp. 41–50; Edward Miller, "The Diplomacy of Personalism: Civilization, Culture, and the Cold War in the Foreign Policy of Ngo Dinh Diem," in Christopher E. Goscha and Christian Ostermann (eds.), *Connecting Histories: Decolonization and the Cold War in Asia, 1945–1962* (Stanford, Calif., 2010), pp. 380–382.

[50]Catton, *Final Failure*, p. 25.

Diem's authoritarian governance provoked growing conflict with his own people and concern among Americans. His philosophy of government was succinctly summarized in a line he personally added to the constitution: "The President is vested with the leadership of the nation." He identified *his* principles with the nation's welfare and firmly believed that the people must be guided by the paternalistic hand of those who knew what was best for them. A deeply suspicious person, he rejected compromise. He viewed any opposition as subversion that must be suppressed. Cabinet officers or upper-level civil servants who disagreed with him were promptly dismissed. To appease his American patrons, he occasionally paid lip service to democracy, but in practice he assumed absolute powers. He personally dominated the executive branch of government, reserving to himself total authority for decision making. Unwilling or unable to delegate, he oversaw the operations of the government down to the most minute detail. The executive branch dominated the legislature, which, in any case, was virtually handpicked by careful manipulation of the electoral process. The National Assembly initiated nothing important, and pliantly approved whatever the president submitted.

The government might have survived its authoritarianism had it pursued enlightened policies, but its inability to meet the needs of the people and its ruthless suppression of dissent stirred a rising discontent that eventually brought its downfall. Diem's policies toward the villages—traditionally the backbone of Vietnamese society— failed badly. Land reform was an urgent task, especially in areas such as the Mekong Delta where landlords owned most of the land, and the Viet Minh had implemented sweeping programs. Diem was deeply committed to land reform, but his program was implemented belatedly and in a cautious manner that alienated both peasants and landlords. Only about one-third of the land worked by tenants was redistributed. The ceiling for landlords was set very high. Of the land made available for redistribution only about 40 percent actually changed hands. The program was implemented slowly and its dictates were not always enforced. In seeking to "harmonize" the perhaps irreconcilable interests of peasants and landlords, Diem's government managed to antagonize both. Diem was even more passionately devoted to a land resettlement program, initiated in 1957, that he hoped would create a "human wall" against North Vietnamese infiltration in thinly populated areas of the Mekong Delta and the

Central Highlands as well as relieve population pressures in the cities and expand agricultural production. The program achieved limited success. But tribespeople and ethnic Vietnamese were reluctant to participate. In pushing the program, the regime moved too rapidly and often employed coercion, provoking conflict with its own people and U.S. advisers.[51]

Another "reform" enacted by the government during the 1950s touched off massive resentment in the villages. Diem romanticized villagers as staunchly independent and the forebears of Vietnamese democracy, but he treated them as backward, ignorant, and in need of government direction. In a misguided effort to centralize authority over the villages and check Viet Minh influence, he abolished traditional local elections and began to appoint village and provincial officials. The villagers had enjoyed virtual autonomy for centuries. The fears aroused by the mere presence of outsiders were often heightened by what they did. Many of Diem's appointees were chosen on the basis of personal loyalty; most were poorly trained for their jobs. Some used their positions for personal enrichment. Province chiefs were known to have arrested villagers on trumped-up charges and then forced them to pay bribes for their release.

Diem's vigorous assault against political opponents spawned rising discontent in the cities and the countryside. Newspapers that criticized the government were promptly shut down. Nhu's Vietnam Bureau of Investigation rooted out suspected subversives in a manner that would have made F.B.I director J. Edgar Hoover blanch. Using authority handed down in various presidential ordinances, the government herded into "reeducation centers" thousands of Vietnamese—Communists and non-Communists alike—who were alleged to be threats to public order. The program was originally aimed at Viet Minh "stay-behinds," but it was extended to anyone who dared speak out against the government. The regime admitted to the incarceration of 20,000 people by 1956. The campaign was subsequently intensified. The government "has tended to treat the population with suspicion or coerce it," an American intelligence report concluded in 1960, "and has been rewarded with an attitude of apathy or resentment."[52]

---

[51]Ibid., pp. 50–71
[52]"Special Report on Internal Security Situation in Saigon," March 7, 1960, *USVN*, Book 10, 1267–1280.

IMAGES AND REALITY

In a remarkable display of public–private collaboration, U.S. government officials and private citizens mounted in the 1950s an artful propaganda campaign extolling American good deeds in Indochina and lionizing Diem and South Vietnam. One of the folk heroes of the era, Navy doctor Tom Dooley, played a key role in introducing Americans to Vietnam. In his books and lectures, he portrayed the Vietnamese as childlike people in need of Western help but also as sympathetic figures worthy of U.S. support. He embellished his accounts with horrific—and unsubstantiated—tales of Communist atrocities. His blockbuster best seller about Passage to Freedom, *Deliver Us from Evil*, has been called the *Uncle Tom's Cabin* of the Cold War.[53] The AFV hired a major New York public relations firm to build support for South Vietnam and Diem. Hollywood producers, with the backing of the ubiquitous Lansdale and the AFV, imaginatively transformed English writer Graham Greene's virulently anti-American novel, *The Quiet American*, into a passionately pro-U.S. film starring World War II Medal of Honor winner Audie Murphy, a movie, Lansdale told Diem, that "would help win more friends for you and Vietnam in many places in the world. . . ."[54] Diem himself contributed to the cause by sponsoring exhibits and other events in the United States portraying himself as a worthy successor to Vietnam's national heroes and South Vietnam as a legitimate nation-state and a loyal American ally. [55]

In part no doubt as a result of such propaganda, Diem retained a highly favorable image in the United States until South Vietnam was engulfed by revolution in the early 1960s. It is possible that even those Americans close to the government were unaware until the end of the decade of the extent to which he had alienated his people. In the eyes of most Americans, moreover, his vigorous anti-communism more than compensated for his shortcomings. Apologists such as Professor Wesley Fishel of Michigan State University conceded that Diem had employed authoritarian methods but argued that

[53]Jacobs, *Miracle Man*, pp. 154–157.
[54]Lansdale to Joseph Mankiewicz, March 17, 1956, and Lansdale to Diem, October 28, 1957, Edward Lansdale Papers, Hoover Institution Library, Stanford, Calif.
[55]Matthew Masur, "Exhibiting Signs of Resistance: South Vietnam's Struggle for Legitimacy, 1954–1960," *Diplomatic History* 33 (April 2009): 300–304.

Vietnam's lack of experience with democracy and the threat of communism left him no choice. Ambassador Elbridge Durbrow agreed that Diem's "somewhat authoritarian" government was compatible with U.S. interests and insisted that the United States "look with tolerance" on the government's efforts to develop a political system that conformed to Vietnamese traditions. The American media focused on the stability brought to South Vietnam by the "tough little miracle man." When Diem visited the United States in 1957, he was widely feted. The image persisted even after insurgency had spread across the country. "On his record," *Newsweek*'s Ernest Lindley exclaimed in 1959, "he must be rated as one of the ablest free Asian leaders. We can take pride in our support."[56]

THE ORIGINS OF INSURGENCY

At the very time Americans were extolling the "miracles" wrought by Diem, the revolution that would sweep him from power and in time provoke massive U.S. intervention was taking root. Washington later went to great lengths to prove that the Second Indochina War was the result of "aggression from the north," the determination of North Vietnam to impose communism on its southern neighbor. Antiwar critics insisted, on the other hand, that the southern revolution sprang from indigenous sources and, although assisted by the North, retained substantial independence throughout the war.

A more complex picture of the origins of the insurgency emerges from newly available documentation. In the summer of 1954, southern and northern Viet Minh differed sharply in their assessment of the Geneva Conference. Southern "stay-behinds" complained that DRV diplomats had squandered at the conference table what had been won in the war. They protested partition, which left them exposed, and they feared that they would be abandoned by their northern brethren. By contrast, the Hanoi leadership viewed Geneva as a "big victory" and expressed optimism about the future. France had been defeated and U.S. military intervention averted. The elections provided a mechanism for peaceful unification. Ho Chi Minh was a revered national leader; Bao Dai lacked

---

[56]Durbrow to State Department, December 7, 1959, *FR, 1958–1960*, 1: 269; Ernest K. Lindley, "An Ally Worth Having," *Newsweek*, June 29, 1959, 31.

popular support. The leadership determined to observe the letter and spirit of the Geneva Accords. Such an approach squared with the policies of its major allies, the Soviet Union and China. It would earn the respect of the other Geneva signatories. In any event, the DRV desperately needed the time before the elections to repair damage from the war, consolidate its power, and build socialism in the North. Hanoi thus instructed southern cadres to pursue the revolution by peaceful means, adhere to the Geneva process, and treat other southerners respectfully to help win the elections. Even in 1955, after Diem had emerged from the chaos in Saigon and it seemed clear that elections would not be held, the DRV would go no further than authorize increasingly discontented southerners to step up the political struggle but avoid armed conflict. The "most essential priority" was to focus on the North, which, in the absence of elections, must be built up as a base to liberate the South.[57]

During the next two years, Viet Minh in both halves of Vietnam encountered grave difficulties. The revolution in the South experienced what party histories called its "darkest period." Diem's anti-Communist campaigns executed more than 2,000 suspected Communists, some by the guillotine. Party membership plummeted to precarious levels. "By the time I return, my hair and beard will turn grey," one despairing regroupée concluded a poem.[58] Facing extinction, local leaders appealed for help and increasingly violated the party line by forming militias to forcibly defend themselves, and to even attack the exposed Diemist troops.

In the North, Ho and his cohorts also faced massive problems of reconstruction and nation building. The withdrawal of France and the disruption of trade with southern Vietnam added to the economic woes from eight years of war, leaving shortages of food and consumer goods, rising inflation, and widespread unemployment. A massive land reform program designed to relieve obvious inequities—and extend party control to the villages—was implemented in an especially heavy-handed manner, provoking a rebellion that had to be suppressed by the army. As many as 15,000 dissidents were executed. A campaign to eradicate capitalist influence in the cities sparked dissent among artists and intellectuals.[59] During these

[57]Pierre Asselin, "Choosing Peace: Hanoi and the Geneva Agreement on Vietnam, 1954–1955," *Journal of Cold War Studies* 9 (Spring 2007): 103–118.
[58]Balasz Szaiontai, "Political and Economic Crisis in North Vietnam, 1955–1956," *Journal of Cold War History* 5 (November–December 2005): 415.
[59]Ibid., pp. 404–418.

difficult times, the party itself was increasingly torn between "North-firsters," who wanted to focus on the North, and "South-firsters," who favored mobilizing the North to support the resistance in the South. In December 1956, the factions compromised, agreeing that the North should continue to have priority but authorizing southern insurgents to defend themselves.[60]

Between 1957 and 1960, Hanoi gradually committed itself to the southern insurgency. In March 1957, the DRV approved plans to modernize its own armed forces. More important decisions came in 1959. China's defiance of the Soviet Union in backing wars of national liberation gave heart to South-firsters. The emergence to a leadership position in Hanoi of Le Duan, who had led the fight in the South during the First Indochina War, helped bring about a more aggressive northern posture. Party leaders recognized that revolutionaries in the South were in desperate straits but also that Diem's oppressiveness had created a climate favorable for revolution. They worried that the revolution might be extinguished or might survive and elude their control. Some party leaders may also have concluded that a commitment to war in the South might unify a fractured North.[61] The party thus authorized the resumption of armed struggle and took active measures to support it. With the watchword, "absolute secrecy, absolute security," it established a special force, Group 559, to construct an infiltration route to move personnel and supplies into South Vietnam through Laos—the beginning of the fabled Ho Chi Minh Trail. Along with supplies, it began to send back to the South to assume leadership roles Viet Minh who had come North after Geneva. The Third Party Congress of September 1960 formally approved the shift to armed struggle, assigning liberation of the South equal priority with consolidation in the North. In December 1960, at Hanoi's direction, southern revolutionaries founded the National Liberation Front (NLF), a broad-based organization led by Communists but designed to rally all those disaffected with Diem by promising sweeping reforms and the establishment of genuine independence. North Vietnam carefully concealed its hand, hoping to overthrow Diem by what would appear to be an internal revolution, without provoking U.S. intervention.[62]

---

[60]Lien-Hang T. Nguyen, *Hanoi's War: An International History of the War for Peace in Vietnam* (Chapel Hill, N.C., 2012), pp. 42–43.
[61]Ibid., pp. 44–62.
[62]Ibid., pp. 45–47; Bradley, *Vietnam at War*, pp. 92–94.

In 1960–1961, revolutionary activity surged in the South. The level of violence increased sharply: In 1958, an estimated 700 government officials were assassinated; in 1960, 2,500. In 1959, the insurgents shifted from hit-and-run attacks to full-scale military operations against government-controlled villages and exposed units of the South Vietnamese Army. Intelligence and propaganda networks that had fallen into disuse after Geneva were reactivated. The insurgents launched vigorous campaigns of political agitation in the villages. Largely as a result of Diem's misguided policies, they found a ready audience: The peasants were like a "mound of straw ready to be ignited," a captured guerrilla later told an interrogator.[63] By the time the NLF was formally organized, the Vietcong (a derogatory term meaning "Vietnam Communist," applied to the guerrillas by the Diem regime) had attracted thousands of adherents among the rural population and established a presence in countless villages. Its military forces grew from 2,000 in 1959 to 10,000 in early 1961. By mid-1961, they had pushed Diem's army out of much of the vital Mekong Delta.

On July 8, 1959, in the town of Bien Hoa, the base of the South Vietnamese 7th Infantry Division just north of Saigon, a small band of Vietcong assassins attacked with machine guns and bombs the mess hall where U.S. advisers were watching a feature film on a homemade projector. Sergeant Chester Ovnand, a Texan, and Major Dale Buis, originally from Nebraska, were killed and, several others wounded. The event received little notice at the time, but it assumed great importance in retrospect. That date marked the first Americans killed in the Second Indochina War.

THE IMPENDING CRISIS

Diem's response to the insurgency heightened popular antagonism toward his government. He intensified the anti-Communist campaign in the villages and tightened controls in the cities, arresting scores of alleged dissidents. Once again demonstrating that he was out of touch with rural Vietnam, he launched in the summer of 1959 an ill-fated "agroville" program to combat the rising violence

---

[63]U.S. Congress, Senate, Subcommittee on Public Buildings and Grounds, *Pentagon Papers (Gravel)*, 4 vols. (Boston, 1971), 1 : 329.

in the countryside. The intent was to relocate the peasantry along personalist lines in areas where the army could protect them from guerrilla terror and propaganda. The government sought to make the program attractive by providing the new communities with schools, medical facilities, and electricity. But the peasants deeply resented the forced removal from their homes and lands, which contained the sacred tombs of their ancestors. The government's provisions for their relocation added to their discontent. They were given only about $5.50, which did not cover the cost of the land they were required to purchase. They were forced to work on community projects without compensation. The agroville program was eventually abandoned, but only after it had provoked enormous rural discontent with the government.[64]

Throughout 1960, evidence of the government's fragility mounted. The insurgency grew unchecked in the countryside, and the level of violence increased sharply. In January 1960, at Trang Sup, a village northeast of Saigon, four insurgent companies destroyed a South Vietnamese Army headquarters and seized large stocks of weapons, leaving the army and its U.S. advisers in a state of shock. The regime's unpopularity in Saigon was highlighted in April when a group of non-Communist politicians, many of whom had served in Diem's cabinet, met at the Caravelle Hotel and issued a manifesto bitterly protesting the government's oppressiveness and calling for sweeping reforms. In November, Diem narrowly thwarted an attempted coup by three paratroop battalions presumed to be among the most loyal units of the army. American intelligence reports ominously warned that if present trends continued, the collapse of the regime was certain.

Belatedly perceiving the strength of the insurgency and the inability of the South Vietnamese government and armed forces to cope with it, in 1960 the United States shifted the emphasis of its military programs from conventional warfare to counterinsurgency. U.S. military officials began work on a comprehensive plan to expand the army and Civil Guard and equip and train them for antiguerrilla operations. While this plan was being formulated, the mission in Saigon took piecemeal steps to assist the South Vietnamese. Training programs already in operation were reoriented. Special American teams were sent to train South Vietnamese Ranger Battalions. U.S.

[64]Catton, *Final Failure*, pp. 63–70.

advisers were placed at the regimental level to give on-the-spot advice and assess the capabilities and needs of individual units. Although the shift to counterinsurgency represented a tacit admission that the original advisory program had failed, it did not produce the sort of drastic changes required to defeat the guerrillas. It merely resulted in additional military aid and proposals for bureaucratic reorganization.[65]

In the meantime, civilian officials made gentle and largely unsuccessful attempts to persuade Diem to change his ways. Many Americans, including Ambassador Elbridge Durbrow, feared that unless the president reformed his government and mobilized popular support, the insurgency would overwhelm South Vietnam. He tactfully urged Diem to broaden his government by appointing a new cabinet, relax controls on the press and civil liberties, and pacify the rural population by restoring village elections and making credit easily available. Diem responded noncommittally that the proposals conformed with his own ideas but that it would be "most difficult" to implement them while the government faced internal rebellion.[66] Over the next few weeks, he tightened the controls, clamping down on the army and arresting the politicians who had issued the Caravelle Manifesto.

By the end of the year, Americans in Saigon were thoroughly alarmed by the impending crisis and deeply divided over how to combat it. Durbrow warned Washington that the Saigon government was in "serious danger" and that "prompt and even drastic action" was required to save it. In return for additional military aid, he advised, the United States should insist that Diem institute sweeping reforms.[67] The U.S. military mission in Saigon firmly resisted Durbrow's proposals, which, it claimed, would distract attention from the war and undercut Diem during a critical period. The debate became increasingly bitter. Meetings at the embassy, in the words of a participant, were "barely civil."[68]

Although the experiment in nation building was in obvious jeopardy by the end of the year, the Eisenhower administration did not resolve the debate in Saigon or take any major steps to salvage

---

[65]Spector, *Advice and Support*, p. 372.
[66]Durbrow memorandum, October 15, 1960, *USVN*, Book 10, 1318.
[67]Durbrow to State Department, December 5, 1960, ibid., 1334–1336.
[68]William Colby, *Honorable Men* (New York, 1978), p. 160.

its huge investment. Throughout much of 1960, attention was focused elsewhere. A flare-up over divided Berlin sharpened Cold War tensions in Europe. The Soviet shooting down of an American U-2 spy plane and torpedoing of a summit meeting in Paris provoked a major crisis. The emergence in neighboring Cuba of a revolutionary government headed by Fidel Castro and the establishment of close ties between Cuba and the Soviet Union aroused fears of Communist intrusion in America's backyard. The deterioration in South Vietnam was gradual. A sense of crisis did not develop until late in the year, by which time Eisenhower was already planning to transfer power to the newly elected Democratic administration of John F. Kennedy.

Even then, Laos, rather than South Vietnam, seemed the most urgent problem in Indochina. A mildly pro-Western government had assumed power after Geneva and was given lavish American support. But when it attempted to reach an accommodation with the Pathet Lao insurgents who had fought with the Viet Minh, the United States instigated a right-wing coup. The American-sponsored government launched an ambitious military campaign against the Pathet Lao. But it achieved little success and in 1960 was overthrown by a group of so-called neutralists. Rejecting a compromise, the Eisenhower administration firmly supported its client government and forced the neutralists into an uneasy alliance with the Pathet Lao. By the end of the year, North Vietnam and the Soviet Union had begun to furnish substantial support for the anti-American forces. Intensification of the civil war seemed certain.

In the twilight of his presidency, a deeply concerned Eisenhower pondered U.S. military intervention. Referring to Laos as the "cork in the bottle" whose removal could threaten all of Southeast Asia, the president, as early as September 1959, had grimly warned that it might "develop into another Korea."[69] At a meeting in late 1960, he advised that "we cannot let Laos fall to the Communists, even if we have to fight—with our allies or without them." He seems *not* to have recommended unilateral U.S. intervention to Kennedy in a transition briefing on January 19, 1961, but the

[69]Gordon Gray memorandum, September 14, 1959, Eisenhower Papers, "Cleanup" File, Box 5.

possibility was discussed. Compared with Laos, South Vietnam seemed to be a "back-burner" problem.[70]

Between 1954 and 1961, the United States came full circle in Vietnam. Following Geneva, Eisenhower and Dulles confronted a nearly hopeless situation in southern Vietnam. Some U.S. officials advised abandoning the area, and the administration briefly considered replacing Ngo Dinh Diem. When the prime minister unexpectedly prevailed over his domestic foes, however, the United States assumed from France the burden of nation building and committed itself firmly to his regime. Through the rest of the decade it poured huge sums of money and great effort into constructing in the southern part of Vietnam a bulwark against further Communist expansion in Southeast Asia.

Abysmally ignorant of Vietnamese history and culture, and naively persuaded their way was right, Americans failed to comprehend the perhaps insuperable difficulties of nation building in an area with only the most fragile basis for nationhood. The ambitious programs developed in the 1950s papered over rather than corrected South Vietnam's problems. To have constructed a viable nation in southern Vietnam, moreover, would have required the most enlightened, imaginative, and determined Vietnamese leadership, an ingredient the United States could not provide. Ngo Dinh Diem may well have been the "best available man," as Dulles described him. The United States pinned its hopes exclusively on him and helped him survive the tumultuous years 1954 and 1955.[71] But Diem lacked the qualities necessary for the formidable challenge of nation building. By 1960 he faced a potent internal opposition supported by North Vietnam that he, like the French before him, seemed increasingly incapable of handling.

Through luck as much as anything else, the Eisenhower administration helped keep the Diem regime afloat for six years. Ironically, however, its limited success, exaggerated for public relations purposes, led ultimately to disastrous failure. Throughout the second half of the decade, the administration publicly proclaimed miraculous success

---

[70]The basis for the allegation was the Clark Clifford memorandum of conversation, January 19, 1961, *Pentagon Papers (Gravel)*, 2: 635–637. For a corrective, see Fred I. Greenstein and Richard H. Immerman, "What Did Eisenhower Tell Kennedy about Indochina? The Politics of Misperception," *Journal of American History* 79 (September 1992): 568–587.

[71]Dulles news conference, March 1, 1955, Dulles Papers, Princeton, N.J., Box 99.

where little existed. It applauded South Vietnam's stability while producing a dependent regime that consumed millions of U.S. dollars. This illusion of success "trapped Eisenhower and subsequent U.S. presidents in a frustrating and futile effort to define and defend U.S. interests in Vietnam."[72]

The quirks of the electoral calendar spared Eisenhower from facing the ultimate failure of his policies in Vietnam. Within a short time after taking office, however, John F. Kennedy would have to choose between abandoning what he had called "our offspring" or significantly increasing the American commitment.

---

[72]Anderson, *Trapped by Success*, p. ix

The Self-Immolation of Thich Quang Duc
This classic 1963 photo of the immolation of
Buddhist monk Thich Quang Duc in the streets
of Saigon brought home to Americans the depth
of Vietnamese discontent with the Diem regime,
and it aroused grave concern among Kennedy
advisers and the public about the nation's
growing entanglement in Vietnam.
© *Malcolm Browne/AP Images*

CHAPTER 3

Limited Partnership

Kennedy and Diem, 1961–1963

On the morning of June 11, 1963, Thich Quang Duc, an elderly Buddhist monk, stepped out of a small automobile on a busy Saigon street. As a crowd gathered and other bonzes chanted, Quang Duc assumed the lotus position. Another monk doused him with a highly volatile mixture of gasoline and diesel fuel. Silently and without expression, Quang Duc touched a lit match to his saturated robes. Instantaneously, he burst into flames; within minutes his body was charred and lifeless. Making clear whose attention they sought, Buddhist demonstrators held aloft banners in English proclaiming "Buddhist Priest Burns for Buddhist Demands." Alerted to the event, U.S. reporters were on the scene. Their grim pictures would soon appear in newspapers and on television screens across the world.

The self-immolation of Quang Duc highlighted in the most graphic way the summer 1963 breakdown of U.S. policy in Vietnam. To reverse a rapidly deteriorating situation, the administration of John F. Kennedy in late 1961 had established a "limited partnership" with the Diem government, taking a giant step toward direct U.S. participation in the Second Indochina War. U.S. escalation slowed but did not suppress the National Liberation Front (NLF) insurgency. As the American presence increased dramatically, tensions with the Saigon government mounted. The sudden outbreak of Buddhist protests against alleged Diemist persecution in May 1963 vastly complicated an already tenuous situation. The so-called Buddhist crisis strained to the breaking point relations between Diem and his U.S. patron. It thrust Vietnam to the forefront of policymaking in Washington. It set in motion a tragic chain of events that would lead to the overthrow and killing of Diem and his brother, Ngo Dinh Nhu. Combined with the stunning assassination of Kennedy himself just weeks later, these climactic developments dramatically transformed the war and America's role in it.[1]

THE NEW FRONTIER AND THE COLD WAR

When JFK took office in January 1961, the Cold War seemed to have reached a critical stage. The struggle of hundreds of new nations to break from their colonial past and establish modern institutions unleashed chaos across much of the globe. The rhetoric and actions of the erratic Soviet premier Nikita Khrushchev suggested a new Communist boldness, even recklessness, and a determination to exploit the prevailing instability. Soviet-American confrontation broadened and intensified in the late 1950s. The development of awesome new weapons added an especially frightful dimension. Over the long haul, nationalism proved a more powerful force than communism or democratic capitalism. Within two years the eruption of the Sino-Soviet split would starkly expose the myth of a monolithic Communist "bloc." In 1961, however, the fate of the world appeared to hang in the balance, and Kennedy took office certain that America's survival depended on its capacity to defend "free" institutions. Should it falter, he warned, "the whole world, in my opinion, would inevitably begin to move toward the Communist bloc."[2]

Promising to assert firm, vigorous leadership, and calling upon Americans to become "watchmen on the walls of freedom," Kennedy vowed to meet the perils of the new era. The youngest person ever to be elected president, the former senator from Massachusetts had been born to wealth and privilege. Bright, handsome, and witty, he had been decorated for heroism in the Pacific theater in World War II. He had served without particular distinction in Congress, where he gained a reputation as a playboy. The author of several books on history and politics, he took a keen interest in foreign policy as a house member and a senator and also acquired a special curiosity about Indochina. He had been an avid backer of Diem, but a visit to Saigon in late 1951 had also aroused a certain skepticism that would influence his handling of Vietnam policy.

[1]A.J. Langguth, *Our Vietnam: The War, 1954–1975* (New York, 2000), pp. 214–215.
[2]Quoted in Seyom Brown, *The Faces of Power* (New York, 1969), p. 217.

The new president gathered about him a youthful, energetic corps of advisers from the top positions in academia and industry, activists who shared his commitment to "get the country moving again." The New Frontiersmen accepted without question the basic assumptions of the containment policy, but they also believed they must take the initiative in meeting the Communist threat rather than simply reacting to it.[3] Coming to political maturity during World War II, they were alarmed by the danger of another global holocaust but also exhilarated by the challenge of leading the nation through perilous times. They shared a deep sense of duty to their country and a Wilsonian view that destiny had singled out the United States to defend the democratic ideal. Pragmatic centrists, they believed that no problem was without solution. They were self-confident to the point of arrogance.[4]

Kennedy and his advisers also recognized that domestic politics demanded a successful foreign policy. During the campaign of 1960, in strident tones the senator had accused Eisenhower of indecisiveness and promised to regain the initiative in the Cold War. Having won the most narrow of electoral victories, he was keenly aware of his vulnerability. Especially in his first two years, he kept a wary eye on his domestic flank. He was ever sensitive to Republican charges of weakness or appeasement.

The administration set out at once to meet the challenges of the Cold War. The president ordered a massive buildup of nuclear weapons and long-range missiles to establish a credible deterrent to Soviet nuclear power. Persuaded that Eisenhower's heavy reliance on nuclear weapons had left the United States muscle-bound in many diplomatic situations, Kennedy also expanded and modernized the nation's conventional military forces to permit a "flexible response" to various types and levels of aggression. Certain that the emerging nations would be the major battleground in the struggle between freedom and communism, the administration also devoted much attention to developing an effective response to guerrilla warfare—"an international disease" the United States must learn to "destroy." Kennedy took a keen personal interest in the theory, tactics, and weapons of counterinsurgency warfare and covert

[3]Henry Fairlie, *The Kennedy Promise* (New York, 1973), p. 72.
[4]Thomas G. Paterson, "Bearing the Burden: A Critical Look at JFK's Foreign Policy," *Virginia Quarterly Review* 54 (Spring 1978): 197.

operations. He encouraged his advisers to read the writings of revolutionaries such as Mao Zedong and Castro adviser Che Guevara and pushed the armed services to develop means to combat their tactics. He also felt that America had to strike at the heart of the disease. Some of his top advisers, such as economist Walt Whitman Rostow of the Massachusetts Institute of Technology (MIT), had pioneered so-called modernization theory and insisted that, through generous foreign aid programs and assistance in economic development, the United States could steer the new nations away from communism and toward the Free World.[5]

Vietnam stands as the most tragic legacy of the global activism of the Kennedy era. The president had labeled it the "cornerstone of the Free World in Southeast Asia." In his eyes and those of many of his advisers, South Vietnam was a test case of America's determination to uphold its commitments in a menacing world and its capacity to meet the new challenges posed by guerrilla warfare in the emerging nations. He had joined in the attacks on Truman for "losing" China and was extremely sensitive to the political damage that could come from the loss of additional Asian real estate. Thus he was even less willing than Truman and Eisenhower to permit the fall of Vietnam to communism.

Inheriting from Eisenhower an increasingly dangerous if still limited commitment, he plunged deeper into the morass. Kennedy did not eagerly take up the burden in Vietnam; his actions there contrast sharply with his rhetoric. In settling the major policy issues, he was cautious rather than bold, hesitant rather than decisive, and improvisational rather than carefully calculating. He delayed making a firm commitment for nearly a year and then acted only because the shaky Diem government appeared on the verge of collapse. Wary of the domestic and international consequences of a negotiated settlement but unwilling to risk full-scale involvement, he chose a cautious middle course, expanding the American role while trying to keep it limited. In the short run, such a policy offered numerous advantages, but it was also delusive and dangerous. It encouraged Diem to continue on his self-destructive path while leading Americans to believe they could secure a favorable outcome without

[5]John McCloy and Walt W. Rostow quoted in Fairlie, *Kennedy Promise*, pp. 132, 264; James M. Carter, *Inventing Vietnam: The United States and State Building, 1954-1968* (New York, 2008), pp. 115–117.

paying a heavy price. It significantly narrowed the choices, making extrication more difficult and creating a self-supporting argument for a larger and more dangerous commitment.

YEAR OF CRISES

Throughout the presidential campaign, Kennedy had stressed the perils the nation confronted, but he appears to have been unprepared for the severity of the problems he inherited. Khrushchev's threat to resolve the status of divided Berlin on his own terms held out the possibility of a superpower confrontation. In January 1961, the Soviet premier delivered a seemingly militant speech avowing his support for wars of national liberation. In fact, the statement defied Kremlin hard-liners and the more aggressive Chinese by renouncing conventional war. It may even have been intended to reassure the West. To the untutored ears of the inexperienced Kennedy administration, however, it appeared a virtual declaration of war. Stepped-up Soviet aid to Castro's Cuba and insurgents in the Congo and Laos seemed to confirm the magnitude of the threat. Such was the siege mentality that gripped the White House in early 1961 that JFK on one occasion greeted his advisers by grimly asking, "What's gone against us today?"[6]

Vietnam was not regarded as a major trouble spot in the administration's first hundred days. It was only in January, after reading a gloomy report by Edward Lansdale, that Kennedy learned of the steady growth of the insurgency and the increasing problems with Diem. Lansdale predicted a large-scale insurgent offensive before the end of the year, but he concluded optimistically that a "major American effort" could frustrate the Communist drive for power. Persuaded, like Truman and Eisenhower before him, that Vietnam was vital to America's global interests, Kennedy routinely approved an additional $42 million to support an expansion of the South Vietnamese Army.[7]

By the end of April, Kennedy's staff was again closely watching Vietnam. Acting on Ambassador Elbridge Durbrow's advice, the

[6]Quoted in Walt Whitman Rostow, *The Diffusion of Power: An Essay in Recent History* (New York, 1972), p. 170.
[7]McGeorge Bundy to Rostow, January 30, 1961, John F. Kennedy Papers, National Security File, Box 192, John F. Kennedy Library, Boston, Mass.

president had conditioned the assistance granted in January on the institution of military and political reforms. But Diem had balked, and after three months the aid program remained stalled and the war languished.

At the same time, major foreign policy setbacks in Cuba and Laos appeared to increase the importance of Vietnam. A clandestine effort to overthrow Castro ended in disaster at the Bay of Pigs, leaving Kennedy in a state of acute shock and his administration profoundly shaken. After the Bay of Pigs, Kennedy was suspicious of the Joint Chiefs of Staff (JCS) and the intelligence community; he therefore rejected various proposals to put troops into Laos to stave off the impending defeat of the American-sponsored government. The military warned that protecting U.S. troops sent to Laos against possible Chinese or North Vietnamese countermoves might require extreme measures, even the use of nuclear weapons. The country was landlocked, a poor choice for intervention from a logistic standpoint. More important, most Americans viewed Laotians as lazy, lacking in national unity, and singularly devoid of a martial spirit, and they were reluctant to go to war for a people who seemed unwilling to defend themselves. Ambassador to India John Kenneth Galbraith contemptuously warned that as a "military ally the entire Laos nation is clearly inferior to a battalion of conscientious objectors from World War I." Moreover, as JFK himself repeatedly pointed out, it would be difficult to explain to the American public why he sent troops to remote Laos when he had refused to send them to nearby Cuba. Without explicitly ruling out a military solution, in late April Kennedy broke sharply with Eisenhower's policy and concluded that a negotiated settlement was the best he could get in Laos. The United States agreed to participate in a peace conference at Geneva.[8]

More than anything else, the decision to negotiate in Laos led the administration to reassess its policy in Vietnam. Along with its refusal to send U.S. aircraft or troops to salvage the Bay of Pigs operation, its unwillingness to intervene militarily in Laos

[8]Galbraith to Kennedy, May 10, 1961, Kennedy Papers, Office File, Box 29. For the Laos decisions, see Seth Jacobs, "'No Place to Fight a War': Laos and the Evolution of U.S. Policy toward Vietnam, 1954–1963," in Mark Philip Bradley and Marilyn B. Young (eds.), *Making Sense of the Vietnam Wars: Local, National, and Transnational Perspectives* (New York, 2008), pp. 53–62, and William J. Rust, *Before the Quagmire: American Intervention in Laos, 1954–1961* (Lexington, Ky., 2012), pp. 260–261.

appeared to increase the symbolic importance of taking stands elsewhere. The administration had captured the attention of the nation with its self-conscious activism but had little to show for it. "At this point we are like the Harlem Globetrotters," National Security Adviser McGeorge Bundy conceded, "passing forward, behind, sidewise, and underneath. But nobody has made a basket yet."[9] Kennedy confided to *New York Times* columnist Arthur Krock that he had to make certain that "Khrushchev doesn't misunderstand Cuba, Laos, etc. to indicate that the United States is in a yielding mood on such matters as Berlin."[10] Moreover, with the outcome of the Laos negotiations uncertain, it seemed urgent to prepare a fallback position in Southeast Asia. Vietnam appeared a better place than Laos to make a stand.

Despite its growing concern with Vietnam, the administration did not institute major policy changes or drastically expand American commitments in the spring of 1961. The president authorized a modest increase of 100 advisers in the Military Assistance and Advisory Group (MAAG) and dispatched to Vietnam 400 Special Forces troops to train the Vietnamese in counterinsurgency techniques. Convinced in light of the Laos negotiations that Diem had to be handled with special care, Kennedy recalled Durbrow, the foremost advocate of hard bargaining tactics, and sent Vice President Lyndon B. Johnson to Saigon to give personal assurances of American support. To back up its diplomacy without provoking domestic or international concern, the administration launched covert warfare in Indochina. The United States sent clandestine teams of South Vietnamese across the seventeenth parallel to attack enemy supply lines, sabotage military and civilian targets, and agitate against the Hanoi regime. At the same time, the CIA initiated a "secret war" in Laos, arming some 9,000 Hmong, an ethnic group in that country's mountain region, for actions against the Ho Chi Minh trail in what would become one of the largest paramilitary operations ever undertaken.[11]

[9]Fairlie, *Kennedy Promise*, p. 180.

[10]Krock memorandum of conversation with Kennedy, May 5, 1961, Arthur Krock Papers, Seeley G. Mudd Manuscript Library, Princeton, N.J., Box 59.

[11]For the beginnings of the Laos secret war, see Timothy N. Castle, *At War in the Shadow of Vietnam* (New York, 1993), especially pp. 39–44; and Jane Hamilton-Merritt, *Tragic Mountains* (Bloomington, Ind., 1993), pp. 70–112. See also Richard H. Shultz Jr., *The Secret War against Hanoi* (New York, 1999).

The reappraisal of the spring of 1961 was more important for the questions raised than for the solutions provided. The administration's decisions reflected, in the words of Rostow, a calculated policy of "buying time with limited commitments of additional American resources."[12] But many officials feared that this policy might not be enough. A task force appointed by Kennedy to review American options began to consider the more drastic measures that might be required if the Laos negotiations broke down or the insurgents launched a major offensive in Vietnam. Among other actions, the task force openly raised the possibility of sending, for the first time since 1954, U.S. combat forces to Vietnam. It also discussed air and naval operations against North Vietnam.

While the administration studied various choices, pressures mounted for expanded American involvement in Vietnam. After a whirlwind trip through East Asia with a major stopover in Saigon, Johnson reported that the decision to negotiate in Laos had shaken Diem's confidence in the United States and warned that if a further decline in morale was to be arrested, "deeds must follow words—soon."[13] After Johnson's visit, Diem himself requested additional aid. He displayed no interest in U.S. combat troops when the vice president discreetly raised the issue. Fiercely independent and keenly aware of the rising opposition to his regime, Diem feared that the introduction of large numbers of American troops would not only provide the NLF a powerful rallying cry but also give the non-Communist opposition critical leverage. Shortly after Johnson departed Saigon, however, Diem warned Kennedy that the situation in Vietnam had become "very much more perilous" and requested sufficient additional American aid and advisers to expand his army by 100,000 troops.[14]

The Cold War intensified in the summer of 1961. During a stormy summit meeting in Vienna in June, Khrushchev again affirmed the Soviet commitment to wars of liberation, reinforcing the administration's fears and its inclination to respond somewhere. He "just beat hell out of me," Kennedy remarked. "If he

---

[12]Rostow, *Diffusion of Power*, p. 270.
[13]Johnson to Kennedy, May 23, 1961, Kennedy Papers, Office File, Box 30.
[14]U.S. Congress, Senate, Subcommittee on Public Buildings and Grounds, *The Pentagon Papers (Senator Gravel Edition)*, 4 vols. (Boston, 1971), 2: 60. Hereafter cited as *Pentagon Papers (Gravel)*.

thinks I'm inexperienced and have no guts . . . we won't get any-where with him. So we have to act."[15] In August, under cover of darkness, the Soviets constructed a steel and concrete wall separating West Berlin from the eastern zone, confronting an already beleaguered Kennedy administration with yet another crisis.

THE TAYLOR–ROSTOW MISSION

In the supercharged atmosphere of mid-1961, some of Kennedy's advisers pressed for escalation in Vietnam. Rostow had long advocated the employment of such "unexploited counterguerrilla assets" as helicopters and the newly created Green Berets. "It is somehow wrong to be developing these capabilities but not applying them in a crucial theater," he advised the president. "In Knute Rockne's old phrase, we are not saving them for the junior prom." He compared the summer of 1961 to the year 1942, when the Allies had suffered defeats across the globe, warning that "to turn the tide" the United States must "win" in Vietnam. If Vietnam could be held, Thailand, Laos, and Cambodia could be saved and "we shall have demonstrated that the Communist technique of guerrilla warfare can be dealt with."[16]

Preoccupied with Berlin, JFK fended off his more belligerent advisers, approving only small additional increments of aid until a dramatic worsening of conditions in the fall of 1961 compelled him to act. Infiltration into South Vietnam doubled to nearly 4,000 in 1961. The NLF drastically stepped up operations in September and for a brief period even seized a provincial capital just fifty-five miles from Saigon. Intelligence analysts reported a substantial increase in the size of regular guerrilla forces. The journalist Theodore H. White noted a "political breakdown of formidable proportions" in South Vietnam.[17] In September, Diem urgently requested additional economic assistance. By early October, both the JCS and the National Security Council (NSC) were proposing the introduction of sizable U.S. combat forces into Vietnam.

---

[15]Michael R. Beschloss, *The Crisis Years* (New York, 1991), p. 225.
[16]Rostow to Kennedy, March 29, 1961, Kennedy Papers, National Security File, Box 192, and June 17, 1961, Kennedy Papers, Office File, Box 65.
[17]Quoted in *Pentagon Papers (Gravel)*, 2: 70.

Kennedy remained cautious. He revealed to Krock a profound reluctance to send American troops to the Asian mainland. He expressed grave doubts that the United States should interfere in "civil disturbances caused by guerrillas," adding that "it was hard to prove that this wasn't largely the situation in Vietnam."[18] Increasingly concerned by the military and political deterioration in South Vietnam but fearful of expanding the U.S. commitment, he dispatched Rostow and his personal military adviser, Gen. Maxwell D. Taylor, to Vietnam to assess conditions firsthand and weigh the need for U.S. forces.

Taylor and Rostow confirmed the pessimistic reports that had been coming out of Saigon for the past month. The South Vietnamese Army was afflicted with a "defensive outlook." The Diem government was disorganized, inefficient, and increasingly unpopular. The basic problem was a "deep and pervasive crisis of confidence and a serious loss in national morale" stemming from developments in Laos, the intensification of guerrilla activity, and a devastating flood in the Mekong Delta. "No one felt the situation was hopeless," Taylor later recalled, but all agreed that it was "serious" and demanded "urgent measures."[19]

Taylor and Rostow recommended a significant expansion of American aid to arrest the deterioration in South Vietnam. They emphasized that the Vietnamese themselves must win the war; but they also concluded that the provision of U.S. equipment and skilled advisers working closely with the government at all levels could result in a "much better, aggressive, more confident performance from the Vietnamese military and civilian establishment."[20] Highly trained advisory groups, strategically placed throughout the South Vietnamese bureaucracy, could help identify and correct major political, economic, and military problems. Improved training for the Civil Guard and Village Self-Defense Corps would free the army for offensive operations. Equipment such as helicopters would give it the mobility to fight more effectively. Taylor and Rostow also advocated what they called a "limited partnership" with the South Vietnamese government, a middle ground between

[18]Krock memorandum of conversation with Kennedy, October 11, 1961, Krock Papers, Box 59.
[19]Maxwell D. Taylor, *Swords and Ploughshares* (New York, 1972), p. 241.
[20]Rostow, *Diffusion of Power*, p. 275.

"formalized advice on the one hand" and "trying to run the war on the other."[21]

The most novel—and ultimately most controversial—of the proposals was to send an 8,000-person "logistic task force" of American soldiers, comprising engineers, medical groups, and the infantry to support them. The ostensible purpose was to assist in repairing the massive flood damage in the Mekong Delta, but Taylor had other, more important motives in mind. Diem continued to resist the introduction of U.S. combat forces, but many government officials and many Americans in Saigon believed that troops were desperately needed. Taylor himself felt a "pressing need to do something to restore Vietnamese morale and to shore up confidence in the United States." The task force would serve as a "visible symbol of the seriousness of American intentions," he advised Kennedy, and would constitute an invaluable military reserve should the situation in South Vietnam suddenly worsen.[22] The humanitarian purpose of the force would provide a convenient pretext for its introduction into Vietnam. It could be removed without embarrassment when its job was completed. Taylor and Rostow emphasized that their proposals constituted minimum steps. If they were not enough, the United States might have to dispatch combat troops or launch offensive operations against North Vietnam.

The proposal for a flood relief force aroused especially heated discussion among Kennedy's advisers. Some candidly admitted that it was a subterfuge. Some feared that the introduction of combat troops in any form might jeopardize the Laos negotiations or provoke escalation in Vietnam. Others questioned whether such a force would be large enough or, given its announced purpose of flood relief, capable of restoring morale. Should it come under attack, the United States would face the more difficult choice of supporting it with additional forces or withdrawing it altogether. "If we commit 6–8,000 troops and then pull them out when the going gets rough we will be finished in Vietnam and probably all of Southeast Asia," one NSC staffer warned.[23] There was general

[21]Taylor to Kennedy, November 3, 1961, in Department of State, *Foreign Relations of the United States, 1961–1963* (Washington, D.C., 1988), 1: 493. Hereafter cited as *FR* with date and volume number.

[22]Taylor, *Swords and Ploughshares*, p. 239.

[23]Robert Johnson to Bundy, October 31, 1961, Kennedy Papers, National Security File, Box 194.

unhappiness with the "half-in, half-out" nature of the proposal. Top State Department officials expressed major reservations about committing troops in any form. Secretary of Defense Robert McNamara, the JCS, and McGeorge Bundy used the Taylor proposal to develop more far-reaching recommendations, urging Kennedy to make an unequivocal commitment to prevent the fall of South Vietnam and then be prepared to introduce large-scale U.S. combat forces "if that should become necessary for success."[24]

While the Taylor–Rostow report was circulating in Washington, Undersecretary of State Chester Bowles and the veteran diplomat W. Averell Harriman, the chief negotiator on Laos, promoted a very different course. Harriman expressed grave doubt that Diem's "repressive, dictatorial and unpopular regime" could survive under any circumstances and warned that the United States should not "stake its prestige in Vietnam." Bowles admonished that the United States was "headed full blast up a dead end street." The two men thus pressed Kennedy to defer any major commitment to Diem. If the Laos negotiations proceeded smoothly, the United States could then expand the conference to include Vietnam and seek an overall settlement based on the 1954 Geneva Agreements.[25] The Taylor–Rostow report for the first time since 1954 posed a clear-cut choice between a major escalation of the conflict and possible extrication from Vietnam.

In a way that would become institutionalized, JFK opted for a cautious, middle-of-the-road approach. He flatly rejected a negotiated settlement. Throughout the year, Republicans and right-wing Democrats had charged him with weakness, and Kennedy feared that a decision to negotiate on Vietnam would unleash domestic political attacks as rancorous and destructive as those after the fall of China in 1949.

Administration strategists also felt that in a divided and dangerous world the United States must establish the credibility of its commitments. Should it appear weak, allies would lose faith and

[24]Dean Rusk and Robert McNamara to Kennedy, November 11, 1961, *Pentagon Papers (Gravel)*, 2: 110–116.
[25]Harriman to Kennedy, November 11, 1961, Kennedy Papers, National Security File, Box 195; Chester Bowles, *Promises to Keep* (New York, 1971), p. 409; Stephen Pelz, "John F. Kennedy's 1961 Vietnam War Decisions," *Journal of Strategic Studies* 4 (December 1981): 378.

enemies would be emboldened to further aggression, a process that could leave the awful choice of a complete erosion of America's world position or nuclear war. By late 1961, Kennedy and many of his advisers were convinced that they must prove their toughness to Khrushchev. "That son of a bitch won't pay any attention to words," the president remarked during the Berlin crisis. "He has to see you move."[26]

Although determined to appear tough, Kennedy firmly resisted the proposal to send combat troops. He questioned the psychological value of Taylor's flood relief force. He speculated—prophetically, as it turned out—that the commitment of some men would only lead to requests for more. "The troops will march in; the bands will play; the crowds will cheer," he told Arthur M. Schlesinger Jr., "and in four days everyone will have forgotten. Then we will be told we have to send in more troops. It's like taking a drink. The effect wears off, and you have to take another."[27] He also rejected McNamara's proposal for a major verbal commitment to prevent the fall of South Vietnam, noting that a commitment without troops could bring the worst of both worlds. He expressed deep concern about taking on simultaneously major obligations in Europe and Southeast Asia. He was especially bothered by the prospect of direct involvement in a war whose origins were so "obscure" in an "area 10,000 miles away against 16,000 guerrillas with a native army of 200,000, where millions have been spent for years with no success." On several occasions, he expressed uncertainty that he could secure congressional and allied support to wage such a war.[28]

Kennedy would go no further than approve Taylor's recommendations to increase significantly the volume of American assistance and the number of advisers in hopes this would arrest the military and political deterioration in South Vietnam. To oversee implementation of the new program, the administration created a Military Assistance Command Vietnam (MACV) and elevated the top military official to equal status with the ambassador. It took these steps in full recognition that it was violating the Geneva Accords of 1954. On December 15 it released a "white paper"

[26]Quoted in Paterson, "Bearing the Burden," 206.
[27]Quoted in Arthur M. Schlesinger, Jr., *A Thousand Days* (Boston, 1965), p. 547.
[28]Notes on NSC meeting, November 15, 1961, *FR, 1961–1963*, 1: 607–608.

detailing North Vietnamese breaches of the Geneva Agreements that justified its own response.[29]

In undertaking Taylor's "limited partnership" with South Vietnam, the administration at first took a hard line with Diem. American officials had long agreed that his repressive and inefficient government constituted a major obstacle to defeating the insurgency. Reluctant to commit American personnel, money, and prestige to a "losing horse," as Secretary of State Dean Rusk put it, the administration instructed the embassy in Saigon to inform Diem that approval of the new aid program would be contingent on specific promises to reorganize and reform the government and permit the United States a share in decision making.[30]

The U.S. demands provoked a crisis in Saigon. Accustomed to getting what he wanted with no strings attached, Diem was stunned by Washington's new approach. He perceived that the sort of political reforms the United States sought could lead to his own demise. He angrily protested the pittance of money and equipment offered and lashed out at the proposals for a new relationship, bluntly informing Ambassador Frederick Nolting that South Vietnam "did not want to be a protectorate."[31] The Kennedy administration responded by holding up shipments of military equipment and instituting a quiet search for a possible replacement for Diem. The two sides came close to a break before the United States retreated. Nolting advised that a "cool and unhurried approach is our best chance of success."[32] The State Department could identify no one who appeared capable of filling Diem's shoes. Persuaded, as JFK conceded, that "Diem is Diem and the best we've got," the United States backed down.[33] The new relationship was redefined to mean simply that one party would not take action without consulting the other; the emphasis was shifted from reform to efficiency. The two governments agreed on an innocuous statement affirming these points. The crisis passed.

[29]Department of State, *A Threat to the Peace: North Viet Nam's Effort to Conquer South Viet Nam* (Washington, D.C., 1961).

[30]Rusk to State Department, November 1, 1961, Kennedy Papers, National Security File, Box 194; *Pentagon Papers (Gravel)*, 2: 120.

[31]Nolting to State Department, November 18, 1961, Kennedy Papers, National Security File, Box 165.

[32]Nolting to State Department, November 29, 1961, Kennedy Papers, National Security File, Box 195.

[33]Quoted in Benjamin Bradlee, *Conversations with Kennedy* (New York, 1976), p. 59.

Kennedy's decisions of 1961 mark yet another critical turning point for U.S. policy in Vietnam. Properly wary of deeper military involvement in a conflict he suspected might not be winnable, the president, primarily for political reasons, still refused to abandon the struggle. Rejecting the extremes of combat troops and negotiations, he settled for a limited commitment of aid and advisers. His caution was well placed, but his 1961 decisions increased direct American involvement and the commitment of U.S. prestige. He recognized from the start, moreover, that these limited steps might not be enough to save South Vietnam. Events would demonstrate that the commitments, once made, could not easily be kept limited. The new commitments marked a giant step toward America's assumption of responsibility for the war, a step symbolized by the creation of a formal military command.[34]

In instituting their new partnership, the United States and Diem entangled themselves more tightly in their fateful web. American frustration with Diem was understandable, but in searching for a more manageable replacement, U.S. officials arrogantly presumed to know what was best for South Vietnam. By assuming greater responsibility for the war, they undercut the nationalist claims on which Diem's success ultimately rested. Diem perceived that he could not defeat the insurgency and stay in power without U.S. support, but he recognized the dangers and tried desperately—and ultimately unsuccessfully—to avoid his ally's suffocating embrace. The U.S.–South Vietnam agreements of late 1961 thus opened the way for conflicts that would make a mockery of the word *partnership* and would have tragic consequences for all concerned.[35]

PROJECT BEEFUP

Their differences settled, at least for the moment, the United States and South Vietnam launched a two-pronged campaign to defeat the insurgency. To assert their independence from the United States

---

[34]Michael Cannon, "Raising the Stakes: The Taylor-Rostow Mission," *Journal of Strategic Studies* 12 (June 1989): 153–158.
[35]Kennedy sought to solidify the middle course in Vietnam and in other areas through what became known as the "Thanksgiving Day Massacre," in which the "dovish" Bowles was removed as undersecretary of state and the "hawkish" Rostow was sent to the State Department.

and gain the support of the rural population in the war against the NLF, Diem and Nhu energetically promoted a Strategic Hamlet program. The plan has sometimes mistakenly been attributed to U.S. and British influence, and the regime did consult British counterinsurgency expert Sir Robert Thompson, in part to counterbalance rising American intrusion. But the program had indigenous roots, and Diem and Nhu deliberately left the Americans out as a way of demonstrating South Vietnamese self-reliance. The aim was not only to defeat the NLF but also to carry out a revolution in the villages and chart a distinctively Vietnamese path to modernity. Peasants from scattered villages would be brought together into hamlets surrounded by moats and bamboo stake fences and guarded by military forces. The hamlets would protect the people against NLF terror and also provide the means for a social and economic revolution based on local self-rule and self-sufficiency. The reinstitution of village elections, land reform, and the building of schools and medical facilities would persuade villagers that the government offered more than the insurgents. Restoring village autonomy, displacing the old elite, and encouraging economic development through self-help projects would bind the villagers together as a community, leaving the guerrillas as outsiders facing a hostile population. Diem and Nhu envisioned a truly nationalist revolution that would restore the villages to their traditional place in Vietnamese life. They hoped that the Strategic Hamlet Program would reduce their dependence on the United States. In their most grandiose vision, it would unify all of Vietnam under their control.[36]

To support the counterinsurgency program, the United States, in what was called "Project Beefup," drastically expanded its role in Vietnam. The Military Assistance and Advisory Group was replaced by an enlarged and reorganized military command headed by Gen. Paul D. Harkins. American military assistance more than doubled between 1961 and 1962 and included such major items as armored personnel carriers and more than 300 military aircraft. Kennedy authorized the use of defoliants to deny the guerrillas cover and secure major roads, as well as the limited use of herbicides to destroy enemy food supplies.

---

[36]Philip E. Catton, *Diem's Final Failure: Prelude to America's War in Vietnam.* (Lawrence, Kans., 2002), pp. 86–98, 118–128.

The number of U.S. "advisers" jumped from 3,205 in December 1961 to more than 9,000 by the end of 1962. Highly trained professionals, in many cases veterans of World War II and Korea, they epitomized the global commitment and can-do spirit of the Kennedy era. Their casual dress—brightly colored caps, shoulder holsters, and bandoliers—reflected their unusual mission. They stoically endured the harsh climate and the dysentery (promptly dubbed "Ho Chi Minh's revenge"), confident that they were not only defending Vietnam against a Communist takeover but also preparing themselves for the wars of the future. "It's as important for us to train as the Vietnamese," a helicopter pilot informed an American journalist.[37]

The advisers performed varied, ever-widening tasks. Special Forces units conducted Civic Action programs among the Montagnards of the Central Highlands. Helicopter pilots dropped detachments of Army of the Republic of Vietnam (ARVN) troops into battle zones deep in the swamplands and picked up the dead and wounded after engagements. Americans went with Vietnamese trainees on bombing and strafing missions and, when the Vietnamese ran short of pilots, flew the planes themselves. Army officers and enlisted personnel conducted expanded training programs for the ARVN and the Civil Guard. Advisers down to the battalion level fought with ARVN units on combat missions.

Initiating a pattern that would come to stigmatize the U.S. war in Vietnam as a whole, the Kennedy administration went to considerable lengths to deceive the American public about the extent and nature of its growing involvement. It refused to divulge the actual number of "advisers" sent to Vietnam and continued to insist that they were advisers long after they were actively engaged in combat. Elaborate schemes were devised to maintain that fiction. Low-ranking Vietnamese enlisted men were placed in aircraft merely to provide cover for U.S. pilots. Vietnamese pilots sat next to Americans so that combat casualties could be publicized as training accidents. Advisers going on ground operations were authorized to shoot back if fired upon. Americans even selected the names for combat operations. While actually waging war in Vietnam, the Kennedy administration emphatically denied it. The president himself insisted that the United States had not

[37]Quoted in Richard Tregaskis, *Vietnam Diary* (New York, 1963), p. 149.

sent to Vietnam combat forces in the "generally understood sense of the word" and that U.S. advisers were not involved in combat. When the truth inevitably came out, the administration ordered officials in Saigon to clamp down on the press to minimize the possibility of harmful stories.[38]

Even as the United States and South Vietnam escalated the war, the NLF expanded its grip on the countryside. The Communist Party spearheaded the revolution in the South. Gradually replacing—or purging—the cadres who had fought the French, it recruited a new generation of revolutionaries, many of them poor peasants, young, idealistic, and deeply committed to the cause. The new members were rigorously indoctrinated and required to engage in intense self-criticism. They were schooled to put cause before self: The individual was "no more than a grain of sand in the desert," according to party dogma. The intricate NLF network was tightly organized from top to bottom. Skilled propagandists, the insurgents effectively exploited local grievances to stir up class hatred and mobilize the peasantry against the Saigon government. In some liberated areas, the party enacted land reform that benefited many peasants. Taxes were low and sometimes came in the form of voluntary contributions. Local cadres were schooled to behave properly toward the peasants, to win over their "hearts and minds" (a phrase used by the Americans as well). The NLF also employed violent means to eliminate the best and worst of government officials, in each case strengthening its own position. Party membership almost doubled during this period, exceeding the highest numbers during the French war. Popular support for the insurgency peaked. In late 1961, the NLF raised military struggle to the same level as political agitation. Building a complex military organization extending from local militia platoons to regional main force units, it cleverly used subterfuge and intimidation to expand the area under its control.[39]

For a time in the summer of 1962, South Vietnam wrested the momentum from the insurgents. Buoyed by the new weapons and

[38]Howard Jones, *Death of a Generation: How the Assassinations of Diem and JFK Prolonged the Vietnam War* (New York, 2003), pp. 152–159.

[39]David W. P. Elliott, *The Vietnamese War: Revolution and Social Change in the Mekong Delta 1930–1975* (Armonk, N.Y., 2007), pp. 137–178; Eric Bergerud, *The Dynamics of Defeat: The Vietnam War in Hau Nghia Province* (Boulder, Colo., 1991), pp. 54–68, 82–84.

U.S. advisers, the ARVN launched major military operations. The Strategic Hamlet Program threatened insurgent control in some areas and retook villages that had been "liberated." New weapons, such as armored personnel carriers and helicopters, at first intimidated the guerrillas, causing them some defeats and forcing them into hiding. In the fall of 1962, in the critical Mekong Delta region south of Saigon, party leaders expressed grave concern.

The U.S.–South Vietnamese counteroffensive produced no more than fleeting gains. Even with aircraft and sophisticated electronic equipment, it proved frustratingly difficult to locate enemy bases in the dense forests and swampy paddies of Vietnam. The very nature of airphibious operations—an air strike followed by the landing of troops—gave advance warning of an attack, often permitting the enemy to slip away. The insurgents quickly adapted to the helicopters. Sometimes, they stood and fought, and they learned to bring down the slow, clumsy aircraft with small arms. Other times, they would lie in hiding until the aircraft departed and then ambush the landing force. In late 1962, party leaders concluded that "if we want to survive, we have to attack them, and only by attacking them can we survive." They ordered military forces to stay on the move and employ deception and their superior mobility to keep ARVN units off-balance. More important, they were instructed to stand and fight when challenged.[40] Gradually, they regained the initiative. NLF operations became increasingly bold and began to inflict heavy losses. As the fighting became more costly, ARVN commanders, apparently under orders from Diem, reverted to their old caution, increasingly relying on airpower and refusing to risk their troops in battle.

The NLF resurgence was dramatically manifested in January 1963 in one of the most important battles of the Second Indochina War. A U.S. adviser, the aggressive and charismatic Lt. Col. John Paul Vann, persuaded his ARVN division commander to attack three NLF units near the village of Ap Bac. But the South Vietnamese dallied for a day, enabling the insurgents to learn of the attack and prepare deadly defenses. The ARVN outnumbered the NLF by 10 to 1—the textbook ratio for fighting guerrillas. But at the first sign of resistance, the attackers balked. One group refused to advance. Others failed to block enemy escape routes. Smaller NLF

[40]Elliott, *Vietnamese War*, p. 178.

units encircled the attackers and inflicted huge losses on them and the relief forces sent by helicopter. The battle ended, ingloriously, with the South Vietnamese firing on one another while the NLF slipped away. The vastly superior ARVN forces suffered 61 dead and 100 wounded; two helicopters were shot down. The NLF left only 3 bodies behind. Thinking in entirely conventional terms, the MACV claimed victory because the enemy had vacated the field of battle, a view scathingly dismissed by some skeptical American journalists and top White House advisers. The battle proved to the NLF that they could stand up to and defeat even those ARVN forces with U.S. equipment and advisers. Morale soared. Ap Bac reversed the trend of U.S.–South Vietnamese gains and started the GVN on a downhill slide. It represented a major turning point in the war.[41]

The political implications of techniques employed in military operations also increasingly disturbed some Americans. It was difficult to distinguish between insurgents and innocent civilians, and ARVN soldiers, their lives constantly under threat, were not inclined to make fine distinctions. Civilians, even women and children, were gunned down, giving the NLF a powerful propaganda weapon. The bombing and strafing of villages suspected of harboring guerrillas and the use of napalm and defoliants turned villagers against the government. American and South Vietnamese military officials insisted that air cover was essential to ground operations, however, and Diem and General Harkins vigorously promoted the use of napalm. It "really puts the fear of God into the Vietcong," the general exclaimed. "And that is what counts."[42]

The much ballyhooed Strategic Hamlet Program also produced meager results. A similar plan had worked well in Malaya, where Malay villages were fortified against Chinese insurgents, but in Vietnam the hamlets were to be erected against Vietnamese, many of whom had lived among the villagers for years. The issuance of more than seven million laminated identification cards proved a less-than-adequate safeguard against infiltration. In theory, the program was meant to prevent the massive relocation of peasants from sacred ancestral lands, the flaw of the ill-fated agroville plan. But in

[41]The classic account is Neil Sheehan, *A Bright Shining Lie* (New York, 1988), pp. 212–256. The NLF perspective is set forth in Elliott, *Vietnamese War*, pp. 179–184.
[42]Quoted in Roger Hilsman, *To Move a Nation* (New York, 1967), p. 442.

the delta region, where villagers lived in scattered settlements, the hamlets could not be established without displacement. The large-scale uprooting of the peasantry added to the discontent that had pervaded the rural population since Diem's ascent to power.

The plan was poorly implemented. The Saigon government did not set clear goals and outline the means to achieve them. The result was poorly designed hamlets. In contrast to the NLF, which worked patiently and with painstaking attention to detail, Diem and Nhu naively underestimated the difficulty of the task and tried to do too much too quickly. They established hamlets in areas where no real security existed, and the vulnerable settlements were quickly overrun or infiltrated by the NLF. Many of the hamlets lacked adequate defenses. Adviser Roger Hilsman encountered several spread over such large areas that a full division would have been required to protect them. "But the defenders," he recalled, "were only a few old men, armed with swords, flintlocks, and half a dozen American carbines."[43] In some areas, enemy agents who had infiltrated the South Vietnamese government deliberately sabotaged the hamlets for which they had responsibility.

In the hands of Diem and Nhu, moreover, the program did nothing to bind the people to the government. Land reform was implemented poorly, if at all, and many peasants were left landless. The United States allocated substantial funds for the institution of services in the hamlets, but inefficiency and corruption kept much of the money from its destination. The government lacked qualified people to staff the program, and many incompetent and corrupt officials represented it at the village level. Instead of building a community, they drove and coerced the villagers to achieve unrealistic goals, provoking resistance and flight to the NLF.[44]

The Strategic Hamlet Program failed to achieve its goal of winning the war at the "rice roots." As a means of protecting the villagers from direct attack, it enjoyed some limited, short-term success. Among the Montagnards in the Central Highlands, where the United States assumed responsibility, it played a constructive role. By early 1963, however, even its most ardent supporters agreed that it was fundamentally flawed. In addition, the NLF, fearing that even limited government success would threaten its base among

[43]Ibid., p. 456; Catton: *Diem's Final Failure.* pp. 128 ff.
[44]Catton, *Diem's Final Failure,* pp. 128 FF.

the rural population and leave its members as "fish on the chopping block," launched a systematic and effective campaign against key hamlets, creating specially trained units to destroy them by direct attack or infiltration.[45]

Some Kennedy advisers continued to insist that an effective counterinsurgency program required sweeping political reforms, but Diem stubbornly resisted. To appease his American "partners," he instituted token reforms such as the creation of a council of economic advisers. Instead of broadening his government, as the Americans urged, he retreated more and more into isolation, relying almost exclusively on Nhu, a frail and sinister man who tended toward paranoia and delusions of grandeur. The two men personally controlled military operations and directed the Strategic Hamlet Program. They brooked no interference from their American advisers. Nhu's wife, the beautiful, ambitious, and acid-tongued Tran Le Xuan (often referred to by Americans as the Dragon Lady, a racially charged stereotype applied to strong Asian women, and the name of a leading character in a popular comic strip of the time) increasingly assumed the role of spokesperson for what by 1962 had become a narrow family oligarchy. Madame Nhu sponsored a "Social Purification Law" that prohibited, among other things, dancing, suggestive dress, public displays of affection, and birth control.

The suspicious and beleaguered Ngos tightened rather than relaxed the controls. The National Assembly pliantly passed laws prohibiting all types of public gatherings, weddings and funerals included, unless approved by the government in advance. The regime imposed on Americans as well as Vietnamese the most rigorous censorship. Diem angrily terminated the contract of the Michigan State University advisory group when several of its members, on returning to the United States, wrote articles that he branded "untrue, unfair, and tendentious."[46] The veteran *Newsweek* correspondent Francois Sully was expelled from Saigon for critical remarks about Madame Nhu.

[45]William J. Duiker, *The Communist Road to Power in Vietnam* (Boulder, Colo., 1981), p. 214; "Second Informal Appreciation of the Status of the Strategic Hamlet Program," September 1, 1963, Kennedy Papers, National Security File, Box 202.

[46]Wesley Fishel to John Hannah, February 17, 1962, Kennedy Papers, National Security File, Box 196.

OPTIMISM AND UNCERTAINTY

Throughout 1962, Vietnam remained for the Kennedy admininstration an operational rather than a policy problem. Preoccupied with more urgent matters, such as the Soviet military buildup in Cuba, top U.S. officials devoted little attention to Vietnam. Having decided the hard questions of policy in 1961, they did not consider fundamental changes. Kennedy flatly rejected Rostow's proposal to put pressure on the Russians to stop the infiltration of soldiers and supplies from North Vietnam. He ignored Galbraith's warnings that the United States was becoming entrapped in a "long drawn out indecisive involvement" and might "bleed as the French did."[47]

As late as the end of 1962, a reappraisal appeared unnecessary, because both the embassy and the military command in Saigon exuded optimism. To some extent, as Ambassador Nolting once conceded, their bullishness derived from a "whistle while we work" mentality that was necessary to sustain morale amid setbacks and frustration.[48] In time, however, they came to believe their own rhetoric. Their confidence was clearly misplaced. They appeared, at best, fools, at worst, dissemblers. But the flaws in the program were more apparent later than at the time. Strangers in an unfamiliar country, they depended for information on the South Vietnamese government, which produced impressive statistics to back claims of progress. Nolting and Harkins erred badly in accepting these figures at face value, but the conflict did not lend itself to easy analysis; they, like other observers, were impressed by the change of climate since 1961, when the Diem government had appeared on the verge of collapse. American policy was working, they argued. With time and patience, victory was attainable.

In late 1962, the American press corps in Saigon began to challenge the official optimism. Brash young correspondents such as David Halberstam of the *New York Times* and Neil Sheehan of United Press International did not question the importance of containing communism in Vietnam. Despite government efforts at obfuscation, they sniffed out the facts of growing U.S. involvement. They argued, with increasing force, that the war was being lost. They denounced the Diem government as corrupt, repressive, and

[47]Galbraith to Kennedy, April 4, 1962, Kennedy Papers, National Security File, Box 196.
[48]Nolting to Harriman, November 19, 1962, *FR, 1961–1963,* 2: 738.

unpopular and the Strategic Hamlet Program as a sham. They questioned official reports of military progress, arguing that government statistics were grossly inflated and that the ARVN was conducting "office-hours warfare," launching perfunctory operations during the day and returning to its bases in the evening. They insisted that the war could not be won as long as the United States persisted in its foolish policy of "sink or swim with Ngo Dinh Diem." The angry, defensive response of the embassy and the military command—"Get on the team!" a top military official demanded of one dissident journalist—only enraged the reporters and provoked charges that the government was deliberately deceiving the American people about the war.[49]

Other observers raised even more troublesome questions. Kennedy's former Senate colleague Mike Mansfield visited Vietnam at the president's request and returned in December 1962 with a highly pessimistic appraisal. In a formal, published statement, Mansfield noted that he could find little progress since his last visit in 1955. In a private report to Kennedy he was even more blunt, observing that Diem seemed exhausted, out of touch with reality, and under the sway of his brother, Nhu, and expressing grave concern about deeper U.S. entanglement in Vietnam, even a full-scale entanglement such as the French war. Shortly after Christmas, the two men discussed the report at length aboard Kennedy's yacht off Palm Beach. The president was angry and red-faced, Mansfield recalled, in part because the report questioned his policies, in part because he agreed with his former Senate colleague. Ambassador Nolting later called the Mansfield report "the first nail in Diem's coffin."[50]

Mounting criticism of U.S. Vietnam policy aroused grave concern in Washington. The administration had attempted to keep its involvement under wraps, but the rising toll of American deaths and the critical newspaper accounts raised troublesome questions. U.S. officials spent hours investigating the journalists' reports and answering their allegations. Kennedy himself attempted, unsuccessfully, to get the *Times* to recall Halberstam. The president was

[49]The attitudes of the dissident journalists and their experiences are chronicled in David Halberstam, *The Making of a Quagmire* (New York, 1964). See also Clarence R. Wyatt, *Paper Soldiers* (New York, 1993), pp. 77–127.
[50]Mike Mansfield oral history interview, Kennedy Papers; Jones, *Death of a Generation*, p. 216.

stung by Mansfield's report, but he could not ignore the warnings of a trusted friend. He immediately dispatched Hilsman and Michael Forrestal, a member of the White House staff, on a fact-finding mission to Vietnam.

The Hilsman–Forrestal report of early 1963 struck a middle ground between the harsh criticism of the journalists and the rosy optimism of the embassy. The two men expressed serious reservations about the effectiveness of ARVN military operations, found flaws in the implementation of the Strategic Hamlet Program, and conceded that Diem had become increasingly isolated from the people. They concluded that the United States and South Vietnam were "probably winning" but quickly added that the war would "probably last longer than we would like" and "cost more in terms of both lives and money than we had anticipated."[51] Despite a generally pessimistic appraisal and cautiously optimistic conclusions, Hilsman and Forrestal found U.S. policy sound in its conception and recommended only tactical changes to ensure more effective implementation. Their report reinforced doubts about the reliability of official estimates of progress but kept alive hopes that the United States might yet achieve its goals.

Throughout the spring of 1963, optimism and uncertainty coexisted uneasily in Saigon and Washington. The embassy and the military command continued to exude confidence. Harkins even informed a gathering of top officials in Honolulu in April that the war might be over by Christmas. Intelligence analyses were much more cautious, warning that the military situation remained fragile and unpredictable. In the White House, in the lower echelons of the Washington bureaucracy, and among some Americans in Vietnam, there was a gnawing uncertainty about how the war was really going and severe doubt, if it was not going well, about which way to turn.

Growing evidence of Vietnamese–American tension compounded the uncertainty. The tension existed at all levels and was probably inevitable given the rapid U.S. buildup in Vietnam and the vastly different approaches of the two peoples. Restless and impatient, the Americans were eager to get on with the job and were frustrated by the inertia that pervaded the government and

---

[51]Hilsman–Forrestal report, January 25, 1963, *FR, 1961–1963*, 3: 50–52.

army of South Vietnam. They sought to bypass the central government and deal directly with the villagers, thus, in effect, taking control of the war. Their arrogance was frequently manifested, one U.S.
adviser conceded, by an attitude of "Get out of my way, I'd rather
do it myself!" Proud and sensitive, having only recently emerged
from Western rule, the Vietnamese bristled at the presumptuous-
ness of the newcomers who sought to tell them how to run their
country. "Daily friction leads to no more love left," a Saigon newspaper philosophized in the spring of 1963.[52]

Relations at the top levels grew particularly tense. The
Americans urged "democratic" reforms to secure popular support,
they said, but Diem perceived that such reforms would undermine
rather than strengthen his regime. Trapped in the dilemma he had
feared from the start, he recognized that the American presence,
although necessary to hold the line against the NLF, had introduced
another—perhaps pivotal—element into the already volatile mix.
He became more and more sensitive to U.S. criticism. Diem and
Nhu were increasingly troubled by the growing number of Americans and their apparent efforts to run the war. They protested
infringements of Vietnamese sovereignty and fretted about a new
colonialism. "All these soldiers," Diem complained to the French
ambassador. "I never asked them to come here. They don't even
have passports."[53] Diem and Nhu concluded that the United States
posed as great a threat to them as the NLF and began to think in
terms of reducing their dependence on their ally. In May 1963, Nhu
publicly questioned whether the United States knew what it was
doing in Vietnam and proposed that U.S. forces might be reduced
by as many as 5,000 soldiers. He also began to explore, through a
Polish intermediary, the possibility of a settlement with Hanoi
based on American withdrawal from Vietnam.[54] Kennedy was
increasingly sensitive to South Vietnamese anger. "Those people
hate us," he told a journalist. "They are going to throw our asses
out of there at almost any point."[55] Some of his advisers began to

---

[52]Chester Cooper, *The Lost Crusade: America in Vietnam* (New York, 1970), p. 207; Ellen
Hammer, *A Death in November* (New York, 1987), p. 33.

[53]Quoted in Hammer, *Death in November*, p. 121.

[54]Memorandum of conversation at the White House, April 4, 1963, *FR, 1961–1963*,
3: 198–200.

[55]Quoted in Reeves, *President Kennedy*, pp. 484–485.

see Diem and Nhu as major obstacles to winning the war in South Vietnam and therefore as expendable.

In this atmosphere of confusion and mounting conflict, the Kennedy administration began to consider the possibility of withdrawing some troops from Vietnam. As early as the spring of 1962, presumably with the president's approval, Secretary of Defense McNamara had initiated planning for a phased withdrawal of U.S. forces as part of a larger effort to institute long-range defense planning and reduce waste in the defense budget. The secretary especially feared a long-range, open-ended, and increasingly expensive commitment, as in South Korea. McNamara and others also saw troop withdrawals as a means to gain leverage with the Saigon government and assure Congress and the public that the United States was not hopelessly entangled in Vietnam.

Some former Kennedy advisers claim that the president's interest in troop withdrawals confirms his concern about an open-ended commitment and even *his* determination to extricate the United States from Vietnam after he had been reelected. "If I tried to pull out completely now from Vietnam," he reportedly explained to Mansfield, "we would have another Joe McCarthy red scare on our hands."[56] Others argue that he was determined to leave Vietnam even if it meant losing the war and that he had devised a secret plan to disguise his intentions until after the election. Such arguments go too far. There is no evidence to support the notion of a secret plan for extrication, and the extent to which Kennedy was committed to troop withdrawals remains unclear. In a conversation with McNamara in May 1963, the president did affirm that his commitment to the withdrawal of a planned 1,000 troops later in the year depended on success in the war.

THE BUDDHIST CRISIS

At the very time Kennedy and Diem were having sober second thoughts about their fateful partnership, an upheaval among Buddhists in the major cities of South Vietnam suddenly introduced

[56]Kenneth P. O'Donnell and David F. Powers, *"Johnny, We Hardly Knew Ye": Memories of John Fitzgerald Kennedy* (New York, 1973), p. 16; Newman, *JFK and Vietnam*, pp. 236–237, 321–325; Marc J. Selverstone, "It's a Date: Kennedy and the Timetable for a Vietnam Troop Withdrawal," *Diplomatic History* 34 (June 2010): 485–495.

a dramatic new threat to the Diem regime and new complications for an already faltering American policy. The affair began on May 8, seemingly inadvertently, when government troops fired into crowds gathered in Hue to protest orders forbidding the display of flags on the anniversary of Buddha's birth. The May 8 incident stirred new and vigorous protest. Buddhist leaders, such as charismatic Thich Tri Quang, accused the government of religious persecution and demanded religious freedom. Diem at first sought to conciliate the Buddhists, but hotheads on both sides, including his older brother Ngo Dinh Thuc, the Catholic Archbishop of Hue, and Tri Quang, made any resolution difficult. A provocative anti-Buddhist statement by Madame Nhu's Women's Solidarity Movement in early June stirred things up again, leading to the self-immolation of Quang Duc on June 11 and a full-fledged crisis.

From that fiery moment, the Buddhist protest emerged into a powerful, deeply rooted political movement that threatened the very survival of the Diem government. The protests of 1963 grew out of a Buddhist revival that had begun in the 1920s and sought to restore Buddhism to a central place in Vietnamese life. The revival aspired to unify Vietnam's disparate Buddhist groups into a strong national movement deeply engaged in the shaping of Vietnamese society. By the 1960s, Buddhist leaders were increasingly alarmed by the direction the Diem government was moving and saw his personalist agenda as inimical to their aspirations.[57] The immolation of the elderly monk spurred wider protests in South Vietnam. Students in the universities and high schools, including some Catholics, joined in mass demonstrations, and discontent spread to the army. As the Buddhists became more confrontational, the government abandoned any thought of conciliation. Diem dismissed the protests as Communist-inspired; Madame Nhu called the immolations "barbecues" and offered to furnish the gasoline and matches for more. By midsummer, South Vietnamese society appeared on the verge of disintegration.

The crisis brought consternation to a Washington already uneasy over its Vietnam policy. The administration was caught off guard by the protest, surprised by the response it touched off, and shocked by the self-immolation of Quang Duc. Fearing that these

---

[57]Edward Miller, "Religious Revival and the Politics of Nation Building: Reinterpreting the 1963 'Buddhist Crisis' in South Vietnam." Paper in possession of author.

ominous new developments might undercut domestic support for the war and further endanger a counterinsurgency program many suspected was already failing, the administration frantically attempted to reconcile the two sides, sending numerous emissaries to talk with Buddhist leaders and pressing Diem to take conciliatory measures.

Such efforts produced meager results. The Americans could never really determine what the Buddhists wanted; Diem and Nhu were obdurate. Diem defiantly proclaimed that he would not permit himself and his country to be humiliated, even if the Americans "trained their artillery on this palace." Nhu instructed the Americans that it was impossible to fight a war with a guilty conscience and appealed for an aid program without strings such as the one provided during World War II, when the United States assisted Soviet dictator Joseph Stalin without approving his regime.[58] Diem and Nhu compared the crisis of 1963 to that with the sects in 1955, which, they claimed, also, the United States had not understood and which they had successfully suppressed by force. The demonstrations and immolations continued; in all, seven monks met fiery deaths. While Madame Nhu and the government-controlled Saigon press issued shrill tirades against the Buddhists and the United States, Nhu's police carted off hundreds of protesters to South Vietnam's already bulging jails.

By the late summer, the Kennedy administration was increasingly troubled and deeply divided. The Buddhist mind remained "terra incognito," one Kennedy adviser later conceded, but most Americans agreed that Diem's response had been provocative.[59] Some feared that there was no real alternative to Diem and that a change in government might bring even greater chaos to South Vietnam. Others retained confidence in Diem himself, blaming the problems on Nhu and his wife and arguing that the damage might yet be repaired if they could be removed. Still others began to view the Buddhist crisis as symbolic of basic, uncorrectable defects in the regime and concluded that the United States must face the possibility of a change.

An incident in late August clinched the issue as far as Diem's American opponents were concerned. Nolting's appointment as

[58]Embassy Saigon to State Department, June 24, 1963, *FR, 1961–1963,* 3: 413; Memorandum of conversation, Nhu and Robert Manning, July 17, 1963, ibid., 500–501.
[59]Cooper, *Lost Crusade,* p. 210.

ambassador expired in the summer of 1963. During his farewell visit, Diem had assured him, as a personal favor, that no further repressive measures would be taken against the Buddhists. But on August 21, Nhu's U.S.-trained Special Forces carried out massive raids in Hue, Saigon, and other cities, ransacking the pagodas and arresting more than 1,400 Buddhists. Whether Diem approved the raids in advance remains unclear, but in the eyes of most Americans, his subsequent refusal to disavow Nhu's actions placed the onus squarely on him. These latest actions, just days after the solemn pledges to Nolting, appeared to the anti-Diemists a "deliberate affront" that demanded a firm response. Since the Kennedy administration had taken office, consideration had been given to Diem's replacement. Americans assumed as a matter of course a right and, indeed, a duty to intervene in South Vietnamese affairs as they saw fit. "We could not sit still and be the puppets of Diem's anti-Buddhist policies," Hilsman later recalled.[60]

Shortly after the raid on the pagodas, moreover, a group of South Vietnamese Army generals reopened secret contacts already established with CIA agents in Saigon. The most recent incident made clear, they warned, that Nhu would stop at nothing. Reporting evidence that he was not only planning their execution but also discussing with Hanoi a deal that would sell out the independence of South Vietnam, the generals inquired how the United States might respond should they move against the government. The anti-Diem group in Washington was undoubtedly alarmed that Nhu was making overtures to Hanoi; such reports reinforced their conviction that something must be done. More important, perhaps, the inquiries suggested that there was, after all, an alternative.

The generals' overtures arrived in Washington on a Saturday, when many top officials were out of town, and Hilsman, Forrestal, and Harriman seized the opportunity to execute what Taylor later described as an "egregious end run."[61] They prepared a tough, if somewhat ambiguous, cable instructing the newly appointed ambassador, Henry Cabot Lodge Jr., to give Diem an opportunity to rid himself of Nhu, but adding that if he refused, the United States must "face the possibility that Diem himself cannot be preserved." They also instructed Lodge to make clear to the generals that the United States would not continue to support Diem if he refused to cooperate and that it would provide them with "direct support in any interim period of breakdown of central government mechanism."[62] These last words left deliberately vague what the United States might do and under what circumstances, but the thrust of the message was unmistakable: If Diem remained obdurate, the United States was prepared to dump him. The cable was cleared with Kennedy, then vacationing on Cape Cod. The president's endorsement was apparently used to secure the acquiescence of responsible officials in the Defense Department.

Lodge wasted no time implementing his instructions. From the day he set foot in Saigon, he had concluded that a change of government was necessary. He shared Hilsman's outrage at the August 21 incident. He had no doubt, he later recalled, that the raid on the pagodas "marked the beginning of the end of the Diem regime."[63] His convictions were reinforced by his first meeting with Diem. When he warned that the regime's handling of the Buddhists was endangering American support for South Vietnam, Diem gave him a long lecture on the difficulties of governing a nation with a "dearth of educated people." The embassy subsequently contacted the generals through a CIA agent—"so the official American hand would not show"—offering assurances of support should they succeed in overthrowing the government but warning that the United States would not assist them in undertaking a coup or "bail them out" if they got into trouble.[64]

Kennedy and his top advisers returned on Monday to a capital rife with tension. Charges and countercharges flew back and forth. Some senior officials accused those who had been in charge of effecting major policy changes behind their back. "This shit has got to stop," the president himself upbraided Forrestal at one point. Over the next four days, a chastened and somewhat more collaborative team of advisers struggled through endless meetings to hammer out

[62]Telegram, August 24, 1963, U.S. Congress, House Committee on Armed Services, *United States–Vietnam Relations, 1945–1967: A Study Prepared by the Department of Defense* (Washington, D.C., 1971), Book 12, 536–537.

[63]Lodge oral history interview, Kennedy Papers.

[64]Forrestal to Kennedy, August 26, 1963, Kennedy Papers, Office File, Box 128; Neil Sheehan et al., *The Pentagon Papers as Published by the New York Times* (New York, 1971), pp. 195–196. Hereafter cited as *Pentagon Papers (NYT)*. See also memorandum, "Contacts with Vietnamese Generals," October 23, 1963, Lyndon B. Johnson Papers, Lyndon B. Johnson Library, Austin, Tex., DSDUF, Box 2; and Thomas L., Aherm, Jr. "CIA and the House of Ngo: Covert Action in South Vietnam, 1954–1963(u)" (DVD, 2009).

a policy. All agreed that Nhu must go, but Ambassador Nolting continued to vigorously defend Diem. Those who backed a coup urged a positive response to the generals' queries. Others conceded an urgent need for more reliable information about the coup plotters and expressed doubts whether a coup could succeed. Should an uprising take place, McNamara stressed, the United States must figure out "how we make this thing work." With misgivings, the administration decided to make one last approach to Diem to get rid of Nhu. But it did not alter the policy agreed upon over the previous, frantic weekend. "We're up to our hips in mud out there," JFK affirmed. Congress might "get mad" if the United States colluded with coup plotters, but "they'll be madder if Vietnam goes down the drain." Uncertain about the generals but not willing to let the possibility of a successful coup slip away, the administration offered encouragement without any tangible support or even a firm commitment. Lodge was instructed to inform the generals that the United States would "support a coup which has [a] good chance of succeeding but plans no direct involvement of U.S. Armed Forces." He was authorized to announce publicly and at his own discretion a reduction in aid to Diem, the signal the generals had requested as an indication of Washington's support.[65]

While U.S. officials in Washington and Saigon nervously awaited the generals' response, the plans for a coup gradually unraveled. The leaders of the plot could not secure the support of key army units in the Saigon area. Despite the assurances given by the CIA go-between, they remained uncertain of American backing. On August 31, they informed Harkins that the coup had been called off. "There is neither the will nor the organization among the generals to accomplish anything," Lodge cabled Washington with obvious disappointment.[66]

NO TURNING BACK

Although the August plot came to nothing, it marked another major turning point in U.S. policy in Vietnam. Many officials had grave reservations about the desirability, feasibility, and possible

[65] Memoranda of these meetings and actual tape recordings may be found at http://www. gwu.edu/~N5archiv/NSAEBBI/NSABB302/index.htm
[66]Quoted in *Pentagon Papers (Gravel)*, 2: 240.

consequences of a coup, but the anti-Diemists had been able to bind them to their point of view. By making such a commitment, the administration encouraged opponents of the regime and made difficult, if not impossible, any real reconciliation with Diem. As Lodge put it, the United States was "launched on a course from which there is no respectable turning back."[67]

The Diem regime remained defiant. Nhu sent his wife out of the country, perhaps as much for her personal safety as to appease the United States. But he stubbornly refused to resign. Lodge described him as a "lost soul, a haunted man who is caught in a vicious circle. The Furies are after him." The monkish Diem sought to discredit the Buddhist protest by claiming that the pagodas had been turned into bordellos where obscene photographs had been discovered and virgins were being despoiled.[68] The regime made no effort to conciliate the Buddhists or the United States.

Over the next four weeks, the Kennedy administration heatedly debated its options. Hilsman and others argued that there was no chance of stabilizing South Vietnam as long as Nhu remained. They warned that Nhu might already be committed to a deal with Hanoi that would force the United States out of Vietnam. The administration must therefore apply firm pressure, including aid cuts, to compel Diem to remove Nhu and adopt the changes in policy necessary to defeat the NLF. Others, such as Nolting, advocated a final attempt at reconciliation. The failure of the August coup made clear, they argued, that there was no real alternative to Diem. The president was unlikely to remove Nhu, even under the most severe American pressure. Cuts in aid would only hurt the war against the Vietcong, antagonize the South Vietnamese people, and further destabilize the country. There was still a chance, they concluded, that if the United States repaired its relations with the government, the war might be won.

A "fact-finding" mission to South Vietnam added to the confusion. Gen. Victor Krulak of the Defense Department played down the possibilities of a coup and advised that the war could be won if the United States firmly supported Diem. In contrast, Joseph Mendenhall of the State Department reported a "virtual breakdown of the civil government in Saigon," warned of a possible religious

[67]Lodge to Rusk, August 29, 1963, ibid., 738.
[68]Lodge to Rusk, September 9, 1963, *FR, 1961–1963*, 4: 142; Lodge to Rusk, September 19, 1963, ibid., 259.

war between Catholics and Buddhists, and concluded that there
was no chance of defeating the guerrillas unless, "as a minimum,
Nhu withdrew or was removed from the government." "You two
did visit the same country, didn't you?" Kennedy remarked with
obvious exasperation.[69]

The administration by this time was more divided on Vietnam
than it had been on any other issue. "My God, my government's
coming apart," Kennedy exclaimed on one occasion. Such was the
confusion and perplexity that at one point, in a moment of frustration, Attorney General Robert Kennedy blurted out the ultimate
question, wondering aloud whether any South Vietnamese government was capable of winning the war and whether the United
States should not begin to extricate itself from an impossible tangle.
The question was both appropriate and timely. The disarray in
South Vietnam was reaching a point where both factions in the
administration may have been right—the country could not be stabilized with or without Diem.

Adding to the confusion, major international developments
raised the enticing—to some, frightening—possibility of a negotiated settlement in Vietnam. Following the Cuban missile crisis, the
most dangerous face-off of the Cold War, the Soviet Union and the
United States took the first awkward steps toward detente with the
negotiation of a nuclear test ban treaty. The missile crisis also cata-
lyzed the shift from a bipolar to a multipolar world. The long-
simmering ideological and power struggle between the USSR and
China came out into the open, with momentous implications for the
Cold War. In the West, French leader Charles de Gaulle staked out a
course independent of the United States. Seeking to promote
France's prestige generally, its influence in its former colony,
Vietnam, and a Vietnamese peace that might be extended to other
areas, de Gaulle in late August—just as the Buddhist crisis wors-
ened and Washington began to contemplate the overthrow of
Diem—proposed an ambitious neutralization scheme.[70] His aim was
a unified Vietnam, free of U.S. and Chinese influence, and occupy-
ing a neutral, Yugoslavia-like position in Asia. Paralleling de
Gaulle's ploy, the Polish diplomat Mieczyslaw Maneli explored with

[69]Hilsman, *To Move a Nation*, p. 502.
[70] Yuko Torikata, "Reexamining de Gaulle's Peace Initiative on the Vietnam War,"
Diplomatic History, 5 (November 2007): 916–922.

DRV leaders Pham Van Dong and Ho Chi Minh, on the one hand, and Nhu, on the other, the possibility of a negotiated settlement.[71]

This flurry of diplomacy produced little beyond rumor. Nhu seems to have used the prospect of negotiations mainly as leverage against the United States. There is little to indicate that he was serious about a settlement. Ho and Pham Van Dong appeared receptive to economic and cultural exchanges with the South and even negotiations based on a U.S. withdrawal. "We are realists," Pham told Maneli. But they would have had to persuade the party's hardliners, such as increasingly influential First Secretary Le Duan. Maneli did not even have the backing of his own government, and the Soviet Union distanced itself from his diplomacy. Both North and South Vietnam appear to have distrusted him. The United States at this juncture was adamantly opposed to negotiations. Rumors of Nhu's conversations with Maneli and possibly NLF agents contributed to U.S. support for a coup. Kennedy and his advisers suspected that de Gaulle's overture might be motivated by anti-Americanism. They especially feared that, given South Vietnam's present weakness, neutralization would lead to unification under North Vietnamese domination. The Laos neutralization agreement, signed in July 1962, had broken down in less than a year, and North Vietnam had quickly resumed using Laos as a supply route. Far from offering a model for neutralization, the Laos agreement confirmed in U.S. eyes the limits of negotiations. Kennedy told Laotian leader Souvanna Phouma that de Gaulle's proposals were "fine" for "the future" but did not seem realistic for the "present."[72]

In any event, despite Robert Kennedy's despairing question, most Americans were still persuaded that the war could somehow be won. To JFK, the middle ground still seemed open, and the "safe course, in his view, was to stay the course," as Fredrik Logevall has written, at least until he was reelected, even if it required overthrowing Diem.[73] The chief result of the rumors of peace was to

---

[71] Margaret K. Gnoinska, "Poland and Vietnam, 1963: New Evidence on the Maneli Affair," *Cold War International History Project Working Paper* 45 (March 2005).

[72] Quoted in David Kaiser, *American Tragedy: Kennedy, Johnson, and the Origins of the Vietnam War* (Cambridge, Mass., 2000), pp. 357–358. On the importance of Laos, See Rust, *Before the Quagmire*, pp. 267–269.

[73] Fredrik Logevall, *Choosing War: The Lost Chance for Peace and Escalation of War in Vietnam* (Berkeley, Calif., 1999), p. 42.

sharpen the U.S. desire to get rid of Nhu. The attorney general's question was not raised again. The administration drifted along, divided against itself, uncertain of its direction, in truth rushing headlong toward a coup.

THE OVERTHROW OF NGO DINH DIEM

After more than a month of debate, in early October Kennedy settled on a short-run policy that, characteristically, split the difference between the two extremes promoted by his advisers. Still quite uncertain what was going on in South Vietnam, he dispatched Taylor and McNamara to Saigon to get a firsthand appraisal. The mission took place in an atmosphere that can only be described as surreal. It's report was actually drafted before the group left Washington. In Saigon, the chain-smoking Diem subjected the visitors to a two-hour monologue, including predictions of South Vietnam's becoming a "model democracy" and a spirited defense of Mme. Nhu: "One cannot deny a lady the right to defend herself when she has been unjustly attacked." Taylor arranged a tennis match with Gen. Duong Van Minh at the Saigon Officers Club to assess the prospects for a coup. It produced nothing but tennis, and the Americans concluded that the dissidents had "little stomach" for overthrowing the government. The visitors were deluged with hopelessly conflicting reports on the war, leaving McGeorge Bundy "with a lasting skepticism of the ability of any man, however honest, to interpret accurately what was going on." [74] Probably after discussions with Lodge, Taylor and McNamara rejected any notion of conciliating Diem on grounds that it would reinforce his belief that he could bend the United States to his will. The only feasible course was to apply "selective pressures," including cuts in U.S. aid. Such an approach probably would not sway Diem to remove Nhu, but it might persuade him to stop oppressing political dissenters. Overly optimistic about the progress of the counterinsurgency effort, Taylor and McNamara concluded that if Diem could be brought around, the insurgency might be reduced to "something little more than organized banditry." Based on such optimism, they also recommended the phased withdrawal of U.S. troops back to the January

[74]Jones, *Death of Generation,* pp. 369–375.

1961 level by the end of 1965 with the first installment of 1,000 men to leave later in the year. "We need a way to get out of Vietnam," McNamara averred. "This is a way of doing it." With the election a year away and eager to reassure the public and Congress, Kennedy approved the withdrawal plan without conditioning it on military success.[75]

Although it badly misjudged the actual conditions in South Vietnam, the McNamara–Taylor report formed the basis of subsequent U.S. policy. The relative quiet in the countryside in late 1963 resulted from a deliberate North Vietnamese–NLF attempt to encourage negotiations rather than from the effectiveness of the counterinsurgency program. Taylor and McNamara underestimated the prospects of a coup and overestimated the efficacy of applying pressure to Diem. Kennedy approved their recommendations on October 5. Over the next few weeks, the administration gradually implemented the policy of "selective pressures." Lodge remained away from the presidential palace, insisting that Diem must come to him. In the meantime, the administration recalled the CIA station chief in Saigon, John Richardson, known among Vietnamese and Americans as a close friend of Nhu; cut off funds to Nhu's Special Forces; and suspended shipments of tobacco, rice, and milk under the commodity import program.

A number of Kennedy advisers later emphatically denied that these measures were designed to stimulate a coup, and in the most literal sense, they were correct. The McNamara–Taylor report had explicitly rejected encouragement of a coup. The aid cuts were designed to pressure Diem. The administration was not as innocent as its defenders have maintained, however. Hilsman later conceded that "some of the things that we did encouraged the coup, some we intended as pressure on Diem, although we knew it [sic] would encourage a coup."[76] Kennedy and his advisers would have been naive indeed if they did not recognize that the recall of Richardson, whom the generals had feared would tip off the August plot, and the cuts in aid, the very signal of support the generals had requested earlier, would influence Diem's opponents. And the timing is significant. The aid cuts were instituted after the generals had once again inquired how the United States would respond to a coup.

[75]Ibid., pp. 380–384.
[76]Hilsman oral history interview, Kennedy Papers.

The measures taken during October encouraged the generals to step up their planning and seek further assurances from the United States.

Once aware that the generals were again planning a coup, the administration did nothing to discourage them. The response to their inquiry was sufficiently vague to salve the consciences of those who preferred a coup but hesitated to accept direct responsibility for it, and to satisfy the reservations of those who remained wary of dumping Diem. But the instructions offered the assurances the generals sought. Lodge was authorized to inform the plotters that although the United States did not "wish to stimulate a coup," it would not "thwart a change of government or deny economic and military assistance to a new regime if it appeared capable of increasing [the] effectiveness of the military effort, ensuring popular support to win [the] war and improving working relations with the U.S."[77]

His administration sharply divided to the very end, Kennedy stuck by his compromise policy. Harriman, Hilsman, and others felt that Diem must go. Vice President Johnson, top CIA and Pentagon officials, and Harkins continued to insist that there was no real alternative and that Diem's removal would bring chaos to South Vietnam. They also felt, as Harkins put it, that it was "incongruous" after nine years of supporting Diem "to get him down, kick him around and get rid of him."[78] Kennedy himself vacillated, adhering to the policy of not overtly supporting a coup but not discouraging one either. In this case, not to decide was to decide, and by leaving matters in the hands of Lodge, whose views were well known, the president virtually ensured the outcome. The major fear among Kennedy and some of his advisers in the anxious days of late October seems to have been that the coup might fail, provoking Diem, in Robert Kennedy's words, to "tell us to get the hell out of the country" and sending U.S. policy in Vietnam and indeed Southeast Asia "down the road to disaster." A successful coup, others warned, might impede prosecution of the war. Although he sought evidence that a coup could succeed, Kennedy seemed content to leave in Lodge's hands a decision whether to call it off or delay it.[79]

---

[77]CIA to Lodge, October 6, 1963, *Pentagon Papers (Gravel)*, 2: 769.
[78]Quoted in ibid., 785.
[79]Ken Hughes, "The Tale of the Tapes: JFK and the Fall of Diem," *The Boston Globe Magazine*, October 24, 1999, pp. 14 ff.

Throughout the last week of October, Saigon was gripped with tension and deluged with rumors as the various actors played out their complicated—and ultimately tragic—drama. Determined to avoid the mistakes of 1960 and August 1963, the generals lined up their forces with the closest attention to every detail. Keenly aware that the "elephants were crashing in the jungle," Nhu concocted an elaborate scheme to keep himself and his brother in power by staging a fake coup and using it as an excuse for eliminating suspected opponents. To complicate matters still further, in the last hours before the real coup, Diem suddenly turned conciliatory, inquiring of Lodge at their last meeting what the United States wanted of him. Whether he was merely trying to buy time or had concluded that he must place himself in the hands of his ally is unclear. In any event, his apparent concession came too late.

While Diem was talking with Lodge early in the afternoon of November 1, the generals seized key military installations and communications systems in Saigon, compelled the surrender of Nhu's Special Forces, and demanded the resignation of Diem and Nhu. The coup plotters—and the United States—had hoped for a peaceful transition with the former leaders going into exile far from Vietnam, thereby helping to secure international support for the new government. Reluctant to be tied to the coup, the Kennedy administration left matters largely in the hands of the generals. The coup leaders made slapdash arrangements for such an outcome and completely underestimated their adversaries. Diem and Nhu adamantly refused to resign. With a briefcase full of U.S. money, they fled the palace through a secret underground passage and were transported by car to a Catholic church in Cholon, the Chinese district. Early the next morning, All Souls Day (the Day of the Dead), they received communion. Furious with Diem and Nhu's escape and tipped off as to their whereabouts, the generals sent an armored vehicle to capture them. Their hands were bound and they were thrown in the back of the truck. Presumably on the generals' orders, they were shot in the head and repeatedly stabbed by a hit man who had once been Nhu's bodyguard. Diem was buried in an unmarked grave in a cemetery next to the house of the U.S. ambassador.[80]

---

[80]Jones, *Death of a Generation*, pp. 416–419, 428–429, 435.

Throughout the coup, the United States followed to the letter its promises "not to thwart a change of government." American officials later insisted that they knew nothing of the timing or exact plans for a coup. In fact, CIA agent Lucien Conein maintained close contact with the generals in the planning stages through clandestine meetings at a dentist's office. He had telephone contact with them while the coup was taking place. The United States refused even to intervene to ensure the personal safety of Diem and Nhu. Lodge was considerably less than candid in the telephone conversation with Diem when he pretended ignorance of Washington's attitudes. During the last pathetic phone call, Lodge offered to help, but he then went off to bed, leaving matters in the hands of the coup forces. Perhaps he accepted at face value the generals' pledges to spare Diem and Nhu. He may have feared that any action taken on behalf of the brothers would be interpreted as a violation of the earlier U.S. assurances not to interfere.

The news of the coup and the bloody deaths of the Ngos evoked mixed reactions. In Saigon, jubilant crowds smashed statues of Diem, danced in the streets, and covered ARVN soldiers with garlands of flowers. "Every Vietnamese has a grin on his face today," Lodge excitedly informed Washington. In the ancient Vietnamese tradition, the mandate of heaven had passed. Among Americans there was a sense of relief and satisfaction. Lodge, the primary architect, hailed the coup as a "remarkably able performance in all respects." Some Washington officials agreed and went to great lengths to distinguish this "acceptable" coup from the "unacceptable" military takeovers then sweeping Latin America. Lodge went further, extolling the coup as a "useful lesson" in the way people "on the side of freedom," with U.S. help, could "clean their own house," eliminating the "autocrats" and "Colonel Blimps" as a way to prevent being taken over by Communists.[81]

The deaths of Diem and Nhu were deeply unsettling. The generals first attributed them to "accidental suicide," but photographs of the two mutilated bodies, hands tied behind their backs, made clear, as McGeorge Bundy sarcastically put it, that this was "not the

---

[81]Lodge to State Department, November 2, 1963, *FR, 1961–1963*, 4: 526; Memorandum for record of White House meeting, November 1, 1963, *FR, 1961–1963*, 4: 518; Lodge to State Department, November 3, 1963, ibid., 546–548; Lodge to State Department, November 6, 1963, ibid., 577–578.

preferred way to commit suicide." Some of Kennedy's advisers accepted the deaths as a matter of course. "Revolutions are rough. People get hurt," Hilsman told a reporter.[82] But Kennedy himself was profoundly troubled. When he learned of the slaying of Diem and Nhu, Taylor later recalled, "he leaped to his feet and rushed from the room with a look of shock and dismay on his face which I had never seen before."[83] When someone justified the deaths on the grounds that the two men were tyrants, the president retorted that "they did the best they could for their country." People close to him found Kennedy more depressed than at any time since the Bay of Pigs and speculated that he realized that Vietnam had been his greatest foreign policy failure.[84]

Just three weeks later, Kennedy himself was assassinated in Dallas. His defenders, many of whom would become outspoken opponents of the Vietnam War, would later argue that he was planning to extricate the United States from what he had concluded was a quagmire. Kennedy undoubtedly harbored deep-seated doubts about the prospects for success in South Vietnam, and he had adamantly opposed the commitment of U.S. combat troops. On Laos and other issues, he had shown flexibility. He had grown demonstrably more secure in office. A good case can therefore be made that when faced with the collapse of South Vietnam in 1964–1965, he might have sought a diplomatic solution.[85] At the same time, there is no persuasive evidence that he was committed to a full-scale withdrawal. He had resisted negotiations as firmly as he opposed combat troops. In a speech to be given on the day of his death, he conceded that commitments in Third World nations could be "painful, risky, and costly," but, he added, "we dare not weary of the test." The plan for a phased withdrawal approved by Kennedy in October was designed to meet different needs. It was reaffirmed at a policy conference in Honolulu on November 20. The first

[82]Memorandum of White House meeting, November 4, 1963, *FR, 1961–1963,* 4: 555–556; Hilsman quoted in Marguerite Higgins, *Our Vietnam Nightmare* (New York, 1965), p. 225.

[83]Taylor, *Swords and Ploughshares,* p. 301.

[84]Reeves, *President Kennedy,* p. 651; Schlesinger, *A Thousand Days,* pp. 997–998.

[85]For arguments that Kennedy would have responded differently than Johnson, see Logevall, *Choosing War,* pp. 396–400; Lawrence Freedman, *Kennedy's Wars: Berlin, Cuba, Laos, and Vietnam* (New York, 2000), pp. 400–413; and Kaiser, *American Tragedy,* pp. 3–5, 121, 265.

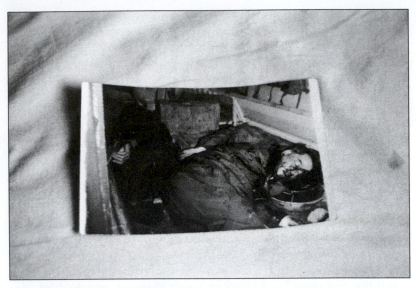

The Killing of Diem and Nhu
South Vietnamese president Ngo Dinh Diem and his brother Ngo Dinh
Nhu, disguised as priests to facilitate their planned escape, are pictured
here in the back of an armored personnel carrier after their assassination by
the perpetrators of the coup that removed them from power. Aware that
the United States had not done enough to save the lives of the Ngo
brothers, President John F. Kennedy was visibly shaken by their violent
death. Less than a month later, JFK himself was slain by an assassin in
Dallas.
© *Bettmann/CORBIS*

increment of 1,000 men was quietly removed the next month.
But National Security Action Memorandum (NSAM) 273, also
drafted in Honolulu, strongly reaffirmed the importance of South
Vietnam to American security and the necessity of waging the war
vigorously, including even attacks on North Vietnam. U.S. officials
dismissed as "folly" proposals from leading journalists and a Soviet
diplomat for the neutralization of South Vietnam. Its present weakness would make it easy prey for a rapacious North. Some
Americans keenly felt that complicity in the coup and the bloody
deaths of Diem and Nhu imposed upon the United States greater
responsibility for the fate of South Vietnam, complicating the prospect of withdrawal. Hilsman, in fact, reassured a worried South

Vietnamese official on November 27 that the United States would "keep in Viet-Nam whatever forces are necessary for victory."[86] Kennedy seems to have remained as conflicted as ever. On the day before he died, he indicated that he wanted a "complete and profound review" of U.S. involvement in Vietnam to determine how to implement a "gradual shift in our presence" there, a comment Forrestal interpreted as the president's way of considering various options without making a firm decision.[87]

What Kennedy might have done can never be known, of course, and his administration must be judged on what it actually did during its brief tenure. The president and most of his advisers uncritically accepted the assumption that a non-Communist South Vietnam was vital to America's global interests. Their rhetoric, in fact, strengthened the hold of that assumption. That the president never devoted his full attention to Vietnam, as his defenders claim, seems clear. He reacted to crises and improvised responses day to day, seldom examining the implications of his actions. Although apparently troubled by growing doubts, he refused, even after the problems with Diem had reached a crisis point, to face the hard questions. His cautious middle course significantly enlarged the American role and commitment in Vietnam. Like most of his advisers, he acted on the arrogant presumption that the United States knew best what was right for Vietnam. "In the name of the struggle against the Viet Cong," Ellen Hammer has written, the Americans "claimed the right to intervene as they chose" and overthrew the Diem government primarily because it resisted their advice.[88] With the coup, the United States assumed direct responsibility for the South Vietnamese government. Whatever his fears or his ultimate intentions, Kennedy bequeathed to his successor a problem eminently more dangerous than the one he had inherited.

[86]Herbert S. Parmet, *JFK: The Presidency of John F. Kennedy* (New York, 1984), p. 336; State Department to Embassy Saigon, November 27, 1963, *FR, 1961–1963*, 4: 640.
[87]Andrew Preston, *The War Council: McGeorge Bundy, the NSC, and Vietnam* (Cambridge, Mass., 2006), pp. 130, 132–140.
[88]Hammer, *Death in November*, p. 211.

LBJ and HHH President Lyndon Baines Johnson and an out-of-his-comfort-zone vice-president-elect Hubert H. Humphrey celebrate their 1964 electoral success on horseback at the LBJ Ranch in Texas. The presidential helicopter is in the background. Johnson's decisive victory encouraged him to pursue his expansive vision of Great Society domestic reform and freed him to escalate the war in Vietnam. Humphrey opposed escalation in 1965, opening a rift with LBJ that would widen when the vice president ran for president in 1968.

LBJ Library

CHAPTER 4

Enough, but Not Too Much

Johnson's Decisions for War, 1963–1965

Between November 1963 and July 1965, Lyndon Baines Johnson transformed a limited commitment to assist the South Vietnamese government into an open-ended commitment to preserve an independent, non-Communist South Vietnam. Johnson inherited from Kennedy a rapidly deteriorating situation in South Vietnam. Fearing that large-scale involvement might jeopardize his chances of election in 1964 and threaten his beloved Great Society domestic programs, he temporized for more than a year, expanding American assistance and increasing the number of advisers in hopes that a beefed-up version of his predecessor's policy might somehow stave off disaster. South Vietnam's survival appeared more in doubt than ever after Johnson's reelection, however, and over the next nine months he made his fateful decisions, authorizing a sustained air offensive against North Vietnam and dispatching ground forces to stem the tide in the South. By July 1965, the United States was committed to a major war on the Asian mainland.

A "BIG JUICY WORM"

The overthrow of Diem culminated a very bad year in South Vietnam. Following Ap Bac, National Liberation Front (NLF) military forces regained the momentum held only briefly by the Army of the Republic of Vietnam (ARVN). The insurgents continued to chip away at the already shaky Strategic Hamlet Program. In parts of the vital Mekong Delta, the government's position had declined significantly before the Buddhist crisis erupted in Saigon. Through a kind of circular effect, the onset of chaos in the capital in the summer of 1963 undercut the government's hold in the rural areas, and the erosion of its strength in the countryside further threatened an increasingly embattled Diem regime. The November coup exacerbated the position of the Government of Vietnam (GVN) across the board. The army suffered from confusion and waning morale and the officials in the villages from weakened authority. The strategic hamlets completely collapsed. By the end of the year the Saigon government verged on disintegration.[1]

These obvious signs of decay in South Vietnam posed for the Hanoi leadership grave dangers—and enticing opportunities. A complete government collapse might provoke large-scale American intervention, even combat troops. But South Vietnam's growing weakness also opened the possibility that a major escalation of the political and military struggle might produce victory in the South. In a late 1963 change of power as significant as the one that had already occurred in Saigon, a group headed by the hardline First Secretary Le Duan had seized control from moderates such as Ho Chi Minh. In what turned out to be a colossal miscalculation, the new leaders gambled upon a go-for-broke strategy to gain a total victory that would leave the United States no choice but to withdraw. Moving to the third stage of revolutionary warfare before the second stage of equilibrium had been achieved, Hanoi's hawks ordered a stepping up of political struggle in the South to spark a mass popular uprising. They increased the size of the North Vietnamese Army (NVA) to 300,000 men, for the first time readied regular units for infiltration into the South, and vastly expanded the flow of equipment and supplies down the Ho Chi Minh Trail. In making these decisions, Le Duan shunted aside cautious pragmatists such as the venerable Ho (he would remain an essential figurehead and would undertake important diplomatic missions but henceforth would have negligible influence on policy). The party's Ninth Plenum approved this aggressive course in December 1963. With these decisions, the hawks gained control of the war and mounted an intense campaign of oppression to stamp out dissent at home.[2]

---

[1]David W.P. Elliott, *The Vietnamese War: Revolution and Social Change in the Mekong Delta, 1930–1975* (Armonk, NY, 2006), pp. 188–193.
[2]Ibid, pp. 195–197; Lien-Hang T. Nguyen, *Hanoi's War: An International History of the War for Peace in Vietnam* (Chapel Hill, NC, 2012), pp. 65–67.

For Johnson and the United States, the road to war was longer and more tortuous. After listening to Ambassador Lodge's gloomy assessment of the postcoup prospects of the Saigon regime on November 24, 1963, the new president claimed to feel like a catfish that had just "grabbed a big juicy worm with a right sharp hook in the middle of it." Johnson vowed to meet the Communist challenge, however, and insisted that he would not let Vietnam go the way China had gone in 1949. He instructed Lodge to "go back and tell those generals in Saigon that Lyndon Johnson intends to stand by our word." Two days later, NSAM 273 incorporated this pledge into policy by declaring that the "central objective of the United States" was to assist the "people and Government" of South Vietnam "to win their contest against the externally directed and supported communist conspiracy." This reaffirmation of the U.S. commitment to South Vietnam tied LBJ's policies to those of his predecessor. But the vow to "win" went a step further. The revised document also initiated planning for expanded operations against North Vietnam, opening the possibility for a major U.S. escalation of the war.[3]

During the first months of Johnson's presidency, the situation in South Vietnam further deteriorated. Some Americans had naively assumed that the removal of Diem and Nhu would restore domestic harmony and promote political unity, but the effect was quite the opposite. Diem had systematically destroyed the opposition, and his death left a gaping vacuum. Buddhists and Catholics constituted the most coherent groups in the cities, but their hatred of each other was implacable, and neither represented a viable political force. The Buddhists were splintered into a bewildering array of factions. Although tightly disciplined, the Catholics had no political program or mass appeal. The coup released long-pent-up forces. In the months that followed, new groups proliferated, but they were leaderless and hopelessly fragmented.

In the countryside, decay remained the norm. The removal of Diemist controls over information made clear that the statistics compiled by the government to demonstrate progress had been grossly in error. The insurgents controlled more people and

---

[3]Bill Moyers, "Flashbacks," *Newsweek*, February 10, 1975; Howard Jones, *Death of a Generation: How the Assassinations of Diem and JFK Prolonged the Vietnam War* (New York, 2003), p. 446.

territory than had been assumed. The Strategic Hamlet Program was in shambles, many of the key hamlets in the critical Mekong Delta having been torn down either by guerrillas or by their own occupants. The situation was "very disturbing," McNamara warned Johnson in late December. Unless the trend could be reversed within the next few months, South Vietnam might be lost.[4]

The junta that assumed power after the coup did little to arrest the decline. It inherited a bureaucratic structure atrophied by "dry rot and lassitude." The twelve army officers who formed the Military Revolutionary Council (MRC) had been educated in France and had spent much of their careers in French service. They lacked political experience and indeed confidence in their own political skills. During the planning for the coup, they several times told their American contact that the United States should "take care of the political part." As they floundered about, however, Lodge ordered U.S. officials to keep their distance, a move designed to demonstrate the new government's independence that deprived it of much-needed American help. Suspicious of each other and of competing factions within the army, and uncertain which way to move, the MRC isolated itself in its headquarters near Saigon's Tan Son Nhut Airport. Those few actions it took merely added to the confusion. The removal of Diem's province chiefs, for example, brought paralysis to local administration.[5]

The new government lasted less than three months. Presumably to get him out of Saigon, MRC leaders had sent to Da Nang Maj. Gen. Nguyen Khanh, described by one of his coconspirators as "highly deceitful" and a "complete opportunist." In late January, Khanh informed a CIA contact that some of the generals who backed neutralization of South Vietnam along lines proposed by France were planning a coup. No evidence has ever been found to support Khanh's claims. He was likely acting to advance his own ambitions. By affirming that the United States opposed neutralization, the U.S. agent may have given him a green light for a coup of his own. The U.S. military command was disappointed in the

[4]Robert McNamara to Johnson, December 21, 1963, in Department of State, *Foreign Relations of the United States, 1961–1963* (Washington, D.C., 1991), 4: 1. Hereafter cited as *FR* with date and volume number.

[5]Henry Cabot Lodge to Johnson, January 1, 1964, *FR 1964–1968*, 1: 1; Thomas L. Ahern Jr., "The CIA and the House of Ngo: Covert Action in South Vietnam, 1954–1963" (DVD, 2009), pp. 175, 179.

junta's lack of aggressiveness and may have welcomed Khanh's scheme. At the very least, the United States did nothing to stop him. On January 29, 1964, a group of officers headed by Khanh overthrew the ineffectual junta.[6]

The coup reinforced Washington's growing doubts about its client state. Devious, opportunistic, and ambitious, Khanh in a notably checkered career had supported the Viet Minh and the French and had worked for and against Diem. His reliability must have been suspect. Putting the best face on a bad situation, some Americans comforted themselves that he was an able military commander and that, at least in contrast to Diem and the junta, he was "our boy." Lodge speculated that one-man rule might be preferable to a divided junta, and he was encouraged by Khanh's pledges to act decisively. Nothing would please the United States more, Lodge informed the general, than "the sight of an oriental chief of state who wanted to go fast and did not hesitate to kick people in the rear end." Khanh's response—he hoped he would "pick the right rear ends to kick"—could not have offered much reassurance. And Lodge conceded that it would be premature to predict a long life for the new government.[7] The United States quickly recognized Khanh, but with little enthusiasm and even less confidence.

The Khanh government faced truly staggering problems. Military operations and the Strategic Hamlet Program had come to a complete standstill. The government's authority was nonexistent throughout much of the countryside, and near anarchy prevailed in the cities. In Saigon the "atmosphere fairly smelled of discontent," Gen. William Westmoreland later recalled, with "workers on strike, students demonstrating, the local press pursuing a persistent campaign of criticism of the new government."[8] As NLF incidents increased in number and boldness, the capital took on all the appearances of an armed camp. Government buildings, stores, and even cafés were surrounded by barbed wire, while soldiers stood guard in concrete sentry boxes reinforced with sandbags. Khanh himself took up residence in a house on the Saigon River, where he

[6]Ahern, "CIA and the House of Ngo," p. 189; Thomas L. Ahern Jr., "CIA and the Generals: Covert Support to Military Government in South Vietnam" (DVD, 2009), pp. 9–18; A. J. Langguth, *Our Vietnam: The War, 1954–1975* (New York, 2000), pp. 275–278.
[7]Lodge to Secretary to State, February 5, 1964, DDRS (75) 215A.
[8]William C. Westmoreland, *A Soldier Reports* (Garden City, N.Y., 1976), p. 63.

could flee by boat if necessary. American intelligence warned that unless the new government took charge immediately and dealt with its problems effectively, South Vietnam had, "at best, an even chance of withstanding the insurgency menace during the next few weeks or months."[9]

VIETNAM, THE GREAT SOCIETY, AND WORLD ORDER

To Lyndon Baines Johnson and the advisers around him, the crisis of early 1964 could not have been less welcome. Johnson had assumed office in a moment of great national tragedy. He set as his first task conducting an orderly transition and restoring national calm. He attached great importance to passage of Kennedy's legislative agenda, long stalemated in Congress, both as a memorial to the fallen leader and as a springboard to launch his own reform program and campaign for election in his own right. From this standpoint, a crisis in Vietnam could only be regarded as an intrusion.

But it was an intrusion that had to be handled effectively. From the outset, Johnson personalized the struggle in Vietnam. The new president was an extraordinarily complex individual. A physically imposing man, he had an ego and ambitions the size of his native Texas. A remarkably adroit politician, brilliant legislator, and highly successful Senate majority leader, he was a driven man, prodigiously energetic, single-minded, manipulative, often overbearing. At the same time, he could be generous, warm, and compassionate toward other people. He was fiercely loyal to those who stood by him. "He had as many sides to him as a kaleidoscope," Dean Acheson once observed, an "unbelievable combination of sensitivity and coarseness, of understanding and obtuseness."[10] Despite his considerable accomplishments, Johnson remained profoundly insecure, especially in the area of foreign policy. He viewed the emerging crisis in Vietnam as a crucial test of strength for his personal prestige, his authority as president of the United States and leader of the Free World, and indeed for his manhood.

---

[9]Quoted in *Pentagon Papers (Gravel)*, 3: 42.
[10]Quoted in Clark Clifford with Richard Holbrooke, *Counsel to the President: A Memoir* (New York, 1991), p. 386.

Recognizing his foreign policy inexperience, he retained and relied heavily on Kennedy's advisers. Secretary of State Dean Rusk, Secretary of Defense Robert McNamara, and National Security Adviser McGeorge Bundy had all played prominent roles in shaping Kennedy's Vietnam policy. They had a deep personal stake in upholding it. Indeed, they felt very strongly that expansion of the American commitment since 1961 had itself significantly increased the importance of holding the line there.

Johnson linked Vietnam inextricably to his domestic political fortunes. He saw the commitment there as a vital part of the Kennedy program that he was sworn to uphold. He had been at the center of the political bloodletting that had followed the fall of China in 1949. He was certain that the "loss" of Vietnam would produce an even more explosive upheaval, a "mean and destructive debate," he later commented, "that would shatter my Presidency, kill my administration, and damage our democracy."[11] Early in his presidency, he set out to create what he called the Great Society, the most ambitious legislative program of domestic reforms since Franklin Roosevelt's New Deal. He also tied Vietnam to the realization of these goals, fearing that if he showed weakness, southern conservatives who opposed his domestic programs, especially his commitment to racial equality, would attack him with a vengeance. "If I don't go in now and they show later that I should have," he predicted, "then they'll . . . push Vietnam up my ass every time."[12]

In the eyes of Johnson and his key advisers, Vietnam remained vital to America's larger foreign policy goals. Policymakers had begun to perceive by 1964 the extent to which major changes in world politics were challenging long-standing Cold War assumptions. In particular, open squabbling between the Soviet Union and China undermined the assumption that in Vietnam as elsewhere, the United States confronted a monolithic communism united in its drive for world domination.

Most foreign policy experts still believed, however, that it was essential to hold the line in Vietnam. The ethos of the Cold War, by this time deeply ingrained, put a premium on toughness and viewed compromise as a sign of weakness, retreat as a sign of cowardice. The United States must continue to display to the major Communist

[11]Doris Kearns, *Lyndon Johnson and the American Dream* (New York, 1976), p. 252.
[12]Brian VanDeMark, *Into the Quagmire* (New York, 1991), pp. xv, 60.

powers its certainty of purpose and strength of will. A firm stand in Vietnam would discourage any Soviet tendencies toward adventurism and encourage the nascent trend toward détente with the United States. It was especially important to contain the presumably more aggressive and reckless Chinese. Policymakers also believed that the way the United States responded to "Communist provocations" in Vietnam would have "profound consequences everywhere." If the United States did not protect Vietnam, Secretary of State Rusk insisted, its "guarantees with regard to Berlin would lose their credibility."[13] Turbulence in the Third World, especially in Southeast Asia and the Western Hemisphere, appeared to pose serious dangers to American credibility and world order. Firmness in Vietnam would ensure stability in a strife-torn world by demonstrating that violent challenges to the status quo would be resisted.

In the spring and early summer of 1964, LBJ was deeply conflicted about Vietnam. As South Vietnam continued to come apart, his military advisers pressed him to attack North Vietnam—even China. Dovish senators such as Mike Mansfield and the influential journalist Walter Lippmann urged him to accept de Gaulle's neutralization scheme as a way to get out of an impossible tangle. The president's candid telephone conversations with friends and advisers reveal his frustration—indeed his torment. In talking with McNamara, he yearned for some "military mind" who could devise a plan to "trap those guys [Viet Cong] and whip the hell out of them." Yet he conceded to others that "I shudder at getting too deeply involved there. . . ." A major escalation could produce another Korea or even World War III. "It's damned easy to get into a war," he prophetically observed on one occasion, "but it's going to be awfully hard to extricate yourself if you get in." At times, he questioned the intrinsic value of Vietnam. "What the hell is Vietnam worth to me?" he would ask. "What is Laos worth to me?" "But if you start running from the Communists," he would answer, "they may just chase you into your own kitchen. . . ." "We're there, and being there we've got to conduct ourselves as men." He expressed certainty that the "loss" of Vietnam would provoke his impeachment by Congress. "I don't think it's worth fighting for," he confided to Bundy, "and I don't think we can get out." "It's just

[13]Memorandum of conversation, Rusk and French ambassador, July 1, 1964, *FR, 1964–1968*, 1: 536.

the biggest damn mess that I ever saw," he told his old friend and Senate mentor Richard Russell of Georgia.[14]

MORE OF THE SAME

Despite his anguish over Vietnam, the president was not prepared to employ American military power on a large scale in early 1964. Like Kennedy and Eisenhower before him, he had no enthusiasm for a massive engagement of American forces on the Asian mainland. He and his advisers also feared that Americanization of the war would further undercut the self-reliance of the Vietnamese. The introduction of large-scale U.S. forces in Vietnam would provoke much hostile propaganda throughout the world. Most important, it might cause major disruptions at home, threatening Johnson's legislative program and his campaign for the presidency. He therefore turned down proposals developed by the Joint Chiefs of Staff (JCS) for air and ground operations against North Vietnam.

After a major policy review in mid-March, the president concluded that the "only realistic alternative" was "to do more of the same and do it more efficiently."[15] NSAM 288, approved March 17, did state U.S. objectives in more sweeping terms, emphasizing as the essential goal the preservation of an independent, non-Communist South Vietnam. The administration still hoped that its program of military and economic assistance would be workable, however, and at this point merely attempted to make it more effective. Aware that the most urgent problem was the weakness of the South Vietnamese government, Washington publicly affirmed its support for Khanh and privately advised the U.S. mission to do everything possible to avert further coups. NSAM 288 also called for a national mobilization plan to put South Vietnam on a war footing and for significantly increasing the size of its armed forces. The president appointed Gen. William Westmoreland, a paratrooper and veteran of World War II and Korea, to replace the ineffectual and perennially optimistic Harkins. Over the next nine months, the United States increased its "advisers" from 16,300 to 23,300 and expanded its economic

[14]Randall B. Woods, *LBJ—Architect of American Ambition* (New York, 2006), p. 510; Edward C. Keefer, "LBJ Calling," *Diplomatic History* 24 (January 2010): 205.
[15]Kearns, *Johnson*, p. 196.

assistance by $50 million. "As far as I am concerned," Johnson advised Lodge in April, "you must have whatever you need to help the Vietnamese do the job, and I assure you that I will act at once to eliminate obstacles or restraints wherever they may appear."[16]

Although the administration did little more than reaffirm existing policy in the spring of 1964, its attention was shifting increasingly toward North Vietnam. The change reflected a growing concern over the infiltration of people and supplies from the North and mounting frustration with ground rules that permitted Hanoi to support the insurgency with impunity. Some U.S. officials seem also to have concluded that action against the North might somehow compensate for the lack of progress in the South. Others wished to signal Hanoi that it would pay a high price for its continued intervention. Although covert operations in North Vietnam had been notably unsuccessful, they were expanded in early 1964 to include intelligence overflights, the dropping of propaganda leaflets, and OPLAN 34A commando raids conducted by South Vietnamese guerrillas along the North Vietnamese coast. The administration also intensified its planning to prepare U.S. forces for possible "border control" operations into Cambodia and Laos, "tit-for-tat" retaliatory bombing raids into North Vietnam, and a series of "graduated overt pressures" against North Vietnam, including air attacks against military and industrial targets. Firm warnings were delivered to Hanoi through Canadian intermediaries that continued support for the insurgency could bring great devastation to North Vietnam itself. At a National Security Council (NSC) meeting on March 17, top administration officials expressed confidence that increased military and economic aid would be enough to stem the tide in South Vietnam. They also agreed that failure of the program outlined in NSAM 288 might compel them to take the war to North Vietnam.[17]

The spring 1964 program, like those before it, produced meager results. Under U.S. supervision, Khanh developed ambitious plans for bringing the government down to the village level, but there was a vast gap between planning and implementation. In many areas the NLF was so firmly entrenched that it could not be

[16]Johnson to Lodge, April 4, 1964, Johnson Papers, Lyndon Baines Johnson Library, Austin, Texas, National Security File, Country File: Vietnam, Box 3.
[17]Summary record of NSC meeting, March 17, 1964, Johnson Papers, National Security File, NSC Meetings File, Box 1.

dislodged except by massive force. Where it could function freely, the government was hampered by a shortage of skilled officials and by what one American described as "outmoded concepts, directives and practices, bureaucratic constipation, [and] insufficient on-the-spot resources."[18] As a result of spiraling desertion rates, the strength of the ARVN remained well below the figure authorized before the projected increase. The army won a few minor engagements in the early summer, but it was never able to gain the initiative. American officials publicly praised Khanh's "able and energetic leadership." Khanh dutifully followed U.S. suggestions for gaining popular support, visiting numerous villages and cities and even making a series of "fireside chats."

Although a word from well-placed Americans could topple governments in Vietnam, it could not create stability; mere speeches were inadequate to bring together South Vietnam's disparate political forces. Catholics and Buddhists mobilized against each other and agitated against a government neither trusted. After a period of quiescence, the students began to stir again. The government itself was rent by internal dissension, and a coup plot in July failed only because the United States made known its opposition. Maxwell Taylor, who replaced Lodge as ambassador in midsummer, reported in August that "the best thing that can be said about Khanh's government is that it has lasted six months and has about a 50-50 chance of lasting out the year."[19]

Hanoi responded defiantly to American warnings. There is no reason to suppose that the North Vietnamese leaders wanted war with the United States. Rather, they hoped that intensification of aid to the NLF would topple the South Vietnamese government, leaving the United States no choice but to abandon its ally. They may have dismissed the various U.S. "signals" as bluff. In any event, they were not prepared to abandon their long-sought goal in the face of American threats. In the spring and summer of 1964, North Vietnam mobilized its own forces for war, intensified transformation of the Ho Chi Minh Trail into a modern logistical network capable of handling large trucks, and stepped up preparation of units of its own regular army for infiltration into South Vietnam. Premier Pham Van Dong

[18]William Colby memorandum, May 11, 1964, Johnson Papers, National Security File, Country File: Vietnam, Box 3.
[19]Quoted in *Pentagon Papers (Gravel)*, 3: 82.

bluntly informed Canadian Blair Seaborn in June that the stakes were as high for North Vietnam as for the United States and that the NLF and its supporters were prepared to endure regardless of the cost. If the United States insisted on war, he concluded with a ringing declaration, "We shall win!"[20]

Under these circumstances, Americans increasingly looked north for a solution they could not find in the south. Alarmed by the persistent lack of progress in South Vietnam, annoyed by Hanoi's defiant response, and fearful that the North Vietnamese might seek to exploit the administration's presumed immobility in an election year, by mid-summer 1964 some of Johnson's advisers had developed a full "scenario" of graduated overt pressures against the North, according to which the president, after securing a congressional resolution, would authorize air strikes against selected North Vietnamese targets. Rusk and McNamara finally rejected the program for fear that it would "raise a whole series of disagreeable questions" that might jeopardize passage of civil rights legislation, but the proposals indicate the drift of official attitudes during this period.[21]

TONKIN GULF

The administration implemented much of the proposed "scenario" in early August in response to a series of dramatic events at sea. The president and his advisers portrayed the so-called Tonkin Gulf incidents as unprovoked attacks on U.S. ships innocently steaming in international waters. In fact, as part of the DeSoto Patrols, the destroyer *USS Maddox* was engaged in electronic espionage in the Gulf of Tonkin, sometimes venturing into North Vietnamese waters. One of its objectives was to gauge the reaction of enemy radars to OPLAN 34A operations carried out by South Vietnamese gunboats under U.S. supervision. These boats had bombarded the nearby islands of Hon Me and Hon Ngu the evening of August 1.

[20]George C. Herring (ed.), *The Secret Diplomacy of the Vietnam War: The Negotiating Volumes of the Pentagon Papers* (Austin, Tex., 1983), p. 8.

[21]McNamara–Rusk memorandum, June 11, 1964, Johnson Papers, National Security File, Country File: Vietnam, Box 4. For a full discussion of these events see Andrew L. Johns, "Opening Pandora's Box: The Genesis and Evolution of the 1964 Congressional Resolution on Vietnam," *Journal of American-East Asian Relations*, 6 (Summer–Fall 1997): 186–201.

Correctly assuming that the *Maddox* was connected with these attacks, local North Vietnamese commanders ordered torpedo boats to close with the destroyer the following afternoon. In a brief and decisive engagement, the gunboats launched torpedoes, the *Maddox* opened fire, and aircraft from the nearby *USS Ticonderoga* joined the fray. The North Vietnamese boats were badly damaged but managed to limp back to shore.

Johnson was reportedly enraged when he learned of the encounter, but no retaliation was ordered. "The other side got a sting out of this," Rusk remarked. "If they do it again, they'll get another sting."[22] To avoid any appearance of weakness and to assert traditional claims to freedom of the seas, the administration ordered the *Maddox* to resume operations in the Gulf of Tonkin and sent the destroyer *C. Turner Joy* to support it. The United States may not have been seeking to provoke another attack, but it did not go out of its way to avoid one either. The administration kept the destroyers close to North Vietnamese shores, where they were vulnerable to attack. Eager for "open season" on a nation already looked upon as the enemy, responsible military officials in the area were choosing targets for retaliatory raids before reports of a second attack began to come in.

On the night of August 4, while operating in heavy seas some sixty miles off the North Vietnamese coast, the *Maddox* and the *Turner Joy* suddenly reported being under attack. The initial reports were based on sonar and radar contacts, both unreliable under the adverse weather conditions, and on sightings of torpedoes and enemy searchlights on a night one seaman described as "darker than the hubs of Hell." The captain of the *Maddox* later conceded that evidence of an attack was less than conclusive. North Vietnamese gunboats may have been operating in the area, but no evidence has ever been produced to demonstrate that they committed hostile acts. It is now certain that no second attack took place.

Had it not been an election year or had the president and his advisers been in a less pugnacious mood, the administration might have viewed the conflicting evidence as reason for caution. But the election campaign was gearing up and hawkish Republican candidate Barry Goldwater was already indulging with special fervor in

---

[22]Quoted in John Galloway, *The Gulf of Tonkin Resolution* (Rutherford, N.J., 1970), p. 52. The authoritative study is Edwin E. Moïse, *Tonkin Gulf and the Escalation of the Vietnam War* (Chapel Hill, N.C., 1996). See also John Prados, "Essay: 40th Anniversary of the Gulf of Tonkin Incident," http://www.gwu.edu/~nsarchiv/NSAEBB132/essay.htm.

the quadrennial Cold War exercise of talking tough and branding his opponent as weak. Committed to showing their determination to a recalcitrant Hanoi, U.S. officials had been poised to strike back since the first encounter in the gulf. The JCS insisted that the United States must "clobber" the attackers. After the initial reports of another attack, they worked out a series of retaliatory options ranging from limited air strikes against North Vietnamese naval installations to the mining of parts of their coastline. When the president met with his advisers early that afternoon, there seemed little doubt an attack had occurred. The CIA cautiously speculated that the North Vietnamese might be responding defensively and out of "pride" to attacks on their territory. Top officials insisted rather that Hanoi was trying to make the United States appear a "paper tiger." Rusk labeled the attack an "act of war." Determined to prove their toughness—to American voters and North Vietnamese leaders— Johnson and his advisers agreed, as McNamara put it, that "we cannot sit still as a nation and let them attack us on the high seas and get away with it." They decided upon a "firm, swift retaliatory [air] strike" against North Vietnamese torpedo boat bases.[23]

Although serious questions were raised later in the day about the alleged attacks, the administration stuck by its decision. "FLASH" messages from the *Maddox* cautioned that "freak weather effects" on the radar and sonar, as well as "overeager" sonarmen, may have accounted for many of the reported torpedo attacks and enemy contacts. Contradicting earlier messages, the commander of the *Maddox* also admitted that there had been no "visual sightings." A "complete evaluation" of all the evidence should be made before retaliation was ordered. McNamara postponed the air strike temporarily to make "damned sure that the attacks had taken place." By late afternoon, however, he was convinced, on the basis of evidence that now appears quite dubious. Ignoring the belated uncertainty of the men on the scene, the secretary of defense accepted at face value the judgment of the commander in chief of the Pacific fleet, Adm. U.S. Grant Sharp, in Honolulu, whose certainty was based on the first reports from the *Maddox* and intercepts of North Vietnamese messages indicating that two patrol boats had been

[23] "Chronology of Events, Tuesday, August 4 and Wednesday, August 5, 1964, Tonkin Gulf Strike," Johnson Papers, National Security File, Country File: Vietnam, Box 18; Summary notes of 538th NSC meeting, August 4, 1964, Johnson Papers, National Security File, NSC Meetings File, Box 1; Rusk to Taylor, August 8, 1964, DDRS(75)845-H.

"sacrificed." It is now clear that the intercepts, which provided the clinching evidence, referred to the August 2 attacks. Recently released documents have also revealed that after transmitting to Washington highly misleading information based on bad translations of the intercepts, National Security Agency (NSA) operatives sought to cover their error by sending only information confirming that a second attack had occurred.[24]

McNamara and his military advisers did not knowingly lie about the alleged attacks, but they were obviously in a mood to retaliate. They seem to have selected from the conflicting evidence those parts that confirmed what they wanted to believe. Accepting McNamara's conclusions without question, in the late afternoon Johnson authorized retaliatory air strikes against North Vietnamese torpedo boat bases and nearby oil storage dumps. Described by the Joint Chiefs as a "pretty good effort," the strikes destroyed or damaged twenty-five patrol boats and 90 percent of the oil storage facilities at Vinh.[25]

The president also seized a golden opportunity to secure passage of a congressional resolution authorizing him to take "all necessary measures to repel any armed attacks against the forces of the United States and to prevent further aggression." His purpose was to indicate to Hanoi that the nation was united in its determination to stand firm in South Vietnam. The resolution also served immediate domestic political needs. The show of force and the appeal for national support permitted him to disarm Goldwater, who had vigorously urged escalation of the war, and to demonstrate that he could be firm in defending American interests without recklessly expanding the war. In presenting its case, however, the administration deliberately deceived Congress and the American people. Nothing was said about the covert raids. Official reports indicated that the *Maddox* was engaged in routine patrols in international waters. The incidents were portrayed as "deliberate attacks" and "open aggression on the high seas."

Congress responded quickly and pliantly. Senator Wayne Morse (Oregon Democrat) raised some embarrassing questions about the OPLAN 34A raids and the mission of the American

[24]*New York Times*, October 2, December 2, 2005.
[25]"Chronology of Events," Johnson Papers, National Security File, Country File: Vietnam, Box 18; "Transcripts of Telephone Conversations, 4–5 August," Johnson Papers, National Security File, Country File: Vietnam, Box 228.

destroyers. Senator Ernest Gruening (Alaska Democrat) attacked the resolution as a "predated declaration of war," and Senator Gaylord Nelson (Wisconsin Democrat) attempted to limit the grant of authority to the executive branch. During a period when America's national interests seemed constantly in peril, however, Congress had grown accustomed to approving presidential initiatives without serious question. The crisis atmosphere seemed to leave no time for debate. "The American flag has been fired upon," Representative Ross Adair (Indiana Republican) exclaimed. "We will not and cannot tolerate such things."[26] The Senate debated the resolution less than ten hours, during much of which time the chamber was less than one-third full. By his own admission more concerned with the challenge posed by Goldwater than with giving a blank check to Johnson, Senator J. William Fulbright (Arkansas Democrat) carefully shepherded the resolution through, choking off debate and amendments. The vote in the Senate was an overwhelming 88 to 2; only Morse and Gruening dissented. Consideration in the House was even more perfunctory, passage taking a mere forty minutes and the vote being unanimous.

From a domestic political standpoint, Johnson's handling of the Tonkin Gulf incident was masterly. His firm but restrained response to the alleged North Vietnamese attacks won broad popular support, his rating in the Louis Harris poll skyrocketing from 42 to 72 percent overnight. He neutralized Goldwater on Vietnam, a fact that contributed to his overwhelming electoral victory in November. Moreover, this first formal congressional debate on Vietnam brought a near-unanimous endorsement of the president's policies and provided him an apparently solid foundation on which to construct future policy.

In time, Johnson would pay a heavy price for his easy victory. U.S. prestige was now publicly and more firmly committed not merely to defending South Vietnam but also to responding to North Vietnamese provocations. By attacking North Vietnamese targets, the president temporarily silenced his hawkish critics inside and outside government, but in doing so he had broken a long-standing barrier against taking the war to the North. The first steps taken, the next ones would be easier. Johnson's victory in Congress may have encouraged him to take the legislators lightly in making

[26]Quoted in Anthony Austin, *The President's War* (Philadelphia, 1971), p. 98.

future policy decisions on Vietnam. But the overwhelming vote for the resolution obscured searching questions raised in the debate from the left about the centrality of America's interests in Vietnam and the limits of its power and from the right about the incremental nature of the administration's policies. Such questions would set the contours of a debate on Vietnam that would rage in the months to come. And when the administration's case for reprisals later turned out to be less than overwhelming, many members of Congress correctly concluded that they had been deceived. The president's resounding triumph brought enormous, if still hidden, costs.[27]

Unknown to the United States, the Tonkin Gulf incident also raised the stakes on the other side. Rather than deterring North Vietnam, Johnson's forceful response led it to step up its efforts in the South. Encouraged by signs of continued deterioration in South Vietnam and persuaded that the United States was on the verge of expanding the war, Hanoi decided in September 1964 to send to the South the first units of its own regular army to support a push for victory before the spring of 1965. In yet another major miscalculation, the North Vietnamese hoped to accomplish their goal before the United States could intervene directly in the war, thus avoiding a major conflict with a great power. Shortly after, North Vietnamese leaders went to Moscow and Beijing to seek additional support. The Soviet Union was still cautious but found itself under increasing pressure to do something or lose its leadership position to the Chinese. While urging the North Vietnamese to prepare for a long war, China was more forthcoming, mobilizing forces along its border with North Vietnam and significantly expanding its military and economic assistance.[28]

The Johnson administration did not follow up the Tonkin Gulf reprisals with additional attacks against North Vietnam. The president was not about to jeopardize his political fortunes by escalating the war. Having established his determination to defend American interests with force if necessary, he emphasized in the final months of the campaign his wish to limit American involvement if possible. "We seek no wider war," he stated in numerous speeches.

[27]Andrew L. Johns, *Vietnam's Second Front: Domestic Politics, the Republican Party, and the War* (Lexington, Ky., 2010), pp. 67–69.
[28]Ang Cheng Guan, "The Vietnam War, 1962–1964: The Vietnamese Communist Perspective," *Journal of Contemporary History* 35 (October 2000): 617; William J. Duiker, *Ho Chi Minh: A Life* (New York, 2000), pp. 540–542.

At the same time, political turmoil in South Vietnam made caution essential. Attempting to exploit the Tonkin Gulf affair to save his political skin, Khanh on August 6 assumed near-dictatorial powers and imposed severe restrictions on civil liberties. Thousands of Saigonese took to the streets, and when an angry mob forced Khanh to stand atop a tank and shout "Down with dictatorships," the humiliated general resigned. For days, near anarchy reigned: Mobs rampaged through the streets, Buddhists and Catholics waged open warfare, and gangs of thugs fought and pillaged with hatchets and machetes. Behind the scenes, politicians and generals, Khanh included, jockeyed for power.

Under these circumstances, the administration refused to escalate the war. By early September, the U.S. Air Force and the Marine Corps were vigorously pressing for extended air attacks against North Vietnam. Ambassador Taylor and others conceded that such steps would have to be taken in time, but they argued that it would be too risky to "overstrain the currently weakened GVN by drastic action in the immediate future." Johnson concurred, stating that he did not wish to "enter the patient in a 10-round bout, when he was in no shape to hold out for one round." While keeping other options open, the administration decided merely to continue its covert operations against North Vietnam and to be ready to respond to North Vietnamese provocations on a "tit for tat basis."[29] LBJ remained sufficiently concerned about the approaching election and the internal situation in South Vietnam that he refused to retaliate when NLF guerrillas on November 1 attacked the U.S. air base at Bien Hoa, killing four Americans and destroying five aircraft.

DECISIONS FOR WAR

Johnson's reluctance would soon change. Scholars now agree that late 1964–early 1965 was the pivotal period in his escalation of the Vietnam War.[30] During this time, the president fundamentally

[29]McGeorge Bundy memorandum for the record, September 14, 1964, Johnson Papers, National Security File, Country File: Vietnam, Box 6.

[30]See, for example, Logevall, *Choosing War;* David Kaiser, *American Tragedy: Kennedy, Johnson, and the Origins of the Vietnam War* (New York, 2000); and H. R. McMaster, *Dereliction of Duty: Lyndon Johnson, Robert McNamara, the Joint Chiefs of Staff, and the Lies That Led to Vietnam* (New York, 1997).

altered the U.S. commitment by initiating the regular bombing of North Vietnam and by sending the first U.S. ground combat troops to South Vietnam. Some of his advisers doubted that even these steps would be enough, but they believed that to maintain its international credibility, the United States should do everything it could as the "good doctor" to save the ailing patient, South Vietnam. Johnson, Rusk, McGeorge Bundy, and McNamara seem to have hoped that by gradually increasing the bombing and injecting U.S. forces into the ground war they could coerce North Vietnam into abandoning the southern insurgency. This strategy of gradual escalation, which drew on the recent experience of the Cuban missile crisis, was based on the dubious assumption that North Vietnam would give up its goals rather than risk complete destruction. The result for the United States was an irreversible commitment to a major war and Americanization of the conflict in South Vietnam.

Johnson was not forced into war by the exigencies of domestic or international politics. Public opinion in late 1964 was apathetic and permissive. Growing numbers of Americans opposed a major war. Although there was also opposition to withdrawal, the public would likely have gone along with a skillfully executed disengagement. Some leading political figures and major newspapers endorsed drastic escalation, but by early 1965 many others had become increasingly concerned about the prospect of war and favored deescalation and a negotiated settlement. Johnson's political position was as strong as it would ever be. He had just won an overwhelming electoral victory and had firm control of Congress. The administration often maintained that it was in Vietnam to prove its reliability to its allies. In fact, America's major allies doubted the importance of Vietnam and were even more skeptical that the United States could succeed there with military force. When the administration launched a "many flags" campaign in the spring of 1964 to get support from its allies, only Australia enthusiastically agreed to provide troops.[31]

The administration chose war for other reasons. A resolute Cold Warrior, Secretary of State Rusk believed that the United States must stand firm in Vietnam to contain an aggressively expansionist China. Johnson shared Rusk's concern and feared even more the political backlash from right-wing Republicans and southern Democrats

[31]Logevall, *Choosing War*, pp. 275–279, 304–305.

should he falter in Vietnam. For the president, the Great Society remained the highest priority. He continued to worry that a retreat on Vietnam would jeopardize his cherished domestic goals. For personal reasons, he also found the possibility of failure intolerable.

Another leader might also have gone to war in these circumstances, but the *way* the United States went to war in early 1965—"by stealth"—bore the distinctive LBJ brand.[32] This approach was partly a result of personality and modus operandi. A cloakroom operator rather than a master of debate, the former Senate majority leader did not like open and freewheeling discussion. His ego and insecurity led him to personalize dissent and opposition. He was determined to keep control in his own hands. He also feared that a potentially divisive debate on Vietnam would distract attention from the domestic issues he wished to focus on. Thus, while taking major steps toward war, Johnson carefully and skillfully silenced public debate. He obscured the significance of what he was doing. By stressing the continuity of his policies and emphasizing that he was giving equal attention to military measures *and* negotiations, he encouraged both "hawks" and "doves" to believe that he was moving in their direction. By deceit and obfuscation, he brilliantly mobilized a consensus behind his policies while blurring what these policies actually were.

The process began even before the election. On November 2, the day before Americans went to the polls, Johnson authorized intensive planning for future action in Vietnam, a "crucial step in the country's entry into a new war."[33] By the end of that month, a firm consensus had emerged among his advisers that the United States must soon undertake a carefully orchestrated bombing attack against North Vietnam. U.S. officials disagreed among themselves on the reasons for the bombing, some viewing it as a way of boosting morale in South Vietnam, others as a means of reducing infiltration from the North, and still others as a weapon to force Hanoi to stop supporting the insurgency. They also disagreed on the type of bombing campaign. The military pressed for a "fast and full squeeze"—massive attacks against major industries and military targets. Civilians advocated a "slow squeeze"—a graduated series of attacks beginning with infiltration routes in Laos and slowly extending to

[32]Ibid., pp. 273, 314–315.
[33]Kaiser, *American Tragedy*, p. 355.

North Vietnam. Despite warnings from intelligence sources that bombing would not decisively affect the war in the south, most of Johnson's advisers endorsed the use of airpower in some form.

Only Undersecretary of State George Ball vigorously dissented. An experienced diplomat who as counsel to the French embassy had observed firsthand that nation's defeat in Indochina, Ball insisted that airpower would not solve the American dilemma in Vietnam. He doubted it would either improve morale in the South or compel Hanoi to give in. He also warned that in response to U.S. escalation North Vietnam might pour its virtually unlimited human resources into the struggle and China might intervene. Most important, after the process of escalation had been initiated, the United States could not be sure of controlling events. "Once on the tiger's back," Ball concluded, "we cannot be sure of picking the place to dismount."[34]

Ball's argument had little impact in Washington, and by the end of November Johnson's senior advisers had formulated concrete proposals for the use of American military power. Rejecting the more extreme program of the JCS, they advocated a two-phase plan of gradually intensifying air attacks. The first phase, to last roughly a month, consisted of limited bombing raids against infiltration routes in Laos, along with reprisal strikes against North Vietnamese targets in response to any provocation. In the meantime, Taylor would use the promise of air attacks against North Vietnam to persuade the South Vietnamese to put their house in order. Once an acceptable level of stability had been attained, the United States would move into phase two, a large-scale air offensive against North Vietnam lasting from two to six months, to be followed if necessary by a naval blockade.

Johnson approved the program in December, a "momentous decision," historian Fredrick Logevall has emphasized, perhaps the most important of the war.[35] On December 1, the president approved immediate initiation of phase one bombing operations in Laos. Still reluctant to move too far too fast, he subsequently approved in principle the launching of retaliatory strikes and phase two bombing operations when the situation warranted. Those operations required a substantial deployment of ground combat forces, and the president also endorsed this highly significant measure.

[34]George W. Ball, *The Past Has Another Pattern* (New York, 1982), pp. 380–385.
[35]Logevall, *Choosing War*, pp. 270–273.

In approving what amounted to decisions for war, Johnson demanded absolute secrecy, covering his tracks so skillfully that he deceived his contemporaries and misled a generation of historians. Recognizing that even with his huge electoral mandate he would have only a brief honeymoon period to achieve his ambitious legislative goals, he was unwilling to permit the war to thwart his Great Society. If he had to go to war, he would do everything possible to obscure and conceal it. He made it a matter of "highest importance" that the December decisions be kept from the public. Speaking figuratively but firmly, he threatened to "shoot at sunrise" anyone who leaked sensitive information about the war.[36]

For the same reasons, he continued to move cautiously for more than a month. He was loathe to escalate too rapidly in view of his campaign assurances of no wider war. South Vietnam was still in turmoil, and he refused to send U.S. troops when the South Vietnamese were "acting as they are." He and his advisers also feared that U.S. reprisals might provoke further NLF attacks at a time when South Vietnam was "too shaky" to withstand a "major assault." He thus instructed Taylor to do everything possible to get the South Vietnamese to pull together. He refused even to retaliate when, on Christmas Eve, the NLF bombed a U.S. officers' quarters at the Brinks Hotel in Saigon, killing two Americans and injuring thirty-eight.[37]

ROLLING THUNDER

By the end of January, the president could delay no longer. One of the major arguments against escalation—the weakness of South Vietnam—had become the most compelling argument for it. After Khanh's resignation, a civilian government had been formed, but it could not consolidate its position. Upon returning to Saigon, Taylor informed South Vietnam's leaders that the United States would escalate the war if they could stabilize the government. The answer came immediately when Vice Air Marshal Nguyen Cao Ky and General Nguyen Chanh Thi executed yet another coup. Outraged,

[36]Kaiser, *American Tragedy*, p. 379; McMaster, *Dereliction of Duty*, p. 195.
[37]Meeting on Vietnam, December 1, 1964, Johnson Papers, Meeting Notes File, Box 1; Lyndon B. Johnson, *The Vantage Point* (New York, 1971), p. 121.

Taylor lectured the young officers as a drill instructor might talk to recruits. Perhaps something was wrong with his French, he snarled sarcastically, because his listeners had obviously not understood him. "Now you have made a real mess," he added angrily. "We cannot carry you forever if you do things like this."[38]

The harsh reprimand produced some "shame-faced grins," Taylor recalled, but no results.[39] The military finally agreed to cooperate with civilian politicians to form a new government, but Buddhist leaders refused to participate and launched a new round of demonstrations, hunger strikes, and immolations that took on increasingly anti-American tones. Protesters publicly demanded Taylor's resignation. Five thousand students sacked the U.S. Information Service library in Hue. Rumors of coup plots abounded. U.S. officials began to fear that a new government could emerge from the chaos and negotiate with the enemy on the basis of a U.S. withdrawal. In the meantime, NLF regular forces decimated two elite South Vietnamese units in major battles. Combined with reports that North Vietnamese regular units were now entering the South, the defeats aroused growing fear that the enemy had decided to launch an all-out attack that South Vietnam could not withstand.

By the end of January, most of Johnson's advisers agreed that the threat to the South and the ominous military danger required the United States to bomb the North. Throughout the month, Taylor bombarded Washington with warnings that failure to take drastic action could only lead to "disastrous defeat." McGeorge Bundy played a decisive role in moving Johnson toward a major escalation of the war. Since 1961, Bundy had radically transformed the role of the NSC, creating a smaller, more streamlined State Department within the office of the president. As National Security Adviser, he increasingly served as a policy coordinator who framed options for his boss. By late 1964, Bundy had established himself as one of Johnson's most influential foreign policy advisers. He had also grown more hawkish on Vietnam. A staunch supporter of improved relations with the USSR, he feared that by shattering U.S. credibility the collapse of South Vietnam would irreparably compromise any prospect of détente. It would also heighten China's aggressiveness.

---

[38]Quoted in Neil Sheehan et al., *The Pentagon Papers as Published by the New York Times* (New York, 1971), pp. 371–381. Hereafter cited as *Pentagon Papers (NYT)*.
[39]Maxwell D. Taylor, *Swords and Ploughshares* (New York, 1972), p. 330.

In early 1965, he set out to end the indecision and delay. His January 27 "fork in the road" memorandum—"an explosive document," McNamara later recalled—remains a landmark on America's road to war in Vietnam. Speaking in "apocalyptic" language, he warned, much like Taylor, that continuation of existing policy would lead to "disastrous defeat." The choice was between using U.S. military power to change Communist policy or seeking negotiations "aimed at salvaging what little could be preserved." He favored the more aggressive option, pushing for retaliatory air strikes at the first opportunity followed by phase two bombing operations.[40]

Undoubtedly with great reluctance but also with firm resignation, Johnson concurred. "Stable government or no stable government we'll do what we have to do," he vowed. It was the decisive moment—Johnson moving to implement the program he had approved in principle in December. He dispatched Bundy to Saigon to see what further military action should be taken. Recognizing that a pretext for escalation would be useful, he resumed DeSoto Patrols in the Gulf of Tonkin.[41]

The awaited incident came on land instead of at sea. On February 7, NLF units attacked a U.S. Army barracks in Pleiku and a nearby helicopter base, killing nine Americans, wounding 126, and destroying five aircraft. That evening, after a meeting of less than two hours, the administration decided to strike back. Only Senator Mansfield dissented, arguing that the United States might provoke Chinese intervention. Johnson brusquely dismissed Mansfield's argument. "We have kept our guns over the mantel and our shells in the cupboard for a long time now," he exclaimed with obvious impatience. "I can't ask our American soldiers out there to continue to fight with one hand behind their backs."[42] The president ordered the immediate implementation of FLAMING DART, a plan of reprisal strikes already drawn up by the JCS. Later that day and again the following day, American aircraft struck North Vietnamese military installations just across the seventeenth parallel. When, on February 10, the NLF attacked an American enlisted men's quarters

---

[40]Andrew Preston, *The War Council: McGeorge Bundy, the NSC, and Vietnam* (Cambridge, Mass., 2006), pp. 39–53, 165–167; Kaiser, *American Tragedy*, pp. 387–393; Logevall, *Choosing War*, p. 317.

[41]Kaiser, *American Tragedy*, p. 392.

[42]Johnson, *Vantage Point*, p. 125.

at Qui Nhon, the president ordered another, even heavier series of retaliatory air strikes.

Within less than forty-eight hours, the administration moved from reprisals to a sustained, graduated program of air attacks against North Vietnam, the fundamental aim of which was to persuade Hanoi to refrain from intervention in South Vietnam. Mansfield, some top State Department officials, Vice President Hubert H. Humphrey, and even members of Bundy's staff strongly opposed such a move. But most U.S. officials mistakenly viewed the Pleiku attack as a direct challenge issued by North Vietnam that must be met (more than thirty years later, a former NLF officer revealed to a number of Americans, this author included, that he had ordered the attack on his own authority). McNamara and his top advisers, the JCS, Gen. Westmoreland, and Ambassador Taylor strongly supported a sustained bombing program. The normally cool and detached Bundy visited Pleiku the day of the attack and was deeply shaken by the carnage he witnessed. Henceforth, he pushed for escalation with a new passion, warning that "without new U.S. action defeat appears inevitable—probably not in a matter of weeks or even months, but within the next year or so." Assistant Secretary of Defense John McNaughton, who had accompanied Bundy to Vietnam, agreed, arguing that "measured against the costs of defeat the program would be 'cheap,'" and even if it failed to turn the tide, "the value of the effort" would "exceed the costs."[43] The next day, apparently without extended debate, the administration approved ROLLING THUNDER, the program of gradually intensified air attacks Bundy and McNaughton had advocated.

The administration deceived the American public in explaining the reasons for and significance of its decision. Officials from the president down justified the air strikes as a response to the Pleiku attack and emphatically denied any change of policy. It is abundantly clear, however, that Pleiku was the pretext for rather than the cause of the February decision. The possibility of a South Vietnamese collapse appeared to demand the adoption of a policy some Americans had been advocating for more than two months. It was, therefore, simply a matter of finding the right opportunity to justify measures to which the administration was already committed. Pleiku provided such an opportunity, although it could as

[43]Preston, *War Council*, pp. 176–179.

easily have been something else. "Pleikus are like streetcars," McGeorge Bundy later remarked, by which he meant that if you missed one, another would be along shortly.[44] Despite the administration's disclaimers, the February decisions marked a major watershed in the war. The initiation of regular bombing attacks advanced well beyond the limited tit-for-tat reprisal strikes of Tonkin Gulf and provided a built-in argument for further escalation should that become necessary.

Indeed, almost as soon as the bombing program got under way, there were pressures to expand it. The initial attacks achieved meager results, provoking Taylor to complain that ROLLING THUNDER had constituted but a "few isolated thunder claps" and to call for a "mounting crescendo" of air strikes against North Vietnam.[45] Intelligence reports ominously warned that the military situation in South Vietnam was steadily deteriorating. At the present rate the government might soon be reduced to a series of islands surrounding the provincial capitals. From the outset, Johnson had insisted on maintaining tight personal control over the air war—"They can't even bomb an outhouse without my approval," he is said to have boasted.[46] But in response to these urgent warnings, he permitted gradual expansion of the bombing and relaxation of the restrictions under which it was carried out. The use of napalm was authorized to ensure greater destructiveness, and pilots were permitted to strike alternative targets without prior authorization if the original targets were inaccessible. In April, American and South Vietnamese pilots flew a total of 3,600 sorties against North Vietnamese targets. The air war quickly grew from a sporadic, halting effort into a regular, determined program.

GROUND TROOPS, ENCLAVES, AND PEACE MOVES

The expanded air war also provided the pretext for the introduction of U.S. ground combat forces into Vietnam. Anticipating retaliatory attacks for ROLLING THUNDER, Gen. Westmoreland in late February urgently requested two Marine landing teams to protect the air

[44]Quoted in Anthony Lake (ed.), *The Vietnam Legacy* (New York, 1976), p. 183.
[45]*Pentagon Papers (Gravel)*, 3: 335.
[46]Westmoreland, *Soldier Reports*, p. 119.

Marines Land at Da Nang
Shortly after 9:00 a.m. on March 8, 1965, Marines from the 3rd Battalion,
9th Marine Expeditionary Force, splashed ashore in rough seas at Da Nang.
They were the first U.S. ground combat troops sent to Vietnam. With their
arrival, the United States crossed a major threshold in its escalation of the war.
The Marines were originally "tasked" to guard the air base at Da Nang. But in
less than a month, President Lyndon Johnson secretly authorized them to
move out and engage enemy soldiers in combat.
© *AP Images*

base at Da Nang. Although he conceded the importance of protecting the base, Taylor expressed grave concern about the long-range
implications of Westmoreland's request. He questioned whether
American combat forces were adequately trained for guerrilla warfare in the Asian jungles and warned that the introduction of such
forces would encourage the ARVN to pass military responsibility to
the United States. Most important, the introduction of even small
numbers of combat troops with a specific and limited mission
would violate a ground rule the United States had rigorously
adhered to since the beginning of the Indochina wars. Once the first
step had been taken, it would be "very difficult to hold [the] line."[47]

[47]*Pentagon Papers (Gravel)*, 3: 418.

Taylor's objections were prophetic, but they were ignored. Months before, the president had approved in principle the introduction of ground combat forces. The need appears to have been so pressing and immediate, the commitment so small, that the decision was made routinely, with little discussion of its long-range consequences. After less than a week of apparently perfunctory debate, LBJ approved Westmoreland's request. On March 8, two battalions of Marines, fitted out in full battle regalia, with tanks and 8-inch howitzers, splashed ashore near Da Nang, where they were welcomed by South Vietnamese officials and by pretty Vietnamese girls passing out leis of flowers. It was an ironically happy beginning for what would be a wrenching experience for the two nations.

As Taylor had predicted, once the first step had been taken, it was very difficult to hold the line. Alarmed by the slow pace of the ARVN buildup and fearful of a major enemy offensive in the Central Highlands, Westmoreland concluded by mid-March that if the United States was to avert disaster in Vietnam, there was "no solution . . . other than to put our own finger in the dike."[48] He therefore advocated the immediate commitment of two U.S. Army divisions, one to the highlands, the other to the Saigon area. The Joint Chiefs forcefully endorsed Westmoreland's request. Long impatient with the administration's caution and eager to assume full responsibility for the war, they even went beyond Westmoreland, pressing for the deployment of as many as three divisions to be used in offensive operations against the enemy.

The administration now found itself on what McNaughton called "the horns of a trilemma." The options of withdrawal and a massive air war against North Vietnam had been firmly rejected. It was apparent by mid-March, however, that the bombing campaign approved in February would not produce immediate results. Westmoreland's urgent warnings raised fears that further inaction might lead to a South Vietnamese collapse. Many administration officials therefore reluctantly concluded that they must introduce U.S. ground forces into Vietnam. They fully appreciated, on the other hand, the possible domestic political consequences of the sort of commitment Westmoreland proposed. And Taylor ominously warned that to place major increments of forces in the highlands would invite heavy losses, even an American Dien Bien Phu.

[48]Westmoreland, *Soldier Reports*, p. 126.

The administration resolved its "trilemma" with a compromise, rejecting the military proposals but still approving a significant commitment of ground forces and an enlargement of their mission. At a conference in Honolulu in late April, McNamara, Taylor, and the Joint Chiefs agreed on a hastily improvised strategy to "break the will of the DRV/VC [Democratic Republic of Vietnam/Viet Cong] by depriving them of victory." The bombing would be maintained at its "present tempo" for six months to a year. But the conferees agreed, as McNamara put it, that bombing "would not do the job alone."[49] They therefore decided that some 40,000 additional U.S. ground combat forces should be sent to Vietnam.

These forces were not to be used in the highlands or given an unrestricted mission, as Westmoreland and the Joint Chiefs had advocated, but would be used in the more cautious "enclave strategy" devised by Taylor. Deployed around the major U.S. bases, their backs to the sea, they would be authorized to undertake operations within fifty miles of their base areas. The administration hoped this limited commitment would deny the enemy a knockout blow, thus allowing time for the South Vietnamese buildup and for the bombing to take its toll. Although the April decisions stopped short of the commitment urged by the military, they advanced well beyond the original objective of base security and marked a major step toward large-scale involvement in the ground war. The new strategy shifted emphasis from the air war against North Vietnam to the war in the south. By adopting it, the administration at least tacitly committed itself to expand its forces as the military situation required.

By this time Johnson recognized that achievement of U.S. objectives in Vietnam would require a sustained and costly commitment, but he still refused to submit his policies to public or congressional debate. Many administration officials shared a view widely accepted at the height of the Cold War that foreign policy issues were too complex and too important to be left to an indifferent and ignorant public and a divided and unwieldy Congress. LBJ seems to have feared that a declaration of war might trigger a Chinese or Soviet response or increase domestic pressures for an unlimited conflict in Vietnam. He particularly feared, as he later put it, that a

[49]McNamara to Johnson, April 21, 1965, Johnson Papers, National Security File, Country File: Vietnam, Box 13.

congressional debate on "that bitch of a war" would destroy "the woman I really loved—the Great Society."[50] The president's unparalleled knowledge of Congress and his confidence in his renowned powers of persuasion encouraged him to believe that he could expand the war without provoking a backlash. The repeated deference of the Congress to executive initiatives gave him no reason to anticipate a major challenge.

Johnson thus took the nation into war in Vietnam by indirection and dissimulation. The bombing was publicly justified as a response to the Pleiku attack and the broader pattern of North Vietnamese "aggression" rather than as a desperate attempt to halt the military and political deterioration in South Vietnam. The administration never publicly acknowledged the shift from reprisals to "sustained pressures." The dispatch of ground troops was explained solely in terms of the need to protect U.S. military installations. Not until June, when it crept out by accident in a press release, did officials publicly concede that American troops could undertake offensive operations.

Although the administration effectively concealed the direction of its policy, the obvious expansion of the war, particularly the bombing, attracted growing criticism. White House mail ran heavily against the bombing. A few newspapers joined the *New York Times* in warning of the cost of "lives lost, blood spilt and treasure wasted, of fighting a war on a jungle front 7,000 miles from the coast of California." Prominent Democratic senators such as Frank Church, Mike Mansfield, and George McGovern urged the president to search for a negotiated settlement. Professors at the University of Michigan, Harvard, and Syracuse conducted all-night teach-ins; students on various campuses held small protest meetings and distributed petitions against the bombing; and on April 17, in a portent of things to come, 20,000 students gathered in Washington to march in protest against the war.

Escalation also aroused widespread criticism abroad and brought forth, even from some of America's staunchest allies, appeals for restraint. United Nations Secretary General U Thant of Burma had been trying for months to arrange private talks between the United States and North Vietnam. When the administration ignored his overtures and initiated the bombing, he publicly

[50]Quoted in Kearns, *Johnson*, p. 251.

charged that Washington was withholding the truth from the American people. In early April, seventeen nonaligned nations issued an "urgent appeal" for negotiations without precondition. Great Britain, as cochair of the Geneva Conference, called upon the parties to the conflict to state their terms for a settlement. In a move that infuriated Johnson, Canadian Prime Minister Lester Pearson, speaking on American soil, appealed to Washington to stop the bombing and work for a peaceful settlement.

The administration quickly responded to its critics. White House aides organized "Target: College Campuses," sending their "best young troops" to speak at universities and bringing professors and student leaders to Washington for "seminars."[51] The president invited dissident members of Congress and newspaper editors and representatives of foreign governments in for sessions that sometimes lasted for three hours, vigorously defending his policies and reminding his visitors of past favors. Administration spokespersons publicly replied to critics, revealing from the start an abrasiveness and arrogance that would steadily widen the gap between Washington and opponents of the war. Addressing the American Society for International Law, Rusk expressed incredulity at the "stubborn disregard of plain facts by men who are supposed to be helping our young to learn . . . how to think."[52]

The administration also sought to disarm its critics by several well-publicized peace initiatives. In a speech at Johns Hopkins University on April 7, LBJ affirmed that the United States was prepared to enter into "unconditional discussions." He also dangled before Hanoi the offer of a billion-dollar economic development program for the Mekong River valley region, a program "on a scale even to dwarf our TVA," he claimed. "Ho [Chi Minh] will never be able to say 'No,'" a president accustomed to winning over recalcitrant senators with offers of dams and roads confidently exclaimed to an aide.[53] In early May, he approved a five-day bombing pause, accompanied by private messages to Hanoi indicating that the diminution of North Vietnamese and NLF military activity could lead to a scaling back of U.S. bombing.

[51]Jack Valenti to McGeorge Bundy, April 23, 1965, Johnson Papers, National Security File, Country File: Vietnam, Box 13.
[52]Quoted in *Time*, April 30, 1965, 29.
[53]*Public Papers of the Presidents of the United States, Lyndon B. Johnson, 1965* (Washington, D.C., 1966), 1: 394–399; Langguth, *Our Vietnam*, p. 355.

Johnson was undoubtedly sincere in his desire for peace, but the spring 1965 initiatives were designed as much to silence domestic and international critics as to set in motion determined efforts to gain a peace settlement. Despite his offer to participate in "unconditional discussions," the United States did not wish to begin serious negotiations at a time when its bargaining power was so weak. Indeed, it had not even begun internal discussions to formulate a negotiating position. The president also made clear in his April 7 speech that the United States would not compromise its fundamental objective of an independent South Vietnam, which meant, by implication, a non-Communist South Vietnam. And U.S. officials were aware that the North Vietnamese would not negotiate on that basis.

Hanoi was even less inclined than Washington to negotiate at this stage of the war. Ideology provided hard-liners such as Le Duan confidence in the ultimate triumph of their revolution. Hard experience made them leery of diplomacy. They vividly recalled the period after the 1954 Geneva Conference when, in their view, the great powers had cheated them of the victory they had won on the battlefield. Like the United States, North Vietnam feared that a willingness to negotiate might be interpreted by the other side as a sign of weakness. As with their American counterparts, party leaders harkened back to World War II for historical lessons. "We do not want a Munich which will spare us from war now but bring dishonor upon us," Premier Pham Van Dong told a French diplomat in April 1965.

Hanoi was especially disinclined toward negotiations at this time because it was certain it was winning. The go-for-broke strategy adopted in late 1963 appeared to be paying rich dividends. The NLF had intensified its political struggle in South Vietnam and had initiated a shift to big-unit military operations. In a relatively short time it had enlarged the liberated zone from the Central Highlands to the Mekong Delta, controlling about one-half the people and territory of South Vietnam. Big-unit operations increasingly exposed the vulnerability of the ARVN. In May 1965, at Binh Gia north of Saigon, NLF main forces mauled two South Vietnamese battalions, as at Ap Bac validating their ability to defeat large enemy units. Not surprisingly, Le Duan sensed an "opportune moment" when South Vietnam might be defeated before the United States could intervene in force, leaving it no choice but to withdraw. In response to Johnson's John Hopkins speech, North Vietnam did release a Four Point program for negotiations, but like the U.S. peace moves, this ploy was aimed mainly at world opinion. It denounced the U.S. bombing pause as a "worn-out trick of deceit and threat" and stepped up rather than reduced its military and political activities in South Vietnam.[54]

U.S. peace moves did help still domestic and foreign criticism, at least temporarily, and the administration used the respite to solidify congressional support. On May 4, Johnson requested $700 million for military operations in Vietnam and made clear that he would regard a vote for the appropriation as an endorsement of his policies. The basic decisions had already been made, of course, and the president did nothing to clarify the policy he was actually pursuing. It was very difficult for the legislators to vote against funds for troops in the field. Congress approved the request quickly and without dissent. Johnson would later cite this vote, along with the Tonkin Gulf Resolution, to counter those critics who said he had not given Congress an opportunity to pass on his Vietnam policy.

CULMINATION

In the three months after the May bombing pause, the Johnson administration took the final steps toward an open-ended commitment to war. Despite the bombing, continued increases in aid, and the infusion of ground forces, the military situation deteriorated drastically. At this most critical phase of the war, the ARVN verged on disintegration. Desertion rates among draftees in training centers ran as high as 50 percent. Discouraged by the failure of the bombing and increasingly inclined to "let the Americans do it," the officer corps became even more cautious. The high command was "close to anarchy" from internal squabbling and intrigue.[55] Bolstered by as many as four regiments of North Vietnamese regulars, the NLF took the offensive in May. It's resounding victory at Binh Gia increased Westmoreland's already pronounced doubts about the ARVN's capabilities, and the heavy losses completely upset his

[54]Elliott, *Vietnamse War,* pp. 217, 223, 225; Nguyen, *Hanoi's War,* pp. 73–79; Pierre Asselin, "We Don't Want a Munich: Hanoi's Diplomatic Strategy, 1965–1968" *Diplomatic History* 36 (June 2012): 548–561.

[55]William Depuy memorandum for the record, March 9, 1965, and memorandum to Westmoreland, April 13, 1965, William Depuy Papers, U.S. Army Military History Institute, Carlisle Barracks, Pa., Folder D(65).

plans for building it up. By the end of May, he concluded that major increments of U.S. forces were essential to avert defeat.

The political situation showed no signs of improvement. Khanh had continued to play a dominant role after his resignation in August 1964, resuming the premiership for a brief period and then taking command of the armed forces. After more than a year at or near the center of power, during which he had sharply exacerbated the divisions in South Vietnam, the embattled general finally withdrew in February 1965 and, to the relief of the Americans, accepted an appointment as "roving ambassador." Following an impossibly confusing series of coups and countercoups, a civilian government was formed by Phan Huy Quat, and relative quiet prevailed for a time. When Quat shook up his cabinet in May, however, the so-called Young Turks, Vice Air Marshal Ky and Gen. Nguyen Van Thieu, finally emerged from the shadows, dissolving the government and assuming power.

The new government, the fifth since the death of Diem, would survive far longer than any of its predecessors, but at the outset its future seemed uncertain. Thieu, who assumed command of the armed forces, was respected by the Americans as a capable military leader, and Taylor regarded him as a man of "considerable poise and judgment."[56] The prime minister, Ky, was another matter entirely. Customarily attired in a flashy flying suit with a bright purple scarf and an ivory-handled pistol hanging ostentatiously on his hip, the flamboyant, mustachioed air marshal had a well-earned reputation for "drinking, gambling and chasing women," as well as for speaking out of turn and using the air force for personal political intrigue.[57] The Americans found it hard to take Ky seriously and saw little cause for optimism in his rise to power. The Ky–Thieu directorate "seemed to all of us the bottom of the barrel, absolutely the bottom of the barrel," Assistant Secretary of State William Bundy later recalled.[58]

Under these circumstances, Johnson's advisers again began pressing for vigorous action to stave off certain defeat. Long frustrated by the restrictions on the bombing, Westmoreland, the Joint Chiefs, and Walt Rostow of the State Department urged intensification of the air war. The present level of bombing, they contended,

[56]Taylor, *Swords and Ploughshares*, p. 345.
[57]CIA memorandum, October 8, 1964, Johnson Papers, National Security File, Country File: Vietnam, Box 7.
[58]William Bundy oral history interview, Johnson Papers.

was merely inconveniencing Hanoi, and U.S. restraint had allowed it to strengthen its offensive and defensive capabilities. Rostow, in particular, argued that victory could be attained if the United States would strike North Vietnam's industrial base.

Westmoreland and the Joint Chiefs advocated a drastic expansion of American ground forces and the adoption of an offensive strategy. More certain than ever that South Vietnam lacked sufficient military strength to hold the line on its own, Westmoreland, with the support of the Joint Chiefs, requested an additional 150,000 U.S. troops in early June. Traditionalists in their attitude toward the use of military power, Westmoreland and the Joint Chiefs had opposed the enclave approach from the start and now insisted on an aggressive, offensive strategy. "You must take the fight to the enemy," Gen. Earle Wheeler, the JCS chairman, affirmed. "No one ever won a battle sitting on his ass."[59] Indeed, by the summer of 1965, even Taylor conceded, as he later put it, that "the strength of the enemy offensive had completely overcome my former reluctance to use American ground troops in general combat."[60]

Only Ball and Washington attorney Clark Clifford, a frequent personal adviser to Johnson, vigorously opposed a major commitment of U.S. ground forces. Ball expressed profound doubt that the United States could defeat the enemy "or even force them to the conference table on our terms, no matter how many hundred thousand white, foreign (U.S.) troops we deploy." He warned that approval of Westmoreland's proposals would lead to a "protracted war involving an open-ended commitment of U.S. forces, mounting U.S. casualties, no assurances of a satisfactory solution, and a serious danger of escalation at the end of the road." Once the United States was committed, there could be no turning back. "Our involvement will be so great that we cannot—without national humiliation—stop short of achieving our complete objectives." Clifford concurred, urging the president to keep U.S. forces to a minimum and probe "every serious avenue leading to a possible settlement." "It won't be what we want," he concluded, "but we can learn to live with it."[61]

[59]Henry Graff, *The Tuesday Cabinet* (Englewood Cliffs, N.J., 1970), p. 138.
[60]Taylor, *Swords and Ploughshares*, p. 347.
[61]Ball to Johnson, July 1, 1965, in Sheehan et al., *Pentagon Papers (NYT)*, pp. 449–454; Clifford to Johnson, May 17, 1965, Johnson Papers, National Security File, Country File: Vietnam, Box 16.

The clinching argument for a decision already virtually made was provided by McNamara after another whirlwind visit to Saigon in early July. The secretary of defense underscored the pessimistic reports from Westmoreland and Taylor and warned that to continue "holding on and playing for the breaks" would only defer the choice between escalation and withdrawal, perhaps until it was "too late to do any good." McNamara conceded that the expansion of American involvement would make a later decision to withdraw "even more difficult and costly than would be the case today." On the other hand, it might "stave off defeat in the short run and offer a good chance of producing a favorable settlement in the longer run." The secretary recommended the gradual deployment of an additional 100,000 combat forces.[62]

In late July, Johnson made his fateful decisions, setting the United States on a course from which it would not deviate for nearly three years and opening the way for eight years of bloody warfare in Vietnam. The president did not approve the all-out bombing campaign urged by Westmoreland and the Joint Chiefs. He and his civilian advisers continued to fear that a direct, full-scale attack on North Vietnam might provoke Chinese intervention. They also felt that the industrial base around Hanoi was a major trump card for the United States. The threat of its destruction might thus be more useful than destruction itself. The administration approved Westmoreland's request to use B-52 bombers for saturation attacks in South Vietnam and permitted a gradual intensification of the bombing of North Vietnam. Sorties increased from 3,600 in April to 4,800 in June, and would continue to grow thereafter. Johnson kept tight control over the bombing, personally approving the targets and restricting attacks to the area south of the twentieth parallel.

At the same time, the president authorized a major commitment of ground forces and a new strategy for their deployment. Determined to prevail in Vietnam and increasingly alarmed by the reports of military and political decline, he authorized in July the immediate deployment of 50,000 troops to South Vietnam. Recognizing that this would not be enough, he privately agreed to commit another 50,000 before the end of the year and, implicitly at least, committed himself to furnish whatever additional forces might be

---

[62]Johnson, *Vantage Point*, pp. 145–146.

needed later. Johnson also authorized Westmoreland to "commit U.S. troops to combat independent of or in conjunction with GVN forces in any situation when . . . their use is necessary to strengthen the relative position of GVN forces."[63] These decisions mark the culmination of a process initiated in December 1964. In July 1965, the president made an open-ended commitment to employ American military forces as the situation demanded. And by giving Westmoreland a free hand, he cleared the way for the United States to assume the burden of fighting in South Vietnam.

Significantly, in making these decisions, the Johnson administration all but ignored the object of its concern, its South Vietnamese ally. The Saigon government was not consulted on the decisions to bomb North Vietnam and introduce major increments of U.S. combat forces. The most that was done was to brief its leaders on the steps being taken and request their concurrence. Former ambassador Bui Diem later noted the absence of communication between allies, the "unself-conscious arrogance" of the Americans, and the impotence of the South Vietnamese, who acquiesced in the Americanization of the war against their better judgment and despite the fact that they had just emerged from years of foreign domination. "The Americans came in like bulldozers," Bui Diem observed, "and the South Vietnamese followed their lead without a word of dissent, for the most part without a thought of dissent."[64]

The president also refused to inform his own people. Some U.S. officials implored him to place the July decisions squarely before the nation. The JCS pressed for mobilization of the reserves and calling up the National Guard to make clear, as Wheeler later put it, that the United States was not becoming engaged in "some two-penny military adventure."[65] McNamara was sufficiently concerned about the domestic political implications to urge Johnson to declare a state of national emergency and ask Congress for an increase in taxes—in short, without seeking a declaration of war, to put the nation on a war footing. Johnson himself apparently toyed with the idea of securing another congressional resolution explicitly endorsing his policies. Some of his advisers proposed a "full scenario" of actions to explain the war to the public and promote public support. "How

[63]Sheehan et al., *Pentagon Papers (NYT)*, p. 412.
[64]Bui Diem with David Chanoff, *In the Jaws of History* (Boston, 1987), pp. 127, 153.
[65]Earle Wheeler oral history interview, Johnson Papers.

do you send young men there in great numbers without telling why?" former ambassador Henry Cabot Lodge Jr. asked.[66]

After extensive deliberation, the president rejected all such steps. His attorney general assured him that he had the power to commit forces without going to Congress.[67] He continued to fear that anything resembling a declaration of war might provoke the Soviet Union and China. Most important, his civil rights and Medicare bills were then at crucial stages in the legislative process, and congressional approval was pending on numerous other proposals. Johnson was determined to establish his place in history through the achievement of sweeping domestic reforms. He feared that seeking from Congress authority to wage war in Vietnam would destroy his dreams of a Great Society at home. He thus informed his staff that he wished the decisions implemented in a "low-keyed manner in order (a) to avoid an abrupt challenge to the Communists, and (b) to avoid undue concern and excitement in the Congress and in domestic public opinion."[68]

To avoid undue excitement, the president continued to deceive the nation as to the significance of the steps he was taking. To make his decisions more palatable to potential waverers, he and his aides issued dire warnings that failure to act decisively would result in playing into the hands of those who wanted to take drastic measures, the "Goldwater crowd," who were "more numerous, more powerful and more dangerous than the fleabite professors."[69] To appease skeptics such as Mansfield, Johnson implied that he would give equal priority to seeking a diplomatic settlement, without divulging his certainty that such efforts were doomed to failure. Although he had approved the immediate deployment of 100,000 troops followed by another 100,000 in 1966, he revealed publicly only that he was sending 50,000. He made that move as painless as possible by refusing to call up the reserves and increase taxes. He announced his decision on July 28 at a noon press conference instead of at prime time and lumped it in with other items in a

---

[66]Quoted in VanDeMark, *Into the Quagmire*, p. 207.
[67]Nicholas Katzenbach to Johnson, June 10, 1965, Johnson Papers, National Security File, Country File: Vietnam, Box 17.
[68]Benjamin Read memorandum, July 23, 1965, Johnson Papers, National Security File, Country File: Vietnam, Box 16.
[69]McGeorge Bundy to Johnson, July 14, 1965, Johnson Papers, Diary Backup File, Box 19.

way that obscured its significance. He continued to deny that he had authorized any change in policy and did not give a clear indication—even in the sense that he understood it at the time—of what lay ahead. His tactics reflected his continuing determination to achieve his goals in Vietnam without sacrificing the Great Society and his certainty that he could accomplish both tasks at once.

The July decisions represented the culmination of a year and a half of agonizing over America's Vietnam policy and stemmed logically from the administration's refusal to accept the consequences of withdrawal. Johnson feared the domestic consequences of failure in Vietnam. He and his top advisers also believed that to withdraw from Vietnam would encourage disorder throughout the world and drastically weaken American influence. Men of action and achievement, leaders of a nation with an unbroken record of success, they were unwilling to face the prospect of failure. If the United States pulled out of Vietnam, Johnson warned on one occasion, "it might as well give up everywhere else—pull out of Berlin, Japan, South America."[70]

In making the July commitments, the administration saw itself moving cautiously between the extremes of withdrawal and total war; it sought, in Johnson's words, to do "what will be enough, but not too much." The president and his advisers did not seek the defeat of North Vietnam. They did not "speak of conquest on the battlefield . . . as men from time immemorial had talked of victory," the historian Henry Graff recorded. They sought rather to inflict sufficient pain to compel the enemy to negotiate on terms acceptable to the United States—in Johnson's Texas metaphor, to apply sufficient force until the enemy "sobers up and unloads his pistol."[71]

Displaying the consummate political skill that had become his trademark, Johnson in the last week of July molded a consensus for his Vietnam policy. He appears to have been committed from the outset to take steps that would give the United States "the maximum protection at the least cost."[72] During the week of July 21–28,

[70]John D. Pomfret memorandum of conversation with Johnson, June 24, 1965, Arthur Krock Papers, Seeley G. Mudd Manuscript Library, Princeton, N.J., Box 59.
[71]Graff, *Tuesday Cabinet*, pp. 54, 59.
[72]Summary notes of National Security Council meeting, June 11, 1965, Johnson Papers, National Security File, NSC Meetings, Box 1.

however, he gave the JCS and Ball their days in court, listening carefully to their arguments and raising numerous probing questions before rejecting their proposals for large-scale escalation and withdrawal.[73] In meetings with the congressional leadership, he promised conservatives to hold the line in Vietnam, while reassuring liberals that he would not permit the war to get out of hand. "I'm going up old Ho Chi Minh's leg an inch at a time," he told Senator George McGovern.[74] Johnson's middle course probably reflected the ambivalent aspirations of the American public and Congress. The president went to war with support that appeared to be solid.

As the president himself had predicted, getting into war would be much easier than getting out. The administration's decisions of 1964 and 1965 were based on two fatal miscalculations. In seeking to do what would be "enough but not too much," LBJ and his advisers never analyzed with any real precision how much would be enough. When Ball warned that it might take as many as a half million troops, McNamara dismissed the figure as "outrageous."[75] JCS estimates of the forces needed and time required turned out to be not far off the mark. But the president devoted his energy to neutralizing the military politically rather than seeking their views; the Joint Chiefs hesitated to press on him the truth as they saw it for fear it might deter him from war. They hoped, once they got a foot in the door, to chip away at the presidential restrictions until they got the type of war they wanted. The decisions of December 1964 through July 1965 also took place in a strategic vacuum, scant consideration being given to a precise formulation of goals and how U.S. power might best be used to achieve them.[76] Leaders of the most powerful nation in the history of the world, many U.S. officials could not conceive that a small, backward country could stand up against them. It would be like a congressional filibuster, Johnson once speculated, "enormous resistance at first, then a steady whittling away, then Ho [Chi Minh] hurrying to get it over with."[77]

[73]Larry Berman, *Planning a Tragedy: The Americanization of the War in Vietnam* (New York, 1982), pp. 128–129.
[74]George McGovern, *Grassroots* (New York, 1977), pp. 104–105.
[75]Benjamin Read oral history interview, Johnson Papers.
[76]McMaster, *Dereliction of Duty*, pp. 257, 261, 275, 301.
[77]Kearns, *Johnson*, p. 266.

Miscalculating the costs that the United States would incur, the administration could not help but overestimate the willingness of the nation to pay. On July 27, 1965, Mansfield penned a long, eloquent, and prophetic warning to his old friend and political mentor. He advised Johnson that Congress and the nation supported him because he was president, not because they understood or were deeply committed to his policy in Vietnam, and that there lingered beneath the surface a confusion and uncertainty that could in time explode into outright opposition.[78] Mansfield correctly perceived the flimsiness of Johnson's backing. As long as U.S. objectives could be obtained at minimal cost, Americans were willing to stay in Vietnam. When the war turned out to last much longer and cost much more than had been anticipated, however, the president's support would wither away. The advocates of escalation and withdrawal he had parried so skillfully in July 1965 would turn on him.

Johnson disregarded Mansfield's admonitions. After months of uncertainty, he had set his course. In July 1965, quietly and without fanfare, he launched the United States on what would become its longest, most frustrating, and most divisive war. The nation responded with a sense of relief that the steps taken were not more costly and drastic. Reflecting the mood of the moment, *Newsweek* noted the absence of "hot tides of national anger" and remarked on the "strange, almost passionless war" the United States was waging in Vietnam. "There are no songs written about it," the magazine concluded, "and the chances that any will seem remote," a prophecy that turned out to be tragically off the mark.[79]

[78]Mansfield to Johnson, July 27, 1965, Johnson Papers, National Security File, National Security Council Histories: Deployment of Major U.S. Forces to Vietnam, July 1965, Box 40.
[79]*Newsweek*, August 9, 1965, 17–18.

President Johnson
The commander-in-chief has just listened to a
tape sent from Vietnam by his son-in-law
Charles Robb describing an ambush in which
GIs were killed. His growing distress at the
inconclusive and intractable war mirrored that
of the country in 1967.
LBJ Library

CHAPTER 5

On the Tiger's Back

The United States at War, 1965–1967

While visiting the aircraft carrier *Ranger* off the coast of Vietnam in 1965, Robert Shaplen overheard a fellow journalist remark: "They just ought to show this ship to the Vietcong—that would make them give up."[1] From Lyndon Johnson in the White House to the GI in the field, the United States went to war in 1965 in much this frame of mind. The president had staked everything on the unexamined assumption that the enemy could be quickly brought to bay by the application of American military might. The first combat troops to enter Vietnam shared similar views. When "we marched into the rice paddies on that damp March afternoon," Marine Lt. Philip Caputo later wrote, "we carried, along with our packs and rifles, the implicit conviction that the Viet Cong would be quickly beaten."[2]

Although by no means unique to the Vietnam War, this optimism does much to explain the form that American participation took. The United States never developed a strategy appropriate for the war it was fighting, in part because it assumed that the mere application of its vast military power would be sufficient. The failure of one level of force led to the next and then the next, until the war attained a degree of destructiveness no one would have thought possible in 1965. Most important, the optimism with which the nation went to war accounts more than anything else for the great frustration that subsequently developed in and out of

---

[1]Robert Shaplen, *The Lost Revolution: The U.S. in Vietnam, 1946–1966* (New York, 1966), p. 186.
[2]Philip Caputo, *A Rumor of War* (New York, 1977), p. xii.

government. Failure never comes easily, but it comes especially hard when success at little cost is anticipated.

Within two years, the optimism of 1965 had given way to deep and painful frustration. By 1967, the United States had nearly a half million combat troops in Vietnam. It had dropped more bombs than in all theaters in World War II and was spending more than $2 billion per month on the war. Some American officials persuaded themselves that progress had been made, but the undeniable fact was that the war continued. Lyndon Johnson thus faced an agonizing dilemma. Unable to end the war by military means and unwilling to make the concessions necessary to secure a negotiated settlement, he discovered belatedly what George Ball had warned in 1964: "Once on the tiger's back we cannot be sure of picking the place to dismount."

American strategy in Vietnam was improvised rather than carefully designed and contained numerous contradictions. The United States went to war in 1965 to prevent the collapse of South Vietnam, but it was never able to relate its tremendous military power to the fundamental task of establishing a viable government in Saigon. The administration insisted that the war must be kept limited—the Soviet Union and China must not be provoked to intervene—but the president counted on a quick and relatively painless victory to avert unrest at home. That these goals might not be compatible apparently never occurred to Johnson and his civilian advisers. The United States injected its military power directly into the struggle to cripple the insurgency and persuade North Vietnam to stop its "aggression." The administration vastly underestimated the enemy's capacity to resist, however, and did not confront the crucial question of what would be required to achieve its goals until it was bogged down in a bloody stalemate.

Although the president and his civilian advisers set limits on the conduct of the war, they did not provide firm strategic guidelines for the use of American power. Left on its own, the military fought the conventional war for which it was prepared, without reference to the peculiar conditions in Vietnam. Westmoreland and the Joint Chiefs chafed under the restraints imposed by the civilians. Sensitive to Gen. Douglas MacArthur's fate in Korea, however, they would not challenge the president directly or air their case in public. On the other hand, they refused to develop a strategy that accommodated the restrictions imposed by the White House;

instead, they attempted to break the restrictions down one by one until they got what they wanted. The result was considerable ambiguity in purpose and method, growing civil–military tension, and a steady escalation that brought increasing costs and uncertain gain.[3]

ROLLING THUNDER

The United States relied heavily on bombing.[4] Airpower doctrine emphasized that the destruction of an enemy's war-making capacity would force that enemy to come to terms. The limited success of strategic bombing as applied on a large scale in World War II and on a more restricted scale in Korea raised serious questions about the validity of this assumption. The conditions prevailing in Vietnam, a primitive country with few crucial targets, might have suggested even more questions. The air force and navy advanced unrealistic expectations about what airpower might accomplish, however, and clung to them long after experience had proven them unjustified. The civilian leadership accepted the military's arguments, at least to a point, because bombing was cheaper in lives lost and therefore more palatable at home, and because it seemed to offer a quick and comparatively easy solution to a complex problem. Initiated in early 1965 as much from the lack of alternatives as from anything else, the bombing of North Vietnam was expanded over the next two years in the vain hope that it would check infiltration into the South and force North Vietnam to the conference table.

The air war gradually assumed massive proportions. The president firmly resisted the Joint Chiefs' proposal for a knockout blow, but as each phase of the bombing failed to produce results, he expanded the list of targets and the number of strikes. Sorties against North Vietnam increased from 25,000 in 1965 to 79,000 in 1966 and 108,000 in 1967; bomb tonnage increased from 63,000 to 136,000 to 226,000. Throughout 1965, ROLLING THUNDER concentrated on military bases, supply depots, and infiltration routes in the southern part of the country. From early 1966 on, air strikes

[3]George C. Herring, *LBJ and Vietnam: A Different Kind of War* (Austin, Tex., 1994), pp. 26–62.
[4]The best analyses of the air war are Mark Clodfelter, *The Limits of Air Power: The American Bombing of North Vietnam* (New York, 1989), and Earl H. Tilford Jr., *Setup: What the Air Force Did in Vietnam and Why* (Maxwell Air Force Base, Ala., 1991).

were increasingly directed against the North Vietnamese industrial and transportation systems and moved steadily northward. In the summer of 1966, Johnson authorized massive strikes against petroleum storage facilities and transportation networks. A year later, he permitted attacks on steel factories, power plants, and other targets around Hanoi and Haiphong as well as on previously restricted areas along the Chinese border.

The bombing inflicted an estimated $600-million damage on a nation still struggling to develop a viable, modern economy. The air attacks crippled North Vietnam's industrial productivity and disrupted its agriculture. Some cities were virtually leveled, others severely damaged. Giant B-52s, carrying payloads of 58,000 pounds, relentlessly attacked the areas leading to the Ho Chi Minh Trail, leaving the countryside scarred with huge craters and littered with debris. The bombing was not directed against the civilian population, and the administration publicly maintained that civilian casualties were minimal. But the CIA estimated that in 1967 total casualties ran as high as 2,800 per month and admitted that these figures were heavily weighted with civilians; McNamara privately conceded that civilian casualties were as high as 1,000 per month during periods of intensive bombing. A British diplomat later recalled that by the fall of 1967 there were signs among the civilian population of the major cities of widespread malnutrition and declining morale.[5]

The manner in which airpower was used in Vietnam virtually ensured that it would not achieve its objectives. Whether, as the Joint Chiefs argued, a massive, unrestricted air war would have worked remains much in doubt. In fact, the United States had destroyed most major targets by 1967 with no demonstrable effect on the war. Nevertheless, the administration's gradualist approach gave Hanoi time to construct an air defense system, protect its vital resources, and develop alternative modes of transportation. Gradualism encouraged the North Vietnamese to persist despite the damage inflicted upon them.

North Vietnam demonstrated great ingenuity and dogged perseverance in coping with the bombing. Civilians were evacuated from the cities and dispersed across the countryside; industries and

---

[5]Raphael Littauer and Norman Uphoff (eds.), *The Air War in Indochina* (Boston, 1972), pp. 39–43. For a firsthand account of the impact of the bombing, see John Colvin, "Hanoi in My Time," *Washington Quarterly* (Spring 1981): 138–154.

The Mu Gia Pass
The Mu Gia Pass through the Annamite cordillera was a major entry point from North Vietnam into Laos on the fabled Ho Chi Minh Trail. An estimated 66 percent of North Vietnamese truck traffic went through it. Identifying the pass as a point of possible enemy vulnerability, the United States bombed it relentlessly, leaving the moonscape portrayed here in 1968. After each bombing, the North Vietnamese quickly repaired the damage, and the Mu Gia Pass was never closed for any significant length of time.
© *Hoang Van Sac/AP Images*

storage facilities were scattered and in many cases concealed in caves and under the ground. The government claimed to have dug more than 30,000 miles of tunnels, and in heavily bombed areas the people spent much of their lives underground. An estimated 500,000 North Vietnamese, many of them women and children, worked full-time repairing bridges and railroads. Piles of gravel were kept along the major roadways, enabling "Youth Shock Brigades" to fill craters within hours after the bombs fell. Concrete and steel bridges were replaced by ferries and pontoon bridges made of bamboo stalks, which were sunk during the day to avoid detection.

Truck drivers covered vehicles with palm fronds and banana leaves and traveled at night, without headlights, guided only by white markers along the roads. B-52s blasted the narrow roads through the Mu Gia Pass leading to the Ho Chi Minh Trail, but to American amazement trucks moved back through within several days. "Caucasians cannot really imagine what ant labor can do," one American remarked with a mixture of frustration and admiration.[6]

Losses in military equipment, raw materials, and vehicles were more than offset by drastically increased aid from the Soviet Union and China. U.S. escalation did not force the two Communist rivals back into a close alliance, as George Ball had warned. Nevertheless, along with their increasingly heated rivalry, it permitted Hanoi to play one against the other to get increased aid and prevent either from securing predominant influence.

Until 1965, the Soviet Union had remained detached from the conflict, but the new leaders who overthrew premier Nikita Khrushchev in October 1964 took a much greater interest in Vietnam, and U.S. escalation presented challenges and opportunities they could not ignore. The bombing created a need for sophisticated military equipment that only the Soviets could provide, giving them a chance to wean North Vietnam from dependence on China. At a time when the Chinese were loudly proclaiming Soviet indifference to the fate of world revolution, the direct threat to a Communist state posed by U.S. escalation required the Russians to prove *their* credibility. The expanding war provided opportunities for the USSR to undermine U.S. prestige, tie down both of its major rivals, test its own weapons under combat conditions, and analyze the latest U.S. military hardware. The Soviets were nervous about escalation of the war and especially feared a nuclear confrontation like the 1962 Cuban missile crisis. They resented North Vietnam's stubborn independence, bemoaned the fact that their massive aid did not purchase commensurate influence with Hanoi, and complained of the way the North Vietnamese used their freighters in Haiphong harbor as shields against U.S. bombing. But the Russians steadily expanded their support. Up to January 1, 1968, they furnished more than 1.8 billion rubles in assistance to North

---

[6]Quoted in Townsend Hoopes, *The Limits of Intervention* (New York, 1970), p. 79. For North Vietnam's response to the air war, see Jon M. Van Dyke, *North Vietnam's Strategy for Survival* (Palo Alto, Calif., 1972).

Vietnam, 60 percent of which was for military aid that included such modern weapons as fighter planes, surface-to-air missiles (SAMs), and tanks. Three thousand Soviet technicians took direct part in the war effort, some of them manning antiaircraft batteries and SAM sites and actually shooting down U.S. aircraft.[7]

For China also, the war with the United States—especially the air war—presented challenges and opportunities. The Chinese had supported North Vietnam since the Geneva Conference. At a time when they were asserting leadership of the world revolutionary movement, they could not help but view U.S. escalation as a "test case for 'true communism.'" They deemed the defense of North Vietnam essential to their own security. By rallying his people to meet an external threat, party chairman Mao Zedong also sought to mobilize support for his radicalization of China's domestic policies. Like the Soviets, the Chinese feared a confrontation with the United States, and they had vivid memories of losses suffered in the Korean War. They therefore let it be known through public statements and intermediaries that should the United States invade North Vietnam they would send their own forces. They also made clear through words and deeds their full support for their ally. Under agreements worked out in 1964 and 1965, approximately 320,000 Chinese engineering and artillery troops helped the Vietnamese build new highways, railroads, and bridges to facilitate the transport of supplies from China and manned antiaircraft positions to defend the existing network from American attack. The Chinese also provided huge quantities of vehicles, small arms and ammunition, uniforms and shoes, rice and other foodstuffs, even volleyball and table tennis equipment for the recreation of North Vietnamese troops. In contrast to the First Indochina War, the wary Vietnamese did not permit their powerful allies to control their decision making. They developed into an art form the exploitation of divisions between the Soviet Union and China. Although eager supplicants, they were also tough negotiators who held out for what they most needed rather than accept outright what others offered. Assistance from the Soviet Union, China, and ten other Communist-bloc nations made up roughly 60 percent of North Vietnam's budget between 1965 and 1967, thus sustaining its

[7]Ilya V. Gaiduk, "The Vietnam War and Soviet-American Relations, 1964–1973: New Russian Evidence," *Cold War International History Project Bulletin* (Winter 1995/1996): 232, 250–258.

war economy. It helped North Vietnam counter U.S. air attacks, replaced equipment lost through the bombing, and freed Hanoi to send more of its own troops to the South. The consistent underestimation of its volume and importance by U.S. intelligence led top officials to believe that North Vietnam was more vulnerable to U.S. military pressure than it was.[8]

Other factors reduced the effectiveness of the bombing. Heavy rains and impenetrable fog forced curtailment of missions during the long monsoon season, from September to May. Pilots claimed to be able to bomb with "surgical" precision, but the weather and techniques that had not advanced much since World War II made for considerable inaccuracy. Many targets had to be bombed repeatedly before they were finally destroyed. As they came closer to Hanoi and Haiphong, U.S. aircraft ran up against a deadly air defense system. Soviet SAMs and MiG fighters did not score a high kill rate, but they threw off bombing patterns and forced pilots down to altitudes where they confronted heavy flak and small-arms fire. One U.S. pilot described North Vietnam as the "center of hell with Hanoi as its hub."[9]

Despite the extensive damage inflicted on North Vietnam, the bombing did not achieve its goals. It absorbed a great deal of personnel and resources that might have been diverted to other military uses. It hampered the movement of troops and supplies to the South, and its proponents argued that infiltration would have been much greater without it. Official American estimates nevertheless conceded that infiltration increased from about 35,000 soldiers in 1965 to as many as 90,000 in 1967, even as the bombing grew heavier and more destructive. North Vietnamese Army (NVA) and National Liberation Front (NLF) troops required only 34 tons of supplies a day from outside South Vietnam, "a trickle too small for airpower to stop."[10] It is impossible to gauge with any accuracy the psychological impact of the bombing on North Vietnam, but it did not destroy Hanoi's

---

[8]James G. Hershberg and Chen Jian, "Informing the Enemy: Sino-American 'Signaling' and the Vietnam War," in Priscilla Roberts, ed., *Behind the Bamboo Curtain* (Stanford, Calif., 2006), pp. 193–257; Harish C. Mehta, "Soviet Biscuit Factories and Chinese Financial Grants: North Vietnam's Economic Diplomacy in 1967 and 1968," *Diplomatic History* 36 (April 2012): 316, 318–320, 324.

[9]Quoted in Clodfelter, *Limits of Air Power*, pp. 131–132.

[10]Tilford, *Setup*, p. 113.

determination to prevail. It gave the leadership a powerful rallying cry to mobilize the civilian population in support of the war.

By 1967, the United States was paying a heavy price for no more than marginal gains. The cost in bombs of a B-52 mission ran to $30,000 per sortie. The direct cost of the air war, including operation of the aircraft, munitions, and replacement of planes, was estimated at more than $1.7 billion during 1965 and 1966, a period when aircraft losses exceeded 500. Overall, between 1965 and 1968 the United States lost 950 aircraft costing roughly $6 billion. According to one estimate, for each $1 of damage inflicted on North Vietnam, the United States spent $9.60. The costs cannot be measured in dollars alone. Captured U.S. fliers gave Hanoi hostages who would assume increasing importance in the stalemated war. The continued pounding of a small, backward country by the world's wealthiest and most advanced nation gave the North Vietnamese a propaganda advantage they exploited quite effectively. Opposition to the war at home increasingly focused on the bombing, which, in the eyes of many critics, was at best inefficient, at worst immoral.

SEARCH AND DESTROY

American ground operations in the South also escalated dramatically between 1965 and 1967. Even before he had significant numbers of combat forces at his disposal, Westmoreland had formulated the strategy he would employ until early 1968. It was a strategy of attrition, the major objective of which was to locate and eliminate NLF and North Vietnamese regular units. Westmoreland has vigorously denied that he was motivated by any "Napoleonic impulse to maneuver units and hark to the sound of cannon," but "search and destroy," as his strategy came to be called, did reflect traditional U.S. Army doctrine. In Westmoreland's view, North Vietnam's decision to commit large units to the war left him no choice but to proceed along these lines. He did not have sufficient forces to police the entire country, nor was it enough simply to contain the enemy's main units. "They had to be pounded with artillery and bombs and eventually brought to battle on the ground if they were not forever to remain a threat." The helicopter provided a means to quickly deliver large numbers of U.S. troops over difficult terrain to get at enemy forces, and "airmobility" became a major instrument of search and destroy. Westmoreland's aim was to attain a "crossover point" where the United States was killing enemy forces faster than they could be replaced. That achieved, he reasoned, the South Vietnamese government could stabilize its position and pacify the countryside. The adversary would have to negotiate on terms acceptable to the United States.[11]

Westmoreland's aggressive strategy required steadily increasing commitments of personnel. To secure some of the needed troops and give international respectability to its commitment in Vietnam, the Johnson administration mounted a "many flags" campaign among its allies, pressing them to commit forces and dangling subsidies, arms packages, and trade deals as inducements. The president himself got into the act, warning allied diplomats in 1967 of a "brush fire" in their backyard. If "you're wise . . . ," he advised them, "you'll help me stamp it out before it reaches you. It will reach you," he concluded ominously, "before it reaches me."[12]

The results, from the U.S. perspective, were disappointing. America's European allies saw in a way the Johnson administration never did the dubiousness of its cause in Vietnam. They questioned whether the stakes were as high as the United States claimed or whether its credibility was really on the line. On the contrary, they feared that America might suffer more from a failed intervention than from a face-saving withdrawal. In any event, they doubted, given the weakness of South Vietnam, that even a massive injection of U.S. power could do more than delay an inevitable defeat. Except for France, America's major European allies did not openly oppose U.S. policy in Vietnam, but they adamantly refused, despite relentless pressure and Johnson's personal arm-twisting, to provide even the token military forces the administration requested. "Are we the sole defenders of freedom in the world," the presidency plaintively asked in 1965.[13]

---

[11]William C. Westmoreland, *A Soldier Reports* (Garden City, N.Y., 1976), pp. 149–150; Gregory A. Daddis, *No Sure Victory: Measuring U.S. Army Effectiveness and Progress in the Vietnam War* (New York, 2011), pp. 17, 91–92.

[12]New Zealand embassy, Washington, to Ministry of External Affairs, November 3, 1967, EA 478/4/8, Records of the New Zealand Ministry of External Relations and Trade, Wellington, N.Z.

[13]George C. Herring, "Fighting Without Allies," in Marc Jason Gilbert, ed., *Why the North Won the Vietnam War* (New York, 2002), p. 80.

Even in the Pacific region the results were disappointing. The most hawkish of the allies at the outset of the war, Australia sent 8,000 soldiers and paid for them itself. Although dependent on the United States for its very survival, South Korea drove a hard economic bargain for the 60,000 troops it provided. Others were reluctant to refuse but also uneager to make large commitments. New Zealand doubted that the United States could achieve its goals in Vietnam but recognized that U.S. departure from the region would leave a "strategic task of frightening dimensions." To appease Washington, Wellington sent an artillery battery as a token. Thailand also committed a small "volunteer" contingent; the Philippines an engineering battalion; and Nationalist China small, highly trained units for covert operations. As the war dragged on inconclusively and became more unpopular throughout the world, even the Pacific allies grew more reluctant to succumb to U.S. blandishments, pleading budgetary constraints and domestic politics as excuses. When Maxwell Taylor and Clark Clifford visited the region in 1967 seeking additional forces, they found allied leaders "friendly but usually cautious and defensive," talking more about what they had done in the past than about what they would do in the future. Allied forces in Vietnam peaked at around 71,000 in early 1969.[14]

The United States thus provided the bulk of the forces, and even before the 1965 buildup had been completed, Westmoreland requested sufficient additional troops to bring the total to 450,000 by the end of 1966. Although the administration retained tight control over the air war, it gave its field commander broad discretion in developing and executing the ground strategy. It saw no choice but to give him most of the troops he asked for. In June 1966, the president approved a force level of 431,000 to be reached by mid-1967. While these deployments were being approved, Westmoreland was developing requests for an increase to 542,000 troops by the end of 1967.

Furnished with thousands of fresh American troops and a massive arsenal of modern weaponry, Westmoreland took the war to the enemy. He accomplished what has properly been called a "logistical miracle," constructing virtually overnight the facilities to handle huge numbers of U.S. troops and enormous volumes of

[14]Clifford-Taylor report, August 5, 1967, Johnson Papers, Lyndon Baines Johnson Library, Austin, Tex., National Security File, Country File: Vietnam, Box 91.

Total U.S. Military Personnel in South Vietnam

Date	Army	Navy	Marine Corps	Air Force	Coast Guard	Total
31 Dec. 1960	800	15	2	68	—	About 900
31 Dec. 1961	2,100	100	5	1,000	—	3,205
30 June 1962	5,900	300	700	2,100	—	9,000
31 Dec. 1962	7,900	500	500	2,400	—	11,300
30 June 1963	10,200	600	600	4,000	—	15,400
31 Dec. 1963	10,100	800	800	4,600	—	16,300
30 June 1964	9,900	1,000	600	5,000	—	16,500
31 Dec. 1964	14,700	1,100	900	6,600	—	23,300
30 June 1965	27,300	3,800	18,100	10,700	—	59,900
31 Dec. 1965	116,800	8,400	38,200	20,600	300	184,300
30 June 1966	160,000	17,000	53,700	36,400	400	267,500
31 Dec. 1966	239,400	23,300	69,200	52,900	500	385,300
30 June 1967	285,700	28,500	78,400	55,700	500	448,800
31 Dec. 1967	319,500	31,700	78,000	55,900	500	485,600
30 June 1968	354,300	35,600	83,600	60,700	500	534,700
31 Dec. 1968	359,800	36,100	81,400	58,400	400	536,100
30 Apr. 1969	363,300	36,500	81,800	61,400	400	*543,400
30 June 1969	360,500	35,800	81,500	60,500	400	538,700
31 Dec. 1969	331,100	30,200	55,100	58,400	400	475,200
30 June 1970	298,600	25,700	39,900	50,500	200	414,900
31 Dec. 1970	249,600	16,700	25,100	43,100	100	334,600
30 June 1971	190,500	10,700	500	37,400	100	239,200
31 Dec. 1971	119,700	7,600	600	28,800	100	156,800
30 June 1972	31,800	2,200	1,400	11,500	100	47,000
31 Dec. 1972	13,800	1,500	1,200	7,600	100	24,200
30 June 1973	**	**	**	**	**	**

*Peak strength.
**Totals for all five services combined less than 250.
Source: U.S., Department of Defense, OASD (Comptroller), Directorate for Information Operations, March 19, 1974.

equipment. The Americans who fought in Vietnam were the best-fed, best-clothed, and best-equipped army the nation had ever sent to war.

In what Westmoreland described as the "most sophisticated war in history," the United States attempted to exploit its technological superiority to cope with the peculiar problems of a guerrilla war. To locate an ever-elusive enemy, the military used small, portable radar units and "people sniffers" that picked up the odor of human urine. IBM 1430 computers were programmed to predict likely times and places of enemy attacks. Herbicides were used on a wide scale and with devastating ecological consequences to deprive the guerrillas of natural cover. C-123 RANCHHAND crews, with the sardonic motto "Only You Can Prevent Forests," sprayed more than 100 million pounds of chemicals such as Agent Orange over millions of acres of forests, destroying an estimated one-half of South Vietnam's timberlands and leaving horrendous human and ecological costs. C-47 transports were converted into terrifying gunships (called "Puff the Magic Dragon" after a popular folk song of the era) that could fire 18,000 rounds a minute.

The United States relied heavily on artillery and airpower to dislodge the enemy at minimal cost, and it waged a furious war against NLF and North Vietnamese base areas. "The solution in Vietnam is more bombs, more shells, more napalm . . . till the other side cracks and gives up," observed Gen. William Depuy, one of the principal architects of "search and destroy."[15] From 1965 to 1967, South Vietnamese and U.S. airmen dropped more than a million tons of bombs on South Vietnam, twice the tonnage dropped on the North. Retaliatory bombing was employed against some villages suspected of harboring guerrillas. Airpower was used to support forces in battle according to the "pile-on concept," in which U.S. troops encircled enemy units and called in the aircraft. "Blow the hell out of him and police up," one officer described it.[16] A much greater proportion of the air strikes comprised what was loosely called interdiction—massive, indiscriminate raids, primarily by B-52s, against enemy base areas and logistics networks. Entire areas of South Vietnam were designated

[15]Quoted in Daniel Ellsberg, *Papers on the War* (New York, 1972), p. 234.
[16]Quoted in Littauer and Uphoff, *Air War*, p. 52.

Free Fire Zones, which could be pulverized without regard for the inhabitants.

North Vietnam more than matched U.S. escalation. If the United States fought a limited war for limited objectives, Hanoi, by contrast, fought an all-out war for national survival and victory. Although their bold gamble had backfired, its leaders stuck doggedly to their strategy. They mobilized the entire resources of their nation for what they called the "Anti-American Resistance for National Salvation" and pledged to fight until the enemy was defeated and South Vietnam liberated. "The greater the escalation of USA troops," premier Pham Van Dong boldly proclaimed, "the greater would be [our] victory." At least at the outset, the war was popular in the North. The initial mobilization program doubled the number of NVA troops from around 200,000 to more than 400,000. North Vietnam significantly stepped up the infiltration of men and supplies into the South. Recognizing that their very survival was at stake, North Vietnamese leaders developed a sophisticated strategy of *dau tranh* ("struggle") that sought to integrate the military, political, and diplomatic dimensions of war. North Vietnamese and NLF strategists often disagreed on how aggressively to pursue the war in the South and to what extent the North Vietnamese rear area should be put at risk. But they concurred that the South Vietnamese government and army and American public opinion were their enemies' most vulnerable points. They attempted through intensive guerrilla and main unit operations to put maximum military pressure on the South Vietnamese and keep U.S. casualties high in hopes that Americans would weary of the war.[17]

Infiltration into South Vietnam was crucial to victory, and the fabled Ho Chi Minh Trail was the key to infiltration. From the beginning of the American war, the North Vietnamese committed vast human and material resources to expanding and improving this vital lifeline. What had been a primitive footpath with elephants sometimes used as a mode of conveyance was transformed by the late 1960s into a complex and sophisticated network of arteries into South Vietnam, with some paved roads capable of handling heavy trucks

---

[17]Lien-Hang T. Nguyen, *Hanoi's War: An International History of the War for Peace in Vietnam* (Chapel Hill, N.C., 2012), pp. 74–76; Pierre Asselin, " 'We don't want a Munich': Hanoi's Diplomatic Strategy, 1965–1968," *Diplomatic History* 36 (June 2012): 548, 551.

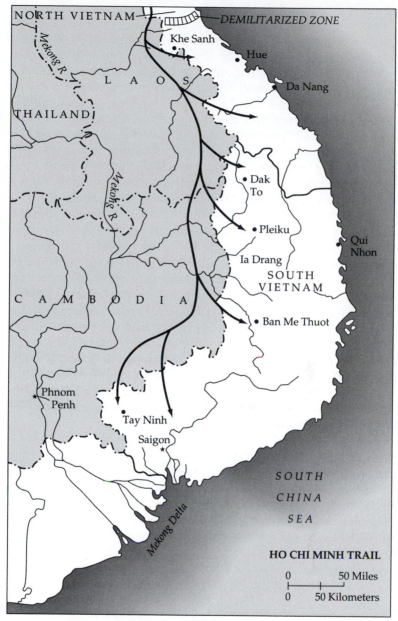

NORTH VIETNAM

DEMILITARIZED ZONE

Khe Sanh

Hue

L A O S

Da Nang

THAILAND

Mekong R.

Mekong R.

Dak
To

Pleiku

Qui
Nhon

Ia Drang

SOUTH
VIETNAM

C A M B O D I A

Ban Me Thuot

Phnom
Penh

Tay Ninh

Saigon

SOUTH
CHINA
SEA

Mekong Delta

HO CHI MINH TRAIL

0   50 Miles

0   50 Kilometers

Map by Jeffrey L. Ward. Reprinted with permission of Simon & Schuster from
Our Vietnam—Nuoc Viet Ta: A History of the War: 1954–1975 *by A. J.*
Langguth, p. 397. Maps Copyright © 2000 by Jeffrey L. Ward.

and with rest stations at numerous points. Thousands of workers, including women and children, devoted much of their lives to keeping the roads open. For the porters and soldiers who went to South Vietnam, the trip remained arduous. Depending on the means of travel, the 600-mile trek could take from two weeks to six months. It was fraught with peril from deadly tigers and bears, from the terror of American B-52 bombing, and especially from the scourge of malaria. Many way stations soon had cemeteries that marked the danger. During peak periods in the late 1960s, North Vietnam could move an estimated 400 tons of supplies per week and as many as 5,000 soldiers a month into South Vietnamese battle zones.

Throughout 1965 and 1966, the North Vietnamese and NLF attempted to keep the Americans off balance, thereby disrupting search-and-destroy operations. In 1967, they engaged U.S. forces in major actions around the demilitarized zone, giving themselves short supply lines and convenient sanctuary and hoping to draw the Americans away from the populated areas and leave the countryside vulnerable to the NLF. Tactically, the North Vietnamese relied on ambushes and hit-and-run operations and sought to "cling to the belts" of the Americans in close-quarter fighting to minimize the impact of the vastly superior U.S. firepower. Like their NLF counterparts, the North Vietnamese were capable fighters. "Damn, give me two hundred men that well disciplined and I'll capture this whole country," one U.S. adviser commented after a major battle in the Central Highlands in late 1965.[18]

During 1966 and 1967, intensive fighting took place across much of South Vietnam. Along the demilitarized zone, Marines and North Vietnamese regulars were dug in like the armies of World War I, pounding each other relentlessly with artillery. In the jungle areas, small American units probed for the hidden enemy in a manner comparable to the Pacific island campaigns of World War II. Increasingly, however, Westmoreland concentrated on large-scale search-and-destroy operations against enemy base areas. Operation CEDAR FALLS, a major campaign of early 1967, sent

---

[18]Quoted in the *New York Times*, October 28, 1965. William J. Duiker, *The Communist Road to Power in Vietnam* (Boulder, Colo., 1981), pp. 240–256, contains a persuasive assessment of North Vietnamese strategy. The story of the Ho Chi Minh Trail is well told in John Prados, *The Blood Road: The Ho Chi Minh Trail and the Vietnam War* (New York, 1999).

The Destruction of Ben Suc
The village of Ben Suc was a major NLF supply center in the notorious Iron Triangle northwest of Saigon. The NLF had dominated this area for years, and in 1967 the United States set out to save it by destroying it. More than 6,000 civilians were forcibly evacuated from Ben Suc, after which the village was bombed by B-52s for four days. Two Army divisions then moved in. Ben Suc ceased to exist. *Time* magazine reported that "even a crow flying across the Triangle will have to carry lunch from now on." The NLF quickly returned to the Iron Triangle, however, and it became a staging area for the 1968 Tet Offensive.
© *Time & Life Pictures/Getty Images*

some 30,000 U.S. troops against the Iron Triangle, an NLF stronghold just north of Saigon. After B-52s saturated the area, American forces surrounded it, and helicopters dropped large numbers of specially trained combat troops into the villages. Following removal of the population, giant Rome plows with huge spikes on the front leveled the area, destroying what remained of the vegetation and leaving the guerrillas no place to hide. The region was then burned and bombed again to destroy the miles of underground tunnels dug by the insurgents.

It remains difficult to assess the results of U.S. ground operations from 1965 to 1967. American troops fought well, despite the

NLF Tunnel System
During the wars with France and the United States, the Viet Minh and later
the National Liberation Front dug by hand thousands of miles of tunnels
that connected villages and linked staging areas to battle zones. Inside
these underground fortresses were supply depots, ordnance factories,
hospitals, printing presses, sleeping quarters, kitchens, and even theaters
for propaganda plays.

miserable conditions under which the war was waged—dense
jungles and deep swamps, fire ants and leeches, booby traps and
ambushes, an elusive but deadly enemy. In those instances where
main units were actually engaged, the Americans usually prevailed. There was no place in South Vietnam where the enemy
enjoyed security from U.S. firepower. It was clear by 1967 that the
infusion of American forces had staved off what had appeared in
1965 to be certain defeat.

In a war without front lines and territorial objectives, where
"attriting the enemy" was the major goal, the "body count" became
the index of progress. Most authorities agree that the figures were
notoriously unreliable. The sheer destructiveness of combat made it
difficult to produce an accurate count of enemy killed in action. It
was impossible to distinguish between guerrillas and noncombatants, and in the heat of battle American "statisticians" made little
effort. "If it's dead and Vietnamese, it's VC, was a rule of thumb in
the bush," Philip Caputo has recalled.[19] Throughout the chain of
command there was heavy pressure to produce favorable figures,
and padding occurred at each level until by the time the numbers

[19]Caputo, *Rumor of War*, p. xviii.

North and South Vietnam at War
From The Eye Witness History of the Vietnam War 1961–1975 *by George Esper, copyright © 1983 by Villard Books. Used by permission of Villard Books, a division of Random House.*

reached Washington, they bore little resemblance to reality. Even with an inflated body count—and estimates of padding range as high as 30 percent—it is clear that the United States inflicted huge losses on the enemy. Official estimates placed the number as high as 220,000 by late 1967. Largely on the basis of these figures, the American military command insisted that the United States was winning the war.

As with the air war, the strategy of attrition had serious flaws. It assumed that the United States could inflict intolerable losses on the enemy while keeping its own within acceptable bounds, an assumption that flew in the face of past experience with land wars on the Asian continent and the realities in Vietnam. An estimated 200,000 North Vietnamese reached draft age each year, and Hanoi was able to replace its losses and match each American escalation. Moreover, the conditions under which the war was fought permitted the enemy to control its casualties. The North Vietnamese and NLF remained extraordinarily elusive and were generally able to avoid contact when it suited them. They fought at times and places of their own choosing and on ground favorable to them. If losses reached unacceptable levels, they simply melted into the jungle or retreated into sanctuaries in North Vietnam, Laos, and Cambodia.

The massive application of U.S. military power took a heavy toll on North Vietnam. The still fragile nation suffered huge setbacks in economic development. As casualties mounted and the bombing inflicted growing damage, war-weariness supplanted the initial surge of enthusiasm in the North. Dissent arose from some who wanted to spare North Vietnam the destruction of U.S. bombs and others like Gen. Vo Nguyen Giap, the hero of Dien Bien Phu, who deplored the waste of NVA main units in the South and pressed for a defensive, protracted war strategy.[20]

The arrival of U.S. troops with their enormous firepower dramatically altered the war in South Vietnam. American military operations battered some NLF main units, compounded supply problems, disrupted the party's organizational network, and even caused defections among its leadership. U.S. escalation forced the Front to impose conscription to fill its ranks and higher taxes to meet its most urgent needs, alienating the people on whose backing it relied. The costs of war for peasants in many areas began to exceed the benefits they had derived from the revolution. Growing competition between the Front and the Government of Viet Nam (GVN) for their loyalty along with the impact of U.S. firepower

[20]Nguyen, *Hanoi's War*, pp. 76–79.

forced them to struggle merely to survive and made life increasingly untenable in some areas. Support for the revolution dropped sharply from its 1963–1964 peak. Some peasants' search for cities and towns, along with the demoralization of the civilian population, deprived the NLF of its base.[21]

Still, the United States could gain no more than a stalemate. Despite popular grumbling and intraparty dissent, the Hanoi leadership pressed on with its aggressive strategy. The North Vietnamese and NLF had been hurt, in some cases badly, but their main forces had not been destroyed. The NLF political structure was damaged but still intact. The NLF and North Vietnam retained the strategic initiative and could strike quickly when and where they chose. In the South, in 1966 and 1967 the NLF shifted from costly engagements with U.S. forces to attacks on the Army of the Republic of Viet Nam (ARVN), deemed an enemy point of vulnerability, and on the towns and cities, to force the enemy to disperse its forces and demonstrate to refugees that there was no safe haven. Westmoreland did not have sufficient forces to wage war against the enemy's regulars and control the countryside. Even in areas such as the Iron Triangle, when American forces moved on to fight elsewhere, the insurgents quietly slipped back in. It all added up to a "state of irresolution," Robert Shaplen observed in 1967.[22]

Skeptics increasingly questioned whether the progress made was not more than offset by the consequences of large-scale U.S. military operations. In 1966 alone, unexploded American bombs and shells provided the guerrillas with enough explosives to kill as many as 1,000 people. The massive bombing and artillery fire disrupted the agriculture on which the South Vietnamese economy depended, produced huge civilian casualties, and drove millions of noncombatants into hastily constructed refugee camps or into the already overcrowded cities. American military operations further undermined the social fabric of an already fragile nation and alienated the people from a government that never had a firm base of popular support. "It was as if we were trying to build a house with a bulldozer and wrecking crane," one U.S. official later observed.[23]

[21]Elliott, *Vietnamese War*, pp. 229–231, 236–238, 248, 269, 298–300.
[22]Robert Shaplen, *The Road from War: Vietnam, 1965–1970* (New York, 1970), p. 167.
[23]Stephen Young, quoted in W. Scott Thompson and Donaldson D. Frizzell, *The Lessons of Vietnam* (New York, 1977), p. 225.

Americanization of the war also had a debilitating effect on the South Vietnamese Army. Westmoreland had called for American forces because he doubted the battle-worthiness of the ARVN. Once he had them, he relied primarily on them. During the period of U.S. military preponderance, the ARVN was largely shunted aside, relegated to lesser operations and population control, chores its officers considered demeaning and took on with considerable reluctance. The sense of inferiority thus engendered did nothing to resolve the problems of morale and leadership that had always been the ARVN's curse. Much time and money were spent training and equipping the South Vietnamese from 1965 to 1967, but it was all in the American mold, preparing them to fight the kind of war the Americans were waging. The ARVN thus became more than ever dependent on the United States. It was ill-prepared to assume the burden of the fighting at some later, unspecified date.

The United States paid a heavy price for limited gains. In many operations vast quantities of firepower were expended, sometimes with negligible results. The ammunition costs of the war were "astronomical," Army Chief of Staff Harold Johnson later recalled, and some surveys revealed that as much as 85 percent of the ammunition used was unobserved fire, "a staggering volume."[24] Although the United States killed 700 guerrillas in the CEDAR FALLS operation, the enemy main force escaped. American casualties were small compared with Vietnamese, but the number killed in action rose to 13,500 by late 1967. Swelling draft calls and mounting casualties brought rising opposition to the war at home.

Thus, despite the impressive body count figures, it was clear to many observers by mid-1967 that the hopes of a quick and relatively inexpensive military victory had been misplaced. Each American blow "was like a sledgehammer on a floating cork," the journalist Malcolm Browne observed. "Somehow the cork refused to stay down."[25] By this point, the United States had nearly 450,000 troops in Vietnam. Westmoreland conceded that even if his request for an additional 200,000 soldiers was granted, the war might go on for as long as two years. If not, he warned, it could last five years or even longer.

[24]Harold Johnson oral history interview, U.S. Army Military History Institute, Carlisle Barracks, Pa.
[25]Malcolm W. Browne, *The New Face of War* (Indianapolis, Ind., 1968), p. ix.

THE "OTHER WAR":
NATION BUILDING AND PACIFICATION

While drastically expanding its military operations in Vietnam, the United States also grappled with what many had always regarded as the central problem: construction of a viable South Vietnamese nation. Ky surprised skeptics by surviving in office for more than six months. Persuaded that it finally had a solid foundation upon which to build, the U.S. administration in early 1966 decided to make clear its commitment and press Ky to reform his government. At a hastily arranged "summit" meeting in Honolulu, Johnson publicly embraced a somewhat embarrassed Ky, symbolizing the new commitment, and secured his agreement to a sweeping program of reform. The president left no doubt of the importance he attached to the pledges. The Honolulu communiqué was a "kind of bible," he declared. He would not be content with promises or "high-sounding words." There must be "coonskins on the wall."[26]

No sooner had Ky returned to Saigon than he faced a stiff internal challenge. Quiescent for nearly a year, the Buddhists viewed Honolulu as a clear sign that Ky, with American support, would attempt to maintain absolute power, and again they took to the streets. As in 1963, the demonstrations began in Hue and were led by Buddhist monks, but they quickly spread to Saigon and drew together the many groups dissatisfied with the regime: students, labor unions, Catholics, and even factions within the army. The demonstrations took on an increasingly anti-American tone. Signs reading END FOREIGN DOMINATION OF OUR COUNTRY appeared in Hue and Da Nang. An angry mob burned the U.S. consulate in Hue. Fire fighters refused to extinguish the blaze.

The Buddhist crisis exposed the fragility of the Saigon government and the weakness of the U.S. position in Vietnam. The existence of a virtual civil war within an insurrection dampened the hopes that had begun to develop for Ky's government. The protesters advocated the holding of elections and the restoration of civilian government, goals to which the United States could hardly take exception. The State Department nevertheless feared that giving in

---

[26]Transcript of Johnson briefing, February 8, 1966, Johnson Papers, National Security File, International Meetings File: Honolulu, Box 2.

to the Buddhists would "take us more rapidly than we had envisaged down a road with many pitfalls." Rusk instructed the embassy to persuade moderate Buddhist leaders to drop their "unrealistic demands" because of the "grave danger of simply handing the country over to the Viet Cong."[27]

The conflict in I Corps, the northern military section of South Vietnam, almost forced a reassessment of U.S. policy. Although they attempted to remain neutral, the U.S. Marines stationed in the area came under fire several times from ARVN units sympathetic to the Buddhists and from those loyal to Ky. On occasion the troops had to threaten to use force to defend themselves against one side or the other. The Marines naturally expressed "bitterness and disgust" that while they were putting their lives on the line to save South Vietnam, the South Vietnamese were fighting each other.

For the only time between 1965 and 1968, this second Buddhist crisis provoked serious discussion in Washington of a possible U.S. withdrawal from Vietnam. In response to events in I Corps, U.S. public opinion polls revealed a sharp decline in popular support for the war and Johnson's handling of it. Legislators from both parties and both ends of the political spectrum expressed anger at the anti-American tones of the protests and dismay at the political chaos in South Vietnam. Some called for negotiations to end the war, others for a U.S. withdrawal. Even President Johnson conceded that in the event of a GVN collapse or a Buddhist takeover, the United States might *have* to leave South Vietnam. He ordered his aides to consider various fallback options and be prepared to make "terrible choices."[28] The military drew up contingency plans. McNamara's close friend and top aide John McNaughton recommended that the United States use the "semi-anarchy in Vietnam as a foundation for disengagement." On one occasion, his boss seemed to agree, blurting out, "I want to give the order to our troops to get out of there so bad I can hardly stand it."[29]

[27]Rusk to Embassy Saigon, March 16, 1966, Johnson Papers, National Security File, Country File: Vietnam, Box 28; Rusk to Embassy Saigon, April 5, 1966, Johnson Papers, National Security File, Country File: Vietnam, Box 29.
[28]Robert J. Topmiller, *The Lotus Unleashed: The Buddhist Peace Movement in South Vietnam, 1964–1966* (Lexington, Ky., 2002), pp. 71–91.
[29]Ibid, pp. 93–116; Benjamin T. Harrison and Christopher L. Mosher, "The Secret Diary of McNamara's Dove: The Long-Lost Story of John T. McNaughton's Opposition to the Vietnam War," *Diplomatic History* 35 (June 2011): 525.

Acting without approval from Washington, an embattled Ky eventually solved the American dilemma and saved his own skin by dispatching a thousand South Vietnamese marines to Da Nang to suppress the rebellion. The Buddhists gave way in the face of superior force and withdrew in sullen protest. Although annoyed by Ky's independence, the administration was relieved and more than satisfied with the outcome. The president "categorically thrust aside the withdrawal option," William Bundy recalled, and "we all relaxed."[30]

In the aftermath of the Buddhist crisis, Americans and Vietnamese struggled to live up to the lofty promises of Honolulu. From Washington's standpoint, pacification was a top-priority item. Improving the South Vietnamese standard of living was the one area of the war that struck a responsive chord in Johnson. A populist reformer at heart, he identified with the people of South Vietnam and deeply sympathized with their presumed desire for political freedom and economic progress. Like most of his colleagues, he believed it was necessary to win the support of the people to defeat the NLF. He felt a keen personal need to endow the war with some higher purpose. He could wax eloquent about such topics as inoculation programs, educational reform, and the use of American expertise to teach the Vietnamese to raise larger hogs and grow more sweet potatoes. "Dammit," he exploded on one occasion, "we need to exhibit more compassion for these Vietnamese plain people. . . . We've got to see that the South Vietnamese government wins the battle . . . of crops and hearts and caring."[31] Under intensive prodding from Washington, the Americans and South Vietnamese devised an ambitious Revolutionary Development (RD) program, consciously imitative of NLF techniques, in which teams of fifty-nine people trained in propaganda and social services would go into the villages, live with the people, and carry out hundreds of tasks to build popular support for the government and undermine the guerrillas.

Revolutionary Development encountered many of the problems that had frustrated earlier pacification programs. The creaking Saigon bureaucracy and poor coordination between Americans and

[30]William Bundy oral history interview, Johnson Papers. .
[31]Jack Valenti, *A Very Human President* (New York, 1973), p. 133; Lady Bird Johnson, *A White House Diary* (New York, 1970), pp. 370–371.

Vietnamese hampered administration of the plan. It was impossible to recruit sufficient participants in a country short of skilled personnel, and less than half the cadres needed actually went into training. Candidates were trained on a mass-production basis for a mere three months and in most cases were inadequately prepared for the formidable task that lay ahead. Once in the field, the RD teams were frustrated by local officials who regarded them as a threat. Funds promised for many projects never reached their destination. Having seen so many other programs come and go, the villagers greeted the arrivals with a mixture of apathy and caution. Because of the chronic personnel shortage, many cadres were often shifted to new areas before their work was completed, and any gains were quickly erased. Good performance by RD teams was sometimes undercut by the behavior of ARVN units that extorted taxes and fees from the villagers and stole chickens and pigs. When asked what would most help pacification in his area, one U.S. adviser responded: "Get the 22nd [ARVN] Division out of the province."[32]

The fundamental problem was the absence of security. The U.S. military was preoccupied with the shooting war and gave little attention to what became known as "the other war" (the term itself suggested the absence of coordination between pacification and military operations). In most cases, the ARVN was incapable of providing security; in some areas it was part of the problem. Sometimes, RD teams would make progress, only to have it nullified when American aircraft bombed their villages. Cadres were frequently sent into insecure areas, where they were harassed and terrorized by guerrillas. Many fled. Those who stayed and worked effectively with the people were often found with their throats slit. During a seven-month period in 1966, 3,015 RD personnel were murdered or kidnapped.[33]

Under these circumstances, pacification achieved little. Roads were repaired, schools built, and village elections held, but even on the basis of the highly inaccurate methods used to measure progress, the number of "pacified" villages increased by a mere 5 percent in

[32]Daniel Ellsberg memorandum, March 30, 1966, John P. Vann Papers, U.S. Army Military History Institute, Carlisle Barracks, Pa.
[33]Douglas A. Blaufarb, *The Counterinsurgency Era: U.S. Doctrines and Performance* (New York, 1977), pp. 205–242, contains a full discussion of the Revolutionary Development program. See also Thomas L. Ahern Jr., *Vietnam Declassified: The CIA and Counterinsurgency* (Lexington, K.Y., 2010), pp. 191–219.

the first year. To revive the program, Johnson placed it under the immediate authority of the U.S. military command in the spring of 1967. Westmoreland persuaded a reluctant ARVN to commit the bulk of its forces to rural security. These changes would eventually produce better results, but at a time when the vast American military effort had attained nothing better than a stalemate, the failure of pacification was especially discouraging.

In at least one area, the two nations did live up to the goals of the Honolulu communiqué: a new constitution was drafted and national elections were held. The Americans did not presume that the export of democracy would solve South Vietnam's problems. On the contrary, many agreed with Lodge (who had returned for a second tour as ambassador) that the establishment of real democracy in a land with no Western democratic traditions was "clearly an impossible task." Some feared that a genuinely open political process would lead to chaos. The Americans nevertheless felt that a new constitution and elections would give South Vietnam a better image and might, in Lodge's words, "substitute a certain legitimacy for the hurly-burly of unending coups."[34]

The Ky regime dutifully followed American advice, but in a way that ensured its own perpetuation. Elections for a constituent assembly were so tightly circumscribed that the Buddhists boycotted them. The assembly met in early 1967 and turned out a polished document, based on American and French models and including a Bill of Rights. The government nevertheless insisted on a strong executive and on provisions permitting the president to assume near-dictatorial powers in an emergency, which could be declared at his discretion. Those branded Communists or "neutralist sympathizers" were disqualified from office. The president was to be elected by a plurality, ensuring that opposition candidates did not band together in a runoff.

Throughout the preelection maneuvering, the United States quietly but firmly supported the government's efforts to remain in power. The State Department expressed concern about the wholesale disqualification of opposition candidates, but Lodge prevailed with his argument that the "GVN should not be discouraged from taking moderate measures to prevent [the] elections from being used as a

---

[34]Henry Cabot Lodge Jr., *The Storm Has Many Eyes* (New York, 1973), p. 215.

vehicle for a Communist takeover."[35] The most serious challenge came from bitter internal squabbling, which was resolved only under intense pressure from the United States and after a long meeting, filled with histrionics, in which Ky tearfully gave way and agreed to run for the vice presidency on a ticket headed by Gen. Thieu.

The September 1967 elections were neither as corrupt as critics charged nor as pure as Johnson claimed. The regime conducted them under conditions that made defeat unlikely. There was evidence of considerable last-minute fraud. But the large turnout and the fact that elections had been held in the midst of war were cited by Americans as evidence of growing political maturity. What stands out in retrospect is the narrowness of the government's victory. The Thieu–Ky ticket won 35 percent of the vote, but Truong Dinh Dzu, an unknown lawyer who had run on a platform of negotiations with the NLF, won 17 percent. The elections may have provided the regime with a measure of respectability, but they also underscored its continued weakness. In a nation where political authority derived from the will of heaven and popular support was an obligation, the narrowness of the victory could only appear ludicrous. Many Vietnamese cynically regarded the entire process as "an American-directed performance with a Vietnamese cast."[36]

THE IMPACT OF AMERICANIZATION

While the United States and South Vietnam struggled to resolve old problems, Americanization of the war created new and equally formidable problems. Those Americans who visited South Vietnam for the first time were stunned by the sheer enormity of the U.S. effort, a huge, sprawling, many-faceted military–civilian apparatus, generally uncoordinated, in which all too frequently the various components worked against rather than in support of one another. By late 1967, the United States had almost a half million troops in Vietnam. The civilian side of the war also expanded to elephantine proportions, with an aid program of $625 million, which was one-fourth of the economic assistance given to the entire world, and 6,500 American

[35]U.S. Congress, Senate Subcommittee on Public Buildings and Grounds, *The Pentagon Papers (The Senator Gravel Edition)* (4 vols., Boston, 1971), 2: 384.
[36]Shaplen, *Road from War*, p. 151.

civilians working in various capacities. Presidential speechwriter Harry McPherson spoke of the "colossal size of our effort." White House aide John Roche described the American presence as "just unbelievable," the "Holy Roman Empire going to war," and observed sarcastically that cutting its size by two-thirds might increase its efficiency by 50 percent.[37]

One of the most serious—and most tragic—problems caused by Americanization of the war was that of refugees. The expansion of American and enemy military operations drove an estimated four million South Vietnamese, roughly 25 percent of the population, from their native villages. Some drifted into the already teeming cities; others were herded into shabby refugee camps. The United States furnished the government with some $30 million a year for the care of the refugees, but much of the money never reached them. Resettlement programs were initiated from time to time, but the problem was so complex that it would have taxed the ingenuity of the most imaginative officials. In any event, nothing could have compensated the refugees for the loss of their homes and lands. A large portion of South Vietnam's population was left rootless and hostile. The refugee camps became fertile breeding grounds for insurgent fifth columns.

The sudden infusion of a half million U.S. troops, thousands of civilian advisers, and billions of dollars had a profoundly disruptive effect on a young and still very fragile nation. To support its enormous military machine and facilitate operations against the enemy, the United States poured millions of dollars into South Vietnam's primitive infrastructure. It upgraded roads and expanded and modernized unloading facilities at Saigon and other port cities. It built enormous barracks complexes at base areas across the country. The vast, sprawling, twenty-five-square-mile "instant city" of Long Binh, just north of Saigon, included hospitals, restaurants and snack bars, a post exchange, bowling alleys, movie theaters, swimming pools, basketball courts—and the notorious Long Binh Jail (called, naturally, the LBJ). Saigon's enlarged Tan Son Nhut Airport soon became one of the busiest in the world. It also housed the Vietnamese and U.S. military commands and was dubbed the "Little Pentagon." The price tag for infrastructure in 1966 alone was $1.4 billion.[38]

[37]Herring, *LBJ and Vietnam*, pp. 20–21.
[38]James M. Carter, *Inventing Vietnam: The United States and State Building, 1954–1968* (New York, 2008), pp. 181–204.

The buildup was so rapid and vast that it threatened to over-whelm South Vietnam. Saigon's ports were congested with ships and goods, and vessels awaiting unloading were backed up far out to sea. The city itself became a "thorough-going boom town," Shaplen remarked, its streets clogged with traffic, its restaurants "bursting with boisterous soldiers," its bars as "crowded as New York subway cars in the rush hour." Signs of the American presence appeared everywhere. Vietnamese children wore Batman tee shirts. Long strips of bars and brothels sprang up overnight around the newly constructed base areas, the one at Bien Hoa became known as Tijuana East. In a remote village near Da Nang, Caputo encountered houses made of discarded beer cans: "red and white Budweiser, gold Miller, cream and brown Schlitz, blue and gold Hamm's from the land of sky-blue waters."[39]

The presence of thousands of Americans spending millions of dollars had a devastating effect on a quite vulnerable Vietnamese economy. Prices increased by as much as 170 percent during the first two years of the buildup, making it impossible for ordinary Vietnamese to make ends meet. The United States eventually con-trolled the rate of inflation by paying its own soldiers in scrip and by flooding the country with consumer goods, but the corrective measures themselves had harmful side effects. Instead of using American aid to promote economic development, South Vietnamese importers bought watches, transistor radios, and motorbikes to sell to people employed by the United States. The vast influx of American goods destroyed South Vietnam's few native industries and made the economy even more dependent on continued outside aid. By 1967, much of the urban population was employed provid-ing services for the Americans.

In the bonanza atmosphere, crime and corruption flourished. Corruption was not new to South Vietnam or unusual in a nation at war, but by 1966 it operated on an incredible scale. Government offi-cials rented land to the United States at inflated prices; required bribes for driver's licenses, passports, visas, and work permits; extorted kickbacks for contracts to build and service facilities; and took part in the illicit importation of opium. The black market in scrip and dollars became a major enterprise. Import licenses for items in the commercial import program became licenses to steal.

---

[39]Shaplen, *Road from War*, pp. 20–21; Caputo, *Rumor of War*, p. 107.

With the connivance of Americans, garbage trucks left PXs loaded with stolen goods to be sold on the black market. On Saigon's PX Alley, an open-air market covering two city blocks and made up of more than 100 stalls, purchasers could buy everything from hand grenades to Scotch whiskey at markups as high as 300 percent. Americans and Vietnamese reaped handsome profits from the illegal exchange of currencies. International swindlers and "monetary camp followers" quickly got into the act. The currency-manipulation racket developed into a "massive financial international network" extending from Saigon to Wall Street, with connections to Swiss banks and Arab sheikhdoms. The pervasive corruption undermined the U.S. aid program and severely handicapped efforts to stabilize the economy of South Vietnam.[40]

American officials perceived the problem, but they could not find solutions. Ky candidly admitted that "most of the generals are corrupt. Most of the senior officials in the provinces are corrupt." But, he would add calmly, "corruption exists everywhere, and people can live with some of it. You live with it in Chicago and New York."[41] The embassy pressed the government to remove officials known to be corrupt, but with little result. "You fight like hell to get someone removed and most times you fail and you just make it worse," a frustrated American explained to journalist David Halberstam. "And then on occasions you win, why hell, they give you someone just as bad."[42] The United States found to its chagrin that as its commitment increased, its leverage diminished. Concern with corruption and inefficiency was always balanced by fear that tough action might alienate the government or bring about its collapse. Lodge and Westmoreland were inclined to accept the situation and deal with other problems.

Tensions between Americans and South Vietnamese increased as the American presence grew. The two peoples approached each other with colossal ignorance. "My time in Vietnam is the memory of ignorance," one GI later conceded. "I didn't know the language.

[40]*New York Times*, November 16, 1966; Abraham Ribicoff to Robert McLellan, January 15, 1969, and memorandum, January 15, 1970, Abraham Ribicoff Papers, Library of Congress, Washington, D.C., Box 432.
[41]Harry McPherson to Johnson, June 13, 1967, Johnson Papers, McPherson File, Box 29.
[42]David Halberstam, "Return to Vietnam," *Harpers* 235 (December 1967): 52.

I knew nothing about the village community. I knew nothing about the aims of the people—whether they were for the war or against it."[43] Indeed, for many Americans, the elementary task of distinguishing friend from foe became a sometimes impossible challenge. "What we need is some . . . kind of litmus paper that turns red when it's near a communist," one U.S. officer, half seriously, half jokingly, told journalist Malcolm Browne.[44] Many Vietnamese found American culture incomprehensible.

Although fighting in a common cause, the two peoples grew increasingly suspicious and resentful of each other. Because of chronic security leaks, the United States kept Vietnamese off its major bases. NLF infiltration of the ARVN's top ranks compelled U.S. officers to keep from their Vietnamese counterparts the details of major military operations. The more the Americans assumed the burden of the fighting, the more they demeaned the martial abilities of their ally. "I wish the southern members of the clan would display the fighting qualities of their northern brethren," a senior U.S. officer observed with obvious scorn.[45] The ARVN indeed became an object of ridicule, its mode of attack best depicted, according to a standard American joke, by the statue of a seated soldier in the National Military Cemetery. Vietnamese slowness to accept American methods exasperated U.S. advisers. "I am sure that if Saigon were left to fend for itself . . . in 20 years this place would be all rice paddies again," one American acidly observed.[46] The apparent indifference of many Vietnamese, while Americans were dying in the field, provoked growing resentment and hatred. The seeming ability of the villagers to avoid mines and booby traps that killed and maimed GIs led to charges of collusion with the enemy.

Vietnamese attitudes toward the foreigners were at best ambivalent. Purveyors of goods and services, from prostitutes to cabbies, preferred to do business with the Americans, who paid them better, provoking great anger among their own people.

---

[43]Quoted in Clark Dougan and Stephen Weiss, *The American Experience in Vietnam* (New York, 1988), p. 62.
[44]Browne, *New Face of War*, p. 46.
[45]General A. S. Collins to Edward F. Smith, November 15, 1966, A. S. Collins Papers, U.S. Army Military History Institute, Carlisle Barracks, Pa.
[46]Curtis Herrick diary, January 13, 1965, Curtis Herrick Papers, U.S. Army Military History Institute, Carlisle Barracks, Pa.

Many Vietnamese appreciated Americans' generosity but objected to their way of doing things. Villagers complained that GIs "acted despicably," tearing up roads and endangering Vietnamese lives by reckless handling of vehicles and firearms. An ARVN major protested that Americans trusted only those Vietnamese who went along with their methods and doled out their aid "in the same way as that given to beggars."[47] Many Vietnamese recognized their need for U.S. help. Some were probably content to let the United States take over the war. But others came to resent the domineering manner of the Americans and viewed the U.S. "occupation" as a "demoralizing scourge," even theorizing that "if we could get rid of the Americans, then we could worry about the Viet Cong." Thoughtful Vietnamese recognized that Americans were not "colonialists," Shaplen observed. But, he added, "there has evolved here a colonial ambience that can sometimes be worse than colonialism itself." To reduce rising tensions between Americans and Vietnamese, Military Assistance Command Vietnam (MACV), in what was called Operation Moose (Move Out of Saigon Expeditiously), began shifting thousands of GI's out of the city in late 1967.[48]

Progress in the critical area of nation building was thus even more limited than on the battlefield. To be sure, the government survived, and after the chronic instability of the Khanh era, that in itself appeared evidence of progress. Survival was primarily a result of the formidable U.S. military presence, however, and did not reflect increased popular support or intrinsic strength. Returning to South Vietnam after an absence of several years, Halberstam was haunted by a sense of déjà vu. There were new faces, new programs, and an abundance of resources. The Americans continued to speak optimistically. But the old problems persisted, and the "new" solutions appeared little more than recycled versions of old ones. "What finally struck me," he concluded, "was how little had really changed here."[49]

[47]Weekly Psyops Field Operation Report, December 2, 1967, Vann Papers, U.S. Army Military History Institute, Carlisle Barracks, Pa.
[48]Shaplen, *Road from War*, p. 154; Jeffrey A. Keith, "Between the Paris of the Orient and Ho Chi Minh City: Imaginings and Reportage in Wartime Saigon, 1954–1975," Ph.D. diss., University of Kentucky, 2011, pp. 164–165.
[49]Halberstam, "Return to Vietnam," p. 50.

WAGING PEACE

The steady expansion of the war spurred strong international and domestic pressures for negotiations, but the military stalemate produced an equally firm diplomatic impasse. American officials later tallied as many as 2,000 attempts to initiate peace talks between 1965 and 1967. Neither side could afford to appear indifferent to such efforts, but neither was willing to make the concessions necessary to bring about negotiations. Diplomacy was one of the key weapons in North Vietnam's arsenal for waging a complex and multifaceted war. It provided a means to gain material support from allies and moral backing from "progressive forces" across the world. It could be used to manipulate world opinion as a way of "isolating the enemy to defeat him." It could even be employed to sway antiwar forces in the United States. Hanoi was always careful to appear open to negotiations and to play the role of aggrieved party. It sought to exploit the various peace initiatives for propaganda advantage.[50] But the leadership continued to count on the United States, like France, to tire of the war and remained confident that it could achieve its essential goals if it persisted. It refused to negotiate without first gaining major concessions from Washington.

Johnson and his advisers also could not ignore the various proposals for negotiations, but they doubted anything would come of them and suspected, with good reason, that Hanoi was expressing interest merely to get the bombing stopped. Despite any firm evidence of results, the president remained hopeful at least until 1967 that North Vietnam would bend to U.S. pressure. He feared that an overly conciliatory stance would be interpreted as a sign of weakness. To defuse international and domestic criticism, Johnson repeatedly insisted that he was ready to negotiate, but he refused to make the concessions Hanoi demanded. As each side invested more in the struggle, the likelihood of serious negotiations diminished.

The positions of the two sides left little room for compromise. The North Vietnamese denounced American involvement in Vietnam as a blatant violation of the Geneva Accords. As a precondition for negotiations, their Four Points required that the United States withdraw its troops, dismantle its bases, and stop all acts of war against their country. The internal affairs of South Vietnam must be resolved by the

[50]Asselin, "Hanoi's Diplomatic Strategy," pp. 550–551.

South Vietnamese themselves "in accordance with the program of the National Liberation Front." North Vietnam was apparently flexible in regard to the timing and mechanism for political change in the South, but on the fundamental issues it was adamant. The "puppet" Saigon regime must be replaced by a government representative of the "people" in which the Front would play a prominent role. Hanoi made clear, moreover, that the "unity of our country is no more a matter for negotiations than our independence."[51]

The United States formally set forth its position in early 1966. "We put everything into the basket but the surrender of South Vietnam," Secretary of State Dean Rusk later claimed, but in fact the administration's Fourteen Points offered few concessions.[52] The United States indicated that it was willing to stop the bombing, but only after Hanoi took reciprocal steps of de-escalation. It would withdraw its troops from the South, but only after a satisfactory political settlement had been reached. The administration accepted the principle that the future of South Vietnam must be worked out by the South Vietnamese. At the same time, it made clear that it would not admit the NLF to the government—that would be like "putting the fox in a chicken coop," Vice President Hubert H. Humphrey asserted.[53] The Fourteen Points conceded merely that the views of the NLF "would have no difficulty being represented," and this only after Hanoi had "ceased its aggression." Beneath these ambiguous words rested a firm determination to maintain an independent, non-Communist South Vietnam.

To silence domestic and international critics and test the diplomatic winds in Hanoi, the administration modified its position a bit in late 1966. Throughout the summer and fall, various third parties struggled to find a common ground for negotiations. After a series of frenzied trips back and forth between Hanoi and Saigon, the Polish diplomat Januscz Lewandowski drafted a ten-point plan for settlement of the conflict. Johnson and his advisers were highly skeptical of the peace moves, which they dismissed as "Nobel Prize fever." They felt that the Lewandowski draft was vague on many

[51]Quoted in Gareth Porter, *A Peace Denied: The United States, Vietnam, and the Paris Agreements* (Bloomington, Ind., 1975), p. 29.

[52]Quoted in Chester Cooper, *The Lost Crusade: America in Vietnam* (New York, 1970), p. 294.

[53]Quoted in Henry Graff, *The Tuesday Cabinet* (Englewood Cliffs, N.J., 1970), p. 67.

critical points and that it gave away too much. The administration could not afford to appear intransigent, however, and it eventually accepted Lewandowski's proposals as a basis for negotiations with the qualification that "several specific points are subject to important differences of interpretation." Responding to Lewandowski's entreaties, the United States also advanced a two-track proposal to provide a face-saving way around Hanoi's opposition to mutual de-escalation. The United States would stop the air strikes in return for confidential assurance that North Vietnam would cease infiltration into key areas of South Vietnam within a reasonable period. Once Hanoi had acted, the United States would freeze its combat forces at existing levels and peace talks could begin.[54]

Code-named MARIGOLD, the Polish initiative ended in fiasco. The extent to which the North Vietnamese were committed to the ten-point plan and were willing to compromise on the basic issues remains unclear. There is ample reason for doubt. But they did agree to ambassadorial-level talks in Warsaw without prior condition and even sent a high-level diplomat to brief their ambassador. American and North Vietnamese representatives were actually scheduled to meet. Several days before the talks were to begin, U.S. aircraft, for the first time in five months, unleashed heavy bombing against targets near Hanoi. The bombing had been scheduled weeks before but was delayed because of bad weather. Distrustful of the Poles and skeptical of the MARIGOLD initiative, Johnson and his top advisers apparently saw no reason to cancel the attacks. Even then, the Warsaw talks appeared ready to proceed, but through a remarkable and still not entirely explainable diplomatic snafu, the two men did not get together. Each felt stood up.[55]

Two weeks later, while diplomats from several countries were frantically trying to keep alive a once promising initiative, another even heavier round of U.S. bombing attacks on Hanoi itself caused extensive civilian casualties and ended any hope of discussions. This round of bombing did result from a conscious decision. Lodge, McNamara, and Undersecretary of State Nicholas Katzenbach all urged the president to refrain from bombing near Hanoi during the most delicate stage of Lewandowski's diplomacy, but he would have none of it.

[54]The most recent account is James G. Hershberg, *Marigold: The Lost Chance for Peace in Vietnam* (Washington, D.C., 2012).
[55]Hershberg, *Marigold*, pp. 281–313.

Like other U.S. officials, he suspected that the entire arrangement was "phony." He insisted that a bombing halt had not been a precondition for the Warsaw talks. Johnson's assessment of North Vietnamese intentions may have been correct, but the December bombings, which came after a long lull forced by bad weather, must have appeared to Hanoi to be a major escalation of the air war timed to coincide with the peace moves. The North Vietnamese had always insisted that they would not negotiate under threat and pressure. They quickly broke off the contact. The Poles felt betrayed, and MARIGOLD withered.

In response to international and domestic pressures, each side in 1967 inched cautiously away from the rigid positions assumed earlier. North Vietnam no longer insisted on acceptance of its Four Points, including a complete American military withdrawal, as a precondition for negotiations, demanding only that the bombing be ended without condition. Hanoi also relaxed its terms for a settlement, indicating, among other points, that reunification could take place over a long period of time. The United States retreated from its original position that North Vietnam must withdraw its forces from the South in return for cessation of the bombing, insisting merely that further infiltration must be stopped. Despite these concessions, the two nations remained far apart on the means of getting negotiations started. And although their bargaining positions had changed slightly, they had not abandoned their basic goals. Each had met with frustration and had incurred heavy losses on the battlefield, but each still retained hope that it could force the other to accept its terms. The two sides thus remained unwilling to compromise on the central issue: the future of South Vietnam. The story of the 1965–1967 peace initiatives, one scholar has concluded, marks "one of the most fruitless chapters in U.S. diplomacy."[56]

THE WAR AT HOME

By mid-1967, Johnson was snared in a trap he had unknowingly set for himself. His hopes of a quick and relatively painless victory had been frustrated. He was desperately anxious to end the war, but he had been unable to do so by force. In the absence of a clear-cut

[56]Allen E. Goodman, *The Lost Peace: America's Search for a Negotiated Settlement of the Vietnam War* (Stanford, Calif., 1978), p. 24.

military advantage or a stronger political position in South Vietnam, he could not do so by negotiation.

As the conflict increased in cost, moreover, he found himself caught in the midst of an increasingly angry and divisive debate, a veritable civil war that by 1967 seemed capable of wrecking his presidency and tearing the country apart. Dissent in wartime is a firmly established American tradition, of course, but Vietnam aroused more widespread and passionate opposition than any other U.S. war. It occurred in a time of social upheaval, when Americans were questioning their values and institutions as at few other periods in their history. It occurred in a time of generational strife. It occurred when the verities of the Cold War were coming into question. The war thus divided Americans as nothing since the debate on slavery a century earlier. It divided businesses, churches and campuses, neighbors and families. It set class against class. As the debate intensified, civilities were increasingly cast aside. Advocates of each side tried to shout the other down, denying basic rights of free speech. Argument was often accompanied by verbal abuse and even physical violence.

At one extreme were the hawks, largely right-wing Republicans and conservative Democrats, who viewed the conflict in Vietnam as an essential element in the global struggle against communism. Should the United States not hold the line, they argued, the Communists would be encouraged to further aggression, and allies and neutrals would succumb to Communist pressures. The United States would be left alone to face a powerful and merciless enemy. Strong nationalists who were certain of America's invincibility and deeply frustrated by the stalemate in Vietnam, the hawks viewed antiwar protest as treason, denounced the restraints imposed on the military, and demanded that the administration do what was necessary to attain victory. "Win or get out," Representative Mendel Rivers (South Carolina Democrat) told President Johnson in early 1966.[57]

At the other extreme were the doves, a vast, sprawling, extremely heterogeneous and fractious group who opposed the war with increasing bitterness and force. The "movement" grew almost in proportion to the escalation of the conflict. It included such diverse individuals as the world-famous pediatrician Dr. Benjamin

[57]Notes on meeting with congressional leadership, January 25, 1966, Johnson Papers, Meeting Notes File, Box 1.

Spock, heavyweight boxing champion Muhammad Ali, actress Jane Fonda, author Norman Mailer, old-line pacifists such as A. J. Muste and new radicals such as Tom Hayden, civil rights leader Dr. Martin Luther King Jr., and conservative Arkansas Senator J. William Fulbright. The doves constituted only a small percentage of the population, but they were an unusually visible and articulate group. Their attack on American foreign policy was vicious and unrelenting. In time, their movement became inextricably linked with the cultural revolution that swept the United States in the late 1960s and challenged the most basic of American values and institutions, leaving divisions that would last into the next century.

College students comprised the shock troops of the movement. Inspired by John Kennedy's idealism and appeals to service, schooled in the civil rights movement, and increasingly outraged by the war and the draft, a small but vocal and highly articulate group of students took the lead in 1965 in openly protesting the war. Brash, self-confident, often self-righteous, they proved skillful propagandists. They fused pop music with protest and in doing so "helped fix the minds of a generation." Only a minority of American college students opposed the war and an even smaller minority actively protested it. Spearheaded by organizations such as Students for a Democratic Society, however, these few students initiated and set the tone for the early antiwar protests, catching the government off guard and leaving it unsure how to respond. They raised public consciousness about the war. Through what has been called "offspring-lobbying," they exerted some influence on their elders. They continued to draw attention even as other groups assumed leadership of the movement.[58]

Although it defies precise categorization, the antiwar movement tended to group ideologically along three principal lines.[59] For pacifists such as Muste, who opposed all wars as immoral, Vietnam was but another phase of a lifelong crusade. For the burgeoning radical movement of the 1960s, opposition to the war extended beyond questions of morality. Spawned by the civil rights

[58]Rhodri Jeffreys-Jones, *Peace Now! American Society and the Ending of the Vietnam War* (New Haven, Conn., 1999), pp. 43–92.

[59]See Charles DeBenedetti with Charles Chatfield, *An American Ordeal: The Antiwar Movement of the Vietnam Era* (Syracuse, N.Y., 1990), and David W. Levy, *The Debate over Vietnam* (Baltimore, 1991), pp. 171–178.

movement, drawing its largest following among upper-middle-class youth on elite college campuses, the New Left joined older leftist organizations in viewing the war as a classic example of the way the American ruling class exploited helpless people to sustain a decadent capitalist system.[60]

Antiwar liberals far exceeded in numbers the pacifists and radicals. Although they did not generally question "the system," they increasingly challenged the war on legal, moral, and practical grounds. Liberals charged that U.S. escalation in Vietnam violated the 1954 Geneva Accords, the United Nations Charter, and the Constitution of the United States. Many liberal internationalists who had supported World War II, Korea, and the Cold War found Vietnam morally repugnant. By backing a corrupt, authoritarian government, they contended, the United States was betraying its own principles. The use of weapons such as cluster bombs, herbicides, and napalm violated basic standards of human behavior. In the absence of any direct threat to American security, the devastation wreaked on North and South Vietnam was indefensible.

Many more liberals questioned the war on practical grounds. It was essentially an internal struggle among Vietnamese, they argued, whose connection with the Cold War was at best indirect. Liberals questioned the validity of the domino theory, especially after the Indonesian army in 1965 threw out the erratic President Sukarno and crushed the Indonesian Communist party. They agreed that Vietnam was of no more than marginal significance to the security of the United States. Indeed, they insisted, the huge investment there was diverting attention from more urgent problems at home and abroad, damaging America's relations with its allies, and inhibiting the development of a more constructive relationship with the Soviet Union. The liberal critique quickly broadened into an indictment of American "globalism." The United States had fallen victim to the "arrogance of power," Fulbright claimed, and was showing "signs of that fatal presumption, that over-extension of power and mission, which brought ruin to ancient Athens, to Napoleonic France and to Nazi Germany."[61]

The various groups that made up the movement disagreed sharply on goals and methods. For some pacifists and liberals,

---

[60]Irwin Unger, *The Movement* (New York, 1974), pp. 35–93.
[61]Quoted in Thomas Powers, *Vietnam: The War at Home* (Boston, 1984), p. 118.

terminating the war was an end in itself; for radicals, it was a means to the ultimate end—the overthrow of American capitalism. Many New Left radicals indeed feared that a premature end to the war might sap the revolutionary spirit and hinder achievement of their principal goal. Most liberals stopped short of advocating withdrawal from Vietnam, much less domestic revolution, proposing merely an end to the bombing, gradual de-escalation, and negotiations. Disagreement on methods was even sharper. Liberals generally preferred nonviolent protest and political action within the system and sought to exclude Communists from demonstrations. Radicals and some pacifists increasingly pressed for a shift from protest to resistance. Some openly advocated the use of violence to bring down a system that was itself violent.

Opposition to the war took many forms. In early 1966, Fulbright's Senate Foreign Relations Committee conducted a series of nationally televised hearings, subjecting administration spokespersons to intense grilling and bringing before viewers such establishment figures and critics of administration policies in Vietnam as Gen. James Gavin and diplomat George F. Kennan, the father of the Cold War containment policy. The hearings got full coverage on all three networks. By challenging the administration's rationale for the war and claims of progress, they forced the public debate LBJ had tried so desperately to avoid and signaled the end of years of executive dominance and congressional acquiescence. They did not convert the public or the Congress, but they made opposition to the war respectable and widened the president's already sizable credibility gap.[62]

There were hundreds of acts of individual defiance. The folk singer Joan Baez refused to pay that portion of her income tax that went to the defense budget. Muhammad Ali declared himself a conscientious objector and refused induction orders, thereby forfeiting his title. Three army enlisted men—the Fort Hood Three—challenged the constitutionality of the conflict by refusing to fight in what they labeled an "unjust, immoral, and illegal war." Army Capt. Howard Levy used the doctrine of individual

[62]Andrew L. Johns, *Vietnam's Second Front: Domestic Politics, the Republican Party, and the War* (Lexington, Ky., 2011), pp. 106–107; Joseph A. Fry, *Debating Vietnam: Fulbright, Stennis, and Their Senate Hearings* (Lanham, Md., 2006), pp. vii, 171–172.

responsibility set forth in the Nuremberg war crimes trials to justify his refusal to train medical teams for combat in Vietnam. Thousands of young Americans exploited legal loopholes, even mutilated themselves, to evade the draft; an estimated 30,000 fled to Canada. Some served jail sentences rather than go to Vietnam. Seven Americans adopted the method of protest of South Vietnam's Buddhists by publicly immolating themselves, as the young Quaker Norman Morrison did directly beneath McNamara's Pentagon office window in November 1965!

Antiwar rallies and demonstrations drew larger crowds in 1966 and 1967, and the participants grew more outspoken. Protestors marched daily around the White House chanting, "Hey, hey, LBJ, how many kids have you killed today?" and "Ho, Ho, Ho Chi Minh, NLF is going to win." Antiwar forces attempted lie-ins in front of troop trains, collected blood for the NLF, and tried to disrupt the work of draft boards, U.S. Army recruiters, and the Dow Chemical Company, producer of the napalm used in Vietnam.

The most dramatic act of protest came on October 21, 1967, with the March on the Pentagon, the culmination of Stop the Draft Week. A diverse group estimated at 100,000 including colorfully arrayed hippies and intellectuals such as Mailer, gathered at the Lincoln Memorial for songs of protest by performers such as Peter, Paul, and Mary and Phil Ochs and speeches proclaiming the beginning of "active resistance." As many as 35,000 protesters subsequently crossed the Potomac and advanced on the Pentagon. The demonstrators were unable to levitate the "nerve center of American imperialism" and exorcise its evil spirits, as radical Abbie Hoffman had promised, but a small group conducted a sit-in. Some carried NLF flags, others smoked marijuana, and a few put flowers in the barrels of the rifles of soldiers guarding the building. Soldiers were challenged to leave their posts. The demonstration ended that evening in violence when federal marshals moved in with clubs and tear gas and arrested nearly 700 demonstrators.[63]

The impact of the antiwar protests remains one of the most controversial issues raised by the war. The obvious manifestations of dissent in the United States undoubtedly encouraged Hanoi to hold out for victory, although there is nothing to suggest that the

[63]Terry H. Anderson, *The Movement and the Sixties: Protest in America from Greensboro to Wounded Knee* (New York, 1995), pp. 178–179.

March on the Pentagon
This picture of an antiwar protestor placing a flower in the barrel of the
rifle of a soldier guarding the Pentagon was taken during the March on the
Pentagon in October 1967, the largest antiwar demonstration to that time.
© *Washington Post/Getty Images*

North Vietnamese would have been more compromising in the
absence of the protests. Antiwar protest did not turn the American
people against the war, as some critics have argued. The effectiveness of the movement was limited by the divisions within its own
ranks. Public opinion polls made abundantly clear, moreover, that a
majority of Americans found the antiwar movement, particularly
its radical and hippie elements, more obnoxious than the war itself.
In a perverse sort of way, the protest may even have strengthened
support for a war that was not in itself popular. The impact of the
movement was much more limited and subtle. It forced Vietnam
into the public consciousness and challenged the rationale of the
war and indeed of a generation of Cold War foreign policies. It
exposed error and self-deception in the government's claims,
encouraging distrust of political authority. It limited Johnson's military options and may have headed off any tendency toward more
drastic escalation. Perhaps most important, the disturbances and
divisions set off by the antiwar movement caused fatigue and

anxiety among the policymakers and the public, thus eventually encouraging efforts to find a way out of the war.[64]

The majority of Americans rejected both the hawk and the dove positions, but as the war dragged on and the debate became more divisive, public concern increased significantly. Expansion of the war in 1965 was followed by a surge of popular support—the usual rally-round-the-flag phenomenon. But the failure of escalation to produce any discernible progress and indications that more troops and higher taxes would be required to sustain a prolonged and perhaps inconclusive war combined to produce growing frustration and impatience.[65] If any bird symbolized the public disenchantment with Vietnam, opinion analyst Samuel Lubell observed, it was the albatross, with many Americans sharing a "fervent desire to shake free of an unwanted burden." The public mood was probably best expressed by a woman who told Lubell: "I want to get out but I don't want to give up."[66]

Support for the war dropped sharply during 1967. By the summer of that year, draft calls exceeded 30,000 per month, and more than 13,000 Americans had died in Vietnam. In early August, the president recommended a 10 percent surtax to cover the steadily increasing costs of the war. Polls taken shortly after indicated that for the first time a majority of Americans felt the United States had erred in intervening in Vietnam. A substantial majority concluded that despite a growing investment, the United States was not "doing any better." Public approval of Johnson's handling of the war plummeted to 28 percent by October.

African Americans opposed the war in numbers much larger than the general population. At first supportive of U.S. involvement, they grew increasingly and understandably dubious about fighting for freedom in Vietnam when they did not have full

---

[64]DeBenedetti and Chatfield, *American Ordeal*, pp. 387–408; Melvin Small, *Johnson, Nixon, and the Doves* (New Brunswick, N.J., 1988), pp. 226–234. For a contrary view see Adam Garfinkle's *Telltale Hearts: The Origins and Impact of the Vietnam Antiwar Movement* (New York, 1995).

[65]Sidney Verba et al., "Public Opinion and the War in Vietnam," *American Political Science Review* 61 (June 1967): 317–333; John E. Mueller, "Trends in Popular Support for the Wars in Korea and Vietnam," ibid., 65 (June 1971): 358–375; and Peter W. Sperlich and William L. Lunch, "American Public Opinion and the War in Vietnam," *Western Political Quarterly* 32 (March 1979): 21–44.

[66]Samuel Lubell, *The Hidden Crisis in American Politics* (New York, 1971), pp. 254–260.

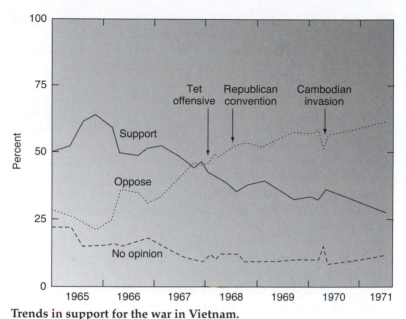

Trends in support for the war in Vietnam.
From John E. Mueller, War, Presidents, & Public Opinion, *p. 56. Copyright © 1985 University Press of America. Reprinted with permission of Rowman & Littlefield Publishers.*

freedom at home. Many came to view the war as a racial conflict whose goal was to oppress another people of color. They felt directly the mounting economic consequences of the war and, despite administration disclaimers, perceived that it was draining funds from government programs that benefited them. "The Great Society has been shot down on the battlefields of Vietnam," King lamented in 1967. African Americans correctly saw themselves as the primary victims of an inequitable selective service system that drafted their sons in disproportionate numbers and used them as cannon fodder. King's speech of April 4, 1967, publicly breaking with the administration over the war, was a signal of revolt. Blacks did not join the antiwar protests in large numbers, but their growing opposition damaged the administration politically. Their resistance to the draft and discontent within the military itself weakened the war effort.[67]

[67]Jeffreys-Jones, *Peace Now,* pp. 94–117. The King quote is from p. 98.

Waning public confidence was mirrored in the press and Congress. A number of major metropolitan dailies shifted from support of the war to opposition in 1967, and even the influential Time-Life publications, fervently hawkish at the outset, began to raise serious questions about the administration's policies. By 1967, Congress was as uneasy with the war—and as divided over it—as the rest of the country. The two political parties were split within their own ranks. Doves and hawks from each at times formed alliances of expediency. Democratic doves had spearheaded the early opposition to the war, and Johnson on occasion had turned to Republicans for crucial support. As the 1968 elections approached, however, Republican hawks and doves increasingly challenged the president's policies. The defection of Kentucky Republican senator Thruston B. Morton in late 1967 was viewed as a "sort of political weather vane" for the nation at large. Admitting that he had once been an "all-out hawk," Morton spoke for the growing number of converts when he complained that the United States had been "planted into a corner out there" and insisted that there would "have to be a change."[68] White House aides nervously warned of further defections in Congress and major electoral setbacks in 1968 in the absence of dramatic changes in the war.[69]

By late 1967, for many observers the war had become the most visible symbol of a malaise that afflicted all of American society. Not all would have agreed with Fulbright's assertion that the Great Society was a "sick society," but many did feel that the United States was going through a kind of national nervous breakdown. The "credibility gap"—the difference between what the administration said and what it did—had produced a pervasive distrust of government. Rioting in the cities, a spiraling crime rate, and noisy demonstrations in the streets suggested that violence abroad had produced violence at home. Increasingly divided against itself, the nation appeared on the verge of an internal crisis as severe as the Great Depression of the 1930s. Anxiety about the war had not

[68]For the shift of 1967, see Johns *Second Front*, pp. 129–139,160–161, 176; Don Oberdorfer, *Tet!* (Garden City, N.Y., 1971), pp. 83–92; and Louis Harris, *The Anguish of Change* (New York, 1973), pp. 60–61.
[69]Walt Rostow to Johnson, August 1, 1967, Johnson Papers, Declassified and Sanitized Documents from Unprocessed Files (DSDUF), Box 2; Harry McPherson to Johnson, August 25, 1967, Johnson Papers, McPherson File, Box 32.

translated into a firm consensus for escalation or withdrawal, but the public mood—tired, angry, and frustrated—posed perhaps a more serious threat to the administration than did the antiwar movement.

THE WAR IN WASHINGTON

The public debate on Vietnam was paralleled by increasingly sharp divisions within the government. Rejecting CIA estimates that played down the success of U.S. military operations, Westmoreland insisted that progress was being made and that the war could be won if the United States used its military power effectively. Although they had beaten down many of the restrictions on the bombing by 1967, the Joint Chiefs remained deeply dissatisfied with the conduct of the air war and angered by the president's continuing refusal to mobilize the reserves. Westmoreland had been given considerable leeway in implementing ground operations, but he resented what he later described as "naive, gratuitous advice" from the "self-appointed field marshals" in the State and Defense Departments. He was frustrated by restrictions that forbade him from going into enemy sanctuaries.[70]

Westmoreland and the Joint Chiefs joined forces in the spring of 1967 to seek a commitment to all-out war. Still confident that search and destroy could succeed, the field commander requested an additional 200,000 troops to step up ground operations against the enemy. The Joint Chiefs urged a limited mobilization of the reserves to secure the new increments. To deny the enemy its sanctuaries, the military pressed for intensive ground and air operations in Cambodia and Laos as well as for an amphibious "hook" across the demilitarized zone into North Vietnam. The Joint Chiefs also advocated intensified bombing of the Hanoi–Haiphong area and the mining of North Vietnamese ports. Presenting a united front, the military urged expansion of the war to force a North Vietnamese defeat.[71]

[70]Westmoreland, *Soldier Reports*, p. 161.
[71]Westmoreland to Joint Chiefs of Staff, March 28, 1967, in Neil Sheehan et al., *The Pentagon Papers as Published by the New York Times* (New York, 1971), pp. 560–565, hereafter cited as *Pentagon Papers (NYT)*; Joint Chiefs of Staff to McNamara, April 20, 1967, ibid., pp. 565–567.

By this time, some of Johnson's civilian advisers were openly advocating the abandonment of policies they had come to regard as bankrupt. Throughout 1966, opposition to the war increased within the administration. Some internal critics, including Bill Moyers of the White House staff and George Ball, quietly resigned, feeling, as James Thomson later put it, "totally alienated from the policy, but helpless as to how to change it."[72] The opposition continued to grow and increasingly centered among the civilians in the Defense Department.

The major proponent of change by the spring of 1967 was, ironically, the secretary of defense, a man intimately associated with a conflict once called "McNamara's war." McNamara seems to have concluded as early as 1965 that the war could not be won in any meaningful sense. In the summer of 1966, he began to fear that the vast expansion of the war was endangering the global security position he had labored so diligently to construct since taking office in 1961. He was troubled by the destructiveness of the war, particularly the civilian casualties, and by the growing domestic opposition, brought home to him in public appearances when he had to shove his way through and shout down protesters. McNamara's reputation as a businessman and public servant had been based on his ability to attain maximum results at minimal cost. By early 1967, he was forced to admit that escalation of the war had not produced results in the major "end products—broken enemy morale and political effectiveness." The South Vietnamese government seemed no more stable than before; pacification had, "if anything, gone backward." The air war had brought heavy costs but limited results, and had cost the United States heavily in terms of domestic and world opinion. "The picture of the world's greatest superpower killing or seriously injuring 1,000 non-combatants a week, while trying to pound a tiny, backward nation into submission on an issue whose merits are hotly disputed, is not a pretty one," he advised Johnson in early 1967.[73] Increases in U.S. troops had not produced correspondingly larger enemy losses. There was nothing to indicate that further expansion of the war would place any real strains on North Vietnamese personnel.

[72]James C. Thomson, "Getting Out and Speaking Out," *Foreign Policy* 13 (Winter 1973–1974), 57.
[73]McNamara to Johnson, May 19, 1967, in Sheehan et al., *Pentagon Papers (NYT)*, p. 580.

Torn between disenchantment with the war and loyalty to his president, McNamara quietly and somewhat hesitantly pressed for basic changes in policy throughout 1967. Arguing that major military targets in North Vietnam had already been destroyed, he proposed either an unconditional bombing halt or restriction of the bombing to the area south of the twentieth parallel. Such a move, he added, would appease critics of the war at home and might lead to serious negotiations. The secretary of defense also advocated a ceiling on troop levels and a shift from search and destroy to a more limited ground strategy based on providing security for the population of South Vietnam.

In somewhat ambiguous terms, he further proposed a scaling down of American political objectives. Inasmuch as the United States had gone to war to contain China, he argued, it had succeeded: The Communist defeat in Indonesia and rampant political turmoil within China itself suggested that trends in Asia were now running in favor of the United States. The administration might therefore adopt a more flexible bargaining position. It could still hope for an independent, non-Communist South Vietnam, but it should not obligate itself to "guarantee and insist upon these conditions." Obliquely at least, McNamara appears to have been suggesting that the United States modify its military strategy and diplomatic stance to find a face-saving way out of Vietnam.[74]

By the summer of 1967, Lyndon Johnson was a deeply troubled man, physically and emotionally exhausted, frustrated by his lack of success, torn between his advisers, uncertain which way to turn. He seems to have shared some of McNamara's reservations. "Bomb, bomb, bomb, that's all you know," he complained to the Joint Chiefs on several occasions.[75] He was worried by Westmoreland's request for more troops. "When we add divisions, can't the enemy add divisions?" he asked the general pointedly in April. "If so, where does it all end?"[76] He remained firmly opposed to mobilizing the reserves.

[74]Ibid., pp. 584–585.
[75]Quoted in Lawrence J. Korb, *The Joint Chiefs of Staff: The First Twenty-Five Years* (Bloomington, Ind., 1976), p. 181.
[76]Excerpt from Johnson–Westmoreland conversation, April 20, 1967, in Sheehan et al., *Pentagon Papers (NYT)*, p. 567.

Johnson could not accept McNamara's recommendations, however. He had gradually lost confidence in his secretary of defense. The relationship had so soured by late 1967 that the secretary gladly accepted an appointment to head the World Bank. Westmoreland continued to report steady progress, moreover, and the president was not ready to concede defeat. He would not consider a return to the enclave strategy—"We can't hunker down like a jackass in a hailstorm," he said—or even a ceiling on the troop level.[77] Although he seems to have agreed that the bombing had accomplished nothing, he was not prepared to stop or even limit it. He refused to risk a confrontation with the hawks or a potentially explosive public debate on the bombing. Moreover, many of those to whom Johnson turned for advice argued strongly against McNamara's recommendations. Rusk, National Security Adviser Rostow, Taylor, Clifford, and McGeorge Bundy all agreed that domestic critics would not be appeased by a bombing halt. Doves, like hawks, had "insatiable appetites," Bundy warned, and if concessions were made to them, they would merely demand more.[78]

Johnson thus continued to cling to the shrinking middle ground between his advisers. He rejected military proposals to expand the war and for 200,000 additional soldiers, approving an increase of only 55,000. No ceilings were set, however, and there was no reassessment of the search-and-destroy strategy. He also turned down McNamara's proposals to limit or stop the bombing. Indeed, to placate the Joint Chiefs and congressional hawks, he significantly expanded the list of targets, authorizing strikes against bridges, railyards, and barracks within the Hanoi–Haiphong "donut" and formerly restricted areas along the Chinese border.

Johnson's decisions of 1967, even more than those of 1965, defied military logic and did not face, much less resolve, the contradictions in U.S. strategy. The bombing was sustained not because anyone thought it would work but because Johnson deemed it necessary to pacify certain domestic factions and because stopping it might be regarded as a sign of weakness. The president refused to give his field commander the troops he considered necessary to

---

[77]Ibid., p. 436.
[78]Bundy to Johnson, ca. May 4, 1967, in Sheehan et al., *Pentagon Papers (NYT),* pp. 569–572.

make his strategy work, but he did not confront the inconsistencies in the strategy itself.

The administration did modify its negotiating position in late 1967. The so-called San Antonio formula backed away from a firm prior agreement on mutual de-escalation. The United States would stop the bombing "with the understanding" that this action would lead "promptly to productive discussions" and that North Vietnam would not "take advantage" by increasing the infiltration of soldiers and supplies across the seventeenth parallel.[79] The administration also indicated its willingness to admit the NLF to political participation in South Vietnam. This softening of the U.S. bargaining position did not reflect the change of goals that McNamara had recommended, however. The commitment to the Thieu regime remained firm. The willingness to deal with the NLF appears to have been based on a hope that it could be co-opted or defeated by political means.

By the end of the year, moreover, Johnson recognized that additional steps would be necessary to hold off disaster. After months of uncertainty, the administration finally concluded in the late summer that slow but steady progress was being made. Officials in Saigon optimistically reported that U.S. operations were keeping the enemy off balance and inflicting enormous losses. The NLF was encountering difficulties in recruiting. The ARVN's desertion rate had declined, and the performance of some units in combat had improved. After months of floundering, pacification seemed to be getting off the ground. Even the generally pessimistic McNamara was moved to comment in July that "there is no military stalemate."[80]

By this time, however, the consensus Johnson had so carefully woven in 1964 was in tatters, the nation more divided than at any other time since the Civil War. Opposition in Congress, as well as inattention and mismanagement resulting partly from the administration's preoccupation with Vietnam, had brought his cherished Great Society programs to a standstill. The president himself was a man under siege in the White House: He was the target of vicious

[79]George C. Herring (ed.), *The Secret Diplomacy of the Vietnam War: The Negotiating Volumes of the Pentagon Papers* (Austin, Tex., 1983), pp. 538–544.
[80]Notes on meeting, July 12, 1967, Johnson Papers, Tom Johnson Notes on Meetings, Box 1.

personal attacks. His top aides had to be brought surreptitiously into public forums to deliver speeches. "How are we going to win?" he asked plaintively at a top-level meeting in late 1967. Anticipating his dramatic March 31, 1968, decision, a despondent LBJ pondered not running for reelection.[81]

Johnson was alarmed by the position he found himself in, stung by his critics, and deeply hurt by the desertion of trusted aides. He angrily dismissed much of the criticism as unfair, and he repeatedly emphasized that his critics offered no alternatives. He recognized that he could not ignore the opposition, however. During the early years, he seems to have feared the hawks more than the doves, but by late 1967 he had changed his mind. "The major threat we have is from the doves," he told his advisers in September 1967.[82] Increasingly fearful that the war might be lost in the United States, he launched a two-pronged offensive to silence his most outspoken enemies and win public support for his policies.

Mistakenly believing that the peace movement was turning the public against the war, the president set out to destroy it. The FBI was already compiling huge dossiers on antiwar and civil rights activists such as Martin Luther King Jr. and Malcolm X, as well as leading peace groups and even the mainstream Protestant National Council of Churches. LBJ also instructed the CIA to institute a program of surveillance of antiwar leaders to prove his suspicions that they were operating on orders from Communist governments. This program, later institutionalized as Operation CHAOS, violated the agency's charter. It led to the compilation of files on more than 7,000 Americans. When the CIA failed to find the links Johnson suspected, he leaked information to right-wing members of Congress that he had such proof, leaving it to them to issue public charges that the peace movement was "being cranked up in Hanoi." As antiwar forces moved from opposition to resistance, the administration's war against them shifted from surveillance to harassment. Law enforcement agencies indicted antiwar leaders such as Dr. Spock for counseling draft resistance. The Internal

[81]Notes on meetings, October 3, 16, 1967, Johnson Papers, Tom Johnson Notes on Meetings, Box 1.
[82]Jim Jones notes on meeting, September 5, 1967, Johnson Papers, Meeting Notes File, Box 2.

Revenue Service examined the tax returns of antiwar leaders and organizations. The FBI recruited informants inside peace organizations, wiretapped telephones, broke into homes and offices, and infiltrated various groups with the object of disrupting their work and causing their members to do things that would further discredit them in the eyes of the public.[83]

At the same time, Johnson mounted an intensive campaign to shore up popular support for the war. From behind the scenes, administration officials organized the ostensibly private Committee for Peace with Freedom in Vietnam, to mobilize the "silent center" in American politics. Johnson's advisers supplied to friendly senators, including some Republicans, information to help answer the charges of congressional doves. A Vietnam Information Group was set up in the White House to monitor public reactions to the war and deal with problems as soon as they surfaced.[84] Recognizing the widespread public perception that the war was a stalemate, the president ordered the embassy and military command in Saigon to "search urgently for occasions to present sound evidence of progress in Vietnam." U.S. officials dutifully responded, producing reams of statistics to show a steady rise in enemy body counts and the number of villages pacified, and publishing captured documents that supported these claims. The White House even arranged for influential citizens to go to Vietnam and observe the progress firsthand.[85]

Westmoreland was brought home in November to reassure a troubled nation. Upon arriving in Washington, he told reporters, "I am very, very encouraged. . . . We are making real progress." In a November 21 speech, he affirmed that although the enemy had not been defeated, it had been badly hurt. "We have reached an important point where the end begins to come into view," he concluded. He even hinted that the United States might begin troop withdrawals within two years.[86]

---

[83]Charles DeBenedetti, "A CIA Analysis of the Anti-Vietnam War Movement: October 1967," *Peace and Change* 9 (Spring 1983): 31–35.

[84]See the extensive correspondence in Johnson Papers, Marvin Watson File, Box 32.

[85]Walt Rostow to Ellsworth Bunker, September 27, 1967, Johnson Papers, DSDUF, Box 4; Eugene Locke to Johnson, October 7, 1967, Johnson Papers, National Security File, Country File: Vietnam, Box 99.

[86]Quoted in Richard P. Stebbins, *The United States in World Affairs, 1967* (New York, 1968), p. 68.

Although his public relations offensive began to show immediate results, Johnson seems to have concluded by the end of the year that a change of strategy in Vietnam might yet be necessary. Pressures for abandoning Westmoreland's search-and-destroy operations mounted throughout 1967. McNamara's civilian advisers pressed for a shift to small-unit patrols that would be more "cost-effective" and would reduce U.S. casualties.[87] In his last major policy memorandum to Johnson, the secretary of defense proposed seeking ways to reduce U.S. casualties and force the South Vietnamese to assume a greater burden of the fighting. Recognizing that public disillusionment threatened not only success in Vietnam but also the internationalist foreign policy the nation had pursued since World War II, a group of leading "establishment" figures, meeting under the auspices of the Carnegie Endowment, proposed a "clear and hold" strategy that would stabilize the war at a "politically tolerable level" and save South Vietnam "without surrender and without risking a wider war."[88]

The major impetus for change came from the so-called Wise Men, a distinguished group of former government officials whom Johnson occasionally called upon for guidance. He appealed to them in early November to advise him on how to unite the country behind the war. The Wise Men generally endorsed existing policies, but they warned that "endless inconclusive fighting" was "the most serious single cause of domestic disquiet." They proposed a ground strategy that would be less expensive in blood and treasure. They advised shifting to the South Vietnamese greater responsibility for the fighting. Former presidential assistant McGeorge Bundy went a step further, advising the president that he had an obligation to "visibly take command of a contest that is more political in its character than any other in our history except the Civil War" and to find a strategy that would be tolerable in cost to the American people for the five to ten years that might be required to stabilize the situation in Vietnam.[89] Johnson would go no further than to privately

[87]Depuy to Westmoreland, October 19, 1967, William Depuy Papers, U.S. Army Military History Institute, Carlisle Barracks, Pa., Folder WXYZ(67).

[88]"Carnegie Endowment Proposals," December 5, 1967, Matthew B. Ridgway Papers, U.S. Army Military History Institute, Carlisle Barracks, Pa., Box 34A.

[89]Jim Jones notes on meeting, November 2, 1967, Johnson Papers, Meeting Notes File, Box 2; Bundy to Johnson, November 10, 1967, Johnson Papers, Diary Backup, Box 81.

commit himself to "review" the conduct of ground operations with an eye toward reducing U.S. casualties and transferring greater responsibility to the South Vietnamese.[90] Even before the Tet Offensive of 1968, he was moving in the direction of what would later be called Vietnamization.

But he did not reevaluate his essential goals in Vietnam. To take such a step would have been difficult for anyone as long as there was hope of eventual success. It would have been especially difficult for Lyndon Johnson. Enormously ambitious, he had set high goals for his presidency, and he was unwilling to abandon them even in the face of frustration and massive unrest at home. It was not a matter of courage. By persisting in the face of declining popularity Johnson displayed courage as well as stubbornness. It was primarily a matter of pride. The president had not wanted the war in Vietnam, but once committed to it he had invested his personal prestige to a degree that made it impossible to back off. He chose to stay the course in 1967 for the same reasons he had gone to war in the first place—because he saw no alternative that did not require him to admit failure or defeat.

While quietly contemplating a change in strategy, Johnson publicly vowed to see the war through to a successful conclusion. "We are not going to yield," he stated repeatedly. "We are not going to shimmy. We are going to wind up with a peace with honor which all Americans seek." At a White House dinner for the prime minister of Singapore, the president expressed his commitment in different terms. "Mr. Prime Minister," he said, "you have a phrase in your part of the world that puts our determination very well. You call it 'riding the tiger.' You rode the tiger. We shall!" The words would take on a bitterly ironic ring in the climactic year 1968.[91]

[90]Johnson memorandum for the record, December 18, 1967, in Lyndon B. Johnson, *The Vantage Point* (New York, 1971), pp. 600–601.
[91]Quoted in Stebbins, *United States in World Affairs, 1967*, pp. 397–398.

Tet, 1968
This classic photo of the street execution of a Vietcong captive by the Saigon police chief brought home to Americans the savagery of the battles of Tet, and aroused growing concern about the type of government and war they were supporting.
© *Eddie Adams/AP Images*

CHAPTER 6

A Very Near Thing

The Tet Offensive and After, 1968

At 2:45 a.m. on January 31, 1968, a team of National Liberation Front (NLF) sappers blasted a large hole in the wall surrounding the U.S. embassy in Saigon and dashed into the courtyard of the compound. For the next six hours, the most important symbol of the American presence in Vietnam was the scene of one of the most dramatic episodes of the war. Unable to get through the heavy door at the main entrance of the embassy building, the attackers retreated to the courtyard and took cover behind large concrete flower pots, pounding the building with rockets and exchanging gunfire with a small detachment of military police. They held their positions until 9:15 a.m., when they were finally overpowered. All nineteen were killed or severely wounded.

The attack on the embassy was but a small part of the Tet Offensive, a massive, coordinated assault against the major urban areas of South Vietnam. In most other locales, the result was the same: The attackers were repulsed and incurred heavy losses. Later that morning, standing in the embassy courtyard amid the debris and fallen bodies in a scene one reporter described as a "butcher shop in Eden," Westmoreland rendered his initial assessment of Tet. The "well-laid plans" of the North Vietnamese and NLF had failed, he observed. "The enemy exposed himself by virtue of his strategy and he suffered heavy casualties." Although his comments brought moans of disbelief from the assembled journalists, from a short-term tactical standpoint Westmoreland was correct: Tet represented

233

a major military defeat for the enemy.[1] As Bernard Brodie has observed, however, the Tet Offensive was "probably unique in that the side that lost completely in the tactical sense came away with an overwhelming psychological and hence political victory."[2] Tet had a tremendous impact in the United States and ushered in a new phase of a seemingly endless war.

GENERAL OFFENSIVE, GENERAL UPRISING

Without full access to North Vietnamese archives, it remains difficult to piece together the origins of the Tet Offensive. As early as the summer of 1966, Hanoi appears to have begun discussing plans for a "general offensive, general uprising," a decisive blow to achieve victory. Such talks were born neither of desperation, as some U.S. commentators later insisted, nor of excessive optimism. They did reflect pressures from the Soviets and the Chinese, whose increasingly bitter conflict put Hanoi in a perilous position. They also reflected growing concern about a military status quo in which North Vietnam was being pummeled by U.S. bombs and the war in the South remained stalemated. Party leaders at least dimly perceived the debate in Washington over possible escalation of the war. Some urged a decisive move before the United States could act. Others hoped to exploit rising antiwar sentiment in the United States and the 1968 presidential election in order to force a change in U.S. policy.[3]

Serious planning began in 1967 and provoked fierce debate within party councils. Some leaders preferred to follow the Soviet line and open negotiations with the United States, at least as a way to get the bombing stopped. In January 1967, Hanoi relaxed its conditions for negotiations. Veteran revolutionaries Ho Chi Minh and Defense Minister Vo Nguyen Giap leaned toward the protracted war strategy favored by China and were especially wary of large-scale

[1]Quoted in Don Oberdorfer, *Tet!* (Garden City, N.Y., 1973), p. 34. For a more recent analysis, see James H. Willbanks, *The Tet Offensive: A Concise History* (New York, 2007).
[2]Bernard Brodie, "The Tet Offensive," in Noble Frankland and Christopher Dowling (eds.), *Decisive Battles of the Twentieth Century* (London, 1976), p. 321.
[3]Merle L. Pribbenow II, "General Vo Nguyen Giap and the Mysterious Evolution of the Plan for the 1968 Tet Offensive," *Journal of Vietnamese Studies* 3 (Summer 2008): 3–10.

military operations, which would impose additional heavy losses on an already war-weary population, or a massive offensive directed at the urban areas of South Vietnam before conditions were ripe. As before, the relentlessly aggressive first secretary Le Duan pressed for much bolder—and more risky—action. Although his daring gamble of 1964 had been thwarted by U.S. military intervention, the first secretary remained certain that the NLF and North Vietnam could strike a decisive blow. He opposed serious negotiations prior to a military victory. To lure U.S. troops away from the major population centers and maintain high enemy casualties, a series of diversionary attacks would be launched in remote areas. These would be followed by coordinated guerrilla assaults against the major cities and towns of South Vietnam to rock the Saigon government to its foundations, ignite a "general uprising" among the people, and shake the will of the United States. Le Duan outflanked Giap by recruiting his second-in-command, Gen. Van Tien Dung, to direct the war in the South. He ignored Ho's repeated objections. Ho and Giap subsequently left the country for extended periods, ostensibly for medical reasons. To ensure full support for their plan, in the summer and fall of 1967 Le Duan and his cohorts executed a brutal purge of party dissidents, incarcerating many of them in Hanoi's Hoa Lo prison (which would later hold U.S. prisoners of war). They whipped up a paranoid frenzy as a basis for political repression. The full plan for a general offensive, general uprising gained final approval in January 1968 just weeks before it was to begin.[4]

Hanoi began executing its plan in late 1967. In October and November, North Vietnamese regulars attacked the U.S. Marine base at Con Thien, across the Laotian border, and the towns of Loc Ninh and Song Be near Saigon and Dak To in the Central Highlands. Shortly after, two North Vietnamese divisions laid siege to the Marine garrison at Khe Sanh near the Laotian border. In the meantime, crack NLF units moved into the cities and towns, accumulating supplies and laying final plans. To undermine the Saigon government, the insurgents encouraged the formation of a "popular front" of neutralists and attempted to entice government officials and troops to defect by offering generous pardons and positions in a coalition government. To spread dissension between

---

[4]Ibid, 13–24; Lien-Hang T. Nguyen, *Hanoi's War: An International History of the War for Peace in Vietnam* (Chapel Hill, N.C., 2012), pp. 88–103.

the United States and Thieu, the front opened secret contacts with the U.S. embassy in Saigon and disseminated rumors of peace talks. Hanoi followed in December 1967 by stating categorically that it would negotiate if the United States stopped the bombing.

The first phase of the plan worked to perfection. Westmoreland quickly dispatched reinforcements to Con Thien, Loc Ninh, Song Be, and Dak To, in each case driving back the North Vietnamese and inflicting heavy losses but dispersing U.S. forces and leaving the cities vulnerable. By the end of 1967, moreover, the attention of Westmoreland, the president, and indeed much of the nation was riveted on Khe Sanh, which many Americans assumed was Giap's play for a repetition of Dien Bien Phu. The press and television carried daily reports of the action. Insisting that the fortress be held at all costs, Johnson kept close watch on the battle with a terrain map in the White House war room. Westmoreland sent 6,000 soldiers to defend the garrison. B-52 bombers carried out the heaviest air raids in the history of warfare, eventually dropping more than 100,000 tons of explosives on a five-square-mile battlefield.

While the United States was preoccupied with Khe Sanh, the North Vietnamese and NLF prepared for the second phase of the operation. The offensive against the cities was timed to coincide with the beginning of Tet, the lunar new year and the most festive of Vietnamese holidays. Traditionally, at Tet, people returned to their native villages and engaged in a week of celebrations, renewing ties with family, honoring ancestors, indulging in meals, and shooting firecrackers. Throughout the war, both sides had observed a cease-fire during Tet. Hanoi correctly assumed that South Vietnam would be relaxing and celebrating, with soldiers visiting their families and government officials away from their offices. While the Americans and South Vietnamese prepared for the holidays, NLF units readied themselves for the bloodiest battles of the war. Mingling with the heavy holiday traffic, guerrillas disguised as Army of the Republic of Vietnam (ARVN) soldiers or as civilians moved into the cities and towns, some audaciously hitching rides on American vehicles. Weapons were smuggled in on vegetable carts and even in mock funeral processions. At Cu Chi in the Iron Triangle, recruits practiced getting inside a replica of the U.S. embassy grounds.

Within twenty-four hours after the beginning of Tet, January 31, 1968, the NLF launched a series of attacks extending from the demilitarized zone to the Ca Mau Peninsula on the southern tip of

Vietnam. In all, they struck thirty-six of forty-four provincial capitals, five of the six major cities, sixty-four district capitals, and fifty hamlets. In addition to the daring raid on the embassy, NLF units assaulted Saigon's Tan Son Nhut Airport, the huge U.S. base at Long Binh, the presidential palace, and the headquarters of South Vietnam's general staff. In Hue, 7,500 NLF and North Vietnamese troops stormed and eventually took control of the ancient Citadel, the interior town that had been the seat of the emperors of the Kingdom of Annam.

U.S.–SOUTH VIETNAMESE RESPONSE

The offensive caught the United States and South Vietnam off guard. American intelligence had picked up signs of intensive enemy activity in and around the cities and had even translated captured documents that, without giving dates, outlined the plan in some detail. The U.S. command was so preoccupied with Khe Sanh, however, that it viewed evidence pointing to the cities as a diversion to distract it from the main battlefield. As had happened so often before, the United States underestimated the capability of the enemy. The North Vietnamese appeared so bloodied by the campaigns of 1967 that the Americans did not conceive they could bounce back and deliver a blow of the magnitude of Tet. "Even had I known exactly what was to take place," Westmoreland's intelligence officer later conceded, "it was so preposterous that I probably would have been unable to sell it to anybody."[5]

Although taken by surprise, the United States and South Vietnam recovered quickly. The timing of the offensive was poorly coordinated. Premature attacks in some towns sounded a warning that enabled Westmoreland to get reinforcements to vulnerable areas. In addition, the NLF was slow to capitalize on its initial successes, giving the United States time to mount a strong defense. In Saigon, U.S. and ARVN forces held off the initial attacks and within several days cleared the city, inflicting huge casualties, taking large numbers of prisoners, and forcing the remnants to melt into the countryside.

---

[5]Quoted in William C. Westmoreland, *A Soldier Reports* (Garden City, N.Y., 1976), p. 321. For a full analysis of the U.S. intelligence failure at Tet, see James J. Wirtz, *The Tet Offensive: Intelligence Failure in War* (Ithaca, N.Y., 1991).

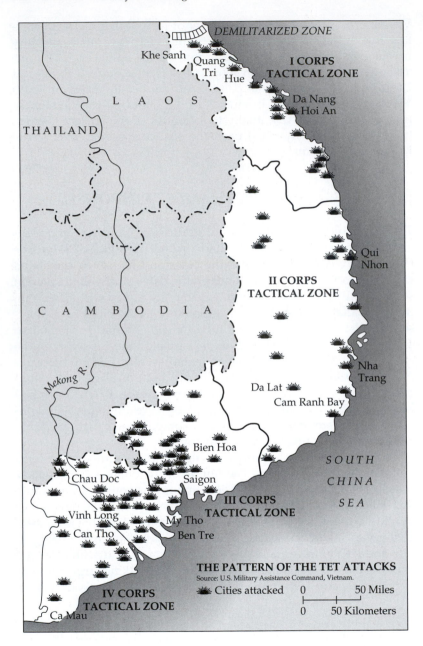

THE PATTERN OF THE TET ATTACKS
Source: U.S. Military Assistance Command, Vietnam.
Cities attacked   0   50 Miles
                   0   50 Kilometers

Hue during the Tet Offensive
This picture shows U.S. Marines walking the streets of Hue after a fierce, month-long battle to regain control from the North Vietnamese and NLF. Once the imperial capital of Annam and a city of great beauty and charm, Hue was left after the 1968 Tet Offensive, in the words of one observer, "a shattered, stinking hulk, its streets choked with rubble and rotting bodies."
© *Archive Photos/Getty Images*

Elsewhere the result was much the same. The ARVN fought better under pressure than any American would have dared predict, and the United States and South Vietnam used superior mobility and fire-power to devastating advantage. The NLF launched a second round of attacks on February 18, but these were confined largely to rocket and mortar barrages against U.S. and South Vietnamese military installations and steadily diminished in intensity.

Hue was the only exception to the general pattern. The liberation of that city took more than three weeks, required heavy bombing and intensive artillery fire, and ranks among the bloodiest and most destructive battles of the war. The United States and South Vietnam lost more than 500 killed, whereas enemy killed in action have been estimated as high as 5,000. The savage fighting caused huge numbers of civilian casualties and created an estimated 100,000 refugees. The bodies of 2,800 South Vietnamese were found in mass graves in and around Hue, the product of NLF and North Vietnamese executions. Another 2,000 citizens were unaccounted for and presumed murdered.

Despite the surprise they attained and their early successes, the North Vietnamese/NLF failed to achieve their major goals. They did not spark the hoped-for urban uprisings. They were not welcomed as liberators. Quite the contrary, many city dwellers rallied to the government. Their poorly coordinated attacks gave the United States and South Vietnam precious hours of warning in some areas. They badly underestimated the U.S. ability to shift forces quickly from one region to another. They were unable to establish any firm positions in the urban areas. Exposed to the full wrath of U.S. firepower, they suffered horrendous casualties, battle deaths being estimated as high as 40,000. The NLF bore the brunt of the fighting at Tet. Its regular units were decimated and would never fully recover. Its political infrastructure suffered crippling losses.

If, in these terms, Tet represented a military defeat for the enemy, it was still a very costly victory for the United States and South Vietnam. ARVN forces had to withdraw from the countryside to defend the cities, inflicting another major setback on pacification. The massive destruction within the cities heaped formidable new problems on a government that had shown limited capacity to deal with the routine. U.S. and South Vietnamese losses did not approach those of the enemy, but they were still very high: In the first two weeks of Tet, the United States lost 1,100 killed in action and South Vietnam 2,300. An estimated 12,500 civilians were killed; Tet created as many as 1 million new refugees. As in much of the war, there was a great deal of destruction and suffering, but no clear-cut winner or loser.

CONFUSION AND UNCERTAINTY

To the extent that the North Vietnamese designed the Tet Offensive to influence the United States, they succeeded, for it sent instant shock waves across the nation. Early wire service reports exaggerated the success of the raid on the embassy, some even indicating that the guerrillas had occupied several floors of the building.

Although these initial reports were in time corrected, the reaction was still one of disbelief. "What the hell is going on?" the venerable newscaster Walter Cronkite, once a strong supporter of the war, is said to have snapped. "I thought we were winning the war!"[6] Televised accounts of the bloody fighting in Saigon and Hue made a mockery of Johnson's and Westmoreland's optimistic year-end reports, widening the credibility gap; cynical journalists openly ridiculed Westmoreland's claims of victory. The humorist Art Buchwald parodied the general's statements in terms of Gen. George Custer at the Little Bighorn. "We have the Sioux on the run," Buchwald had Custer saying. "Of course we still have some cleaning up to do, but the Redskins are hurting badly and it will only be a matter of time before they give in."[7] The battles of Tet raised to a new level of public consciousness basic questions about the war that had long lurked just beneath the surface. The offhand remark of a U.S. Army officer who had participated in the liberation of the Mekong Delta village of Ben Tre—"We had to destroy the town to save it"— seemed to epitomize the purposeless destruction of the war. Candid photographs and television footage of the police chief of Saigon holding a pistol to the head of an NLF captive—and then firing— starkly symbolized the way violence had triumphed over law.

The Tet Offensive left Washington in a state of "troubled confusion and uncertainty."[8] Westmoreland insisted that the attacks had been repulsed and that there was no need to fear a major setback. Administration officials publicly echoed his statements. Johnson and his advisers were shocked by the suddenness and magnitude of the offensive, however, and intelligence estimates were much more pessimistic than Westmoreland. Many officials feared that Tet was only the opening phase of a larger Communist offensive. Some felt that Khe Sanh was still the primary objective, a fear that seemed borne out when the besieging forces renewed their attack in early February. Others feared a major offensive in the northern provinces or a second wave of attacks on the cities. An "air of gloom" hung over White House discussions, Taylor later observed. Gen. Wheeler likened the mood to that following the first Battle of Bull Run.[9]

[6]Quoted in Oberdorfer, *Tet!* p. 158.

[7]*Washington Post,* February 6, 1968.

[8]Townsend Hoopes, *The Limits of Intervention* (New York, 1970), p. 145.

[9]Earle Wheeler oral history interview, Johnson Papers, Lyndon Baines Johnson Library, Austin, Texas.

THE TROOP REQUEST

Out of this uncertainty emerged a Westmoreland request for 206,000 troops that vastly exacerbated the domestic political impact of the Tet Offensive and in time forced basic changes in U.S. policies. The request originated in a strange, almost surreal manner, reflecting divergent concerns within the national security apparatus and lingering confusion about Vietnam. Fearing an all-out enemy assault on Khe Sanh, perhaps being compelled to use tactical nuclear weapons to save the embattled fortress, or even a Dien Bien Phu–like defeat, LBJ vowed to hold the line, even if it required additional troops, expanded air attacks against North Vietnam, or diversionary ground operations in Laos or across the demilitarized zone. From Wheeler's standpoint, a series of possibly connected global threats and the new mood of urgency in Washington provided a timely opportunity to force decisions too long deferred. The Tet Offensive raised the possibility of reinforcements for Vietnam. North Korea's seizure of the U.S. warship *Pueblo* on January 23 and a new flare-up in Berlin aroused concerns about other Cold War hot spots. Available forces were nearly exhausted. Wheeler worried that unless the reserves were mobilized the nation could not meet its expanded commitments. "[If] you need more troops," he advised Westmoreland, "ask for them." Still optimistic, the general initially responded that Khe Sanh was safe. There was no need for nuclear weapons or additional troops.[10]

Under continued prodding from Wheeler, Westmoreland changed his tune, but his ambivalent and sometimes contradictory cables to Washington muddied the waters still further. He remained unclear whether Khe Sanh or the cities posed the greatest threat and what sort of burden the ARVN could assume. He continued to insist that Tet had been an enemy defeat and his forces were safe. But he asked for more troops. He spoke of "heightened risk," even the possibility of North Vietnam trying to seize the northern provinces of South Vietnam, but also of "great opportunity." In picking up on Wheeler's proposal, he left unclear whether he needed more men to avert defeat or to take the offensive against depleted enemy forces, "crush" them, and "materially shorten the war." Two of Westmoreland's cables seemed so different in tone and substance

---

[10]Edward J. Drea, *McNamara, Clifford, and the Burdens of Vietnam, 1965–1969* (Washington, D.C., 2011), pp. 181–182.

that Taylor questioned whether they had been written by the same person. In filtering Westmoreland's requests to Johnson and his civilian advisers, Wheeler painted the situation in much darker terms. Unwilling to "desert" his "commander in time of war"—but also to act "imprudently"—Johnson approved an additional 10,000 troops for Vietnam but also dispatched Wheeler to Saigon to consult with Westmoreland.[11]

Wheeler and Westmoreland conferred in late February and devised a scheme to force the president's hand. Wheeler appears to have been considerably less optimistic about the immediate prospects in Vietnam than Westmoreland, but he agreed that whether Tet provided new opportunities or posed increased dangers, it justified a call for major reinforcements. The two men settled on the figure of 206,000 soldiers, a number large enough to meet any contingency in Vietnam and force mobilization of the reserves. Roughly half of the troops would be deployed in Vietnam by the end of the year; the rest would constitute a strategic reserve. Wheeler raised no objections to a shift to an offensive strategy, but he persuaded the field commander that it would be best to defer such recommendations until the president had approved the new troop level. He was keenly aware of Johnson's opposition to widening the war. He apparently feared that if he presented the case for additional troops on the basis of an optimistic assessment and an offensive strategy, he would be turned down again. Troops, not strategy, offered the "stronger talking point."[12]

Wheeler's report to Washington was deeply pessimistic. Describing the Tet Offensive as a "very near thing," he warned that the initial enemy attacks had almost succeeded in numerous places and had been turned back only by the "timely reaction" of U.S. forces. The North Vietnamese and NLF had suffered heavily, but they had repeatedly demonstrated a capacity for quick recovery. They would probably attempt to sustain the offensive with renewed attacks. Without additional troops, Wheeler concluded, the United States must be "prepared to accept some reverses," a line calculated to sway a president who had already made clear he was not willing to accept defeat. Wheeler insisted that large-scale reinforcements were necessary to protect the cities, drive the enemy from the northern

---

[11]Ibid, pp. 182–183; U.S. Department of State, *Foreign Relations of the United States, 1964–1968,* Vol. 6 (Washington, D.C., 2002), p. 153, fn 2, fn 4; pp. 184–187.

[12]John B. Henry, "February, 1968," *Foreign Policy* (Fall 1971): 21.

provinces, and pacify the countryside. His pessimism may have been sincere; he had never been as confident as Westmoreland. It seems clear, however, that by presenting a gloomy assessment he hoped to stampede the administration into providing the troops to rebuild a depleted strategic reserve and meet any contingency in Vietnam. His proposal reopened in even more vigorous fashion the debate that had raged in Washington throughout 1967.[13]

Wheeler's report shocked an already thoroughly alarmed government. In terms of policy choices, it posed a hard dilemma. The general warned that denial of the request for 206,000 troops could result in military defeat or at least an indefinite continuation of the war. Approval, on the other hand, would force yet another major escalation and impose heavy new demands on the American people in an election year and at a time when public anxiety about Vietnam was already pronounced. At one point in a meeting devoted to the report, an exhausted and emotionally distraught McNamara, in his last hours in office, appealed to his colleagues to "end this thing. . . . It is out of control."[14] Not inclined to make a hasty decision on a matter fraught with such grave implications, Johnson turned the problem over to his new secretary of defense, Clark Clifford, with the grim instruction: "Give me the lesser of evils."

THE CLIFFORD TASK FORCE

Clifford seized the opportunity to carry out a sweeping reassessment of Vietnam policy. The magnitude of the request was such that it demanded careful study. His newness to the job and a need to clarify many fundamental issues also led him in this direction. He quickly began raising at the highest levels questions that had been avoided for years.

The secretary was encouraged by senior civilians in the Pentagon, men such as Paul Nitze and Paul Warnke, who had long been disenchanted with the war and had helped convert McNamara. The Pentagon civilians attacked the request for more

---

[13]Wheeler Report, February 27, 1968, *FR, 1964–1968,* 6: 263–266.
[14]Drea, *McNamara,* p. 184.

troops as another "payment on an open-ended commitment" and questioned whether it would break "Hanoi's will to fight."[15] It would, they warned, encourage "total Americanization of the war" and reinforce the Saigon government's view that the United States would "continue to fight while it engages in backroom politics and permits widespread corruption." Further expansion of the war would also bring increased U.S. casualties and new taxes, risking a "domestic crisis of unprecedented proportions."[16] Clifford's advisers urged the administration to maintain existing limits on the war and give Westmoreland no more than a token increase in troops. Like McNamara in November 1967, they proposed shifting to a "population security" strategy, putting pressure on ARVN to assume a greater burden of the fighting, and scaling back U.S. objectives to permit a "peace which will leave the people of SVN [South Vietnam] free to fashion their own political institutions."[17]

The military bitterly opposed such recommendations. Westmoreland and Wheeler warned that rejection of their proposals would deny the United States an opportunity to exploit a rapidly changing strategic situation. A population security strategy would increase civilian casualties and leave the enemy the initiative.[18] Supported by the Joint Chiefs, they continued to urge expanded military operations that would permit pursuing enemy forces into Laos and Cambodia, pounding North Vietnam by sea and air, and, after an Inchon-type landing, the occupation of parts of North Vietnam north of the demilitarized zone.[19]

Clifford recommended against the military's proposals without resolving the debate on strategy. He was quickly disillusioned with his military advisers. Responding to his relentless questioning, they doubted that an additional 206,000 men would get the job done, acknowledged that North Vietnam could match U.S. escalation, and admitted they could not say when South Vietnam would be able to defend itself. When asked about a plan for victory, they candidly

---

[15]Quoted in U.S. Congress, Senate Subcommittee on Public Buildings and Grounds, *The Pentagon Papers (Senator Gravel Edition)* 4 vols. (Boston, 1971), 4: 558. Hereafter cited as *Pentagon Papers (Gravel)*.
[16]Ibid., 563–564.
[17]Ibid., 564–568.
[18]Ibid., 568.
[19]For the views of the Joint Chiefs, see Clifford notes on meeting, March 18, 1968, Clark Clifford Papers, Lyndon Baines Johnson Library, Austin, Tex.

admitted they had none. "I was appalled," Clifford later wrote. "Nothing had prepared me for the weakness of the military's case."[20] His report kept the strategic issue alive by calling for further study of various alternatives, but it did not address the issues raised by his civilian advisers. The secretary merely recommended the immediate deployment to Vietnam of 22,000 troops, a reserve call-up of unspecified magnitude, and a "highly forceful" approach to get South Vietnam to assume greater responsibility.[21]

THE PRESIDENT'S DECISIONS

The administration accepted Clifford's recommendations. The president and his top civilian advisers had long opposed expansion of the war. They seem to have agreed as early as November 1967 that U.S. forces should not be increased above prevailing levels. In the immediate aftermath of the Tet attacks, Johnson had been ready to send additional troops if necessary to hold the line. But by the time he received Clifford's report, the military situation in South Vietnam seemed well in hand. Westmoreland and Ambassador Ellsworth Bunker reported that U.S. and South Vietnamese forces had fully recovered from the initial shock of the enemy offensive and were ready to mount a major counteroffensive. Under these circumstances, there seemed no need for immediate large-scale reinforcements. Although Johnson did not formally approve Clifford's recommendations at this time, he agreed with them and was prepared to act on them.

The administration also accepted the principle that South Vietnam should do more to defend itself. Johnson's advisers agreed that from a long-range standpoint the key to achieving American objectives was South Vietnam's ability to stand on its own. They had concluded in late 1967 that more should be done to promote self-sufficiency. The ARVN's quick recovery from the initial panic of Tet and its surprising effectiveness in the subsequent battles reinforced the notion that "Vietnamization" might work. Indeed, in the discussions of late February and early March 1968, some of the

---

[20]Clark Clifford, *Counsel to the President,* (New York, 1991), p. 494.
[21]Draft presidential memorandum, March 4, 1968, in *Pentagon Papers (Gravel),* 4: 575–576.

strongest arguments against sending massive reinforcements were that it would encourage the South Vietnamese to do less at a time when they should be doing more and that it would take equipment that might better be used by the ARVN. The administration thus agreed in early March that Thieu and Ky should be bluntly informed that the United States was willing to send limited reinforcements and substantial quantities of equipment but that continued U.S. assistance would depend on South Vietnam's ability to put its house in order and assume a greater burden of the fighting.[22] The decision represented a significant shift in American policy—a return, at least in part, to the principle that had governed U.S. involvement before 1965 and adoption, at least in a rudimentary fashion, of the concept of Vietnamization, which would be introduced with much fanfare by the Nixon administration a year later.

While agreeing in principle to Clifford's recommendations, the administration also began serious consideration of a cutback in the bombing and a new peace initiative. The secretary of defense had recommended against further peace moves in his report. Perhaps as a sop to the military, he had even urged intensification of the bombing. The initiative came from Secretary of State Rusk. Rusk had long felt that the bombing produced only marginal gains at a heavy cost. He proposed that the administration restrict it, without condition, to those areas "integrally related to the battlefield," namely, the supply routes and staging areas just north of the demilitarized zone. Such a move would cost the United States nothing, he argued, because inclement weather in the next few months would severely restrict raids over the northern part of North Vietnam. Bunker had speculated that Hanoi's purpose in launching the Tet Offensive may have been to establish a favorable position for negotiations. In late February, neutral intermediaries had brought several peace feelers to the State Department. Rusk believed that the chances for productive negotiations remained "bleak," but relaxation of the ambiguous San Antonio formula might entice Hanoi to the conference table or at least test its intentions. Even if North Vietnam did not respond positively, domestic critics would be persuaded that the administration was trying to get negotiations under way. The United States could resume air

[22]Schandler, *Johnson and Vietnam*, p. 179.

attacks on Hanoi and Haiphong later, if necessary, the secretary pointed out, probably with increased public support.[23]

Johnson had steadfastly opposed any reduction of the bombing, but he was attracted to Rusk's proposal. The president was certain that North Vietnam had suffered heavily in the Tet Offensive. He appears to have concluded that the United States could undertake negotiations from a vastly strengthened position. He recognized the need to do something to still the growing outcry against the war at home. And he was responsive to the idea because it came from Rusk, a man whose loyalty, caution, and measured judgment he had come to cherish.[24] Johnson later claimed to have accepted the idea of a reduction of the bombing and a new peace initiative as early as March 7. But he was not inclined to move hastily. He remained outwardly noncommittal for several weeks. He urged his advisers to study the matter carefully and develop specific proposals for inclusion in a major speech he was to deliver at the end of the month.

PUBLIC OPINION AND POLITICS

The administration's inclination to move in new directions was strengthened by mounting evidence of public dissatisfaction with the war. Discussion of Vietnam during February and March 1968 took place in an atmosphere of gloom and futility. The media continued to depict events in highly unfavorable and sometimes distorted terms. Early reports of a smashing enemy victory went largely uncorrected. The fact that the United States and South Vietnam had hurled back the attacks and quickly stabilized their position was lost in the image of chaos and defeat.[25] For those television and newspaper commentators who had long opposed the conflict, Tet provided compelling evidence of its folly. "The war in Vietnam is unwinnable," the columnist Joseph Kraft reported, "and the longer it goes on the more the Americans will be subjected to

[23]Ibid., pp. 181–193.
[24]Of Rusk, Johnson once said: "He has the compassion of a preacher and the courage of a Georgia cracker. When you're going in with the marines, he's the kind you want at your side." Max Frankel notes of conversation with Johnson, July 8, 1965, Arthur Krock Papers, Seeley G. Mudd Manuscript Library, Princeton, N.J., Box 1.
[25]For a critical analysis of press and television coverage of Tet, see Peter Braestrup, *Big Story* (New York, 1978).

losses and humiliation." Many opinion makers who had supported the president or had been only mildly critical now came out forcefully against the war. Tet made clear, *Newsweek* commented, that "a strategy of more of the same is intolerable." In a much-publicized broadcast on February 27, Cronkite eloquently summed up the prevailing mood: "To say that we are closer to victory today is to believe, in the face of the evidence, the optimists who have been wrong in the past. To suggest that we are on the edge of defeat is to yield to unreasonable pessimism. To say that we are mired in stalemate seems the only reasonable, yet unsatisfactory conclusion." "If I've lost Cronkite, I've lost the country," a despairing LBJ moaned.[26]

A *New York Times* story of March 10, reporting that the administration was considering sending another 206,000 soldiers to Vietnam, added to the furor. By this time, Johnson had decided to turn down Westmoreland's request, but he had not revealed his intentions publicly, and the story set off a barrage of protest.[27] Critics asked why so many troops were needed and whether more would follow. Skeptics warned that the North Vietnamese would be able to match any American increase. The only thing that would change, NBC's Frank McGee observed, would be the "capacity for destruction." The time had come, he concluded, "when we must decide whether it is futile to destroy Vietnam in the effort to save it."[28]

The possibility of another major troop increase provoked a stormy reaction in Congress. Democrats and Republicans, hawks and doves, demanded an explanation and insisted that Congress share in any decision to expand the war. On March 11 and 12, the Senate Foreign Relations Committee grilled Rusk for eleven hours, dramatically revealing a growing discontent with the administration's policies and a determination to exercise some voice in future decisions. A week later, 139 members of the House of Representatives sponsored a resolution calling for a full review of U.S. policy in Vietnam. The congressional outcry reinforced the administration's conviction that it could not escalate the war without setting off a long and bitter debate. It persuaded some officials, Clifford included, that major steps must be taken to scale down American involvement.[29]

[26]Oberdorfer, *Tet!* pp. 251, 275; Braestrup, *Big Story,* p. 137.
[27]Schandler, *Johnson and Vietnam,* pp. 200–205.
[28]Oberdorfer, *Tet!* p. 273.
[29]Schandler, *Johnson and Vietnam,* pp. 207–217.

Indexes of public opinion also revealed a sharp rise in disillusionment. Support for the war itself remained remarkably steady between November 1967 and March 1968, hovering around 45 percent.[30] But approval of Johnson's conduct of it, which had risen to 40 percent as a result of the 1967 public relations campaign, plummeted to an all-time low of 26 percent during Tet. By March, moreover, an overwhelming majority of Americans (78 percent) believed that the United States was not making any progress in Vietnam. The polls indicated no consensus for either escalation or withdrawal, only a firm conviction that the United States was hopelessly bogged down and a growing doubt that Johnson could break the stalemate.[31]

By mid-March, public discontent had assumed ominous political overtones. Senator Eugene McCarthy of Minnesota, an outspoken dove, had audaciously challenged Johnson's renomination. His surprisingly strong showing in the New Hampshire primary on March 12 suddenly transformed what had seemed a quixotic crusade into a major political challenge. Johnson's name had not been on the ballot, but the party organization had mounted a vigorous write-in campaign for him. When McCarthy won 42 percent of the vote, it was widely interpreted as a defeat for the president. Subsequent analysis revealed that hawks outnumbered doves by a wide majority among McCarthy supporters in New Hampshire. Early appraisals emphasized, however, that the vote reflected a growing sentiment for peace. Within several days a more formidable peace candidate had entered the field. After weeks of hesitation and soul-searching, Senator Robert F. Kennedy of New York announced that he, too, would run against the president on a platform of opposition to the war. With his name, his glamour, and his connections in the party, Kennedy appeared to be a serious threat to Johnson's renomination. Worried party regulars urged the president to do "something exciting and dramatic to recapture the peace issue" and to shift the emphasis of his rhetoric from winning the war to securing "peace with honor."[32]

---

[30]Approval and disapproval of the war were measured by the question "Do you think the United States made a mistake sending troops to Vietnam?"—at best an imperfect way of judging a complex issue.

[31]Louis Harris, *The Anguish of Change* (New York, 1973), pp. 63–64, and Burns W. Roper, "What Public Opinion Polls Said," in Braestrup, *Big Story*, vol. 1, pp. 674–704.

[32]James Rowe to Johnson, March 19, 1968, Johnson Papers, Marvin Watson File, Box 32.

The impact of public opinion on the decision-making process in March 1968 is difficult to measure. Westmoreland and others have charged that a hostile and all-too-powerful media, especially the television networks, snatched defeat from the jaws of victory by turning the public against the war and limiting the government's freedom of action just when the United States had a battered enemy on the ropes.[33] Vietnam was the first television war, to be sure, and it is possible, over a long period of time, that nightly exposure to violence did contribute to public war-weariness. Until the Tet Offensive, however, television coverage of the war had been over-whelmingly neutral or favorable to the government. Because of the isolated and remote nature of combat in Vietnam, it had shown little of the actual horrors of war.[34] The intense and up-close action in the cities at Tet did expose the public more directly to the war, and the coverage was more critical. After the distorted accounts of the embassy battle, coverage was also for the most part more accurate and thus could not help but show the enemy's toughness and tenacity, increase already strong doubts about the South Vietnamese government and army, raise questions about the administration's claims of progress, and widen the president's already yawning credibility gap. It is difficult to measure the impact of television coverage on public attitudes, but it seems probable, as historian Chester Pach has concluded, that coverage of the battles at Tet intensified the "sense of shock, anguish, and uncertainty" felt by Americans and by top government officials.[35]

The Johnson administration itself was at least partially responsible for media and public disillusionment during Tet. Its unduly optimistic pronouncements of 1967 made the shock of Tet greater and further expanded the credibility gap. The president and his advisers

[33]Westmoreland, *Soldier Reports*, p. 410; also Robert Elegant, "How to Lose a War," *Encounter* 57 (August 1981): 73–90.

[34]Excellent analyses that challenge the view of the media as critic and minimize the media's impact on public opinion are Daniel Hallin, *The "Uncensored War": The Media and Vietnam* (Berkeley, Calif., 1986); William M. Hammond, *Public Affairs: The Military and the Media, 1962–1968* (Washington, D.C., 1988); and Clarence R. Wyatt, *Paper Soldiers: The American Press and the Vietnam War* (New York, 1993).

[35]Chester J. Pach Jr. "Tet on TV," in Carole Fink et al. (eds), *1968: The World Transformed* (Washington, D.C., 1998), pp. 55–81; Michael J. Arlen, *The Living Room War* (New York, 1969).

might have challenged the reporting of the media, but their public response to Tet was itself halting and confused, in part because they were uncertain what was happening and how to respond.

The idea that a hypercritical media undercut support for the war just at the point when it could have been won is suspect on more basic grounds. That victory was within grasp, even had Westmoreland been given all the troops he requested, remains highly doubtful. Despite their later claims, many top military officials knew this at the time. They perceived quite clearly the enormous damage the enemy offensive had done to the war effort. They recognized that success was not forthcoming. By making requests they knew would not be approved, in fact, some military leaders may have been trying to put the onus for failure on the backs of the civilians.[36] The influence of public opinion does not appear to have been as great as Westmoreland alleges. None of Johnson's civilian advisers favored expansion of the war and another large troop increase. The president had rejected Westmoreland's proposals even before the public protest reached significant proportions. Evidence of growing popular discontent merely confirmed that it would be disastrous to escalate the war. Public anxiety persuaded some officials that the United States must move toward withdrawal from Vietnam, but the president did not go this far. He eventually concluded that he must make additional conciliatory gestures, but he did not alter his policy in any fundamental way or abandon his goals.

THE GOLD CRISIS

An economic crisis in mid-March, itself in part provoked by the war, also significantly affected post-Tet policy deliberations. Johnson had attempted to finance the war as he had dealt with public opinion—by deceit and trickery—and for the same reason. From the outset, he had a reasonably clear idea what the war would cost, but in dealing with the public and Congress he repeatedly minimized the price tag and refused to ask for new taxes for fear such a request would force cuts in Great Society programs. Until 1967, he financed the war through budgetary sleight of hand.

[36]Robert Buzzanco, *Masters of War: Military Dissent and Politics in the Vietnam Era* (New York, 1996), pp. 316–328.

His tax request of that year was too little and came too late. In any event, as he had feared, an increasingly restive Congress refused to pass it without domestic spending cuts he would not make.

Thus, by March 1968, the United States faced an economic crisis some harried officials compared to the Great Crash of 1929. The war imposed a burden of as much as $3.6 billion a year on a U.S. economy already strained by Great Society spending. Military expenditures stoked inflation and contributed to a spiraling balance-of-payments deficit that weakened the dollar in international money markets and threatened the world monetary structure. A late-1967 financial crisis in Britain, leading to devaluation of the pound, caused further problems, including huge losses from the gold pool. In March 1968, pressure on the dollar mounted again, and gold purchases reached new highs. On March 14, the United States lost $372 million in gold trading. At Washington's urging, the London gold market was closed. The economic crisis in the spring of 1968 marked the beginning of the end of the post–World War II economic boom. It shattered the postwar myth of American invincibility and raised severe doubts among business and government leaders that the nation could do it all and have it all in terms of domestic reform and national defense.[37]

As a result of the gold crisis, Westmoreland's request for additional troops was increasingly linked to the nation's economic woes. Secretary of the Treasury Henry Fowler warned that adoption of Westmoreland's proposals would cost $2.5 billion in 1968 and $10 billion in 1969, adding $500 million to the balance-of-payments deficit and requiring a major tax increase and cuts in domestic programs. Leading organs of business opinion began to question the nation's ability to finance the war at higher or even existing levels. "The gold crisis has dampened expansionist ideas," former Secretary of State Dean Acheson wrote a friend. "The town is in an atmosphere of crisis."[38]

---

[37]Robert M. Collins, "The Economic Crisis of 1968 and the Waning of the 'American Century,'" *American Historical Review* 101 (April 1996): 396–422.
[38]Acheson to John Cowles, March 14, 1968, Dean G. Acheson Papers, Yale University Library, New Haven, Conn., Box 7. The gold crisis is discussed at length in Paul Joseph, *Cracks in the Empire: State Politics in the Vietnam War* (Boston, 1981), pp. 262–266; Gabriel Kolko, *Anatomy of a War* (New York, 1986), pp. 313–320; and Diane B. Kunz, "The American Economic Consequence of 1968," in Fink, *1968*, pp. 83–110.

In this context, some leading "establishment" figures, including the architects of America's major Cold War policies, concluded that the war was doing irreparable damage to the nation's overall national security position. Acheson, W. Averell Harriman, and Nitze, all of whom had served in the Truman administration and had helped formulate the original containment policy, agreed, as Acheson put it, that Vietnam was a dangerous diversion from Europe and that "our leader ought to be concerned with areas that count."[39] Fearing that the nation was hopelessly overextended and that Vietnam was eroding popular support for an internationalist foreign policy, they pressed for a review of Vietnam policy. In a long letter on March 26, Acheson warned the president that the gold crisis and concern about America's "broader interests in Europe" required a "decision now to disengage within a limited time."[40] The old Cold Warriors labored tirelessly behind the scenes to influence the president's decision and converted Clifford to their position.

On March 22, Johnson formally rejected Westmoreland's proposals to seek victory through an expanded war. He was undoubtedly influenced by public opinion and the economic crisis. The steadily improving situation in South Vietnam seems to have been decisive. The Saigon government was responding to American pressures. Stability and order had been restored to the cities. In late March, Thieu announced a massive increase in draft calls that would raise the ARVN's strength by 135,000. The intensity of enemy rocket attacks was steadily diminishing. Enemy forces were withdrawing from the positions established before Tet and splitting into small groups to avoid destruction or capture. In mid-March, Westmoreland informed Johnson of plans for a major offensive in the northern provinces, the central objective of which was to relieve the siege of Khe Sanh.

Under these circumstances, Johnson saw no need for a major increase in American forces. Indeed, he did not even authorize the 22,000 soldiers recommended by Clifford, agreeing merely to deploy 13,500 support troops to augment the emergency reinforcements sent in February. At the same time, he decided to

[39]Quoted in Walter Isaacson and Evan Thomas, *The Wise Men: Six Friends and the World They Made* (New York, 1986), pp. 684, 689.
[40]Acheson to Johnson, March 26, 1968, Acheson Papers.

bring Westmoreland back to Washington to be chief of staff of the army. The general had come under heavy fire for his prophecies of victory and his failure to anticipate the Tet Offensive. Johnson wanted to spare him becoming a scapegoat. The president may also have wished to remove him from the untenable position of fighting a war under conditions he did not approve. The recall of Westmoreland signified the administration's determination to maintain the limits it had placed on the war and, tacitly at least, to check further escalation.

THE MARCH 31 SPEECH

During the last week of March, the internal debate reached a decisive stage and became increasingly sharp and emotional. Some of the president's advisers still insisted that the United States must "hang in there." At one time during the Tet crisis, Rostow had proposed sending to Congress a new Southeast Asia Resolution to rally the nation behind the war. He continued to urge the president to stand firm at what could be a critical turning point. Rusk persisted in working for the partial bombing halt he had outlined in early March. He was concerned by the domestic protest, but he had not despaired of success in Vietnam, nor was he disposed to capitulate to the administration's critics. He believed that the North Vietnamese would reject his proposal, but a conciliatory gesture would show the American people that the administration was doing everything possible to bring about negotiations, thus buying time to stabilize the home front and shore up South Vietnam.

Clifford had moved significantly beyond his position of early March. He was concerned by the apparent damage Vietnam was doing to the nation's international financial position. He was alarmed by the growing domestic unrest, particularly the "tremendous erosion of support" among the nation's business and legal elite. These executives felt the United States was in a "hopeless bog," he reported, and the idea of "going deeper into the bog" struck them as "mad." Although unclear how to proceed, he had set his mind on a "winching down" strategy that would put the United States irreversibly on a course of step-by-step de-escalation. U.S. forces should not be expanded above existing levels and should be used primarily to protect the South Vietnamese population from another enemy offensive. Thieu should be pressed to clean up and broaden his government. Clifford seems also to have been prepared to make major concessions to secure a negotiated settlement. He frankly conceded that the United States might have to settle for the best it could obtain. "Nothing required us to remain until the North had been ejected from the South and the Saigon government had established complete control of all South Vietnam," he later wrote. At a meeting on March 28, he delivered an impassioned plea to initiate the process of de-escalation. Working behind the scenes with Acheson and presidential speechwriter Harry McPherson in what he called a "partnership" to get "our friend out of this mess," he waged an unrelenting battle for the president's mind.[41]

While the debate raged about him, Johnson remained noncommittal. Instinctively, he leaned toward the Rusk position. He was infuriated by the desertion of Clifford, on whose support he had counted. He was deeply opposed to abandoning a policy in which he had invested so much, particularly in view of the improved situation in South Vietnam. Publicly, he continued to take a hard line, proclaiming that "we must meet our commitments in Vietnam and the world. We shall and we are going to win!"[42]

On the other hand, he could not ignore the protest that was building around him. He concluded, gradually and with great reluctance, that some additional conciliatory steps must be taken. In a highly emotional March 26 meeting with Gens. Wheeler and Creighton Abrams, Westmoreland's successor, an obviously embattled commander in chief sought to head off military criticism of his peace moves. In tones that verged on despondency, he lamented an "abominable" fiscal situation, panic and demoralization in the country, near universal opposition in the press, and his own "overwhelming disapproval" in the polls. "I will go down the drain," he gloomily concluded.

Trusted advisers from outside the government seem to have clinched it for Johnson. To move the president from his indecision, Clifford suggested that he call his senior advisory group, the Wise

---

[41]Clark Clifford, "A Viet Nam Reappraisal," *Foreign Affairs* 47 (July 1969): 613; memorandum of conversation with Clifford, March 20, 1968, Krock Papers; Harry McPherson oral history interview, Johnson Papers.

[42]Schandler, *Johnson and Vietnam*, p. 248; Tom Johnson notes on meeting, March 26, 1968, Johnson Papers, Tom Johnson Notes on Meetings, Box 2.

Men, back to Washington for another session on Vietnam. After a series of briefings by diplomatic and military officials on March 26, the group, in a mood of obvious gloom, reported its findings. A minority advocated holding the line militarily and even escalating if necessary, but the majority favored immediate steps toward de-escalation. After its last meeting in November, McGeorge Bundy reported, the group had expected slow and steady progress. This had not happened, and the majority view, as summed up by Acheson, was that the United States could "no longer do the job we set out to do in the time we have left and we must begin to take steps to disengage." The Wise Men disagreed among themselves on what to do, some proposing a total and unconditional bombing halt, others a shift in the ground strategy. Most agreed that the goal of an independent, non-Communist South Vietnam was probably unattainable and favored a move toward eventual disengagement. "Unless we do something quick, the mood in this country may lead us to withdrawal," Cyrus Vance warned.[43] "The establishment bastards have bailed out," a stunned and dispirited Johnson is said to have remarked after the meeting.[44]

Keeping his intentions under wraps until the very end, the president in a televised address on March 31 dramatically revealed a series of major decisions. Accepting Rusk's proposal, he announced that the bombing of North Vietnam would henceforth be limited to the area just north of the demilitarized zone. Responding to the entreaties of Clifford and the Wise Men, however, he went further. "Even this limited bombing of the North could come to an early end," he stressed, "if our restraint is matched by restraint in Hanoi." He named the veteran diplomat W. Averell Harriman his personal representative should peace talks materialize. He made clear that the United States was ready to

---

[43]Summary of notes, March 26, 1968, Johnson Papers, Meeting Notes File, Box 2. The Wise Men were Dean Acheson, George Ball, McGeorge Bundy, Douglas Dillon, Cyrus Vance, Arthur Dean, John McCloy, Omar Bradley, Matthew Ridgway, Maxwell Taylor, Robert Murphy, Henry Cabot Lodge, Abe Fortas, and Arthur Goldberg.

[44]Quoted in Roger Morris, *An Uncertain Greatness: Henry Kissinger and American Foreign Policy* (New York, 1977), p. 44. Johnson was furious with the negative tone of the March 26 briefings. The "first thing I do when you all leave is to get those briefers," he told one of the Wise Men. Notes, March 26, 1968, Johnson Papers, Diary Backup File, Box 95. See also Depuy oral history interview, William Depuy Papers, U.S. Army Military History Institute, Carlisle Barracks, Pa.

discuss peace, any time, any place. In a bombshell announcement that shocked the nation, Johnson concluded: "I shall not seek, and I will not accept, the nomination of my party for another term as your president." He later revealed that for some time he had considered not running for reelection. He was exhausted physically and emotionally from the strains of office. He realized that he had spent most of his political capital and that another term would be conflict-ridden and barren of accomplishment. By removing himself from candidacy, he could emphasize the sincerity of his desire for negotiations and contribute to the restoration of national unity and domestic harmony.[45]

Johnson's speech is usually cited as a major turning point in American involvement in Vietnam, and in some ways it was. No ceiling was placed on U.S. ground forces, and the president did not obligate himself to maintain the restrictions on the bombing. Indeed, in explaining the partial bombing halt to the embassy in Saigon, the State Department indicated that Hanoi would probably "denounce" it and "thus free our hand after a short period."[46] Nevertheless, the circumstances in which the March decisions were made and the conciliatory tone of Johnson's speech made it difficult, if not impossible, for him to change course. March 31, 1968, brought an inglorious end to the policy of gradual escalation.

The president did not change his goals. The apparent American success in the battles of Tet reinforced the conviction of Johnson, Rusk, and Rostow that they could yet secure an independent, non-Communist South Vietnam. "My biggest worry was not Vietnam itself," the president later conceded, "it was the divisiveness and pessimism at home. . . . I looked on my approaching speech as an opportunity to help right the balance and provide better perspective. For the collapse of the home front, I knew well, was just what Hanoi was counting on."[47] By rejecting major troop reinforcements, reducing the bombing, shifting some military responsibility to the Vietnamese, and withdrawing from the presidential race, Johnson

---

[45]*Public Papers of Lyndon B. Johnson, 1968–1969,* 2 vols. (Washington, D.C., 1970), vol. 1, pp. 469–476. On Johnson's decision not to run, see also George Christian memorandum, March 31, 1968, Johnson Papers, Diary Backup File, Box 96.

[46]"March 31 Speech," Johnson Papers, National Security File, National Security Council Histories: March 31, 1968, Speech, Box 47.

[47]Johnson, *Vantage Point,* p. 422.

hoped to salvage his policy at least to the end of his term. He felt certain that history would vindicate him for standing firm. The March 31 speech did not represent a change of policy, therefore, but a shift of tactics to salvage a policy that had come under bitter attack.

The new tactics were even more vaguely defined and contradictory than the old. Johnson's decisions marked a shift from the idea of graduated pressure to the pre-1965 concept of saving South Vietnam by denying the enemy victory. Precisely how this goal was to be achieved was not spelled out. The debate over ground strategy was not resolved. Gen. Abrams was given no strategic guidance. Administration officials generally agreed that ground operations should be scaled down to reduce casualties, but it was not clear how this would contribute to the achievement of American goals. The bombing was to be concentrated against North Vietnamese staging areas and supply lines, but that tactic had not reduced infiltration significantly in the past, and there was no reason to assume it would be more effective in the future. The exigencies of domestic politics required acceptance of the concept of Vietnamization, and the surprising response of the ARVN during Tet raised hopes that it would work. There was little in the past record of various South Vietnamese governments to suggest, however, that Thieu and his cohorts could conciliate their non-Communist opponents and pacify the countryside while effectively waging war against a weakened but still formidable enemy. Negotiations were also desirable from a domestic political standpoint, but in the absence of concessions the administration was not prepared to make, diplomacy could accomplish nothing. Its failure might intensify the pressures the talks were designed to ease. In short, the tactics of 1968 perpetuated the ambiguities and inconsistencies that had marked American policy from the start.

FIGHTING WHILE NEGOTIATING

U.S. policy in the months after Tet makes clear that although the Johnson administration spoke a more conciliatory language and altered its tactics, it did not retreat from its original goals. The president made good on his pledge to negotiate, accepting, after numerous delays, Hanoi's proposal for direct talks. From the outset, however, he refused to compromise on the fundamental issues. In the meantime, the United States kept maximum pressure on enemy forces in South Vietnam, assisted the South Vietnamese in a frantic drive to gain control of the countryside, and made plans for a gradual shift of the military burden to the ARVN. The result was to harden the stalemate, leaving resolution of the problem to the next administration.

Divisions within the U.S. government became even more pronounced during this new phase of the war. Certain, as Westmoreland put it, that the enemy had suffered a "colossal" defeat and that in any negotiations the United States would "hold four aces," North Vietnam "two deuces," Rusk, Rostow, Ambassador Bunker, and the military staunchly opposed concessions and sought to apply intensive military pressure. They feared that the North Vietnamese would use negotiations to divide the United States from its South Vietnamese ally. They insisted that if the administration could shore up the home front and improve its military position in Vietnam, Hanoi could be forced to make major concessions. "We can afford . . . to be tough, patient and not too anxious in our negotiating stance," Bunker affirmed.[48]

Clifford and Harriman, on the other hand, sought to extricate the United States from what they viewed as a hopeless tangle. Certain that the war was crippling America's ability to deal with more important problems and undermining its position as the "standard-bearer of moral principle in the world," they sought through Clifford's "winching down process" mutual de-escalation and disengagement, even at the expense of South Vietnam.[49] A skillful bureaucratic infighter, Clifford attempted to move the president to positions he had not reached. At an April 11 press conference, for example, he stated that a ceiling had been imposed on U.S. ground troops, a policy that the president had not yet approved but could not challenge and that therefore became established.

The battle raged throughout 1968. The two factions fought bitterly over such issues as the U.S. negotiating stance, the scale and purpose of ground operations, and resumption or full curtailment of

[48]Bunker memorandum, "Viet-Nam Negotiations: Dangers and Opportunities," April 8, 1968, W. Averell Harriman Papers, Manuscript Division, Library of Congress, Washington, D.C., Box 521.

[49]Harriman memorandum, "General Review of the Last Six Months," December 10, 1968, Harriman Papers; Clark Clifford, *Counsel to the President: A Memoir* (New York, 1991), pp. 534–536.

the bombing. The stakes were high, the participants exhausted, their nerves frayed. Clifford remembered 1968 as a year that lasted five years; Rusk recalled it as a "blur" and claimed to have survived by a regimen of aspirin, Scotch, and cigarettes. Personal attacks descended to unprecedented levels. The president himself was worn out, increasingly angry and frustrated, more indecisive than usual, at times petulant and petty. Rusk and Rostow's hard line appealed to his "nail that coonskin to the wall" mentality. On occasion, he regretted having made the March 31 speech, and he yearned to bomb Hanoi and Haiphong off the map. A man who thrived on consensus, he could not deal with the bitter divisions among his advisers, and his administration in its last months never developed a thought-out negotiating position. "The pressure grew so intense that at times I felt that the government itself might come apart at the seams," Clifford later recalled. "There was, for a brief time, something approaching paralysis, and a sense of events spiralling out of control."[50]

The Tet Offensive also spurred pressures for negotiations in North Vietnam. The Hanoi leadership was undoubtedly pleased—and perhaps surprised—by its impact in the United States. But Tet had not sparked the hoped-for insurrection in South Vietnam, and it had produced disastrous losses, especially for the NLF. It had also cost crucial Chinese support. Le Duan remained deeply suspicious of diplomacy. He had no intention of compromising on the fundamental issue of the future of South Vietnam. But, like Johnson, he felt compelled to agree to talks, even though the United States had not stopped the bombing completely. Hanoi had always foreseen a time of *dam va danh* ("fighting while negotiating") whose aim was to stimulate "internal contradictions" in the enemy camp. Specifically, North Vietnamese leaders hoped by adding a diplomatic weapon to their arsenal to divide the United States and South Vietnam and exploit surging antiwar sentiment in the United States. Just three days after Johnson's speech, they agreed to meet with the United States to discuss an unconditional end to the bombing.[51]

Hanoi's response caught Washington by surprise. Some U.S. officials suspected a clever diplomatic trap, and the administration was determined not to rush into negotiations. Although LBJ had

---

[50]Clifford, *Counsel to the President*, p. 461; Dean Rusk as told to Richard Rusk, *As I Saw It* (New York, 1990), p. 417.

[51]Nguyen, *Hanoi's War*, pp. 111–115, 120–121.

vowed to send diplomats "to any forum, any time," he rejected Hanoi's proposed sites of Phnom Penh, Cambodia, and especially Warsaw, where he insisted, the "deck would be stacked against us." Despite the accommodating tone of his March 31 speech, the president approached the reality of negotiations with extreme caution. Harriman and Clifford advocated a generous initial offer to get negotiations moving. But Westmoreland and Bunker insisted that the U.S. position in South Vietnam had improved significantly and that the United States would be negotiating from strength. Johnson and his more hawkish advisers sincerely desired peace, but the terms they were prepared to hold out for virtually ensured that nothing would be accomplished. Rusk even spoke of a restoration of the status quo antebellum.[52]

Formal talks finally opened in Paris on May 13 and immediately deadlocked. North Vietnam had little interest in substantive negotiations while the military balance of forces was unfavorable. Its diplomats made clear they were establishing contact with the United States to secure the "unconditional cessation of U.S. bombing raids and all other acts of war so that talks may start." The United States expressed willingness to stop the bombing, but insisted on reciprocal de-escalation. Hanoi continued to reject the American demand for reciprocity and refused any terms that limited its ability to support the war in the South while leaving the United States a free hand there.

To break the impasse, chief American negotiator Harriman subsequently introduced a new proposal. The United States would stop the bombing "on the assumption that" North Vietnam would respect the demilitarized zone and refrain from further rocket attacks on Saigon and other cities and that "prompt and serious talks" would follow. The offer brought no formal response or any indication that one might be forthcoming. American officials complained that the North Vietnamese seemed prepared to sit in Paris "and even read the telephone directory if necessary to keep non-productive talks going." The Joint Chiefs pressed relentlessly for re-escalation,

---

[52]Notes on meeting, May 6, 1968, Johnson Papers, Meeting Notes File, Box 3; Harold Johnson notes on meetings, May 6, 8, 1968, Harold Johnson Papers, U.S. Army Military History Institute, Carlisle Barracks, Pa., Box 127; Andrew Goodpaster oral history interview, U.S. Army Military History Institute, Carlisle Barracks, Pa.

including B-52 strikes against North Vietnamese sanctuaries in Cambodia.[53]

Fearful that the talks might drag on inconclusively, perpetuating the war and exacerbating domestic divisions, Harriman urged the president to compromise. NLF rocket attacks had subsided, and there were indications that significant numbers of North Vietnamese troops had been withdrawn from the South. Harriman argued that the military lull could be interpreted as a sign of de-escalation. He pressed Johnson to stop the bombing and reduce the level of U.S. military activity while making clear the next move he expected from Hanoi. Clifford supported Harriman's proposal, but the military argued that the lull was simply a regrouping for the next offensive and warned that stopping the bombing would endanger American troops. An enraged Johnson flatly rejected Harriman's proposal, privately dismissing it as "mush" and claiming that the enemy was using his "own people as dupes." Meeting with his advisers on July 30, he expressed a wish to "knock the hell" out of the North Vietnamese. At a press conference the following day he threatened that if there were no breakthroughs in Paris, he might be compelled to undertake additional military measures. "Our most difficult negotiations were with Washington and not Hanoi . . . ," one U.S. diplomat later lamented. "We just couldn't convince the President that summer."[54]

The administration also used every available means to strengthen its position in South Vietnam. The air war in South Vietnam reached a new level of intensity, as B-52s and fighter-bombers relentlessly attacked infiltration routes, lines of communication, and suspected enemy base camps. The number of B-52 missions tripled in 1968; the bombs dropped on South Vietnam exceeded one million tons. In March and April, the United States and South Vietnam conducted the largest search-and-destroy mission of the war, sending more than 100,000 troops against enemy forces in the provinces around Saigon. "Charlie [the Vietcong] is being relentlessly pursued night and day and pounded

[53]Notes on National Security Council meeting, May 22, 1968, Johnson Papers, National Security File, NSC Meetings, Box 3; notes on meetings, May 25, 28, Johnson Papers, Meeting Notes File, Box 3.

[54]Quoted in Allan E. Goodman, *The Lost Peace: America's Search for a Negotiated Settlement of the Vietnam War* (Stanford, Calif., 1978), p. 69.

to shreds whenever and wherever we catch him," one U.S. officer exclaimed.[55] The scale of American military operations diminished somewhat in the summer and fall as Abrams shifted to small-unit patrols and mobile spoiling attacks, but throughout the rest of the year the United States kept intense pressure on enemy forces in South Vietnam.

The United States and South Vietnam also launched an Accelerated Pacification campaign to secure as much of the countryside as possible in the event serious negotiations should begin. Abrams committed a major proportion of U.S. and ARVN personnel to the program. Local defense forces were enlarged and given modern military equipment. To use their resources more effectively, the United States and South Vietnam focused on key areas. The Chieu Hoi Program, which offered amnesty and "rehabilitation" to defectors, was intensified, as was the Phoenix Program, a direct attack on the NLF infrastructure through mass arrests. By late 1968, for the first time, the United States and South Vietnam were firmly committed to controlling the countryside.[56]

The United States also pressed forward with Vietnamization. American officials candidly admitted that the South Vietnamese were nowhere near ready to assume the burden of their own defense. "If you took out all the United States . . . forces now," Abrams conceded, "the Government would have to settle for a piece of Vietnam."[57] New plans were nevertheless drawn up to expand and upgrade the South Vietnamese armed forces and gradually shift to them primary responsibility for military operations. The force level was increased from 685,000 to 801,000, training programs were drastically expanded, and ARVN units were given the newest equipment. To improve the combat-readiness of Vietnamese troops and smooth the transition, Abrams employed ARVN and American units in combined operations.[58]

---

[55]Frank Clay to Mr. and Mrs. Lucius Clay, May 15, 1968, Frank Clay Papers, U.S. Army Military History Institute, Carlisle Barracks, Pa.

[56]Douglas S. Blaufarb, *The Counterinsurgency Era: U.S. Doctrines and Performance* (New York, 1977), pp. 264–265; James H. Embrey, "Reorienting Pacification: The Accelerated Pacification Campaign of 1968," Ph.D. diss., University of Kentucky, 1997.

[57]A. J. Langguth, "General Abrams Listens to a Different Drummer," *New York Times Magazine*, May 5, 1968, p. 28.

[58]Jeffrey J. Clarke, *Advice and Support: The Final Years, 1965–1973* (Washington, D.C., 1988), pp. 293–296.

Pacification and Vietnamization were both long-range under-takings, and the frenzied efforts of 1968 could not make up for years of neglect. It was the end of the year before the pacification program got back to where it had been before Tet. The establish-ment of a presence in the villages was not tantamount to gaining the active support of the people, something that could not be accomplished overnight. The ARVN was larger and better equipped, but its basic problems remained uncorrected. Desertions reached an all-time high in 1968; an acute shortage of qualified officers persisted. At the end of the year, American advisers rated two ARVN divisions "outright poor," eight no better than "improv-ing," and only one "excellent."[59] Americans detected among the Vietnamese a stubborn, if quiet, resistance to the whole notion of Vietnamization. Clifford returned from a visit to Saigon "oppressed" by the "pervasive Americanization" of the war. The United States was still doing most of the fighting and paying the cost. "Worst of all," he concluded, "the South Vietnamese leaders seemed content to have it that way."[60]

The post-Tet crash programs significantly altered the military/political balance in South Vietnam. In some rural areas, the people had excitedly rallied to NLF calls for battle in hopes that an intermi-nable war might finally end. They were profoundly demoralized with the outcome. The NLF hold on the countryside was weaker than ever before. Defections increased significantly. The government regained much of what had been lost in the first days of Tet and even extended its influence into new areas. The United States held the mil-itary initiative throughout much of South Vietnam in the last half of 1968. Its fierce and unrelenting spoiling attacks on base areas and supply lines kept the enemy off balance and broke up the remnants of its main force units. The NLF clandestine organization and North Vietnamese main units remained strong enough to mount major operations in May and again in August—the so-called mini-Tet offensives. They also kept up sporadic rocket attacks on the cities. But the United States and South Vietnam were well prepared for the second and third phases of the Tet Offensive and inflicted additional heavy losses on already battered NVA and NLF units.

[59]Robert Shaplen, *The Road from War: Vietnam, 1965–1970* (New York, 1970), p. 250.
[60]Clifford, "Viet Nam Reappraisal," pp. 614–615; also Clifford to Johnson, July 16, 18, 1968, Clifford Papers, Box 5.

Although it improved markedly in the aftermath of Tet, the performance of the government of South Vietnam remained at best uneven. Government and people cooperated to implement Operation Recovery, a massive program to repair the damage done to the cities by the battles of Tet. At American urging, Thieu adopted a new economic program to combat inflation and instituted anticorruption measures to deal with one of South Vietnam's oldest and most pervasive problems. Some optimistic observers concluded late in the year that the government was functioning more effectively than at any other time since the mid-1950s. For every problem attacked, however, others remained unchallenged and new ones surfaced. Land reform progressed at a snail's pace. Tet created thousands of new refugees, and American officials expressed grave concern at the government's apparent indifference to their plight. The prospect of negotiations made Thieu more reluctant than ever to broaden the base of his government. He made some cosmetic changes, appointing a civilian, Tran Van Huong, as prime minister and promising to expand civilian influence in the government. Increasingly, however, he withdrew into himself, trusting no one and making most decisions on his own. "He is his own Nhu," one American complained with more than a touch of resignation.[61]

The possibility of a U.S. withdrawal exacerbated the fragmented political system of South Vietnam. "Divisiveness is still endemic," Robert Shaplen observed in late 1968, "and rivalries exist across the board, in politics, in the Army, among religious groups, and so on." The rivalry between Ky and Thieu intensified, factionalizing much of the government. The Buddhists remained more alienated than ever, demanding the foundation of a "peace cabinet" and urging the soldiers to lay down their arms. Both the Buddhists and the sects appeared to look forward to the collapse of the government so that they could pick up the pieces. New political groups proliferated after the peace negotiations began, but they were dissension-ridden and could not work together. Much of the urban population persisted in its demeanor of watchful waiting. The South Vietnamese, Shaplen concluded, seemed

[61]Quoted in Shaplen, *Road from War*, p. 248. See also William Colby oral history interview, Johnson Papers, and James P. Grant to Ernest Lindley, September 21, 1968, Johnson Papers, National Security File, Country File: Vietnam, Box 101.

"more and more like men who know they are suffering from an incurable malady."[62]

Vietnamese–American tensions heightened in the period after Tet. The government and its supporters angrily protested that they had been railroaded into negotiations before they were ready. Those Vietnamese who had come to depend on the United States expressed bitter fears that they would be left at the mercy of the Vietcong. American service personnel manifested more openly the accumulated frustrations of fighting in a hostile environment a war they could not "win," and the savagery of the battles of Tet and the heavy losses inflamed anti-Vietnamese feelings. A gallows humor solution to the Vietnam dilemma that went the round of fire-bases and GI bars typified the attitude. "What you do is, you load all the Friendlies onto ships and take them out to the South China Sea. Then you bomb the country flat. Then you sink the ship."[63] The savage murder of more than 500 civilians, including women and children, in the village of My Lai by an American company under the command of Lt. William Calley in March 1968 starkly exposed the hostility some Americans had come to feel for all Vietnamese.

YEAR OF ANGUISH

Divisions inside the United States also increased dramatically in an incredible year of tumult and torment. Although the war in Vietnam was only one of numerous causes, it was often the focal point. Campus unrest mounted, some 200 demonstrations erupting at more than 100 colleges during the spring semester alone. The most publicized and violent demonstrations took place at Columbia University in New York City, where radicals took over several buildings and occupied the president's office. After eight days, one thousand police wielding nightsticks forcibly drove out the protesters. The assassination of civil rights leader and antiwar activist Martin Luther King Jr. in April brought latent racial unrest to the surface, provoking rioting, looting, and the burning of

[62]Shaplen, *Road from War,* p. 208.
[63]Michael Herr, *Dispatches* (New York, 1978), p. 59.

buildings in urban areas across the nation. The most visible and destructive rioting was in Washington, D.C., where members of Congress could see the flames of burning neighborhoods from their office windows and soldiers wielded guns on the steps of the Capitol building. Twelve people were killed, an estimated $25 million of damage was done, and the races were further polarized. The assassination of presidential candidate Robert Kennedy in June brought more grief to an already emotionally exhausted nation and seemed a graphic demonstration of the extent to which violence had triumphed.

The Democratic convention in Chicago in August dramatized the stark reality of a nation furiously divided against itself. Within the movement, the left was in the ascendancy. Young radicals of the Youth International Party leaders (Yippies) circulated rumors that the Chicago water supply would be laced with drugs and one thousand protesters would float nude in Lake Michigan. They put forth their own candidate for the presidency, a pig named Pigasus. In return, Chicago's hard-nosed Mayor Richard Daley, mobilized more than 25,000 police, national guard, and army troops to enforce law and order. While antiwar protesters engaged Daley's police in bloody battles in the streets, delegates inside the stormy convention hall bitterly debated the war and other issues. Johnson feared that his preferred candidate, Vice President Hubert H. Humphrey, would be too soft on Vietnam. He even contemplated making himself available for a draft to run again, abandoning the idea only when it was obvious there was little support. The administration micromanaged the convention, insisting on a hard-line plank on the war, splitting an already divided party still further, costing Humphrey crucial support, and proving to some critics that the war could not be ended within "the system." The bloodshed that ran in the streets of "nightstick city" was brought into the homes of Americans each night on television. The nation could "no longer turn away from the fact that the war in Southeast Asia . . . was causing a kind of civil war in the United States."[64]

---

[64]Nancy Zaroulis and Gerald Sullivan, *Who Spoke Up? American Protest against the War in Vietnam, 1963–1975* (New York, 1984), p. 200. See also Terry H. Anderson, *The Movement and the Sixties* (New York, 1995), pp. 183–238; and Maurice Isserman and Michael Kazin, *America Divided* (New York, 2000), pp. 221–240.

THE OCTOBER BOMBING HALT

Largely in response to domestic pressures, Johnson in late 1968 made one last effort to get the peace talks off dead center. The convention in Chicago badly discredited the Democrats. In its aftermath, some party leaders pleaded for a dramatic peace move to assist Humphrey, who lagged well behind Republican candidate, Richard M. Nixon, in the early polls. LBJ had repeatedly insisted that he would not be swayed by political considerations. When Humphrey sought to distance himself from the administration's Vietnam policy, the president expressed preference for a Nixon victory and refused even to see the vice president. But Johnson was sympathetic to the concerns of leading Democrats. He was eventually persuaded that he might be able to break the deadlock in Paris without undue risk. Harriman continued to argue that the military lull in South Vietnam was a clear sign of North Vietnamese interest in substantive negotiations. Abrams affirmed that a bombing halt would not pose a military threat. The North Vietnamese had been badly hurt by the spring campaigns. In any case, the approach of the monsoon season would severely limit the effectiveness of the bombing for several months. To appease the military and keep pressure on North Vietnam, Johnson agreed, in the event of a bombing halt, to redeploy American airpower against North Vietnamese supply lines in Laos. The president, with apparent reluctance, finally committed himself to stop the bombing altogether if some concessions could be obtained from Hanoi.[65]

Over the next few weeks, Harriman diligently negotiated an "understanding." To meet North Vietnam's continuing objections to reciprocity, he indicated that the bombing would be stopped unilaterally. Responding to Soviet pressure and hoping to exploit American presidential politics, Hanoi eventually dropped its insistence on an unconditional bombing halt. The U.S. delegation made clear, however, that the enemy would be expected to stop rocket and mortar attacks on South Vietnamese cities and limit the infiltration of soldiers and supplies across the demilitarized zone. In addition,

---

[65]Johnson, *Vantage Point*, pp. 514–515; memorandum for the record, October 23, 1968, Johnson Papers, Diary Backup, November 11, 1968, Box 115.

the North Vietnamese informally agreed that serious peace talks would begin within four days after the bombing had been stopped. The administration was especially pleased to secure their consent to the Saigon government's participation in the peace talks. To get around North Vietnam's repeated refusal to negotiate directly with the "puppet" Saigon government and Thieu's refusal to join negotiations in which the NLF participated, Harriman devised an ingenious "our side, your side" formula. The negotiations would be two-sided, but each side was free to work out its own composition and to interpret the makeup of the other as it chose. The NLF and the Saigon government could thus participate without recognizing each other as an independent entity. The North Vietnamese refused to commit themselves formally to these "understandings," but they gave private assurances that they would "know what to do" once the bombing had stopped. Hesitant to the end, Johnson finally agreed to "go the last mile" for peace, although administration officials agreed that if the North Vietnamese took advantage of the bombing halt or appeared not to be negotiating seriously, the United States might resume air operations.[66]

Johnson's last-minute peace move became entrapped in election-year maneuvering and intrigue. Although the president and all the candidates had solemnly vowed to keep the war out of politics, the campaign of 1968, in Robert Dallek's words, "produced as much skulduggery and hidden action as any in American history." Humphrey had joined Democratic doves in opposing escalation in 1965. Johnson distrusted him and had his phone tapped. At the outset, LBJ even speculated that he might get more backing on the war from Republicans than from his own party. Nixon had pledged such support, but as the election approached he increasingly feared that his chances might be threatened by an October surprise in Paris. The Nixon campaign team had a "mole" in the White House (who believed he was informing Democratic doves, not Republicans!). Eager for a job no matter who won, Harvard professor and sometime Johnson administration operative Henry A. Kissinger kept the Republicans up to date on developments in Paris. When Nixon learned of the bombing halt, his

---

[66]Johnson, *Vantage Point*, p. 518; notes on meetings, October 14, 31, 1968, Johnson Papers, Meeting Notes File, Box 3.

campaign team, apparently with his authorization, passed messages to President Thieu through Anna Chennault, widow of the legendary founder of China's World War II Flying Tigers and devotee of various right-wing causes, and South Vietnamese ambassador Bui Diem urging him to obstruct peace talks by refusing to participate and hinting that South Vietnam would fare better under a Nixon presidency. When he learned of Republican shenanigans, LBJ put Chennault under surveillance and used CIA and National Security Agency resources to spy on Republicans. Privately, he railed at what he called "treason." He let Nixon know he knew what was going on. But he refused to go public for fear of a constitutional crisis and possible reprisals should Nixon be elected. To do so would also expose his own unsavory practices. LBJ did push ahead with the bombing halt and gave full, if belated, support to Humphrey's campaign.[67]

Nguyen Van Thieu needed little prompting from Republicans. Only forty-four years old at this crucial juncture in his career, he had demonstrated above all else in his rapid rise to military and political power an instinct for survival. He had collaborated with the Viet Minh, the French, and the Americans at various times. He had shown rare cunning in mastering the Byzantine intricacies of South Vietnamese politics. Shrewd and suspicious, he was painfully aware of his dependence on the United States, but he also increasingly recognized that he could not trust his ally. A wily, calculating politician, desperately fearful for his country's future and his own, Thieu probably would have concluded by himself that he would do better with the Republicans than with the Democrats and that delay was essential. Proclaiming that his government was not a "car that can be hitched to a locomotive and taken anywhere the locomotive wants to go," he insisted that he would not meet with the Vietcong and that the American-arranged understanding was a "clear admission of defeat." Hanoi must issue formal assurances that it would de-escalate the war and must negotiate directly with Saigon.[68]

Intensive U.S. pressure failed to budge the embattled South Vietnamese. Johnson sternly warned Thieu on October 30 that if Americans held him responsible for blocking peace, "God help

---

[67]Robert Dallek, *Flawed Giant: Lyndon Johnson and His Times* (New York, 1998), p. 574, and *Nixon and Kissinger: Partners in Power* (New York, 2007), pp. 70–78.
[68]Quoted in Shaplen, *Road from War,* p. 243.

South Vietnam, because no president could maintain the support of the American people." An emotional Thieu stubbornly retorted: "You are powerful. You can say to small nations what you want . . . but you cannot force us to do anything against our interests. This negotiation is not a life and death matter for the US, but it is for Vietnam."[69]

Thieu's obstinacy posed a dilemma for the United States. LBJ recognized that to concede to Saigon's demands would "blow the whole peace effort sky high," perhaps wrecking Humphrey's chances as well.[70] On the other hand, he feared that to negotiate without Saigon, as Harriman and even Rusk urged, offered little prospect of an acceptable settlement and risked Republican charges of a sellout. The president thus announced the bombing halt on October 31 without South Vietnamese approval, but he delayed the opening of formal talks. In the meantime, the United States combined renewed assurances that it would not recognize the NLF or impose a coalition government on South Vietnam with private pressures and eventually a public threat to begin talks without Saigon. After a two-week delay, during which Nixon won a precariously thin victory, Thieu agreed to send representatives to Paris.

Once in Paris, the South Vietnamese raised procedural objections that nullified any hope of a peace settlement. The United States had originally proposed that the delegations be seated at two long tables to emphasize the two-sided nature of the talks. But North Vietnam had demanded a square table with one delegate on each side to underscore its contention that the NLF was a separate party to the talks. To get around this impasse, Harriman had proposed a round table, and the North Vietnamese had acquiesced. But Saigon refused to go along. Thieu may have felt that the issue was of sufficient symbolic or even practical importance to merit resistance, or he may simply have seized on it to stall the talks until a presumably more sympathetic Nixon took office.

Americans railed at South Vietnamese intransigence, and the North Vietnamese mocked U.S. weakness. McPherson lamented that the "American Gulliver is tied down by the South Vietnamese Lilliputians." Outraged at what he later denounced as a "ridiculous

---

[69]Secretary of State to Embassy Saigon, Embassy Saigon to Secretary of State, October 30, 1968, copies in Harriman Papers, Box 554.
[70]Johnson, *Vantage Point*, pp. 517–519.

performance" on the part of the South Vietnamese, Harriman again urged Johnson to negotiate without them. The South Vietnamese had been "coddled and cuddled beyond belief," an impatient and irate Clifford complained. "They're making all the decisions, but we pay, we die, we fight." He pressed Johnson to begin to withdraw U.S. troops irrespective of what Saigon and Hanoi did.[71] North Vietnamese negotiators snidely observed that "usually the man leads the horse. This time the horse is leading the man."[72] The president upheld Thieu's objections, however, and the so-called battle of the tables raged for weeks. Instead of drafting cables at night, the U.S. delegation sketched table designs, the two sides proposing at various times such inventive geometric creations as a broken parallelogram, four arcs of a circle, a flattened ellipse, and two semicircles that touched but did not form a circle. Finally, under pressure from the Soviet Union, Hanoi agreed to a compromise: a round table placed between two rectangular tables. By the time the infamous battle had been resolved, the Johnson administration was in its last days. Any chance of substantive negotiations had passed.[73]

It seems doubtful that South Vietnamese intransigence sabotaged an opportunity for a peace settlement. Hanoi's approach on procedural issues was more flexible in late 1968 than previously, probably because it wanted to get the bombing stopped, possibly because it hoped to extract an acceptable settlement from Johnson before he left office. Its flexibility did not extend to substantive issues, however. There is nothing to indicate that it would have agreed to anything short of an American withdrawal and a coalition government. These terms would not have been acceptable to Johnson. Although he had given in on the bombing halt and was deeply annoyed with Thieu, the president still clung to the goals he had pursued so doggedly since taking office. He made clear to Thieu that he would not

[71]McPherson to Clifford, August 13, 1968, Johnson Papers, McPherson File, Box 53; Clifford notes for meeting with Johnson, November 18, 1968, Clifford Papers, Box 6; Elsey Notes, December 18, 1968, January 4, 1969, Elsey Papers.

[72]Harriman memorandum of conversation with Robert Shaplen, November 30, 1968, Harriman Papers, Box 556.

[73]Harriman to Rusk, December 21, 28, 1968, Harriman Papers, Box 553; Rudy Abramson, *The Life of W. Averell Harriman: Spanning the Century, 1891–1986* (New York, 1992), p. 671.

recognize the NLF or accept a coalition government or some form of cosmetic settlement that would permit an American withdrawal. He seems to have felt that he could still achieve his original goals, and he remained convinced that he had the enemy on the ropes.[74] On the day he ordered the bombing halt, he instructed Abrams to "use his manpower and resources in a maximum effort" to "keep the enemy on the run." "Don't give them a moment's rest. Let the enemy feel the weight of everything you've got."[75] Thus, even if Thieu had gone along from the start, it appears doubtful that any meaningful peace agreement could have been reached in 1968, particularly in view of the short timetable.

The year 1968 ended as it had begun, with deadlock on the battlefield and in diplomatic councils. Each side in the aftermath of Tet saw itself on the offensive seeking a knockout blow against a weakened enemy. In fact, each had suffered enormous losses. In the eight weeks after March 31 alone, 3,700 Americans were killed, an estimated 43,000 enemy. Despite claims of victory, moreover, each combatant was significantly weakened; neither emerged with sufficient leverage to force a settlement. Tet merely hardened the deadlock, and it would take four more years of "fighting while negotiating" before it was finally broken.

In the long run, as historian Ronald Spector has observed, the battles of Tet were decisive "because they were so indecisive."[76] Whatever its costs, Tet represented a major political victory for the enemy because it convinced most Americans that the war could not be won in an acceptable time and at an acceptable cost. Thus, although Johnson clung stubbornly to his goals and refused to make the concessions necessary to get a settlement, he initiated what turned out to be an irreversible process of de-escalation that would in time work in North Vietnam's favor. In a still larger sense,

---

[74]The enemy could "still knock out a window light," Johnson remarked in November, but "they have been out of it since September." Henry Graff, *The Tuesday Cabinet* (Englewood Cliffs, N.J., 1970), p. 163. See also notes on meeting with Nixon, November 11, 1968, Johnson Papers, Tom Johnson Notes, Box 1.

[75]Johnson, *Vantage Point*, p. 523; Lewis Sorley, *Thunderbolt: General Creighton Abrams and the Army of His Times* (New York, 1992), p. 253.

[76]Ronald H. Spector, *After Tet: The Bloodiest Year in Vietnam* (New York, 1993), pp. 311–314.

Comparative Military Casualty Figures

	Killed in Action		Wounded	
Year	U.S.	South Vietnam	U.S.	South Vietnam
1960	0	2,223	0	2,788
1961	11	4,004	2	5,449
1962	31	4,457	41	7,195
1963	78	5,665	218	11,488
1964	147	7,457	522	17,017
1965	1,369	11,242	3,308	23,118
1966	5,008	11,953	16,526	20,975
1967	9,377	12,716	32,370	29,448
1968	14,589	27,915	46,797	70,696
1969	9,414	21,833	32,940	65,276
1970	4,221	23,346	15,211	71,582
1971	1,381	22,738	4,767	60,939
1972	300	39,587	587	109,960
1973	237	27,901	24	131,936
1974	207	31,219	0	155,735
Totals	46,370	254,256	153,313	783,602

Source: Jeffrey J. Clarke, *Advice and Support: The Final Years*, p. 275.

Tet represented the high-water mark of post–World War II American hegemony, that point at which the nation's establishment came to recognize that its international commitments had begun to exceed its ability to pay for them. From this point on, in Vietnam and elsewhere, the United States struggled with the dilemma of scaling back its commitments or finding alternative ways of maintaining its domestic and international well-being at a lower cost.

Richard Nixon and Henry Kissinger
Shown here en route to Europe, Nixon and Kissinger dominated U.S.
policymaking on Vietnam. The two men launched sometimes bold
ventures such as the invasion of Cambodia in 1970 and the Christmas
Bombing of 1972 in an effort to win the war. The best they could do was the
Paris Peace Accords of 1973, an agreement that got the United States out of
Vietnam militarily and gained the return of American POWs but fell short
of the peace with honor Nixon sought. Dependent on each other in many
ways, the two men in time became bitter rivals.
© *Bettmann/CORBIS*

CHAPTER 7

A War for Peace

Nixon, Kissinger, and Vietnam, 1969–1973

"We will not make the same old mistakes," National Security Adviser Henry A. Kissinger proclaimed of Vietnam in 1969. "We will make our own."[1] Kissinger's remark underscored the Nixon administration's determination to find new solutions to an old problem. The self-effacing humor, a Kissinger trademark, suggested a certainty of success. But the prediction turned out to be only partially correct. Kissinger and Nixon did try new approaches, some of which in time produced their own mistakes, but their policy suffered from the same flaws as those of their predecessors. Although disguising it in the rhetoric of "peace with honor," the Nixon administration persisted in the quixotic search for an independent, non-Communist Vietnam. This goal was to be achieved primarily by a massive buildup of South Vietnamese military strength and by the application of military pressure against North Vietnam, methods that had been tried before in various forms and found wanting. The result was four more years of bloody warfare in Indochina, a marked increase in domestic strife, and a peace settlement that permitted American extrication but was neither honorable nor lasting.

PEACE WITH HONOR

U.S. foreign policy in the Nixon–Kissinger era bore the distinct personal imprint of its shapers. The middle-American professional

---

[1]Quoted in Roger Morris, *An Uncertain Greatness: Henry Kissinger and American Foreign Policy* (New York, 1977), p. 4.

politician and the German-born Harvard professor could not have been more different in background, but they shared a love of power and a burning ambition to mold a fluid world and establish their place in history. Nixon was intelligent and hard-working but also tormented, combative, and viciously vindictive. His hatreds burned deeply, especially when fueled by alcohol, which he handled poorly. Kissinger could be outwardly charming and gregarious, but he was also edgy and prone to tantrums. Loners and outsiders in their own professions, the two men were perhaps naturally drawn to each other. Insecure to the point of paranoia, they also became profoundly suspicious of each other and disparaging in the presence of others. In the first years, mutual dependence kept them together, Kissinger depending on Nixon for access to the prominence and power he so craved, Nixon relying on Kissinger to shape his broad designs. Eventually, their suspicions turned into bitter rivalry.[2]

Although both men had reputations as rigid ideologues, they were pragmatic and flexible in their approach to foreign policy. They shared an obsession with secrecy, a zest for intrigue, and a flair for the unexpected move. They also shared a certain disdain for democracy, equating dissent with treason and carrying to extremes the Cold War dogma that national security was too important to be left to an ignorant public and a parochial and cumbersome Congress. Above all, they shared a contempt for bureaucracy. They took the foreign policy controls firmly and exclusively in their own hands and jealously guarded them, using, but rarely relying on or even keeping informed, the rest of the government, and employing deception and backchannel communications to dominate their colleagues. They created an atmosphere of oppressive secretiveness, backbiting, and conspiracy that makes the word *Byzantine* seem tame by comparison.

Their methods spurred extraordinary activities on the part of their advisers merely to keep abreast of what was going on. The Joint Chiefs of Staff, through Chief of Naval Operations Admiral Elmo Zumwalt, used a Navy liaison officer and an enlisted man employed in Kissinger's National Security Council (NSC) office as "spies" to find out what he and the president were up to. Former Wisconsin congressman and Secretary of Defense Melvin Laird reveled in matching wits with Kissinger—and excelled at it. He named loyalists

[2]Robert Dallek, *Nixon and Kissinger: Partners in Power* (New York, 2007), pp. 89–93.

to head the Defense Intelligence Agency and National Security Agency and used them to keep him informed of White House back-channel communications and telephone conversations. He secured from military units handling top-level travel arrangements informa-tion about Kissinger's whereabouts.[3]

The result was a foreign policy sometimes bold and imaginative in conception, often crude and improvisational; sometimes brilliant in execution, sometimes bungling; a policy dedicated to the noble goal of a "generation of peace" but frequently ruthless and cynical in its use of military power and callous in its obliviousness to the enor-mous human costs inflicted at home and especially abroad. The result also was a systematic abuse of power that ultimately forced Nixon's humiliating resignation from the office he had pursued relentlessly throughout his political career.

Prior to taking office, Nixon and Kissinger had firmly defended the American commitment in Vietnam. At the height of the domes-tic debate in 1967, Nixon had insisted that the presence of U.S. troops in Southeast Asia had helped contain an expansionist China and given the "free" Asian nations time to develop stable institu-tions. "Whatever one may think of the 'domino theory,' " he asserted, "it is beyond question that without the American commit-ment in Vietnam, Asia would be a far different place today."[4] Kissinger conceded that the United States may have exaggerated the significance of Vietnam in the early stages of its involvement. "But the commitment of five hundred thousand Americans has set-tled the issue of the importance of Vietnam," he quickly added. "For what is involved now is confidence in American promises."[5]

By 1969, Nixon and Kissinger recognized that the war must be ended. It had become, in the words of a Nixon speechwriter, a "bone in the nation's throat," a divisive force that had torn the country apart and hindered any constructive approach to domes-tic and foreign policy problems.[6] Nixon perceived, moreover, that his ability to extricate the nation from Vietnam would decisively affect his political future and his place in history. "I'm not going to

---

[3]Larry Berman, *Zumwalt: The Life and Times of Admiral Elmo Russell "Bud" Zumwalt, Jr.* (New York, 2012), pp. 312–344.
[4]Richard M. Nixon, "Asia after Vietnam," *Foreign Affairs* 46 (October 1967): 111.
[5]Henry A. Kissinger, "The Vietnam Negotiations," *Foreign Affairs* 47 (January 1969): 219.
[6]William Safire, *Before the Fall* (New York, 1975), p. 121.

end up like LBJ," he once remarked, "holed up in the White House afraid to show my face on the street. I'm going to stop that war. Fast."[7]

The two men nevertheless insisted that the war must be ended "honorably." Simply to pull out of Vietnam, they believed, would be a callous abandonment of those South Vietnamese who had depended on American protection and would be unworthy of the actions of a great nation. As a young Congressman, Nixon had led the right-wing Republican attack on Truman for "losing" China. Like Johnson before him, he feared the domestic upheaval that might accompany the fall of South Vietnam to Communism. The reaction would be "terrible," he told a journalist in May 1969, ". . . we would destroy ourselves if we pulled out in a way that wasn't really honorable."[8]

Most important, Nixon and Kissinger feared the international consequences of a precipitous withdrawal. Even before taking office, they had begun sketching the outlines of a new world order based on American primacy. Their grand design included at least a limited accommodation with the Soviet Union and China. They felt they must extricate the United States from the war in a manner that would demonstrate to these old adversaries resoluteness of purpose and certainty of action, a manner that would uphold U.S. credibility with friends and foes alike. "However we got into Vietnam," Kissinger observed, "whatever the judgment of our actions, ending the war honorably is essential for the peace of the world. Any other solution may unloose forces that would complicate the prospects of international order."[9] Nixon agreed. "The true objective of this war is peace," he affirmed shortly after taking office—with no apparent sense of the paradox—"It is a war for peace."[10]

An "honorable" settlement had to meet several essential conditions. The American withdrawal from Vietnam must be conducted in a way that avoided even the appearance of defeat. There must be no face-saving political settlement designed merely to permit a graceful U.S. exit from Vietnam. Kissinger explicitly rejected the idea of a coalition government, which, he said, would "destroy the existing political structure and thus lead to a Communist takeover."

[7]H. R. Haldeman, *The Ends of Power* (New York, 1978), p. 81.
[8]Quoted in C. L. Sulzberger, *Seven Continents and Forty Years* (New York, 1977), pp. 505–507.
[9]Kissinger, "Vietnam Negotiations," 234.
[10]Sulzberger, *Seven Continents*, p. 507.

Nixon and Kissinger set as their optimum goal a "fair negotiated settlement that would preserve the independence of South Vietnam." At a minimum, they insisted on a settlement that would give South Vietnam a reasonable chance to survive.[11]

Although this objective had eluded the United States for more than a decade, Nixon and Kissinger believed that they could succeed where others had failed. They perceived that the Saigon government could not survive an abrupt American withdrawal, but it appeared stronger than ever in early 1969. With continued U.S. backing, Thieu might hold on indefinitely. The North Vietnamese must recognize, Kissinger reasoned, that they could not eject the United States from Vietnam by force. They might therefore be persuaded to exchange an American withdrawal for a political settlement that would leave Thieu firmly in control.

Nixon and Kissinger were confident, moreover, that they could compel Hanoi to accept terms it had consistently rejected. The Soviet Union had made clear its keen interest in expanded trade with the United States and an agreement limiting strategic arms. This leverage, or "linkage," as Kissinger called it, could be used to secure Russian assistance in getting North Vietnam to agree to a "fair" settlement. Great power diplomacy would be supplemented by the use of force. Nixon felt that military pressure had failed thus far because it had been employed in a limited, indecisive manner. A "fourth-rate power like North Vietnam" must have a "breaking point," Kissinger insisted. He and Nixon were prepared to use maximum force, threatening the very survival of North Vietnam, to get what they wanted.[12] Nixon compared his situation to that faced by Eisenhower in Korea in 1953. He was certain that the threat of "massive retaliation" would intimidate the North Vietnamese as he believed it had the North Koreans. He counted on his image as a hard-line anti-Communist to make the threat credible. "They'll believe any threat of force Nixon makes because it's Nixon," he told one of his advisers. "We'll just slip the word to them that, 'for God's sake, you know Nixon's obsessed about Communism . . . and he has his hand on the nuclear button.' "[13]

[11]Richard M. Nixon, *RN: The Memoirs of Richard Nixon* (New York, 1978), p. 349; Safire, *Before the Fall,* p. 134.

[12]Quoted in Morris, *Uncertain Greatness,* p. 164.

[13]Quoted in Haldeman, *Ends of Power,* p. 83.

The Nixon–Kissinger strategy for ending the war was based on a large dose of wishful thinking. Their concern about U.S. credibility was exaggerated and was based on dubious reasoning to begin with. In any event, as Walter Isaacson has concluded, in their stubborn and ultimately futile pursuit of a settlement that would uphold United States' credibility, they "squandered the true sources of its influence—and of its credibility—in the world: its moral authority, its sense of worthy purpose and its reputation as a reasonable and sensible player." It was naive to assume that they could accomplish what Johnson had failed to do at a time when they had less military power at their disposal and when the patience of the American public had already worn thin. Like their predecessors, they grossly underestimated their adversaries. They also overestimated the willingness and ability of the Kremlin to pressure North Vietnam to accept a settlement favorable to the United States. And the lessons Nixon drew from Eisenhower's ending of the Korean War represented yet another example of misuse of historical analogy by American leaders.[14]

PEACE THROUGH COERCION

With that sublime self-confidence common among leaders new to power, Nixon and Kissinger believed they could end the war within six months to a year. Through French intermediaries, the president conveyed a personal message to the North Vietnamese expressing his desire for peace and proposing as a first step the mutual withdrawal of American and North Vietnamese troops from South Vietnam and the restoration of the demilitarized zone as a boundary between North and South. Kissinger informed Soviet ambassador Anatoly Dobrynin that the administration was eager to negotiate on a variety of urgent topics but bluntly warned that peace in Vietnam must come first.

As a signal to both Hanoi and Moscow that the United States meant business, Nixon ordered intensive bombing attacks against North Vietnamese sanctuaries in neutral Cambodia, a step repeatedly

---

[14]Walter Isaacson, *Kissinger: A Biography* (New York, 1992), p. 161; Edward C. Keefer, "President Dwight D. Eisenhower and the End of the Korean War," *Diplomatic History* 10 (Summer 1986): 267–289.

advocated by the Joint Chiefs of Staff but rejected by LBJ. The military objective was to limit North Vietnam's capacity to launch an offensive against the South, but Nixon's primary motive was to indicate that he would take measures Johnson had avoided, thus frightening Hanoi into negotiating on his terms. Over the next fifteen months, 3,630 B-52 raids were flown, dropping more than 100,000 tons of bombs on Cambodia. The operation was dubbed (with singular inappropriateness) MENU, its individual components BREAKFAST, LUNCH, SNACK, DESSERT. At Nixon's insistence, it was kept secret from the public—and indeed from much of the government—and elaborate methods of bookkeeping were devised to conceal its existence. The bombing of Cambodia did not intimidate Hanoi into making concessions in Paris. The bombing had no perceivable impact on its ability to wage war in South Vietnam, and the area of Cambodia under North Vietnamese control may have increased. The number of civilian deaths may never be known. The bombing drove some Cambodians into the arms of the Communist Khmer Rouge. It helped undermine the already fragile foundations of Cambodian neutrality. When a story on the bombing appeared in the *New York Times* shortly after it was initiated, Nixon, apoplectic with rage and with Kissinger's ardent support, ordered wiretaps on the phones of seventeen government employees and journalists, including some members of Kissinger's staff.[15]

Recognizing that the success of his Vietnam policy hinged on his ability to maintain at least the appearance of unity at home, Nixon mounted a public relations strategy to parallel his secret diplomacy. His aides used extensive polling both to measure and influence public opinion, often framing questions to get the sort of responses they wanted and then publicizing the answers to prove that their policies had popular backing.[16] In May 1969, Nixon unveiled what he described as a "comprehensive peace plan," publicly revealing the proposals he had privately made to North Vietnam and adding his hope that all "foreign" troops might be removed from South Vietnam within a year after the signing of a peace agreement. To make plain his intention of terminating U.S.

[15]Kenton Clymer *Troubled Relations: The United States and Cambodia since 1870* (Dekalb, Ill., 2007), pp. 94–102.
[16]Andrew Z. Katz, "Public Opinion and Foreign Policy: The Nixon Administration and the Pursuit of Peace with Honor in Vietnam," *Presidential Studies Quarterly* 27 (Summer 1997): 499–501.

involvement in the war, he initiated planning for the phased with-drawal of American troops. After conferring with Thieu on Midway Island in June, he announced the immediate withdrawal of 25,000 American combat forces. To emphasize to the Russians, the North Vietnamese, and the right wing at home that he had not gone soft, Nixon delivered several tough speeches, attacking as "new isola-tionists" those doves who argued that the war was diverting the nation from more pressing problems at home and stressing his determination to uphold America's international responsibilities.

Nixon's secret diplomacy and implied military threats wrenched no concessions from North Vietnam. From Hanoi's standpoint, his proposals offered no improvement over those of Johnson. To have accepted them would have represented abandon-ment of goals pursued for a quarter century. National Liberation Front (NLF) and North Vietnamese Army (NVA) units in the South were drastically weakened from the battering absorbed during Tet and its bloody aftermath. The revolution was in its most perilous state since its inception in the late 1950s. The Sino-Soviet split had escalated to actual warfare, leaving Hanoi on its own. In the summer of 1969, North Vietnamese leaders thus reverted to the protracted war strategy favored by Vo Nguyen Giap and Ho Chi Minh, curtailing the level of military attacks in the South and with-drawing some troops back across the demilitarized zone. Hanoi turned to diplomacy to win over world opinion, to keep Nixon from escalating the war, and, in time, to force a unilateral U.S. with-drawal. The leadership agreed to secret talks in Paris but delayed their opening; it instructed negotiators to appear cooperative but not to compromise. Its delegation to the peace talks publicly dismissed Nixon's offer as a "farce" and vowed, if necessary, to sit in Paris "until the chairs rot."[17] Confident that U.S. public opinion would, in time, force Nixon to withdraw unilaterally from Vietnam, Hanoi prepared to wait him out, no matter the cost.

Nixon's peace moves also failed to contain the opposition at home. When it was clear that there would be no breakthrough in

---

[17]Robert Shaplen, *The Road from War: Vietnam, 1965–1970* (New York, 1970), pp. 300–301. The North Vietnamese perspective is well covered in Pierre Asselin, "Revisionism Triumphant: Hanoi's Diplomatic Strategy in the Nixon Era," *Journal of Cold War Studies,* 13 (Fall, 2011): 103–108, and Lien-Hang T. Nguyen, *Hanoi's War: An International History of the War for Peace in Vietnam* (Chapel Hill, N.C., 2012), pp. 129–137.

Paris, public approval of the president's handling of the war dropped sharply. Expressing the growing frustration of the hawks, Senator Richard Russell of Georgia insisted that if the Paris talks did not soon produce results, the United States must make a "meaningful move" against North Vietnam.[18] The organized peace movement, dormant since the Democratic convention of 1968, began to stir again, announcing plans for massive demonstrations in the fall. Congressional doves had remained silent during the administration's first months, giving the president an opportunity to end the war, but by June they began to speak out anew. Republican senator Jacob Javits of New York charged Nixon with pursuing the same "sterile and unsuccessful approach" followed by Johnson; Arkansas senator J. William Fulbright denounced the "new isolationism" speech as "demagogy and personally offensive." Senate doves were not satisfied with Nixon's peace offer and troop withdrawal, and many Democrats rallied behind Clark Clifford's call for the removal of all American forces by the end of 1970. By midsummer, Nixon's brief honeymoon with the Democratic-controlled Congress had ended.

Never one to avoid a fight, Nixon struck back at his foes. White House spokespersons sought to link Democrats and liberals to the radical left, thereby portraying them as dangerous fringe groups. The government prosecuted the ringleaders of the 1968 Chicago protest, the so-called Chicago Seven, initiating a show trial that would take on the solemnity of a circus and would eventually be thrown out of court. The administration used all its public relations skills to draw attention to those who supported the president's policies and discredit those who opposed him. Nixon unleashed his equally combative vice president, Spiro Agnew, for a series of vitriolic attacks against antiwar protesters and the liberal media that allegedly supported them. Believing that student protest derived mainly from narrow self-interest, the administration modified the draft laws, making fewer young men susceptible to being inducted and gradually reducing draft calls.

Nixon's early curiosity about what drove the antiwar protesters evolved into an obsession. He and his top aides developed a voyeurlike and nearly insatiable appetite for information about

[18]Russell to L. M. Thacker, July 26, 1969, Richard M. Russell Papers, University of Georgia Library, Athens, Ga., Dictation File, Box IJ7.

the movement. They spent hours agonizing over how to deal with it and concocted schemes ranging from the bizarre to the sinister, discussing such options as using helicopters to blow out candles held by protesters and hiring thugs to beat protesters up. Above all, the White House viewed the movement as an enemy that must be crushed and launched a systematic campaign to destroy it. The administration increased government surveillance of antiwar organizations and their leaders. The FBI, CIA (through the illegal CHAOS operation initiated by Johnson), and military expanded their surveillance activities, tapping phones and ransacking files of antiwar groups. Like Johnson, Nixon was certain that the Communists were masterminding the movement. When extensive analysis again failed to establish a direct connection, he disparaged the intelligence rather than reexamine his assumptions. The administration went beyond intelligence to infiltration and sabotage. Government agencies spread disinformation to discredit antiwar groups. The Internal Revenue Service and FBI harrassed major organizations and their leaders. Agents working inside these organizations helped disrupt their lawful activity, incited them to violent acts against each other, and engaged in actions to make them look bad.[19]

DUCK HOOK

Fearful that the rising domestic protest might doom his efforts to pressure the North Vietnamese into a settlement, Nixon also improvised in July a "go-for-broke" strategy, an all-out attempt to "end the war one way or the other—either by negotiated agreement or by force." Again through French intermediaries, he sent a personal message to Ho Chi Minh, reiterating his desire for a "just peace" but adding an ultimatum: Unless some progress toward a settlement was made by November 1, he would have no choice but to resort to "measures of great consequence and force." Kissinger again spoke with Dobrynin, warning that "as far as Vietnam is concerned, the train has just left the station and is now headed down

---

[19]Terry H. Anderson, *The Movement and the Sixties* (New York, 1995), pp. 323–325; Tom Wells, *The War Within: America's Battle over Vietnam* (Berkeley, Calif., 1994), pp. 306–377.

the track."[20] On Nixon's orders, Kissinger convened a special, top-secret National Security Council study group to draw up plans (code-named DUCK HOOK) for what he described as "savage, punishing blows" against North Vietnam, including massive bombing attacks on the major cities, a blockade of the ports, and even, possibly, the use of tactical nuclear weapons in certain "controlled" situations. To give force to his warnings, Nixon leaked word to journalists that he was considering such options. He emphatically reiterated LBJs vow that he would not be the first American president to lose a war.[21]

Nixon's ultimatum had no effect. On August 4, in the first of a long series of secret meetings, Kissinger met privately with North Vietnamese diplomat Xuan Thuy. He reiterated Nixon's peace proposals and ultimatum, but Thuy responded with the standard line that the United States must withdraw all its troops and abandon Thieu to secure an agreement. Ho Chi Minh's formal response, written shortly before his death on September 2, 1969, conveyed the same message and was, in Nixon's words, a "cold rebuff." From the president's standpoint, the North Vietnamese were not only intransigent but also deliberately provocative. Hanoi Radio tossed back at the White House statements made by Senate doves that Nixon's policies were prolonging the war and expressed to the "American people" hope that their "fall [peace] offensive" would "succeed splendidly."[22]

Unable to coerce Hanoi into concessions, Nixon was left to choose between a major escalation of the war and a humiliating retreat. He was furious at his adversary's defiance and the domestic criticism he believed had encouraged it. His instinct was to strike back. But some of his advisers implored him not to inflame the opposition at home. More important, after weeks of careful analysis, Kissinger's study group concluded that air strikes and a blockade might not force concessions from Hanoi or even significantly limit its capacity to continue the war in the South. Haunted throughout his career by a near-obsessive fear of failure, Nixon abandoned the plan for "savage, punishing blows" with the greatest reluctance and

[20]Nixon, *RN*, pp. 393–394, 399.
[21]The most complete discussion of the DUCK HOOK planning is in Jeffrey Kimball, *Nixon's Vietnam War* (Lawrence, Kansi., 1998), pp. 158–170.
[22]Nixon, *RN*, pp. 397–399.

only after being persuaded that it would not work. As a limp alternative, he ordered implementation of a military readiness test in hopes that close surveillance of Soviet ships heading for North Vietnam and putting Strategic Air Command (SAC) bombers on high alert would send the requisite signals to Moscow and Hanoi. Neither showed any sign of picking up on the messages.[23]

VIETNAMIZATION

With other options exhausted, Nixon fell back on the Vietnamization policy inherited from Johnson. Within his administration, Secretary of Defense Laird was the prime mover behind Vietnamization—and seems to have given the policy its name. A long-time House member from Wisconsin and hawk on defense issues, Laird had concluded that no military victory was possible in Vietnam and favored, in his own words, "getting the hell out of there."[24] He saw with a clarity others did not the urgency of domestic political reasons for de-Americanizing the war. The United States should drastically increase military aid to bolster South Vietnam's ability to defend itself. A concurrent program of regular U.S. troop withdrawals, sensibly balanced between "too much, too soon, and too little, too late," would persuade Congress and the public that the nation was getting out of Vietnam, buying precious time for Vietnamization to work.[25] After returning from a visit to Saigon in March 1969, where he deemed the rate of progress much too slow, Laird launched a major drive for Vietnamization. Nixon approved his timetable in April. With the nonimplementation of DUCK HOOK, the president settled by default on Vietnamization as his policy to end the war. With more faith than logic, he reasoned that if he could mobilize American opinion behind him, persuade Hanoi that he would not abandon Thieu, and intensify the buildup of South Vietnamese military power, North Vietnam might conclude that it

---

[23]William Burr and Jeffrey Kimball, "Nixon's Secret Nuclear Alert: Vietnam War Diplomacy and the Joint Chiefs of Staff Readiness Test, October 1969," *Cold War History* 3 (January 2003): 113–156.

[24]Dale Van Atta, *With Honor: Melvin Laird in War, Peace, and Politics* (Madison, Wis., 2008), p. 173.

[25]Laird to Nixon, June 2, 1969, Department of State, *Foreign Relations of the United States, 1969–1976*, Vol. 6 (Washington, 2006), p. 264.

would be better to negotiate with the United States now than with South Vietnam later, and he could extract from them the concessions necessary to secure peace with honor.

In a major speech on November 3, Nixon set out to isolate his critics and mobilize popular backing for his policy. He firmly defended the commitment in Vietnam, warning that a pullout would produce a bloodbath in South Vietnam and a crisis of confidence in American leadership at home and abroad. Spelling out his Vietnamization policy in some detail, he offered the alluring prospect that it would not only reduce American casualties but also terminate U.S. involvement in an honorable fashion regardless of what North Vietnam did. Although some members of his staff cautioned against a confrontation with the peace movement, Nixon rejected their advice. He dismissed the protesters as an irrational and irresponsible element and accused them of sabotaging his diplomacy. He openly appealed for the support of those he labeled the "great silent majority." He concluded with a dramatic warning: "North Vietnam cannot humiliate the United States. Only Americans can do that."

The Nixon administration also sought to use the increasingly important prisoner-of-war (POW) issue to build popular support for its Vietnam policies. The families of American prisoners held by North Vietnam had put together several potent and public-relations-savvy organizations to lobby Washington and Hanoi for their release. To give "ordinary people . . . something to be *for*" and counter the antiwar movement, the White House sought to link support for the president's war policies to release of the POWs. Nixon met with prisoner-of-war families. The administration urged Americans to write North Vietnam's delegate to the Paris peace talks to press for their release. U.S. officials helped sponsor advertisements in newspapers and magazines and encouraged the production and use of such items as POW bracelets, postage stamps, and bumper stickers.

Nixon's fall 1969 initiative produced mixed results. Millions of bumper stickers and stamps were sold. The POW campaign further raised the visibility of the issue and heightened public concern about the POWs' release. But it did not generate support for administration policies and actually increased the bargaining value of U.S. prisoners to Hanoi. North Vietnam was able to undercut the president with well-timed and broadly publicized release of POWs, often to representatives of the U.S. antiwar movement. Peace movement leaders countered with the seductive message that the surest way to secure release of the prisoners was for the United States to get out of the war.[26]

The "silent majority speech" nonetheless brought Nixon some short-term gains in the public arena. He placed his opponents on the defensive. By offering a policy that could achieve an honorable peace with minimal American sacrifice, he appeared to have reconciled the contradictory elements in public attitudes toward the war. He cleverly appealed to the patriotism of his listeners and to their reluctance to accept anything resembling defeat. By specifically identifying a "silent majority," he helped to create a bloc of support where none had existed.

The peace movement's fall 1969 "moratoriums to end the war" succeeded spectacularly. Organized mainly by liberals, they attracted millions of sober middle-class citizens. One of the largest expressions of mass protest in the nation's history, they also signaled the new respectability of the movement itself. In contrast to the bedlam and violence of Chicago 1968, the fall demonstrations were peaceful and dignified affairs with religious overtones. Across the nation, church bells tolled, the names of American war dead were called out at candlelight services, and participants solemnly intoned songwriter John Lennon's haunting antiwar chant, "Give Peace a Chance." In Washington's March of Death, thousands of protesters carrying candles walked through high winds and rain from Arlington Cemetery to the Capitol, where they placed in wooden coffins signs bearing the names of GIs killed in Vietnam.

The fall demonstrations did not produce a change in policy. Although alarmed and deeply angered by the protest, Nixon publicly feigned indifference, and his silent majority speech temporarily neutralized the effects of the demonstrations. Low on funds, its leadership increasingly splintered, and demoralized by a crippling sense of helplessness, the organized peace movement in the immediate aftermath of the moratoriums grew quiescent again. The polls indicated solid support for the administration, and in late November pro-Nixon rallies were held in a number of cities. "We've got those liberal bastards on the run now," the president exulted, "and we're going to keep them on the run."[27]

---

[26]Michael J. Allen, *Until the Last Man Comes Home: POWS, MIAS, and the Unending Vietnam War* (Chapel Hill, N.C., 2009), pp. 29–36.

[27]Quoted in Tad Szulc, *The Illusion of Peace* (New York, 1973), p. 158.

VIETNAMIZATION IN PRACTICE

Making Vietnamization work proved a much more formidable task. Whatever they said publicly, U.S. officials undertook the program with grave doubts. Most military experts agreed that without full American assistance, the South Vietnamese could not stand up against the combined threat of the North Vietnamese Army and NLF forces. Gen. Creighton Abrams criticized Vietnamization as "slow surrender" and repeatedly protested the size and pace of U.S. troop withdrawals.[28]

The South Vietnamese also objected to the Nixon policy. Typically, they were not consulted in decisions on and planning for Vietnamization. Although Nixon publicly proclaimed that Thieu had recommended U.S. troop withdrawals, in fact he bitterly opposed them. The South Vietnamese grudgingly acquiesced in what they saw as a political expedient for the United States. But they found the term *Vietnamization* demeaning, protesting that they had been fighting for years before the Americans became involved and even after 1965 had "sacrificed and suffered the most." Some Vietnamese cynically dismissed Vietnamization as a "U.S. Dollar and Vietnamese Blood Sharing Plan." Most saw it as a fig leaf to cover U.S. abandonment.[29]

By the time Nixon formally announced his "new" plan to end the war, Vietnamization had been in effect for more than a year and a half. A tank commander under the legendary Gen. George S. Patton in World War II and the polar opposite of Westmoreland in appearance and leadership style, the gruff, rugged, profane, often unkempt Abrams made major adjustments in fighting the war. He modified Westmoreland's costly and ineffectual search-and-destroy approach for a strategy that integrated combat operations more closely with pacification, and sought mainly to protect the population of South Vietnam. He attempted to curb the excessive and counterproductive use of firepower and the corrupting emphasis on body counts. He shifted from large-scale operations against enemy main-force units to small-unit actions aimed at disrupting the enemy's logistic systems and thereby limiting its ability to take the offensive.[30]

---

[28]Quoted in Isaacson, *Kissinger,* pp. 235–236.
[29]George C. Herring, " 'Peoples Quite Apart': Americans, South Vietnamese, and the War in Vietnam," *Diplomatic History* 14 (Winter, 1990): 17–18.
[30]Lewis Sorley, *A Better War* (New York, 1999), pp. 17–30.

While U.S. combat forces sought to keep the North Vietnamese and NLF off balance, American advisers worked frantically to build up and modernize the South Vietnamese armed forces. The force level, about 850,000 when Nixon took office, was increased to more than 1 million. The United States turned over to South Vietnam huge quantities of the newest weapons: more than a million M-16 rifles, 12,000 M-60 machine guns, 40,000 M-79 grenade launchers, and 2,000 heavy mortars and howitzers. The Vietnamese were also given ships, planes, helicopters, and so many vehicles that one member of Congress wondered whether the object of Vietnamization was to "put every South Vietnamese soldier behind the wheel."[31] Military schools were expanded to a capacity of more than 100,000 students a year. To improve morale and check the desertion rate, the promotion system was modernized, leaves improved, pay scales increased, veterans' benefits expanded, and systematic efforts made to improve conditions in military camps and dependent housing.

The Accelerated Pacification campaign, originally designed as a crash program to extend government control over the countryside prior to negotiations, was institutionalized and expanded in 1969 and 1970. To improve security in the villages, the major weakness of earlier programs, regular forces assigned to pacification were expanded to 500,000 soldiers armed with M-16 rifles and supplemented by a hastily created militia numbering in the thousands. Americans and South Vietnamese also attempted to infuse new life into old programs of village development. Village elections were held, restoring the autonomy that had been taken away in the Diem era. Elected officials were trained in civic responsibilities at the Rural Development Center in Vung Tau and upon graduation were given black pajamas furnished by the CIA. The government turned over to individual villages control of the militia and funds to be used for local projects. Strenuous efforts were made to clear roads, repair bridges, establish schools and hospitals, and expand agricultural production. In March 1970, the government launched an ambitious land reform program through which nearly one million hectares were eventually redistributed.

[31]Thomas Buckley, "The ARVN Is Bigger and Better, But—," *New York Times Magazine*, October 12, 1969, 132.

Vietnamization was in full swing by early 1970, and most observers agreed that significant gains had been made. Almost overnight the South Vietnamese army had become one of the largest and best-equipped in the world. When properly led, moreover, Army of the Republic of Vietnam (ARVN) units fought well. Some American advisers began to detect that, perhaps out of necessity, their performance improved noticeably as U.S. support units were withdrawn. In some areas, improvement in the performance of the separate South Vietnamese militia was even greater than that of the ARVN. American "spoiling" tactics, along with North Vietnam's decision to go on the defensive, left the countryside more secure than at any other time since the war began. The ability of the NLF to tax and recruit had been sharply reduced. NVA units in South Vietnam appeared to be suffering from serious personnel and material shortages. In former guerrilla strongholds, roads were passable at least by day, and the number of terrorist incidents declined markedly. On the surface, at least, the insurgency appeared to be under control. Even long-time skeptics like pacification expert John Vann concluded that "we are now on the right road."[32]

Real progress in Vietnamization remained uncertain. American officials claimed to have "neutralized" as many as 20,000 members of the NLF infrastructure through the Phoenix Program, and NLF operatives later conceded that in some areas Phoenix was "dangerously effective."[33] The figures were grossly inflated, however, and although the insurgents' clandestine apparatus was severely damaged, it remained intact. In addition, the abuses that accompanied the program sometimes generated support for the NLF. American officials also conceded that the gains in security had resulted primarily from U.S. military operations and the enemy stand-down. They wondered whether these factors could be sustained in the face of the withdrawal of U.S. forces and the renewal of enemy attacks.

---

[32]Vann to General Frederick Weyand, January 22, 1970, John P. Vann Papers, U.S. Army Military History Institute, Carlisle Barracks, Pa.

[33]Truong Nhu Tang, *A Vietcong Memoir* (New York, 1985), pp. 201–202. The Phoenix Program was highly controversial during its own time and remains so today. For recent, conflicting assessments, see Dale Andradé, *Ashes to Ashes: The Phoenix Program and the Vietnam War* (Lexington, Mass., 1990); Douglas Valentine, *The Phoenix Program* (New York, 1990); and Mark Moyar, *Phoenix and the Birds of Prey* (Annapolis, Md., 1997).

The biggest question mark remained the government itself. Thieu had skillfully built a durable governing structure comprising Chinese merchants, loyal bureaucrats, and army officers and held together by the glue of corruption. It was, however, a narrowly based operation entirely dependent on the continued infusion of U.S. funds and, ironically, largely resistant to U.S. influence. Despite the frenetic activity in the villages, there was nothing to indicate that the pacification program had generated any real enthusiasm for the Thieu government. One senior U.S. officer observed, moreover, that although significant progress had been made in numerous areas, the government had not yet "succeeded in mobilizing the will and energies of the people against the enemy and in support of national programs."[34]

On paper, the often maligned ARVN appeared a formidable force, but its fundamental weaknesses remained. Many South Vietnamese soldiers were deeply patriotic. That an estimated 200,000 died in combat suggests their willingness to make the ultimate sacrifice. Many others were, at best, ambivalent. In contrast to their NVA brethren, they were not given political education. Some profoundly distrusted their own government. Compelled into service through an inequitable system of conscription out of touch with the dynamics of rural life, they served long enlistments with inadequate provisions for leave. Some soldiers more attuned to the needs of their families and communities than to those of their nation simply left. Desertions peaked in 1969. Poorly trained—in most cases through programs based on U.S. models—they were not well prepared for combat. They endured low pay, poor food, and inadequate medical care. Increases in pay were offset by inflation. In an economy where prostitutes could earn as much in a week as senior military officers in a year, corruption was an accepted means to redress inequities. Some soldiers welcomed Vietnamization as a chance to fight on their own rather than be told what to do by outsiders. Others were painfully aware that, by themselves, they were no match for the enemy. In taking over the war in 1965, the United States had assigned the ARVN a subsidiary role, and it was difficult

[34]Memorandum by General Arthur S. Collins, Fall 1970, A. S. Collins Papers, U.S. Army Military History Institute, Carlisle Barracks, Pa.; see also Report by Vietnam Special Studies Group, January 10, 1970, and Charles S. Whitehouse to William Colby, September 22, 1970, both in Vann Papers.

to reverse the consequences of that move in a short time. A shift in policy driven by U.S. domestic political needs "did not change the fact that we were poorly trained, poorly led, and suffering from low morale," one soldier later recalled.[35]

The "nagging question" was whether the ARVN could fill the vacuum left by departing U.S. troops. Even the better units still hesitated to engage the enemy in sustained combat. Americans belatedly realized that they had made the South Vietnamese dependent. Many U.S. advisers conceded that, at best, much time would be required before the South Vietnamese would be able to stand on their own against the seasoned and well-disciplined (PAVN) soldiers.[36] North Vietnamese negotiator Le Duc Tho openly posed to Kissinger the fundamental question. If the United States could not win with a half million of its own troops, he asked, "How can you succeed when you let the puppet troops do the fighting?" It was a question, Kissinger conceded, that "also torments me."[37]

By the spring of 1970, the contradictions in Nixon's Vietnamization strategy had become all too apparent. The silent majority speech had quieted the opposition temporarily, but Nixon realized that his success was only transient. In March he announced the phased withdrawal of 150,000 troops over the next year in order to "drop a bombshell on the gathering spring storm of anti-war protest."[38] He recognized that this withdrawal, however necessary from the standpoint of domestic politics, would weaken his hand in other areas. Abrams had bitterly protested the new troop withdrawals, warning that they would leave South Vietnam vulnerable to enemy military pressure and could be devastating to the Vietnamization program. Nixon had rather naively hoped that his professed determination to remain in Vietnam indefinitely and the demonstrations of public support that had followed his November 3 speech would persuade the North Vietnamese to negotiate. But there had been no

---

[35]Robert K. Brigham, *ARVN Life and Death in the South Vietnamese Army* (Lawrence, Kans., 2006), especially pp. 98–100.

[36]Collins memorandum, fall 1970, Collins Papers; William Rosson oral history interview, U.S. Army Military History Institute, Carlisle Barracks, Pa.; Jeffrey J. Clarke, *Advice and Support: The Final Years, 1965–1973* (Washington, D.C., 1988), pp. 341–359, provides a balanced and persuasive analysis of Vietnamization.

[37]Quoted in Isaacson, *Kissinger*, p. 253.

[38]Nixon, *RN*, p. 448.

breakthrough in Paris. He recognized that the announcement of additional troop withdrawals would probably encourage Hanoi to delay further. Increasingly impatient for results and still certain that he could end the war by a dramatic show of force, he once more began looking for "initiatives" to "show the enemy that we were still serious about our commitment in Vietnam."[39]

CAMBODIA

The overthrow of Cambodia's neutralist Prince Sihanouk in March by a pro-American clique headed by Prime Minister Lon Nol posed new dangers to the Vietnamization policy and presented enticing opportunities for the initiative Nixon sought. Kissinger has vigorously denied American complicity in the coup, and no evidence has ever been produced to prove that the United States was directly involved. The administration appears not to have been surprised by Lon Nol's move, however, and Washington's long-standing and obvious dislike for Sihanouk and its interest in attacking the North Vietnamese sanctuaries in Cambodia may have encouraged Lon Nol to believe that a successful coup would gain U.S. support.[40]

Kissinger's later claim that the United States intervened in Cambodia only hesitantly and belatedly and only after being persuaded that the North Vietnamese were committed to the destruction of Lon Nol's government appears at best misleading. Shortly after the coup, with U.S. authorization, South Vietnamese units conducted raids across the border into Cambodia. The United States recognized the new Cambodian government and initiated covert military aid. That North Vietnam decided in the aftermath of the coup to take over Cambodia remains unproven today and was open to serious question at the time. On the other hand, from the outset, some U.S. officials were eager to exploit developments in Cambodia. The military for years had urged attacking North

[39]Ibid., p. 445.
[40]The controversy over Cambodia is one of the most bitter and emotional to come out of the war. The respective positions are spelled out in Shawcross, *Sideshow,* especially pp. 112–127, and in Henry A. Kissinger, *White House Years* (Boston, 1979), pp. 457–521.

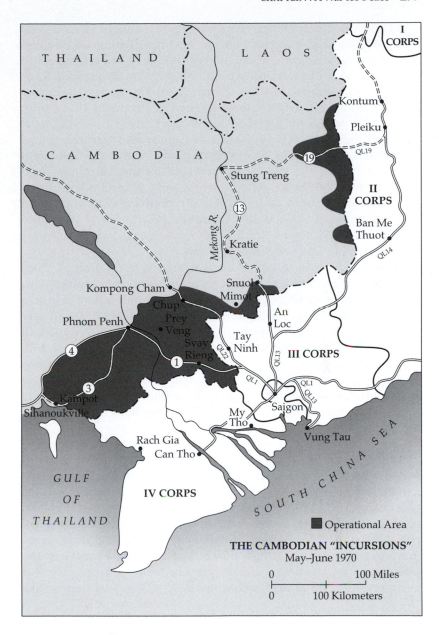

THAILAND

LAOS

I CORPS

Kontum

Pleiku

QL19

CAMBODIA

⑲

Stung Treng

II CORPS

⑬

Mekong R.

Ban Me Thuot

Kratie

QL14

Snuol

Kompong Cham

Mimot

Chup

An Loc

Prey Veng

Tay Ninh

III CORPS

Svay Rieng

QL22

Phnom Penh

④

①

QL1

QL13

①

QL1

③

QL1

QL13

Kampot

My Tho

Saigon

Sihanoukville

Rach Gia

Vung Tau

Can Tho

GULF

SOUTH CHINA SEA

OF

IV CORPS

THAILAND

■ Operational Area

THE CAMBODIAN "INCURSIONS"
May–June 1970

0   100 Miles

0   100 Kilometers

Vietnamese sanctuaries. The change of government in Phnom Penh removed the long-standing concern about violating Cambodian neutrality. Attacks on the sanctuaries could now be justified in terms of sustaining a friendly Cambodian government as well as easing the military threat to South Vietnam. Nixon therefore quickly endorsed a Defense Department proposal that South Vietnamese units with American air support attack an enemy sanctuary on the Parrot's Beak, a strip of Cambodian territory thirty-three miles from Saigon. Even before plans for this operation had been completed, the president approved a more dramatic—and much more risky—move. After nearly a week of careful and apparently agonizing study and over the vigorous opposition of Laird and Secretary of State William Rogers, he approved Abrams's proposal that U.S. forces attack Fishhook, a North Vietnamese base area fifty-five miles northwest of Saigon.

Nixon's decision to send American troops into Cambodia, one of the most important and controversial decisions of his tumultuous presidency, was motivated by a variety of considerations. He was swayed by the military's argument that the operation would buy time for Vietnamization and help sustain a friendly government in Cambodia. On the other hand, he realized that his decision would have a "shattering effect" at home.[41] His willingness to run this risk for uncertain gains reflected, in part, what he called his "big play philosophy," his belief that because the administration was "going to get unshirted hell for doing this at all," it might as well "go for all the marbles."[42]

Rather than fearing the domestic backlash, he seems to have welcomed it. By the spring of 1970, he was embattled at home as well as abroad. The Democratic-controlled Senate had just rejected for the second time his nominee for a Supreme Court vacancy. He was determined to show "those Senators . . . who's really tough."[43]

Most important, he was still confident that he could make peace by threatening Hanoi. Embarrassed by backing down from the November ultimatum, a move that conveyed precisely the wrong message, he seems to have reasoned that widening the war into previously off-limits Cambodia would make clear that, unlike

[41]Kissinger, *White House Years*, p. 449.
[42]Safire, *Before the Fall*, pp. 102–103.
[43]Morris, *Uncertain Greatness*, pp. 174–175.

his predecessor, he would not be bound by restraints. The North Vietnamese would then have to decide "whether they want to take us on all over again," he explained to his staff, and in terms of pressures on them to negotiate, "This was essential."[44]

Preoccupied throughout his career with the urgency of responding to crises, Nixon put himself through an emotional wringer in making the Cambodian decision. Kissinger described him as "overwrought," "irritable," and "defiant."[45] Exhausted from stress and lack of sleep, obviously agitated, at times frenetic and drinking heavily, Nixon repeatedly viewed the epic World War II film *Patton*, apparently as a way of pumping himself up to make a tough decision. The Cambodian crisis represented yet another effort on the part of a profoundly insecure individual to prove his toughness to an ever-widening list of enemies, real and imagined, an opportunity he felt he must seize to demonstrate his courage under fire and show his adversaries that he would not be intimidated. Although he later depicted himself as a voice of reason and a calming influence, Kissinger too, was strung out during this period. He seems to have had reservations about going into Cambodia, but he went along with the president, in part as a way of outflanking Laird and Rogers in the raging turf war that was Nixon's Washington.

The president explained his decision in a belligerent, provocative televised speech on April 30. He justified the Cambodian "incursion" as a response to North Vietnamese "aggression," although Hanoi's intentions remained unclear, and as a necessary action to protect American forces in Vietnam, although he did not explain why an old threat suddenly required such a vigorous response. The real target of the operation, he explained, was the Central Office for South Vietnam (COSVN), the "nerve center" of North Vietnamese military operations, although the Defense Department had made clear to him its uncertainty where COSVN was located or whether it even existed. Anticipating a furor at home, Nixon indicated that he would rather be a one-term president than preside over America's first defeat. He concluded with a bit of inflated rhetoric that appeared to make America's very survival hinge on his Cambodian venture. "If when the chips are down," he warned, "the world's most powerful nation acts like a

[44]Safire, *Before the Fall*, p. 190.
[45]Kimball, *Nixon's Vietnam War*, pp. 204–205.

pitiful helpless giant, the forces of totalitarianism and anarchy will threaten free nations and free institutions throughout the world."[46]

From a military standpoint, Nixon's Cambodian venture produced significant, if limited, results. The U.S. command claimed to have killed some 2,000 enemy troops, cleared more than 1,600 acres of jungle, and destroyed 8,000 bunkers. It uncovered huge caches of supplies and "treasure troves" of intelligence. The incursion rendered the sanctuaries temporarily unusable and vastly complicated North Vietnam's supply problems, thus buying some vital time for Vietnamization. The South Vietnamese army performed very well in most areas. Predictably, on the other hand, the invaders did not locate the elusive COSVN. Americans were also painfully aware that the gains made in Cambodia were no more than "ephemeral." As Abrams himself lamented about the resilience of the enemy, "You give them thirty-six hours and, goddamn it, you've got to start the war all over again."[47] Whatever advantages the operation gained for Vietnamization may have been more than offset by enlargement of the theater of war. At a time when the United States was seeking to scale down its role in Vietnam, it had to divert precious resources to support an even more fragile client state in Cambodia.

In Cambodia itself, U.S. actions contributed to one of the great tragedies of recent history. The United States was not exclusively responsible for Cambodia's misery. North Vietnam had violated Cambodia's precarious neutrality first, and Cambodians of all political factions inflicted their share of suffering on one another. The United States did, however, encourage the Lon Nol government to initiate a war it could not win. The American invasion forced the North Vietnamese to move out of their sanctuaries and into the heartland of Cambodia, threatening the capital, Phnom Penh, and other cities. Whether as a direct or indirect consequence of the U.S. invasion, North Vietnam initiated large-scale support for the Khmer Rouge insurgents fighting Lon Nol. In the particularly brutal civil war that followed, the United States lavishly supported the Cambodian government and unleashed thousands of tons of bombs on Cambodia. The ultimate tragedy was that from

[46]*Public Papers, Richard M. Nixon, 1970* (Washington, D.C., 1971), pp. 405–410.
[47]Quoted in Sorley, *Better War,* p. 204. See also John M. Shaw, *The Cambodian Campaign: The 1970 Offensive and America's Vietnam War* (Lawrence, Kans, 2005).

beginning to end, the Nixon administration viewed its new ally as little more than a pawn to be used to help salvage the U.S. position in Vietnam, showing scant regard for the consequences for Cambodia and its people.[48]

The domestic reaction exceeded Nixon's worst expectations—in tragic ways. The incursion into Cambodia "reignited an antiwar movement that had been smoldering that spring." The unexpected expansion of a war the president had promised to wind down enraged his critics. His intemperate defense of his actions, including a statement indiscriminately branding protesters as "bums," added to the furor. Demonstrations erupted at campuses across the nation. The protest took on new force when four students at Kent State University in Ohio and two at Jackson State College in Mississippi were killed in angry confrontations with the National Guard and police. More than 100,000 demonstrators gathered in Washington the first week of May to protest Cambodia and Kent State. Students at 350 colleges and universities went on strike, and as many as 500 schools were closed down to avert further violence. The Kent State killings provoked outbreaks even at normally conservative and placid institutions. At the University of Kentucky, a building was burned, and student demonstrations were broken up by armed National Guard troops using tear gas.[49]

The Cambodian incursion also provoked the most serious congressional challenge to presidential authority since the beginning of the war. The president had consulted with only a handful of members of Congress, all known to be sympathetic. Many legislators, including Senate Minority Leader Hugh Scott, were outraged at having been kept in the dark. Others were infuriated by Nixon's broadening of the war.[50] In a symbolic act of defiance, the Senate voted overwhelmingly in June to terminate the Tonkin Gulf Resolution of 1964. An amendment sponsored by Senators John Sherman Cooper (Kentucky Republican) and Frank Church (Idaho Democrat) proposed to cut off all funds for American military operations in

---

[48]Clymer, *Troubled Relations*, pp. 109–115.

[49]Anderson, *Movement*, pp. 351–352; Mitchell K. Hall, " 'A Crack in Time': The Response of Students at the University of Kentucky to the Tragedy at Kent State," *Kentucky Historical Register* 83 (Winter 1985): 36–63.

[50]Scott to Kissinger, May 21, 1970, Hugh Scott Papers, University of Virginia Library, Charlottesville, Va., Box 65.

Kent State, 1970
This classic photograph of a young woman kneeling near one of the
students felled by National Guard bullets at Kent State University in Ohio
captured the shock and anguish of a war now come home. The shooting at
Kent State following the invasion of Cambodia sparked massive protests at
colleges and universities across the country.
© *John Filo*

Cambodia after June 30. An even more restrictive amendment sponsored by Senators George McGovern (South Dakota Democrat) and
Mark Hatfield (Oregon Republican) would have required the
administration to withdraw all U.S. forces from Vietnam by the end
of 1971.

Thin-skinned and pugnacious, Nixon throughout his career
had shown a singular capacity to provoke virulent attacks—and
respond in kind. There would be no more "screwing around" with
congressional foes, he instructed his staff. "Don't worry about
divisiveness. Having drawn the sword, don't take it out—stick it in
hard."[51] The president publicly blamed his domestic opponents for
prolonging the war. He bluntly warned congressional leaders that if

---

[51]Safire, *Before the Fall*, p. 190.

"Congress undertakes to restrict me, Congress will have to assume the consequences."[52] He approved one of the most blatant attacks on individual freedom and privacy in American history, the so-called Huston Plan, which authorized the intelligence agencies to open mail, use electronic surveillance methods, and even burglarize to spy on Americans. The agencies subsequently refused to implement this specific plan, but they did use many of its methods in the futile effort to verify suspected links between radical groups in the United States and foreign governments.[53]

The administration rode out the storm. Nixon removed American troops from Cambodia by the end of June, depriving his opponents of their most telling issue; the protests gradually abated. Despite the flurry of activity, Congress was not yet ready to challenge the president directly or assume responsibility for ending the war. The more dovish Senate approved the Cooper–Church amendment, but the House rejected it, permitting the administration to continue air operations in Cambodia and send money and supplies to Lon Nol. The Hatfield–McGovern amendment could not secure a majority of the Senate.

Although Nixon escaped with his power intact, the Cambodian venture tightened the trap he had set for himself. The domestic reaction reinforced his determination to achieve "peace with honor" while sharply limiting his options for attaining it. Cambodia may have bought some time for Vietnamization, but it also imposed clear-cut, if implicit, limits on the future use of American combat forces and increased the pressures for speeding the pace of withdrawal. Divisiveness within the United States increased even beyond the level of 1968, with far-reaching, if still unforeseen, implications for Nixon's future. In the summer of 1970, an embittered president declared war on his enemies: the "madmen" on the Hill, the "liberal" press, the "trash" and "rabble" who marched in protest. "Within the iron gates of the White House, quite unknowingly, a siege mentality was setting in," one of Nixon's aides later stated. "It was now 'us' against 'them.' Gradually, as we drew the circle closer around us, the ranks of 'them' began to swell."[54]

---

[52]Henry Brandon, *The Retreat of American Power* (New York, 1974), pp. 146–147.
[53]Athan Theoharis, *Spying on Americans: Political Surveillance from Hoover to the Huston Plan* (Philadelphia, 1978), pp. 13–39.
[54]Charles W. Colson, *Born Again* (Old Tappan, N.J., 1976), p. 41.

Hoping to break the diplomatic deadlock by going into Cambodia, Nixon seems merely to have hardened it. North Vietnamese and NLF delegates boycotted the formal Paris discussions until U.S. troops had been withdrawn from Cambodia. The secret talks lapsed for months. Hanoi continued to bide its time. The uproar in the United States certainly reinforced its conviction that domestic pressures would eventually force an American withdrawal.

DEADLOCK AND DISSENSION

To resolve his foreign and domestic problems, Nixon launched in October 1970 what he described as a "major new initiative for peace." The proposals he made in a televised speech, while cleverly phrased, offered no concessions on the fundamental issues. Hanoi promptly rejected his call for a cease-fire in place, which, it perceived, would restrict the NLF to areas they now controlled without assuring them any role in a political settlement. In any case, the speech appears to have been designed primarily for the upcoming congressional elections. Nixon followed it up by touring ten states, angrily denouncing the antiwar protesters and urging the voters to elect representatives who would "stand with the President." Even here, the results were disappointing. Several doves were defeated, but the Republicans gained only two seats in the Senate and lost nine in the House.

After two years of continued heavy fighting, intensive secret diplomacy, and political maneuvering, Nixon's position was worse than when he had taken office. The negotiations with North Vietnam remained deadlocked. A National Security Council study of late 1970 grimly concluded that the United States could neither persuade nor force Hanoi to remove its troops from the South. At home, Nixon kept "one step ahead of the sheriff," as he would put it, narrowly heading off restrictions on his war-making powers. But he still faced a hostile and even more determined opposition in Congress and a revived antiwar movement. The situation in South Vietnam remained stable. By the end of the year, however, intelligence reported a sharp increase in the infiltration of troops and supplies into Laos, Cambodia, and South Vietnam, posing an ominous threat to the northern provinces and Hue, where sizable American forces had been withdrawn.

Instead of rethinking a policy that had brought no results, Nixon clung stubbornly throughout much of 1971 to the approach he had improvised the preceding year. To appease critics at home, he speeded up the timetable of American troop withdrawals. Over the protests of Abrams, he ordered the removal of 100,000 troops by the end of the year, leaving 175,000 in Vietnam, of whom only 75,000 were combat forces. To make clear, at the same time, his continued determination to secure a "just" peace and to counter the threat to Vietnamization posed by increased North Vietnamese infiltration and American troop reductions, he stepped up the military pressure against North Vietnam. U.S. aircraft mounted heavy attacks against supply lines and staging areas in Laos and Cambodia. Using as a pretext North Vietnamese firing upon American "reconnaissance" planes, the administration ordered "protective reaction" air strikes against bridges, base camps, and trails across the demilitarized zone and in the Hanoi–Haiphong area.

In February 1971, Nixon again expanded the war, approving a major ground operation into Laos. LAM SON 719 was conceived in the White House and approved over Abrams's vigorous opposition. The objective was the same as in Cambodia—to buy time for Vietnamization by disrupting enemy supply lines—but this time the ARVN assumed the burden of the fighting, with only air support from the United States.

The Laotian operation was at best a costly draw. U.S. intelligence had anticipated only light resistance, but North Vietnam apparently saw an opportunity to strike a body blow at Vietnamization and hurled some 36,000 troops, supported by the newest Russian-made tanks, against the two South Vietnamese divisions that crossed the border. ARVN performed well at first, inflicting huge losses on the enemy, and Abrams now urged that they sustain the attack until the end of the dry season. But Thieu was nervous about his army's losses and refused unless U.S. ground forces joined the battle. In time, the NVA gained the upper hand. After six weeks of the bloodiest fighting of the war, the battered ARVN forces limped back into South Vietnam. Official spokespersons claimed that the ARVN killed as many as 15,000 enemy troops and destroyed North Vietnam's supply network in Laos, thus delaying a major offensive for a year. Nixon and Kissinger continued to delude themselves into claiming a major victory while blaming Abrams for the failures. In fact, the ARVN took a beating, suffering a casualty rate as high as 50 percent and an estimated 2,000 dead. The losses would have been much higher without American air support, which flew one sortie every ten minutes around the clock during the entire operation and dumped 48,000 tons of bombs. Administration assertions that ARVN had conducted an "orderly retreat" appeared ludicrous amid the haste and confusion that accompanied the withdrawal from Laos. The sight of South Vietnamese soldiers clinging desperately to the skids of departing helicopters raised serious questions about the progress of Vietnamization. In the aftermath of the operation, Abrams concluded that South Vietnam could not "sustain large-scale cross border operations . . . without external support."[55]

At home, the protests drew new faces and became more rancorous and unruly. In early 1971, at a Howard Johnson's Motor Lodge in Detroit, the newly formed Vietnam Veterans against the War (VVAW) conducted its "Winter Soldier" investigation of U.S. war crimes; members testified to the atrocities they had seen in the war, such as prisoners being tossed out of helicopters and ears being cut off dead enemy soldiers. In April, in Operation Dewey Canyon III, "a limited incursion into the country of Congress," Vietnam veterans, clothed symbolically in faded uniforms adorned with combat ribbons and peace symbols, gathered in front of the Capitol, told of their own war crimes, and ceremoniously tossed away their medals. Speaking before the Fulbright committee, former Navy lieutenant John Kerry raised a haunting question: "How do you ask a man to be the last man to die for a mistake?"

Several days later, 30,000 self-styled members of the Mayday Tribe descended on Washington with the avowed intention of shutting the government down. They conducted lie-ins on bridges and major thoroughfares and at the entrances of government buildings. Mobs roamed the streets, stopped traffic, and broke windows, creating one of the worst riots in Washington's history.

Many Americans would undoubtedly have preferred that the war simply go away, but by the summer of 1971 the history of a conflict now more than a decade old had begun to come back to haunt the nation. After a long and much-publicized trial, a military court found Lt. William Calley guilty of at "least twenty-two murders" in the My Lai massacre of 1968 and sentenced him to life

[55]Clarke, *Final Years*, p. 473; Sorley, *Better War*, pp. 237–263.

imprisonment, once more bringing before public attention the horrors that had attended the war and setting off a brief but bitter debate on the question of responsibility for alleged war crimes. No sooner had the Calley furor abated than the *New York Times* began publication of the so-called Pentagon Papers, a history of decision making in Vietnam initiated by Robert McNamara in 1967, based on secret Defense Department documents, and leaked by a former Pentagon official, Daniel Ellsberg. The documents confirmed what critics of the war had long been arguing—among other points, that Kennedy and Johnson had consistently misled the public about their intentions in Vietnam and the progress being made.

An increasingly isolated and embattled Nixon responded fiercely to what he regarded as sinister threats to his authority to govern. The White House mounted a major campaign to smear the VVAW and especially Kerry. The Justice Department secured an injunction to prevent the veterans from sleeping on the Mall. The government hauled off to jail some 12,000 Mayday protesters, often without bothering to charge them with any specific offense. Nixon personally intervened in the Calley case while it was still under appeal, ordering Calley released from prison and indicating that he would review the conviction.

The president also took a tough line on the Pentagon Papers. Some of his advisers shrewdly suggested that, because the documents seemed to deal entirely with the Kennedy and Johnson presidencies and would therefore embarrass the Democrats, the administration might best ignore them. But Kissinger flew into a rage, perhaps nervous about his own prior association with Ellsberg, and Nixon, already obsessed with leaks, determined to act. He took the unprecedented step of securing an injunction to stop publication of the Papers. Enraged when the Supreme Court overturned the order, he approved the creation of a clandestine group of "plumbers," ostensibly to plug leaks within the government but in fact to do all kinds of dirty work. Labeling Ellsberg a "rat" (Kissinger called him "the most dangerous man in America today"), Nixon instructed the group to use any means necessary to discredit him. Nixon even discussed the possibility of firebombing and burglarizing the Brookings Institution, a liberal Washington think tank, to determine whether additional classified documents might be held there. Nixon's certainty that he faced a vast and sinister conspiracy intent on destroying him, along with his growing willingness to use any means to fight back, led straight to the Watergate break-in and the demise of his presidency.[56]

Neither Nixon's withdrawal policy nor his vigorous counterattacks against the opposition could stem the war-weariness and general demoralization that enveloped the nation by the summer of 1971. Former Secretary of State Dean Acheson lamented the plight of "this floundering republic." Journalist Robert Shaplen labeled the United States "the sick man of the western hemisphere."[57] While the antiwar movement was splintering into hundreds of groups often in conflict with one another, an antiwar mood increasingly pervaded the nation. Disillusionment with the war reached an all-time high, a whopping 71 percent agreeing that the United States had made a mistake by sending troops to Vietnam and 58 percent regarding the war as "immoral." Nixon's public approval rating on Vietnam had dropped to a low of 31 percent, and opposition to his policies had increased sharply. A near majority felt that the pace of troop withdrawals was too slow. A substantial majority approved the removal of all troops by the end of the year, even if the result was a Communist takeover of South Vietnam.[58]

Congress reflected the growing public uneasiness, although it continued to stop short of decisive action. On two separate occasions, the Senate approved resolutions setting a specific deadline for the removal of all American troops pending Hanoi's release of the prisoners of war. Each time, the House removed the deadline and otherwise watered down the language.

The malaise that afflicted the nation spread to the U.S. armed forces in Vietnam. Until 1969, American GIs had fought superbly, under difficult circumstances. But the failure to call up the reserves and the well-intentioned policy of requiring Americans to serve one-year tours in Vietnam deprived the army of experienced leaders, forced constant turnover in units, and transported to

---

[56]Stanley I. Kutler (ed.), *Abuse of Power: The New Nixon Tapes* (New York, 1998), pp. 1–17; John Prados & Margaret Pratt Porter (eds.), *Inside the Pentagon Papers* (Lawrence, Kans., 2004).

[57]Acheson to Matthew B. Ridgway, July 5, 1971, and Shaplen to Robert Aspey, n.d., both in Matthew B. Ridgway Papers, U.S. Army Military History Institute, Carlisle Barracks, Pa., Box 34B.

[58]Louis Harris, *The Anguish of Change* (New York, 1973), pp. 72–73. See also Charles DeBenedetti with Charles Chatfield, *An American Ordeal: The Antiwar Movement of the Vietnam Era* (Syracuse, N.Y., 1990), p. 298.

Vietnam problems already deeply entrenched in the United States. After the initiation of Nixon's troop-withdrawal policy, moreover, the purpose of the war became increasingly murky to those called on to fight it. Many GIs became much more reluctant to put their lives on the line. Discipline broke down in some units, with enlisted personnel simply refusing to obey their officers' orders. Attempts to assassinate officers in time of war were not unique to Vietnam, but fragging (so called because of the fragmentation grenades often used) reached unprecedented proportions in the Vietnamization period; more than 200 incidents were reported in 1970 alone. The availability and high quality of drugs in Southeast Asia meant that the drug culture that attracted growing numbers of young Americans at home was easily transported to Vietnam. The U.S. command estimated in 1970 that as many as 65,000 American service personnel were using drugs and that 40,000 were hooked on heroin. In addition, the armed services were not immune to the racial tensions that tore America apart in the Vietnam era. Numerous outbreaks of racial conflict in units in Vietnam and elsewhere drew growing attention to the breakdown of morale and discipline. "I need to get this Army home to save it," Abrams moaned to a friend.[59]

Although determined not to be stampeded, Nixon and Kissinger were sufficiently concerned by their predicament to try once again to break the stalemate in Paris. Kissinger expressed repeated fear that the administration might not be able to get through the year without Congress "giving the farm away."[60] Nixon recognized that he would probably need a peace settlement to win reelection, but he hoped to get it far enough in advance to avoid the appearance of desperation or a blatant political maneuver. As a consequence, in May 1971 Kissinger secretly presented to the North Vietnamese the most comprehensive peace offer yet advanced by the United States. In exchange for release of the American prisoners of war, he pledged to withdraw all troops within seven months after an agreement had been signed. The United States also abandoned the concept of mutual withdrawal, insisting only that North Vietnam stop further infiltration in return for the removal of American forces.

---

[59]Quoted in Sorley, *Better War,* 289. An excellent survey of the GI experience is Kyle Longley, *Grunts: The American Combat Soldier in Vietnam* (Armonk, N.Y., 2008).
[60]Quoted in Vernon A. Walters, *Silent Missions* (New York, 1978), p. 516.

This offer initiated the most intensive peace discussions since the war had begun. The North Vietnamese quickly rejected Kissinger's proposal, perceiving that it would require them to give up the prisoners of war (their major bargaining weapon), to stop fighting, and to accept the Thieu regime in advance of any political settlement. Hanoi's delegate, Le Duc Tho, promptly made a counteroffer, however, agreeing to release the POWs simultaneously with the withdrawal of American forces, provided that the United States dropped its support for Thieu prior to a political settlement. Kissinger found the North Vietnamese offer unacceptable, but he was deeply impressed by Tho's serious and conciliatory demeanor and sensed "the shape of a deal" between the two offers. He could "almost taste peace," he remarked excitedly to friends.[61]

The discussions eventually broke down over the issue of the Thieu regime. From the start of the secret talks, the North Vietnamese had insisted on Thieu's removal as an essential precondition for any peace agreement. On several occasions, they had even hinted that the United States might assassinate him. Elections were scheduled to be held in South Vietnam in September. Tho now proposed that if the United States would withdraw its support for Thieu, permitting an open election, it could take the first step toward a settlement without losing face. Uninformed of the substance of the secret talks but sensing just such a deal, Thieu vastly complicated matters by forcing the removal of the two opposition candidates, Nguyen Cao Ky and Duong Van Minh. Thieu's blatant interference in the political process so enraged the American embassy that Ambassador Ellsworth Bunker urged Nixon to publicly disassociate himself from Thieu and privately force him to accept a contested election. Nixon and Kissinger were unwilling to run the risk of abandoning Thieu at this critical juncture, however, and rejected both the North Vietnamese proposal and Bunker's advice. The administration would only declare its "neutrality," a position that was meaningless while Thieu was running unopposed.

After Thieu had been safely reelected, Kissinger attempted to keep the secret talks alive, proposing elections within sixty days after a cease-fire and Thieu's withdrawal one month in advance. From Hanoi's standpoint, this offer was undoubtedly an improvement over earlier ones, but it did not guarantee that Thieu would

[61]Quoted in Marvin and Bernard Kalb, *Kissinger* (Boston, 1974), p. 180.

not be a candidate or that he would be prevented from using the machinery of the government to rig the election. The North Vietnamese thus concluded that it was "necessary not to appear impatient." They promptly rejected the American proposal. The secret talks once again broke off in late November, leaving a frustrated Kissinger to fantasize about building a dam across the Mekong River and flooding all of Vietnam.[62]

Although the negotiations of late 1971 were the most serious yet undertaken, they eventually broke down for the same reasons earlier efforts had failed. Having invested so much blood, treasure, and prestige in a struggle of more than ten years' duration, neither side was yet willing to make the sort of concessions necessary for peace. Perhaps more important, each side still felt it could get what it wanted without compromise.

More than anything else, a stunning, mid-1971 diplomatic turnabout, pulled off with airtight secrecy and announced with great drama and fanfare, doomed any prospect of a negotiated settlement. Nixon had set as an essential part of his Grand Design, a rapprochement with China and the Soviet Union, partly to promote what he called a "generation of peace" but also to isolate North Vietnam from its major allies in hopes of securing an acceptable peace agreement. In July 1971, the administration announced to a shocked world that the president would visit China the following year. The breakthrough in Sino-American relations helped nudge the Kremlin into a summit meeting. These dramatic moves enormously boosted Nixon's confidence, making him less amenable to a deal in 1971.[63]

Chinese and Soviet willingness to talk with the United States evoked from North Vietnamese leaders still bitter memories from Geneva 1954 and angry charges of betrayal. Hanoi correctly perceived that the United States was pursuing "choking warfare" to separate North Vietnam from key allies. Out of necessity, it maintained ties with Moscow and Beijing, but it was not appeased by promises of continued aid. Along with Thieu's reelection, Soviet and Chinese perfidy confirmed Hanoi's inclination to pin its hopes on another major military offensive timed to coincide with the U.S. presidential election. Hanoi's aim was to neutralize the effects of Nixon's détente

[62]Ibid., p. 185.
[63]Nguyen, *War for Peace*, pp. 213–215.

and insulate itself from Soviet and Chinese pressures to compromise. Its hope, encouraged by success in the Laos campaign, was to force a complete ARVN collapse and a favorable settlement. As in 1968, Le Duan and his ally Le Duc Tho were the prime movers. Le Duan's third, high-stakes military gamble, a large-scale, sustained conventional offensive, led by newly acquired Soviet tanks, would be accompanied by political struggle in South Vietnam to gain a "decisive victory." Neither side would achieve its aims in the critical year 1972; each would pay a very high price trying. But they did plunge the war into a final, convulsive phase that would ultimately produce a compromise peace.[64]

THE EASTER OFFENSIVE

On March 30, 1972, North Vietnam launched its invasion of the South. At the time, only 95,000 U.S. forces remained there, only 6,000 of them combat troops. Hanoi correctly reasoned that domestic pressures would prevent Nixon from putting new ground forces into Vietnam. The North Vietnamese timed the invasion to coincide with the beginning of the American presidential campaign in hopes that, as in 1968, by striking a decisive blow they could cripple Nixon as they had Johnson, thus giving them the upper hand in negotiating a settlement. They aimed the offensive directly at ARVN main-force units, hoping to discredit the Vietnamization policy and tie down as many enemy regular forces as possible, enabling the NLF to resume the offensive in the countryside, disrupt pacification, and strengthen its position prior to the final peace negotiations.

In its first stages, the offensive achieved unqualified success. Spearheaded by Soviet tanks, 120,000 North Vietnamese troops struck on three fronts: across the demilitarized zone; in the Central Highlands; and across the Cambodian border northwest of Saigon. Expecting a series of smaller attacks during the Tet holidays, American intelligence—again—completely misjudged the timing, magnitude, and location of the invasion. Achieving near complete surprise, the North Vietnamese routed the thin lines of defending forces and quickly advanced toward the towns of Quang Tri in the north, Kontum in the highlands, and An Loc just sixty miles north

[64]Ibid, pp. 223–236; Asselin, "Revisionism Triumphant," pp. 109–119.

Kim Phuc, 1972
This photograph of Kim Phuc, taken on June 8, 1972, during the furious battles of the Easter Offensive, became one of the defining images of the war. A nine-year-old peasant girl, Kim Phuc was running in terror in a futile effort to escape the napalm clinging to her body after an inadvertant South Vietnamese attack on her village. Used by Hanoi for a time as a poster child for the evils of capitalism, Kim Phuc later defected to Canada. In a moving ceremony on Veteran's Day, 1996, she joined with a former American POW in laying a wreath at the base of the Vietnam Memorial in Washington.
© Nick Ut/AP Images

of Saigon. Thieu was forced to commit most of his reserves to defend the threatened towns, thus freeing the NLF to take the offensive in the Mekong delta and in the heavily populated regions around Saigon.

Although stunned by the swiftness and magnitude of the North Vietnamese strike, Nixon responded with all the force he could muster. Hanoi had mistakenly assumed that his hands would

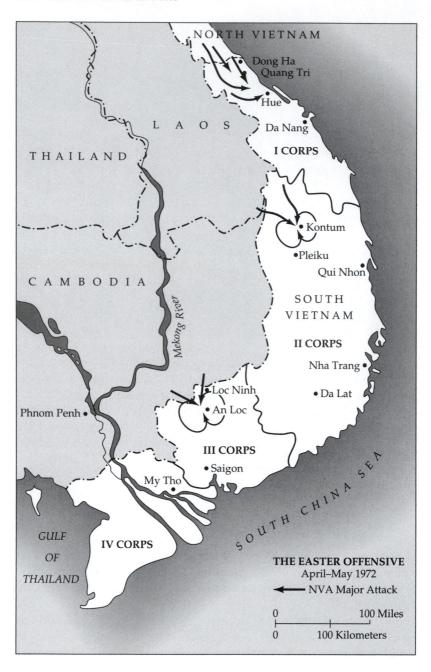

THE EASTER OFFENSIVE
April–May 1972
← NVA Major Attack

be tied by electoral politics. In fact, he viewed what came to be called the Easter Offensive as a brazen and dire threat to his triangular diplomacy, indeed to his presidency. "We're playing a Russia game, a China game, and an election game," he thundered, "and we're not gonna have the ARVN collapse." Eager to give the enemy a "bloody nose," he also sensed an opportunity to revive the end-the-war strategy he had so reluctantly discarded in 1969.[65]

Disillusioned with the military and especially with Laird's Defense Department, Nixon assumed personal control of the U.S. response. Amidst sometimes rambling discussions of great battles past and bold leaders such as Napoleon and Churchill, dotted with praise for each other's toughness (along with rants about the timidity and ineptitude of the U.S. military), he and Kissinger, sometimes with new Joint Chiefs of Staff (JCS) chairman Adm. Thomas Moorer, plotted strategy and oversaw operations. In a massive mobilization effort, they dispatched to the war zone from across the world a vast armada of warships and aircraft, especially the fearsome B-52 bombers. Instead of restricting targets and limiting sorties, as LBJ had done, they ordered the use of maximum firepower. In the first stage, they unleashed a torrent of naval gunfire, artillery, and bombs against North Vietnamese troops in the South and North Vietnam itself, focusing on slowing the NVA advance by knocking out air defenses and crippling logistics with attacks on fuel depots, railyards, and transportation routes from China.[66]

In the meantime, Kissinger met secretly with Soviet premier Leonid Brezhnev. For the first time, he made explicit an American willingness to permit North Vietnamese forces to remain in South Vietnam after a cease-fire. He also held the Soviet Union responsible for the invasion and warned that continuation of the war could severely damage Soviet–American relations and have grave consequences for North Vietnam. The offer and the threats were repeated to Le Duc Tho on May 2.

Still confident of victory, the North Vietnamese flatly rejected Kissinger's offer, leaving Nixon difficult choices. Reporting that Hue and Kontum might soon fall and the "whole thing may be lost," Abrams pressed for intensification of the bombing of North Vietnam

[65]Stephen P. Randolph, *Powerful and Brutal Weapons: Nixon, Kissinger, and the Eastern Offensive* (Cambridge, Mass., 2007), p. 86.
[66]Ibid., pp. 81–101; *FR, 1969–1976*, 6: 154ff.

and even for the mining of Haiphong harbor.[67] On the other hand, Secretaries Laird and Rogers warned that drastic countermeasures could have disastrous domestic consequences. Kissinger worried that the Soviets might cancel Nixon's impending visit to Moscow, undoing months of tedious negotiations on strategic arms limitation and other major issues.

Enraged by Hanoi's defiance and unwilling to accept defeat, Nixon struck back furiously. Still intent on persuading the enemy of his resolve and unpredictability, he set out to demonstrate his willingness to take *"whatever steps* are necessary" to end the war. Johnson lacked the will, he privately boasted (as if to reassure himself). "I have the *will* in spades." More than any one else, Secretary of the Treasury—and LBJ protégé—John Connally persuaded the president to escalate the war regardless of the Moscow summit. Soviet cancellation would not cost him support at home, Connally reasoned, but if he lost the war, he would "lose the country." The result was a "tough watershed decision": to "stop at nothing to bring the enemy to his knees." Where Johnson had fretted about civilian casualties, Nixon instructed Moorer to aim for military targets but "if it slops over, that's too bad." On May 8, he announced to a startled nation the most drastic escalation since 1965: the mining of Haiphong harbor and the massive sustained bombing of North Vietnam. "The bastards have never been bombed like they're going to be bombed this time," he vowed. Throughout the lifetime of what came to be called Operation LINEBACKER, Nixon, dissatisfied with the military's performance in the April bombing, pressed them relentlessly to overcome bad weather and other obstacles to do more and do it better.[68]

Nixon's gamble succeeded, at least to a point. Caught up in an extremely delicate diplomatic game, the two major Communist powers responded cautiously to the events of 1972. Because of their continuing rivalry, neither was prepared to sacrifice North Vietnam on the altar of diplomatic expediency. At the same time, each now viewed the war as a sideshow that must not be allowed to jeopardize the major power realignment then taking place in the world. The Soviet Union continued to provide North Vietnam with massive military and economic assistance. But the summit went ahead

[67]Nixon, *RN*, p. 594.
[68]Randolph, *Powerful and Brutal Weapons*, pp. 158–199; *FR, 1969–1976*, 6: 424–431.

as scheduled. At the outset of Nixon's visit to Moscow in late May, Brezhnev and his colleagues went through the motions of protesting, charging the United States with "sheer aggression" in Vietnam and even comparing the United States to Nazi Germany. The negotiations then proceeded in a cordial and businesslike manner. Major agreements were concluded. The Soviet Union also sent a top-level diplomat to urge Hanoi to make peace. The Chinese protested Nixon's escalation of the war and provided North Vietnam crucial assistance, especially with minesweeping Haiphong harbor. But they, too, urged Hanoi to compromise with the United States.[69]

The domestic reaction also proved manageable. Some media organs strongly backed the president, but others were sharply critical, in some cases reflecting a growing war-weariness among the journalists themselves. Nixon privately fumed at the media for reporting only the bad news and downplaying the good. He set "the discrediting of the press" as a "major objective over the next few months."[70] Senate doves were "shocked," "mad," and "depressed," according to Vermont Republican George Aiken, and another flurry of end-the-war resolutions went into the congressional hopper.[71] But Americans had always considered bombing more acceptable than the use of ground troops, and many felt that the North Vietnamese invasion justified Nixon's aggressive response. As on earlier occasions, the public and Congress rallied around decisive presidential initiatives. The success of the Moscow summit cut the ground from under those who had argued that Nixon's rash actions would undermine détente. Unwilling to leave anything to chance, zealous operatives from the Committee for the Reelection of the President (CREEP) forged thousands of letters and telegrams to the White House expressing approval of Nixon's policies, but even without such antics the president enjoyed broad support. His public approval rating shot up dramatically, Congress did nothing, and he emerged in a much stronger position than before the North Vietnamese invasion.[72]

---

[69]Kissinger, *White House Years*, pp. 1226–1227; Qiang Zhai, *China and the Vietnam Wars, 1950–1975* (Chapel Hill, N.C., 2000), pp. 202–206.
[70]Chester Pach, "'Our Worst Enemy Seems to Be the Press': TV News, the Nixon Administration, and U.S. Troop Withdrawal from Vietnam, 1969–1973," *Diplomatic History* 34 (June 2010): 564.
[71]George Aiken, *Senate Diary* (Brattleboro, Vt., 1976), pp. 55–57.
[72]Harris, *Anguish of Change*, p. 74.

Nixon's decisive response appears also to have averted defeat in South Vietnam. Although the bombing operations ordered in May never fully met his expectations, they far exceeded all previous attacks on North Vietnam. From April to June, U.S. aircraft flew more than 14,000 sorties, and in June alone they dropped 11,200 tons of bombs, including new so-called smart bombs precisely guided to their targets by computers receiving signals from television cameras and laser beams.

The attacks paralyzed the North Vietnamese transportation system and exhausted air defenses. The conventional military tactics employed by the NVA in the summer of 1972 required vast quantities of fuel and ammunition. The bombing and blockade made resupply extremely difficult. Even more critical was U.S. tactical air support in South Vietnam. American aircraft flew round-the-clock missions—B-52 sortie rates reached an unprecedented three per hour each twenty-four hours—pummeling enemy supply lines and encampments. With the crucial assistance of U.S. airpower, the ARVN eventually stabilized the lines in front of Saigon and Hue and even mounted a small counteroffensive.

In the final analysis, the ferocious campaigns of the summer of 1972 merely raised the stalemate to a new level of violence. Both sides endured huge losses—the North Vietnamese suffered an estimated 100,000 casualties, and the South Vietnamese lost as many as 30,000 killed, 78,000 wounded, and 14,000 missing in action—but neither emerged appreciably stronger. Although it fought determinedly at times, the ARVN continued to be afflicted by severe leadership problems, especially in top positions. Its ability to prevail without the support of U.S. airpower was highly suspect. The Easter Offensive again demonstrated, one scholar has concluded, that the " 'strategy' of Vietnamization could never compensate for a lack of national will."[73] North Vietnam had exposed ARVN's continued vulnerability, gained a sizable slice of territory along the Laotian and Cambodian borders that would be important in its final offensive, and retained sizable troops in the South. The NLF scored some major gains in the Mekong Delta. But Hanoi had again badly miscalculated the U.S. response. By spreading its forces over three fronts rather than concentrating on

---

[73]Dale Andradé, *Trial by Fire: The 1972 Easter Offensive, America's Last Vietnam Battle* (New York, 1995), p. 533. See also Sorley, *Better War*, pp. 339–342; and Kimball, *Nixon's Vietnam War*, pp. 324–327.

one, it succeeded nowhere. The North Vietnamese again paid a huge price for their mistakes: Their offensive capabilities were set back for three years. Thieu clung stubbornly to power; the United States remained in South Vietnam.

Frustrated in their hopes of breaking the diplomatic stalemate by military means, by the fall of 1972, each side found compelling reasons to break the military deadlock by diplomacy. The Nixon administration was by no means desperate to get a settlement. The Democrats had nominated George McGovern, an outspoken dove whose extreme views appeared to make him the easiest opponent to defeat and left Nixon substantial room to maneuver. Nonetheless, Nixon and especially Kissinger recognized that an indefinite continuation of the air war could cause problems at home. In any event, U.S. airpower was reeling from months of grueling around-the-clock operations. "My planes are broken," Gen. John Vogt conceded. "We are flat on our ass."[74] War-weary themselves, Nixon and Kissinger were also increasingly frustrated by the persistence of a conflict they had come to see as a major impediment to their larger foreign policy aims and were impatient to uphold their promises to end it.

For North Vietnam, the pressures were more compelling. Through total mobilization, superhuman effort, and amazing adaptability, the nation survived "the second war of US destruction." But it suffered horrendous losses. The bombing and blockade inflicted disastrous effects on its economy and its army in South Vietnam. Its allies pushed ahead with détente with its enemy. The Soviet Union refused to challenge the blockade. Moscow and Beijing pressed Hanoi to gain a settlement by dropping its demand for the ouster of Thieu. Thwarted for the third time in its quest for decisive military victory, the Hanoi leadership made a "watershed" decision of its own in June, shifting from pursuit of military victory in the short run to a diplomatic solution that would enable it to achieve its political aims in the long run. Recognizing that it must seize the opportunity presented by the U.S. election, it sought mainly the removal of all U.S. troops from South Vietnam so that it could deal with Thieu on his own later. By September, when it became obvious that Nixon would win by a landslide, Hanoi realized that it must settle immediately.[75]

[74]Randolph, *Brutal and Powerful Weapons*, p. 329.
[75]Asselin, "Revisionism Triumphant," pp. 120–126.

PEACE IS AT HAND

From late summer on, the two nations inched toward a compromise. When the secret talks resumed in mid-July, Kissinger reiterated the U.S. proposal for a unilateral withdrawal, thus permitting North Vietnamese troops to remain in the South after a cease-fire. He also took a big step away from America's long-standing commitment to Thieu by agreeing to a tripartite electoral commission. Composed of the Saigon regime, the Provisional Revolutionary Government (PRG), the functioning government created by the NLF in 1969 as a rival to the Government of Viet Nam (GVN), and neutralists, this body would work out a settlement after the cease-fire went into effect. In a dramatic and decisive shift in mid-September Tho dropped Hanoi's long-standing demand for the ouster of Thieu, accepting a cease-fire that would leave him in control temporarily but would also grant the PRG political status in the South. Kissinger agreed to a cease-fire and U.S. withdrawal before political arrangements were agreed upon, thus reneging on an earlier promise to Thieu.[76]

During three weeks of intensive, sometimes frantic negotiations, Kissinger and Tho hammered out the fundamentals of an agreement. Within forty-five days after a cease-fire, the United States would withdraw its remaining troops, and North Vietnam would return U.S. POWs. The tripartite National Council of Reconciliation and Concord would then administer elections and assume responsibility for implementing the agreement. The United States would provide for Vietnam $9 billion in aid for reconstruction. By October 11, all but several issues had been resolved. Eager to wrap up the matter as quickly as possible, Kissinger and Tho agreed that these items could be left until later. After consulting with Nixon and Thieu, Kissinger would proceed to Hanoi to initial the treaty on October 22.

In his haste to work out an agreement, Kissinger made several critical mistakes. He had routinely deceived both Vietnams by taking one position with Hanoi and quite another with Saigon. He also badly overestimated Thieu's willingness to do what the United States told him and underestimated Nixon's willingness to go along with Thieu.

---

[76]Pierre Asselin, *A Bitter Peace: Washington, Hanoi, and the Making of the Paris Agreement* (Chapel Hill, N.C., 2002), pp. 62–69.

The imperious and impatient American spent five tension-filled days in Saigon employing what he called "shock tactics," going over the treaty item by item, embellishing its advantages for South Vietnam and issuing only slightly veiled warnings that a refusal to go along would compel the end of American support. Increasingly frustrated that the leader of a mere client state could threaten his grand design, Kissinger complained that Thieu's objections "verge on insanity." While trying to sway the South Vietnamese, he continued to practice masterful self-deception. "We face the paradoxical situation," he wrote Nixon, "that the North, which has effectively lost, is acting as if it had won, while the South, which effectively won, is acting as if it has lost."[77]

Thieu was not appeased. He deeply resented his dependence on the United States. He was frightened at the prospect of abandonment. He was furious that he had not been consulted during the negotiations and especially that he had first learned of the terms through captured NLF documents. He was incensed that the draft Kissinger presented to him was in English. Kissinger's heavy-handed and arrogant efforts to present him with a fait accompli reinforced his already deep-seated suspicion of the United States. Of all the parties concerned, Thieu had the least interest in an agreement providing for an American withdrawal. He found the terms completely unacceptable. He could not go along with an agreement that permitted North Vietnamese troops to remain in the South and that accorded the PRG sovereignty. He brought to Kissinger's attention some notably careless phraseology in the text that accorded the tripartite commission the status of a coalition government. He had been faithful to his ally, he claimed, but now he was being sacrificed. "If we accept the document as it stands, we will commit suicide—and I will be committing suicide." He demanded wholesale changes, including establishment of the demilitarized zone as a boundary between two sovereign states and removal of North Vietnamese troops from the South. Perhaps attempting to repeat his maneuver of 1968 (although McGovern was of no help to him), he sought to drive a wedge between the United States and North Vietnam by blocking the treaty and allowing the war to continue.[78]

---

[77]Quoted in *New York Times*, April 30, 2000.

[78]Ibid.; Kimball, *Nixon's Vietnam War*, pp. 328–332. For the South Vietnamese perspective, see Nguyen Tien Hung and Jerrold L. Schecter, *The Palace File* (New York, 1986), pp. 98–106.

Thieu succeeded for the short term. Exhausted from his arduous negotiations and outraged at this unexpected threat to his handiwork, Kissinger denounced Thieu's demands as "preposterous" and urged Nixon to go ahead without Thieu's cooperation. Concerned primarily with getting the United States out of Vietnam, Kissinger seems to have sought nothing more than a "decent interval" between an American withdrawal and the inevitable North Vietnamese conquest of South Vietnam.

Nixon's views were more complex and ambivalent and tended to shift with his moods. He desperately wanted to end the war—"this cancer eating at us at home, eating at us abroad," he called it. He acknowledged that North Vietnam had made important concessions and that Kissinger's agreement offered a way out. He also painfully recognized that it fell far short of his original goals and that leaving NVA troops in the South after the United States departed would put the GVN at grave risk. Unlike Kissinger, Nixon was not surprised when Thieu balked. South Vietnam's interests clashed fundamentally with those of the United States. He looked down upon his Saigon counterpart and evinced little concern for South Vietnam itself. He suggested to Kissinger at one point that he might string Thieu along until after the election and then "we'll do what we goddamned please." He seems to have been willing, if necessary, to dump Thieu. But appearances were crucial to him, the very essence of what he meant by peace with honor. He did not want the United States and especially the White House to seem responsible for "flushing" the South Vietnamese leader. He also found a separate deal with Hanoi "repugnant" because, he said, "we lose everything we've done." Nixon was angry that by pushing ahead with Hanoi without consulting Saigon, Kissinger had boxed him in. At times he even fantasized that with the election behind him he could force a better deal from North Vietnam. Kissinger sought to keep hopes of an early settlement alive by stating publicly on October 31 that "peace is at hand," but Nixon's refusal to abandon Thieu at this point ensured the breakdown of the October agreement and a new round of negotiations.[79]

For the remainder of the year, Nixon struggled to extricate himself from the bind created by Kissinger and his two Vietnamese adversaries. His landslide reelection gave him some leverage, but

[79]The quotations are from *FR, 1969–1976*, 9: 123; ibid, 8: 1058; and ibid, 9: 419–420.

he also recognized that time was not on his side. Members of Congress, hawks and Republican stalwarts as well as doves, realized that Thieu was responsible for the breakdown of the October agreement and threatened to terminate aid to South Vietnam if the war had not ended by the time the legislature reconvened in January. Nixon's solution to his dilemma was to appear sympathetic to Thieu's demands by seeking modest revisions from North Vietnam while making plain to the South Vietnamese leader that his patience had limits.

In the first phase of its implementation, the strategy failed. Through intermediaries, the president assured Thieu that he was seeking concessions from Hanoi and also promised to respond forcibly should North Vietnam violate any peace agreement. He also warned Thieu that his present course could bring "disaster" to the U.S.–South Vietnamese alliance and threatened "brutal actions" if he did not go along. Apparently determined by this time to sabotage any peace agreement in hopes that the war—and U.S. aid—would continue, Thieu refused to budge and even upped his demands to complete North Vietnamese withdrawal from his country.

The secret discussions resumed in Paris on November 20 in an atmosphere markedly different from when the diplomats had last met. To mollify Thieu, Kissinger raised for reconsideration sixty-nine points, many of them minor but others central to the compromise. He asked for at least a token withdrawal of NVA troops from the South and requested changes in the text that would have weakened the political status of the PRG, restricted the powers of the tripartite commission, and established the demilitarized zone as a virtual boundary. He added a veiled threat that Nixon, having gained a landslide reelection victory, would not hesitate to "take whatever action he considers necessary to protect United States interests."[80] Claiming to have been betrayed, refusing to give in to threats, and determined not to be steamrolled into a disadvantageous agreement, Le Duc Tho angrily rejected Kissinger's proposals and raised numerous demands of his own, even reviving Hanoi's insistence upon the ouster of Thieu.[81]

---

[80]Nixon, *RN*, p. 721.
[81]Kimball, *Nixon's Vietnam War*, pp. 350–351.

For weeks Kissinger and Tho sparred back and forth across the negotiating table in an atmosphere rife with tension and marked by outbursts of anger. Concessions were offered, debated, sometimes heatedly—and then withdrawn. Proposals were revised and re-revised. The negotiations were complicated on the American side by growing suspicion and mutual antagonism between Nixon and Kissinger. Both men were frustrated and exhausted from the unrelenting stress of events. Although still dependent on his chief diplomat to implement his goals, Nixon seethed with resentment that Kissinger was gaining public recognition rightfully his own. He and his new confidant (and Kissinger's top aide) Gen. Alexander Haig railed about the national security adviser's paranoia and mood swings and blamed him for the impasse. The president was planning to reshuffle his cabinet, and Kissinger's place was uncertain. The national security adviser may have pushed a harder line to reestablish his credibility with a distrustful and sometimes vengeful boss.[82]

Strangely, just when peace again seemed in reach—if not at hand—both nations balked. Fearful that the agreement that had seemed so close in October might yet slip away, each side made concessions. By late November, they had crawled back to the essence of the original compromise with only the status of the demilitarized zone unresolved. Certain that Thieu would never accept any proposal that resembled the October agreement, Nixon contemplated—but ultimately rejected—Kissinger's proposal to dump him and sign a bilateral agreement with Hanoi. The North Vietnamese feared that Kissinger's proposal on the demilitarized zone could be read as a permanent dividing line. At a minimum, it could hamper resupply of troops in the South. "We cannot abandon the principle to end the war at all cost," one official insisted. Believing that time was on its side and that Congress might cut off funds for the war, Hanoi refused to compromise, knowingly risking another round of bombing.[83] The talks recessed in mid-December, presumably to resume at the start of the new year.

Weary, frustrated, angry, sometimes using locker room language, Nixon and Kissinger vented their fury at the dilemma

---

[82]Ibid, p. 353; *FR, 1969–1976,* 9: 496.
[83]Asselin, "Revisionism Triumphant," p. 130.

brought upon them by the intransigence of enemy and ally—and by their own mistakes. Kissinger denounced North and South Vietnamese as those "two maniacal parties"; "nuts," he called them. The North Vietnamese were "insolent" and "tawdry." A stubbornly defiant Thieu had "cut off our nose to spite our face," the president raged. He had "destroyed his usefulness" as far as the United States was concerned and must not be permitted to push a great power around. Yet the president continued to believe that abandoning the South Vietnamese leader would cost *him* peace with honor. It would be better, Nixon mused, to continue the alliance with Thieu and "have the Congress do the evil deed." Certain that the LINEBACKER bombings had forced the North Vietnamese into the October agreement, throughout the fall of 1972 Nixon had toyed with the idea of another, even more massive bombing campaign to compel a settlement. When Kissinger returned from Paris, he and the president decided to persist in their strategy but drastically escalate the pressures on both Vietnams. Although South Vietnam had been mainly responsible for the breakdown of the October agreement, the United States would blame the North Vietnamese— and then "bomb the hell out of them." In the meantime, it would develop a "menu" of compelling economic and military pressures to force Thieu to go along with an agreement.[84]

Over the next few weeks, Nixon stepped up the pressure on South Vietnam. He ordered the immediate delivery of more than $1 billion of military hardware, leaving Thieu with, among other assets, the fourth largest air force in the world. Nixon gave "absolute assurances" that if the North Vietnamese violated the peace agreement, he would order "swift and severe retaliatory action." He instructed the Joint Chiefs of Staff to begin immediate planning for such a contingency.[85] At the same time, in Kissinger's words, Nixon sought to "brutalize" Thieu, warning in what he termed his "absolutely final offer" that if South Vietnam rejected the best treaty that could be obtained, the United States would "seek a settlement with the enemy which serves U.S. interests alone."[86]

---

[84]*FR, 1969–1976*, 9: 492, 496, 583, 618–619.

[85]Nixon, *RN*, p. 718; Zumwalt, *On Watch*, pp. 413–414.

[86]H. R. Haldeman, *The Haldeman Diaries: Inside the Nixon White House* (New York, 1994), p. 543; Nixon to Thieu, December 17, 1972, Richard Cheney Files, Gerald R. Ford Library, Ann Arbor, Mich., Box 13.

Thieu continued to defy his more powerful patron, refusing to give Nixon carte blanche to negotiate for him and brazenly informing the press that he had rejected a U.S. ultimatum. Although enraged by the intransigence of an ally he now labeled a "complete SOB," Nixon was not entirely displeased, perceiving that Thieu's defiance gave him ample pretext for a break should it come to that later.[87]

While attempting to bludgeon Thieu into submission, Nixon employed what Kissinger called "jugular diplomacy" against North Vietnam, ordering over the Christmas season a massive dose of bombing against Hanoi and Haiphong. The motive was to force the North Vietnamese to conclude an agreement. But the decision reflected the accumulated anger and frustration of four years. It was also designed to reassure Thieu and reduce North Vietnam's capacity to threaten South Vietnam after a settlement had been concluded. Nixon knew that he must end the war quickly or Congress might take control out of his hands. He was egged on by hardliners such as Connally and Haig. An intensive bombing attack could end the war with a dramatic flourish—a bang rather than a whimper—as Nixon had predicted at the outset of his presidency. It would enable him to portray the peace that had resulted from compromise as a victory for U.S. military power and his own courage and diplomatic skill.[88] It would demonstrate to the North Vietnamese that he was prepared to uphold the peace that was negotiated, thus helping to make any agreement more inforceable.

Between December 18 and 29, Nixon unleashed the most ferocious and devastating air attacks of the war. He made absolutely clear to the Joint Chiefs his determination to inflict maximum damage. "I don't want any more of this crap about the fact that we couldn't hit this target or that one," he lectured Moorer. "This is your chance to use military power to win this war, and if you don't, I'll hold you responsible."[89] During LINEBACKER II, also called the Christmas bombing, U.S. aircraft flew close to 2,000 sorties and dropped nearly 20,000 tons of bombs, exceeding the tonnage for 1969 to 1971. The all-weather, high-flying B-52s, which gave no warning but inflicted enormous destruction, bore the burden of

[87]Haldeman, *Haldeman Diaries*, p. 558.
[88]Kimball, *Nixon's Vietnam War*, pp. 362–364.
[89]Sulzberger, *Seven Continents*, p. 593; Nixon, *RN*, pp. 725–726.

LINEBACKER II. The campaign was designed to cripple North Vietnam's war-making capacity and, by focusing directly on Hanoi and Haiphong, also to destroy it's will by psychological damage and by hitting targets such as radio stations and power plants. Offering a small carrot to go with a heavy stick, Nixon proposed to North Vietnam on December 22 resumption of the Paris talks on January 3, 1973.

The Christmas bombing gave Hanoi strong incentive to return to the conference table (although there is every reason to believe it would have done so anyway). North Vietnamese leaders had expected another round of bombing, but they were caught off guard by the magnitude of the December attacks and by the focus on the major cities. The bombing severely set back North Vietnam's industrial and war-making capabilities. It did not compare in destructiveness to the air attacks on Tokyo, Hiroshima, and Dresden during World War II. U.S. pilots went to some lengths to minimize civilian casualties; large numbers of civilians had already been evacuated from the cities. Still, the destruction in parts of Hanoi and Haiphong was extensive. More than 1,600 civilians were killed and 1,261 injured in what Vietnamese called "the twelve days of darkness." By the end of December, North Vietnam had exhausted its stock of surface-to-air missiles, leaving it more vulnerable to B-52 attack. As at Geneva in 1954 and during the Easter Offensive, China and the Soviet Union again pressed Hanoi to settle with the United States. On December 26, a day on which B-52s dropped 4,000 tons of bombs in fifteen minutes, Hanoi conveyed to Washington its willingness to resume peace talks on January 8.

The Christmas bombing also gave Nixon compelling reasons to return to the negotiating table. In part because of U.S. tactics designed to limit civilian casualties, North Vietnamese air defenses exacted a heavy toll, bringing down fifteen B-52s (nine in the first three days) and eleven other aircraft, leaving ninety-three crew members missing, and creating thirty-one new POWs. North Vietnamese propagandists defiantly labeled the Christmas bombing a "Dien Bien Phu of the skies." The bombing also provoked cries of outrage across the world. The Soviets and Chinese, in marked contrast to their restraint in May, heatedly protested. In a remark that especially stung Nixon, Swedish prime minister Olof Palme compared it as an act of cruelty to those perpetrated by the Nazis.

The reaction at home was one of shock and anger. Critics condemned Nixon as a "madman" and accused him of waging "war by tantrum." Columnist Joseph Kraft denounced the bombing as an act of "senseless terror which stains the good name of America."[90] Many Americans who had accepted the May bombings questioned both the necessity and the unusual brutality of the December attacks, a "sorry Christmas present" for the American people, in the words of Senator Aiken.[91] Nixon's approval rating plummeted to 39 percent overnight. Congressional doves made it clear that when they returned to Washington after the Christmas recess, they would be ready to do battle with the president. "We took the threats from Congress seriously," one of Nixon's aides later observed. "We knew we were racing the clock," and if North Vietnam refused to negotiate, "we faced stern action."[92] Under intense pressure at home and abroad and with the bombing as cover, Nixon readily endorsed Hanoi's acceptance of his proposal to go back to the conference table.

The two parties returned to Paris on January 8 and quickly came to terms. Nixon told Kissinger on January 6 that "almost any settlement would be tolerable." Hanoi desperately wanted the bombing stopped and the United States out and was prepared to accept, in the words of a Vietnamese historian, "a partial victory to create conditions conducive to a complete victory."[93] After four days of marathon negotiations marked by give-and-take on both sides, Kissinger and Tho hammered out an agreement. North Vietnam made important concessions by accepting more restrictive language on the demilitarized zone and by agreeing that the release of PRG prisoners in the South would be tied to the withdrawal of its own troops. While pledging to release U.S. prisoners of war, it secured its primary objectives: the end of the U.S. bombing and withdrawal of the remaining American forces. That accomplished, it could begin to rebuild for yet another stage of the war. Nixon hoped to use the threat of U.S. airpower and the promise of reconstruction aid to North Vietnam to uphold the settlement. His best hope—a pipedream it would turn out—was for a Korea-type

[90]James R. Powell, *Going for Broke: Richard Nixon's Search for "Peace with Honor,"* *October 1972–January 1973,* Ph.D. diss., University of Kentucky, 1997, p. 206.
[91]Aiken, *Senate Diary,* p. 136.
[92]Colson, *Born Again,* pp. 77–79.
[93]Asselin, *Bitter Peace,* p. 155.

outcome with two separate Vietnams that would enable him to claim peace with honor.

This time, the United States imposed the settlement on South Vietnam. Nixon again promised continued aid after the peace agreement and vowed to "respond with full force" if North Vietnam violated its terms. He warned that if Thieu continued to resist he would cut off further assistance and sign the treaty alone. In one especially heavy-handed letter, he reminded Thieu of the fate of Ngo Dinh Diem.[94] To underline the threat, the United States cut off assistance under the Commodity Import Program. The White House also enlisted conservative senators such as Barry Goldwater to make plain to Thieu he had no support in Congress. Thieu stalled right up to the deadline, raised more objections, asked for additional revisions, and even sent agents to the United States to lobby for him, an act that especially infuriated Nixon. Finally, emotional and despondent, he caved in, remarking with resignation, "I have done all that I can for my country." The Saigon government never formally endorsed the treaty, but Thieu made known in a cryptic way he would no longer oppose it.

Nixon and Kissinger later claimed to have achieved the peace with honor to which they had committed themselves in 1969. Despite the perfidy of North Vietnam, the intractability of South Vietnam, and the vicious, unrelenting attacks from their domestic critics, the two men saw themselves as having courageously persisted to secure a peace agreement that extricated the United States from the war, secured the return of American prisoners of war, and kept South Vietnam intact. That peace with honor could have been upheld, they insisted, had not North Vietnam repeatedly violated the Paris agreements and had not a vengeful and feckless Congress, bolstered by the Watergate scandals, prevented the administration from using American power to defend a peace for which so much had been paid in blood and treasure.

In fact, there was no peace. The Paris agreements permitted American extrication from the war and left the Thieu government in place, at least for the moment. But the major question over which the war had been fought—the political future of South Vietnam—was left unresolved. The political mechanism established to resolve it was inherently unworkable. At the time Kissinger and Tho emerged from

[94]Hung and Schecter, *The Palace File*, pp. 73–74.

the Hotel Majestic in Paris smiling broadly at their achievement, the combatants in South Vietnam were busily preparing for the final round. As all sides recognized at the time, the 1973 agreements marked the beginning of yet another phase in the thirty-year struggle for the control of Vietnam.

Nor was there honor. Although South Vietnam was indeed intact when the peace agreement was signed, the presence of 150,000 North Vietnamese troops below the demilitarized zone, along with the U.S. withdrawal and recognition of the PRG, represented huge concessions on the part of the United States, concessions that Thieu saw so clearly as imperiling the existence of his already rickety government. With the use of or the threat of using American airpower, Nixon might have been able to delay the outcome. But U.S. forces would not be deployed in Vietnam again. Even the threat increasingly lacked credibility. This inability to act was in part a result of the Watergate scandal, as Nixon and Kissinger later claimed. What they conveniently omit is that Watergate was the result of illegal actions taken by a paranoid administration and a vindictive president determined to destroy his political enemies. Even without Watergate, Nixon's threats to use American airpower and his promises to Thieu would probably have turned out to be empty. Because Nixon had not consulted with Congress, they were of dubious legality. In any event, once U.S. forces had been removed from Vietnam, a war-weary nation and a rebellious Congress were not inclined to permit them to return. Nixon may have seen this outcome and sought to shift blame for the inevitable fall of South Vietnam to Congress. Or, as Larry Berman has argued, he may have planned through American airpower to maintain a perpetual stalemate.[95] Whatever the case, he failed. Although he had succeeded in buying some time for Vietnamization, he had never built a base of public support to uphold the standards he had set for peace with honor. In the end, his standards had to give way to public unwillingness to invest more resources in a losing cause.[96]

For all concerned, "peace with honor" came at an enormous price. Official U.S. estimates place the number of South Vietnamese battle deaths for 1969 to 1973 at 107,504 and North Vietnamese and NLF at more than a half million. There will probably never be a full

[95]Berman, *No Peace, No Honor,* pp. 9, 204.
[96]Katz, "Public Opinion and Foreign Policy," 507.

accounting of civilians deaths and casualties. The tonnage of bombs dropped on Indochina during these years far exceeded that of the Johnson years, wreaking untold devastation, causing permanent ecological damage to the countryside, and leaving millions of civilians homeless.

The United States suffered much less than Vietnam, but the cost was still substantial. An additional 20,553 Americans were killed in the last four years of the war, bringing the total to more than 58,000. Continuation of the war fueled an inflation that neither Nixon nor his successors could control. The war polarized the American people and poisoned the political atmosphere as no other issue since slavery a century before. Although Nixon had prolonged the fighting four years mainly to uphold America's credibility in the world, the United States emerged from the conflict with its international image substantially tarnished and its people weary of international commitment.

For Nixon, too, the price was steep. In January 1973, at the very moment when he should have been savoring his electoral triumph and his diplomatic successes, he was exhausted, embittered, and isolated, his administration reduced to a "small band of tired, dispirited, sometimes mean and petty men, bickering among themselves, wary and jealous of one another."[97] Ironically, at the very height of their political and diplomatic triumphs, Nixon and Kissinger gave vent to jealousy and backbiting over who deserved the credit. Enraged when Kissinger leaked to the press that he had opposed the Christmas bombing, Nixon characteristically ordered the monitoring of his key adviser's telephone. He was furious that Kissinger shared the Nobel Peace Prize with Le Duc Tho. At the beginning of the second term, the president and his staff were preparing to remove Kissinger from his position.

More than any other single issue, the Vietnam War brought a premature end to the Nixon presidency. The extreme measures he took to defend his Vietnam policies led directly to Watergate, which would eventually force his resignation. Thus, when the final crisis came in 1975, the person who claimed to have achieved peace with honor was no longer in the White House, and the nation was in no mood to defend the agreement he had constructed at such great cost.

[97]Colson, *Born Again*, p. 80.

Veterans at the Wall
Vietnam war veteran Gary Huber of Michigan locates a
friend's name on the Vietnam Veterans Memorial—the
Wall—on Veterans' Day 2002. The war touched the souls
of Americans as few other events in their history. The
stark but moving memorial came to symbolize the
nation's pain and grief and for veterans especially served
as a place for healing and reconciliation.
© AFP/Getty Images

CHAPTER 8

The Postwar War
and the Legacies of Vietnam

The "peace" agreements of January 1973 established a framework for continuing the war without direct American participation. North Vietnam still sought unification of the country on its terms; South Vietnam still struggled to survive as an independent nation; and President Nixon still supported the South's aspirations. The cease-fire existed only on paper.

This last phase of the war was remarkably short. Dependent on the United States from its birth, the Saigon government had great difficulty functioning on its own. Because of the surging Watergate scandals and American war-weariness, moreover, Nixon was not able to live up to his secret commitments to Thieu. Indeed, in August 1974 he was forced to resign. Congress drastically cut back aid to South Vietnam, further eroding the Saigon government's faltering will to resist. When North Vietnam and the National Liberation Front (NLF) mounted a major offensive in the spring of 1975, South Vietnam collapsed with stunning rapidity, dramatically ending the thirty-year war and leaving the United States, on the eve of its third century, frustrated, angry, and bewildered.

THE POSTWAR WAR

The "postwar war" began before peace was proclaimed. The United States had some difficulty arranging with North Vietnam for the return of the 591 prisoners of war, at one point threatening to delay troop withdrawals in the absence of cooperation. By the end of March, the details had been worked out and the POWs were released.

Some had been held more than eight years. All had suffered through horrible living conditions, cruel captors, isolation, beatings, and other forms of torture. Some broke under the stress and made statements demanded by their captors. As a group, however, the POWs bore their captivity with courage, dignity, and remarkable inner strength. They developed ingenious methods to communicate with one another—and to survive. They returned in March 1973 to a heroes' welcome. Jeremiah Denton's understated response—"We are honored to have had the opportunity to serve our country under difficult circumstances"—added to their appeal. That the POWs were singled out as the only true heroes of an unpopular war did a disservice to the thousands of Americans who performed heroic feats, but their dramatic return helped a divided and war-weary nation salvage some pride and redemption.[1]

The return of the POWs and the withdrawal of U.S. troops were the only tangible accomplishments of the teams assigned to implement the peace accords. From the start, efforts to effect a cease-fire proved unavailing. The Vietnamese combatants had not abandoned their goals; they observed the agreements only to the extent that it suited their interests. For Saigon, the agreement permitted, with U.S. assistance, continuation of the war and possible improvement of its position. For Hanoi and the NLF, it provided a political mechanism to win the war.

Buoyed by Nixon's promises, Thieu defied the peace agreement from the outset. The NLF had launched a series of land-grabbing operations immediately before the cease-fire, and Thieu wanted to retrieve as much of the lost territory as possible. Although he controlled an estimated 75 percent of the land and 85 percent of the people when the agreements were signed, he sought to solidify his position while U.S. support remained firm. To secure as much additional territory as possible, he resettled refugees and built forts in contested areas. Army of the Republic of Vietnam (ARVN) units attacked North Vietnamese bases and supply lines. Artillery and aircraft indiscriminately shelled and bombed villages

---

[1]Vernon E. Davis, *The Long Road Home: U.S. Prisoner of War Policy and Planning in Southeast Asia* (Washington, D.C., 2000), pp. 527–528. For a companion official history of the POWs' captivity, see Stuart I. Rochester and Frederick Kiley, *Honor Bound: The History of American Prisoners of War in Southeast Asia, 1961–1973* (Washington, D.C., 1998).

under Provisional Revolutionary Government (PRG) control. During the first three months of "peace," the ARVN lost more than 6,000 soldiers, among its highest casualties during the entire war. Thieu's aggressive approach brought short-term advantages but cost his country over the long run by overextending its forces, putting them on the defensive, and leaving the initiative with the enemy.[2]

North Vietnam and the NLF were more cautious but no less purposeful. Battered and exhausted from the bloody campaigns of 1972, and short of food, ammunition, and personnel, they desperately needed time to regroup. They were also eager to secure a complete— and irreversible—U.S. withdrawal from Vietnam and thus sought to avoid blatant violations of the accords that might provoke a resumption of the bombing or threaten American promises of aid for postwar reconstruction. During the first months after the cease-fire, the PRG attempted to consolidate the territory under its control and to undermine Thieu's position where possible through political agitation. By appearing to support the peace accords, it sought to win sympathy from the war-weary people in South Vietnam, show good faith to win over world opinion, and portray Thieu as the enemy of peace. Meanwhile, North Vietnam quietly infiltrated troops and equipment into the South, built a system of modern paved roads with concrete bridges linking staging areas to strategic zones in South Vietnam, and even constructed a thousand mile pipeline to ensure adequate supplies of petroleum for forces in the field.[3]

The Nixon administration persisted in its commitment to South Vietnam. Shortly after the signing of the peace agreement, the president reaffirmed to Saigon's ambassador America's continuing military, economic, and "spiritual" support and boasted that the United States had a "stick and a carrot to restrain Hanoi."[4] Throughout 1973, the administration employed various subterfuges to maintain a high level of military aid without overtly violating the Paris accords. Instead of dismantling its bases, it transferred title to the South Vietnamese before the cease-fire went into effect.

[2]James H. Willbanks, *Abandoning Vietnam: How America Left and South Vietnam Lost It's War* (Lawrence, Kans., 2004), pp. 190–193. Maynard Parker, "Vietnam: The War That won't End," *Foreign Affairs* 53 (January 1975): 365–366.
[3]Willbanks, *Abandoning Vietnam*, p. 191.
[4]Kissinger memorandum, January 30, 1973, *Foreign Relations of the United States, 1969–1976*, 10: 12–13.

Supplies were designated "nonmilitary" and thus eligible for transfer. The military advisory group was replaced by a team of 50 military and 1,200 civilian advisers, some of the latter hastily discharged from military service and placed in the employ of the Saigon government. The United States kept a formidable armada of naval and airpower in the Gulf of Tonkin, in Thailand, and on Guam. The Nixon administration continued to bomb Cambodia, in part to support the embattled Lon Nol government against a determined Khmer Rouge offensive, and also to maintain the president's reputation for fierceness.

Nixon and Kissinger quickly perceived their waning ability to influence events in Indochina. In March, they contemplated bombing the Ho Chi Minh Trail in response to heavy North Vietnamese infiltration to reaffirm to Hanoi that "we might be trigger happy." But they quickly dropped the idea. The president acknowledged that in the absence of a full-scale invasion of the South, it would be impossible to bomb North Vietnam without provoking an uproar in Congress. Once the last Americans had departed, he ruminated, the public reaction would be "Now for Christ's sake, we're out of Vietnam. Let's don't go back in."[5] Because the United States had provided massive aid to South Vietnam to defend itself, the president further reasoned, Americans would naturally say let them do it. Nixon and Kissinger had viewed postwar aid to North Vietnam as leverage to "get them the hell out" of South Vietnam, as Nixon put it. But they realized that Congress would not be receptive to such a request. The administration lost its carrot in the spring when it suspended discussions on postwar aid in response to continued North Vietnamese infiltration.

Under these circumstances, expectations were adjusted. Kissinger may still have hoped for a decent interval, but he admitted at one point that he did not believe South Vietnam would last through 1974. An interval, perhaps, but hardly decent. Even with the wealth of documentation now available, it remains difficult to fathom Nixon's expectations. Still mainly concerned about U.S. credibility, he once expressed hope that the Saigon government could hang on until events elsewhere began to eclipse Vietnam in importance. "You can't have it collapse immediately," he told

[5]Nixon conversation with Brent Scowcroft, March 20, 1973, ibid, pp. 160–161.

Alexander Haig in late March. Admitting that it was hard to be optimistic, he comforted himself with the notion that his administration had "gone the extra mile" in support of Thieu.[6]

VIETNAM, WATERGATE, AND CONGRESS

By the early summer of 1973, Nixon's ability to dangle carrots or brandish sticks had been further curtailed by an increasingly rebellious Congress. The congressional challenge reflected a pervasive war-weariness and a widespread feeling among Americans that once their troops had been safely removed, the nation should extricate itself entirely from the conflict. Mounting evidence of White House involvement in the Watergate scandal increased Nixon's vulnerability. Republicans joined Democrats in condemning the bombing of Cambodia as illegal. On May 10 the House voted to cut off funds for further air operations. Congress displayed no enthusiasm for reconstruction aid for North Vietnam, especially after returned POWs started to divulge the grim details of their captivity. Doves protested that it would not promote peace; hawks denounced it as "reparations." In the fall of 1973, Congress voted that no funds would be provided until Hanoi gave a full accounting of U.S. personnel missing in action, something it refused to do.

Perceiving the relentless erosion of administration influence over events in Indochina, Kissinger journeyed to Paris once again in May in a last-ditch and ultimately futile effort to persuade Hanoi to observe the cease-fire. Le Duc Tho responded angrily to American charges of violations with countercharges that South Vietnam and the United States were not upholding their commitments. More annoying to Kissinger was when Tho dismissed U.S. accusations as attempts to deceive public opinion, "as you have done with Watergate." Operating without any leverage, Kissinger cobbled together a new agreement that did little more than establish a timetable for implementing the old one. Once again, Thieu balked, stalling for days and refusing to acquiesce until faced with another series of letters containing escalating Nixon threats to cut off U.S. aid to his government. Kissinger subsequently informed a South Vietnamese

---

[6]Haig–Nixon telecon, March 30, 1973; ibid, p. 175; Nixon–Scowcroft telecon, June 12, 1973, ibid, p. 335.

diplomat that he was done negotiating with North Vietnam (a message that may have cheered some Saigon officials): "I am washing my hands of this." Upon returning to Washington he told the press that he was going to reduce his involvement in Indochina affairs "in order to preserve my emotional stability."[7]

Kissinger's remark was more prophetic than he could have realized, for during the summer of 1973 Nixon's power drastically eroded. Ever-widening investigations of what had seemed a routine break-in at the Democratic party headquarters in Washington's posh Watergate Hotel a year earlier had revealed ties between the burglars and the president's reelection committee and even to the White House itself, sensational exposes of other presidential abuses of power, and details of a frenzied administration cover-up. Senate hearings on the Watergate affair were televised by the networks and mesmerized a huge national audience. Nixon's efforts to save his own skin by firing his top aides backfired when some of them divulged yet more about goings-on in the White House.

Nixon's steadily weakening position encouraged more vigorous Congressional efforts to terminate military activities in Southeast Asia. Long-embittered Democrats were encouraged to take on the president, and Republicans were increasingly reluctant to support him. Nixon and Kissinger vigorously defended the bombing of Cambodia as necessary to sustain Lon Nol and uphold the ceasefire. But an overwhelming majority of legislators agreed with Senator George Aiken that the bombing was "ill-advised and unwarranted." Many accepted the outspoken affirmation of Representative Norris Cotton (New Hampshire Republican): "As far as I'm concerned, I want to get the hell out."[8] In late June, Congress approved an amendment requiring the immediate cessation of all military operations in and over Indochina. The House upheld Nixon's angry veto, but the president was eventually forced to accept a compromise extending the deadline to August 15. For the first time, Congress had taken decisive steps to curtail American involvement in the war. "It would be idle to say that the authority

---

[7]Memorandum of conversation, June 15, 1973; ibid, p. 354; Marvin and Bernard Kalb, *Kissinger* (Boston, 1974), p. 432.

[8]George Aiken, *Senate Diary* (Brattleboro, Vt., 1976), p. 198; Kalb and Kalb, *Kissinger,* p. 432.

of the executive has not been impaired," Kissinger remarked with obvious understatement and disappointment.[9]

By the end of 1973, Nixon was virtually powerless. Watergate had reduced his popular approval ratings to an all-time low and left him fighting a desperate rearguard action to save his political life. His complete absorption in his survival rendered him increasingly incapable of dealing with other issues. In November, Congress passed, over another veto, the so-called War Powers Act, a direct response to the abuse of presidential authority in Vietnam. The legislation required the president to inform Congress within forty-eight hours of the deployment of American military forces abroad and to withdraw them in sixty days in the absence of explicit congressional endorsement. Some members of Congress protested that the act conferred on the president a more direct power to commit American troops to war than was provided by the Constitution, but the circumstances under which the debate took place, combined with Watergate and the vote terminating operations in Indochina, made virtually certain the end of direct American involvement in Vietnam. The administration could do little more than mount a covert disinformation program to delude Hanoi into believing that a major offensive on it's part would provoke massive U.S. military retaliation.

A CRUMBLING BASTION

In the meantime, the Paris agreements had become a dead letter. Discussions of a political settlement had begun in early 1973 and continued sporadically throughout the year, but the basic issue—the future of South Vietnam—was nonnegotiable. Thieu proclaimed the "Four Nos": no recognition of the enemy; no coalition government; no neutralization for South Vietnam; no concession of territory. Still confident of U.S. support despite the darkening cloud of Watergate, he formally announced in late 1973 the start of the "Third Indochina War," stepping up ground and air attacks on enemy bases and launching a series of land-grabbing operations in PRG-held territories along the eastern seaboard, in the Iron Triangle, and in the Mekong Delta.

[9]Kalb and Kalb, *Kissinger,* p. 434.

This time North Vietnam and the PRG counterattacked. Fearing a repetition of the late 1950s, when Viet Minh stay-behinds had been close to extermination at the hands of Ngo Dinh Diem, southerners pressed for action. Some North Vietnamese military leaders urged launching an all-out offensive. Having been burned three times and unwilling to give the United States any reason to return to Vietnam, Le Duan and Pham Van Dong responded cautiously. At the twenty-first plenum in July, the party leadership ordered a gradual escalation of the political and military struggle in the South as a prelude to a general offensive. Integrating regular units with local forces, they sought to put maximum pressure on South Vietnam wherever possible and wrest whatever territory they could. Over the next few months, they scored major successes, mauling ARVN units in the Iron Triangle, retaking some territory that had been lost, and seizing additional territory formerly under Saigon's control. The fighting sharply intensified. By the end of 1973 the Third Indochina War was in full swing.[10]

Over the next year, the military balance shifted decisively toward North Vietnam and the NLF. Thieu's "hold at all costs" strategy produced crippling overextension. The more hamlets the Government of Vietnam (GVN) acquired, the more vulnerable it became. More than half of its million-soldier army was tied down in static defense positions and scattered through the northern provinces. They could not attack North Vietnamese supply routes. Modeled after the U.S. Army, the ARVN had a huge logistics tail. Only about 150,000 of its regular forces were actual combat troops. As many as 20,000 of these were "flower soldiers" who had purchased their freedom from fighting. Pay cuts and loss of perquisites spurred an even higher desertion rate. Corruption and weak leadership continued to undermine ARVN effectiveness. Like its mentor, the ARVN had come to rely on airpower and heavy firepower, and the departure of U.S. air units from South Vietnam had weakened its fighting effectiveness. The numbing sense of dependency persisted as the South Vietnamese still insisted on "checking with the Americans," even though it was unclear what Americans should be checked with.[11]

---

[10]Willbanks, *Abandoning Vietnam*, p. 196; Pierre Asselin, *A Bitter Peace: Washington, Hanoi, and the Making of the Paris Agreement* (Chapel Hill, N.C., 2002), pp. 185–186; David W. P. Elliott, *The Vietnamese War: Revolution and Social Change in the Mekong Delta, 1930–1975* (Armonk, N.Y., 2007), pp. 409–410, 414.

[11]Parker, "Vietnam," pp. 366–367; Willbanks, *Abandoning Vietnam*, pp. 201–206.

South Vietnam's perennial economic and political problems had been sharply aggravated by the American withdrawal. Loss of the $400 million the United States spent annually in South Vietnam, reduction of military aid from $2.3 billion in 1973 to about $1 billion in 1974, and a steep rise in worldwide inflation combined to produce an annual inflation rate of 90 percent, massive unemployment, a drastic decline in morale in the armed forces and among the urban population, and an increase in the ever-present corruption. Scavengers stripped the American-built port at Cam Ranh Bay to a bare skeleton. Pilots demanded bribes to fly missions in support of ground troops.

Thieu's policies compounded the problems. In the spring of 1974, he attempted to starve out the enemy by blockading PRG areas and enacting various measures to deny them rice. The so-called Rice War backfired, causing enormous suffering throughout all of South Vietnam, even in Saigon. By 1974, there were three to four million unemployed people in areas controlled by the GVN. The increase in hunger and joblessness stimulated a rise in crime and corruption. The economic crisis of 1974 compounded Thieu's political woes. The Buddhists became more active than at any other time since 1966, agitating for peace and reconciliation with the Communists. The Catholics, the government's most important base of support, organized an anticorruption campaign, the major target of which was Thieu himself. A spirit of defeatism grew among those fence-sitters who had not supported the government but had not actively opposed it either. Growing political unrest spurred demonstrations. The government responded as it always had with jailings and beatings.[12]

By this time, the North Vietnamese Army (NVA) had an estimated 285,000 troops in the South, vast stockpiles of supplies, and a highly sophisticated logistics system that permitted the shifting of regulars, along with tanks and artillery, to any battlefront within hours. The once primitive Ho Chi Minh Trail was now a gravel-paved two-lane highway with way stations every hundred kilometers. North Vietnam had also built a north–south supply route from the demilitarized zone to within one hundred kilometers of Saigon. Still closely watching events in Washington, Hanoi's leaders in late 1973

[12]Ngo Vinh Long, "Post-Paris Struggles and the Fall of Saigon," in Jayne S. Werner and Luu Doan Huynh (eds.), *The Vietnam War: Vietnamese and American Perspectives* (New York, 1993), pp. 206–212.

remained hesitant to launch an end-the-war offensive. But they sharply escalated the fighting, exhorting forces to "attack point by point, grasping partial victories and advancing toward final victory." They assaulted ARVN bases and headquarters and towns held by the GVN. During 1974, they regained the initiative, took substantial new territory, especially in the vital Mekong Delta and land deemed crucial for the final offensive, and gained invaluable combat experience. Throughout the summer and fall, they inflicted heavy losses on South Vietnamese forces, further eroding morale and confidence. By late in the year, the NVA stood poised for the final offensive.[13]

The American abandonment of South Vietnam was manifest by the end of 1974. Nixon was forced to resign in August, removing from power the individual who had promised continued support and leaving a stunned and despondent Thieu to contemplate abandoning the northern part of South Vietnam and building a new nation around the former Cochin China. Throughout the year, Kissinger pleaded with an increasingly defiant Congress to expand military aid to $1.5 billion, insisting that the United States had a moral obligation to South Vietnam and warning that failure to uphold it would have a "corrosive effect on our interests beyond Indochina."

Arguments that had been accepted without challenge for nearly a quarter of a century now fell flat. Runaway inflation in the United States evoked insistent demands for reducing expenditures. Many members of Congress agreed with Senator William Proxmire (Wisconsin Democrat) that there was less need for continued military aid to South Vietnam than for "any other single item" in the budget. Critics insisted that the Thieu government was in no immediate peril and warned that much of the money would line the pockets of Saigon's corrupt bureaucrats. A continuation of massive American military aid would encourage Thieu to prolong the war, whereas a reduction might impress on him the need to seek a political settlement. It was time to terminate America's "endless support for an endless war," Senator Edward Kennedy insisted. In September 1974, Congress approved an aid program of only $700 million, half of which comprised shipping costs.[14]

The aid cuts of 1974 had a devastating impact in South Vietnam. Without the continued large infusion of U.S. funds and

---

[13]Willbanks, *Abandoning Vietnam*, pp. 208–213.
[14]*Congressional Record*, 93d Cong., 2d Sess., 29176–29180.

equipment, the armed forces could not fight the way the Americans had trained them. Air force operations had to be curtailed by as much as 50 percent because of shortages of gasoline and spare parts. Ammunition and other supplies had to be severely rationed. The inescapable signs of waning American support had a crushing effect on morale in an army already reeling under North Vietnamese blows. Desertions reached an all-time high of 240,000 in 1974. The aid cutbacks heightened Thieu's economic and political woes, spurring among many Vietnamese a "growing psychology of accommodation and retreat that sometimes approached despair."[15]

THE END OF THE TUNNEL

From the time of the First Indochina War, overly optimistic French and U.S. officials had promised a light at the end of the tunnel. When that light finally appeared in 1975 it came with a stunning rapidity and brought an outcome that turned a cliché into a cruel irony.

Since the beginning of the postwar war, North Vietnamese and NLF leaders had watched events in South Vietnam and especially in the United States with "an almost obsessive curiosity." In early 1975, they concluded that the opportune moment was at hand.[16] In December 1974, North Vietnamese main units and PRG regional forces had attacked Phuoc Long, northeast of Saigon. Within three weeks they had killed or captured 3,000 ARVN troops, seized huge quantities of supplies, and "liberated" the entire province. The ease of the victory underscored the relative weakening of the ARVN during the past year and made clear, as the North Vietnamese chief of staff, Gen. Van Tien Dung, later put it, that Thieu was now forced to fight a "poor-man's war." Thieu refused to withdraw from Phuoc Long—or send additional troops to defend it. Its fall and America's silent response shattered morale among South Vietnamese civilians and military and left the president fearful of a coup.

Aware from intelligence that Saigon was not expecting a major offensive in 1975, in January Hanoi adopted a two-year plan, a series

---

[15]Guenter Lewy, *America in Vietnam* (New York, 1978), p. 208.
[16]Truong Nhu Tang with David Chanoff and Doan Van Toai, *A Vietcong Memoir* (New York, 1985), p. 225.

of large-scale offensives in 1975 to create the conditions for a general offensive and a general uprising in 1976. U.S. failure to respond to the fall of Phuoc Long confirmed what many North Vietnamese strategists had long suspected, that having pulled out of South Vietnam, the Americans would not "jump back in." After days of sometimes heated debate, the leadership concluded that even if the United States responded with naval and airpower, it could not "rescue the Saigon administration from its disastrous collapse."[17]

The collapse came with a suddenness that surprised even the North Vietnamese. Massing vastly superior forces against the stretched-out ARVN defenders, Dung attacked Ban Me Thuot in the Central Highlands in early March and took it within two days. To secure control of the highlands before the end of the dry season, he moved against Pleiku and Kontum. Belatedly scrapping his hold-everything strategy, a now panicky Thieu ordered a withdrawal from the highlands, a necessary decision, perhaps, but no plans had been formulated, and a retreat is among the most difficult of military maneuvers to execute. The withdrawal quickly turned into a rout. Soldiers deserted to look after their families, thousands of civilians joined the soldiers in flight, clogging the avenues of escape. The breakdown of discipline sparked riots and looting. Hundreds died of hunger and sickness. Much of the army was captured or destroyed, and thousands of civilians died from enemy or friendly gunfire or from starvation in what journalists called the "Convoy of Tears." "It was a true hell," one survivor recalled.[18] Pleiku and Kontum fell within a week. This disastrous, largely self-inflicted defeat cost the Thieu government six provinces, at least two divisions of troops, and the confidence of its army and people. It opened the way for even greater catastrophe in the nation's coastal cities.

Sensing that total victory was now in reach, Hanoi put into effect contingency plans for the conquest of South Vietnam. The important coastal city of Da Nang, normally populated by 300,000 citizens, was crammed with an additional 2 million refugees. When North Vietnamese forces approached the outskirts, the city fell apart. The defending army, along with hundreds of thousands of civilians, fled for Saigon, duplicating on an even larger and more tragic scale the debacle in the highlands. Air evacuation had to be

---

[17]Van Tien Dung, *Our Great Spring Victory* (New York, 1977), pp. 17, 19–20.
[18]Willbanks, *Abandoning Vietnam*, p. 244.

stopped when frantic refugees mobbed the planes. Soldiers looted, and money-hungry citizens charged up to $2 for a glass of water. An estimated 60,000 died trying to get out of Da Nang.

Ten days after the attack had begun and almost ten years to the day after the U.S. Marines had splashed ashore at Da Nang, the two coastal cities were in North Vietnamese hands. South Vietnam had been cut in two and half its army lost without putting up any resistance. Nha Trang and Cam Ranh Bay were abandoned before they were even threatened. Dung now threw all his forces into the "Ho Chi Minh Campaign" to liberate Saigon. Many South Vietnamese were frightened by the prospect of a northern victory but unwilling or unable to do anything to stop it.

The United States was stunned by the collapse of South Vietnam but resigned to the outcome. American intelligence had correctly predicted that the major enemy thrust was not planned until 1976, but the capacity of the South Vietnamese to resist was again overestimated. Washington was shocked by the sudden loss of the central highlands. America's disinclination for further involvement was obvious: On the day Ban Me Thuot fell, Congress rejected President Gerald Ford's request for an additional $300 million in military aid for South Vietnam.

The legislators' vote seems to have accurately reflected the wishes of their constituents. A few diehards issued one last appeal to honor the nation's commitments and defend freedom against Communist aggression. Some Americans raised the specter of a bloodbath in which hundreds of thousands of South Vietnamese would be slaughtered by the Communist conquerors. For the most part, such appeals fell on deaf ears. Weary of the seemingly endless involvement in Vietnam and pinched by an economic recession at home, Americans were not in a generous mood. Why throw good money after bad, they asked. At a time when they themselves were in "desperate financial straits," they saw no reason to sacrifice for a government that was "not only corrupt but grossly wasteful and inefficient." It was about time that the South Vietnamese were made to stand on their own feet, one "fed-up taxpayer" exclaimed. "My God, we're all tired of it, we're sick to death of it," an Oregonian wrote. "55,000 dead and $100 billion spent and for what?"[19]

---

[19]Mrs. J. S. Mozzanini to James J. Kilpatrick, February 6, 1975, and numerous other letters in James J. Kilpatrick Papers, University of Virginia Library, Charlottesville, Va., Box 5.

The fall of Da Nang and Hue and the imminent threat to Saigon did nothing to change Americans' views. Ford gave no thought to employing U.S. air and naval power. To stiffen South Vietnamese morale and shift to the legislative branch blame for a debacle that seemed inevitable, he made a personal appearance before Congress to ask for $722 million in emergency military assistance, setting off a final, bitterly emotional debate on the war. Persisting in the self-delusion that had marked U.S. involvement from the outset, administration officials held out the chimera that additional aid might yet bring about a stalemate and a negotiated settlement within the framework of the Paris accords. Now insisting for the sake of expediency that the domino theory was not valid, Secretary of State Kissinger reiterated the shopworn warning that if America let South Vietnam down, the "impact on the United States in the world would be very serious indeed." The nation must not have on its conscience "pulling the plug" on the South Vietnamese. It must give them some chance to succeed rather than "doom them to lingering deaths."[20]

Such arguments evoked little support. Legislators responded to Ford's speech with stony silence. They retorted heatedly that the South Vietnamese had abandoned more equipment in the northern provinces than could be purchased with the additional funds. No amount of money could save an army that refused to fight. It was time for the United States to end its involvement in "this horrid war."[21] The specter of the Gulf of Tonkin and Watergate hung over the debate. Revelations of Nixon's secret promises to Thieu provoked cries of outrage. Administration efforts to pin the blame on Congress infuriated some who had supported the war. Congress eventually approved $300 million for the evacuation of Americans and for humanitarian purposes and endorsed Ford's request to use American troops to evacuate U.S. citizens from South Vietnam. But it would go no further. "The Vietnam debate has run its course," Kissinger commented with finality on April 17.[22]

---

[20]Notes on cabinet meeting, April 16, 1975, Ron Nessen Papers, Gerald Ford Library, Ann Arbor, Mich., Box 294; memorandum of conversation, Kissinger, Ford, and congressional leaders, March 5, 1975, Kissinger/Scowcroft File, Box A1, Ford Library.
[21]*Congressional Record*, 94th Cong., 1st Sess., 10101–10108.
[22]*New York Times*, April 18, 1975.

The Ho Chi Minh Campaign: North Vietnam's Final Offensive, 1975
Stanley Karnow, *Vietnam—A History*, p. 662.

The growing certainty that the United States would not intervene doomed what glimmer of hope South Vietnam may have had. North Vietnamese forces advanced from Da Nang to the outskirts of the capital in less than a month, meeting strong resistance only at Xuan Loc, where a small but courageous and stubborn ARVN contingent fought desperately against superior numbers and firepower.

With the fall of that town on April 21 and the congressional rejection of Ford's request for aid, the intransigent Thieu finally and reluctantly resigned, bitterly blaming the debacle on his ally. "It is so easy to be an enemy of the United States," he moaned, "but so difficult to be a friend." He was replaced by the aged and infirm Tran Van Huong, who vainly attempted to negotiate a settlement on the basis of the 1973 agreements, and then by the pathetic Duong Van Minh, the architect of the 1963 coup, to whom was left the odious task of surrendering

The End of the Tunnel
This iconic image of a North Vietnamese tank crashing through the gates of Saigon's presidential palace on April 30, 1975, symbolized the fall of South Vietnam and the end of nearly three decades of war in Vietnam. The former capital of the Republic of Vietnam was quickly renamed Ho Chi Minh City in honor of the revered leader of the revolution.
© *AP Images*

unconditionally. On April 30, 1975, enemy tanks crashed through the gates of the presidential palace. NLF soldiers triumphantly ran up their flag over a quickly renamed Ho Chi Minh City. A week earlier, Ford had formally proclaimed at Tulane University in New Orleans what had already become obvious: The Vietnam War was "finished as far as the United States was concerned." When he uttered the word *finished*, the crowd of mostly students cheered robustly, many jumped to their feet, and there was prolonged applause.[23]

The U.S. evacuation of Saigon revealed in microcosm much of the delusion, frustration, and tragedy that had marked the American experience in Vietnam. Some U.S. officials persisted in the belief that the South Vietnamese would mount an effective defense of their country until the North Vietnamese were at the gates of Saigon and clung stubbornly to hopes of a negotiated settlement long after any such possibility had vanished. Ambassador Graham Martin had pronounced upon his appointment in 1973 that he was "not going to Vietnam to give it away to the Communists." He stubbornly supported Thieu long after it was evident that the president had no backing within his own country. Martin thwarted several coup attempts and encouraged Thieu's refusal to resign, resignation being perhaps the only chance of avoiding unconditional surrender.

Fearful of spreading panic in Saigon and hoping to arrange the American exit in a way that "would not add a further disgrace to the sad history of our involvement," Martin delayed implementation of evacuation plans until the last minute.[24]

With Tan Son Nhut Airport unusable, the United States, through Operation FREQUENT WIND, managed to airlift by helicopter 7,100 Americans and South Vietnamese. Many Washington officials were intent on extricating only Americans, but Ford, to his credit, insisted that the United States had a moral obligation to evacuate as many as possible of those South Vietnamese who had worked closely with their ally. U.S. Navy ships transported some 70,000 to ships in the South China Sea, leaving behind 420 who had been promised help. The U.S. evacuation triggered total panic in the city, "a vision out of a nightmare," one participant called it, fraught with unbelievable human agony. Looting and plunder were common. Senior military officers fled, and the remnants of the army, as in the

[23]New Orleans *Times-Picayune,* April 23, 2000.
[24]Martin to Kissinger, April 18, 1975, Kissinger/Scowcroft File, Box A1, Ford Library.

North, simply melted away. Corruption ran rampant, escape often going to the highest bidder. The U.S. Embassy paid enormous fees for exit visas for some of those seeking to flee. Because of delays in implementing the evacuation plan and the unavailability of adequate transport, many who wished to leave could not. The spectacle of U.S. Marines using rifle butts to keep desperate Vietnamese from blocking escape routes and of angry ARVN soldiers firing on the departing Americans provided a tragic epitaph for twenty-five years of American involvement in Vietnam. The indelible image of the last helicopter departing a Saigon rooftop starkly symbolized the U.S. failure. Ford recalled April 30, 1975, as "one of the saddest days of my life"; journalist Evan Thomas later labeled it a "low moment in the American century."[25]

The United States bears a heavy burden of responsibility for the debacle of April 1975. Americans had made the South Vietnamese armed forces dependent and then left them to save themselves before they were ready and without the air support on which they had come to rely. The "peace" agreement of 1973 was designed more to get the United States out of Vietnam than to end the fighting among the Vietnamese. Despite Nixon's protestations of peace with honor, it was fundamentally flawed, especially by leaving more than a hundred thousand North Vietnamese troops in the South. In the two years after the signing of the Paris agreements, the Nixon administration gave Thieu enough support to encourage his defiance but not enough to ensure his survival. Nixon's ill-advised promises were intended to secure Thieu's adherence to the Paris agreements. They encouraged his continued dependence on Washington. They tempted him to reject the admittedly risky choice of negotiations and launch a war he could not win. The reduction of U.S. involvement in the war and subsequent congressional cutbacks of American aid undoubtedly demoralized the South Vietnamese and weakened their capacity to fight. The refusal of the United States to intervene in the final crisis sealed their fate. But Nixon and Kissinger's cynical and self-serving efforts to blame the collapse of South Vietnam on Congress ring hollow. Without consulting Congress, Nixon made *secret* promises that would have

[25]Evan Thomas, "The Last Days of Saigon," *Newsweek,* May 1, 2000, 37–42. The fullest and most up-to-date account is George J. Veith, *Black April: The Fall of South Vietnam, 1973–1975* (New York, 2012).

required congressional assent for implementation, and at a time when it was in full rebellion against a never-ending war and the stretching of presidential powers. An administration that had repeatedly spurned Congress could hardly expect its compliance in time of crisis. Nixon's ability to implement his promises was severely hampered by the Watergate scandals—for which his administration was responsible.

In the final analysis, Vietnamese factors determined the outcome more than anything the United States did or failed to do. The fall of South Vietnam just fifty-five days after the onset of the North Vietnamese offensive was symptomatic of the malaise that had afflicted that ill-fated nation since its birth. The Saigon regime could never quite overcome its origins as a French puppet government. Political fragmentation, the lack of able and far-sighted leaders, and a tired and corrupt elite that could not adjust to the revolution that swept Vietnam after 1945 afforded a fragile basis for nationhood. Given these harsh realities, America's effort to create a bastion of anti-communism south of the seventeenth parallel was probably doomed from the start. The United States could provide money, weapons, and advice, but it could not furnish the ingredients necessary for political stability and military success. The Saigon regime failed to mobilize the people to fight internal subversion and external invasion. Despairing of the ability of the South Vietnamese to save themselves, the United States had assumed the burden in 1965, only to toss it back in the laps of its clients when Americans tired of the war. The dependency of the early years persisted long after the United States had shifted to Vietnamization. To the very end—and despite overwhelming evidence to the contrary—Thieu and his cohorts clung desperately to the belief that the United States would return and rescue them. "Saigon collapsed from within as much as from external assault," historian David Elliott has written, "and fell apart from the top down rather than from the bottom up."[26] Thieu's gross strategic errors and desperate attempts to save himself while his nation was dying suggest that the outcome would probably have been the same whatever the United States had done. Without firm leadership from their president and high command, the South Vietnamese people surrendered to hysteria. The nation simply disintegrated.

[26]Stephen T. Hosmer et al., *The Fall of South Vietnam* (Santa Monica, Calif., 1978), pp. 118–120; Elliott, *Vietnamese War*, pp. 438–439.

The North Vietnamese and the NLF were not superpeople, as they were sometimes portrayed in U.S. antiwar propaganda. They made colossal blunders. They repeatedly miscalculated the United States' response to their actions. Their stubborn determination to prevail, no matter what, inflicted astronomical and sometimes cruel burdens on their own people. Despite their claims to revolutionary zeal, they were at times bitterly divided among themselves. Their leaders also struggled to hold onto power and stamped out dissent with brutal efficiency. Especially toward the end, they faced slackening morale among their army and people, the result of decades of bloody warfare. Still, in waging this conflict they had distinct advantages. From the outset of the revolution, the Communists drew into the fold the most dedicated and able political activists, who provided superior leadership, from the top down to the village level. Le Duan lacked Ho Chi Minh's charisma and international stature, but he shared his predecessor's determination to endure, and he was ruthless in his use of power. Skilled organizers, the North Vietnamese and the NLF tapped the wellsprings of their people's nationalism and mobilized the resources of Vietnam in a total and concentrated effort to achieve their goals. Time after time, defeat after defeat, they demonstrated incredible staying power and resiliency, rebounding for the next round of an endless war. At least until 1972, they exploited the Sino-Soviet split to secure maximum aid while safeguarding their freedom of action. They formulated a sophisticated strategy that blended military, diplomatic, and political means to achieve the long-sought end of liberating the South and unifying the nation. They skillfully employed the concept of protracted war, perceiving that the Americans, like the French, could become impatient and that if they bled long enough, they would grow weary of the war.

CONSEQUENCES AND IMPACT

With the North Vietnamese/NLF victory, the "dominoes" in Indochina quickly toppled. Cambodia fell before South Vietnam, ending a peculiarly brutal war and initiating a period of unbelievable cruelty. Between 1970 and 1972, the United States had spent more than $400 million in support of Lon Nol's government and army. Heavy bombing continued until Congress legislated its end in August 1973. In six months of 1973, the bombing exceeded 250,000 tons, more than was dropped on Japan in all of World War II. Lon Nol's government and army were ineffectual even by South Vietnamese standards, however, and with extensive support from North Vietnam and China, the Khmer Rouge pressed on toward Phnom Penh, using human-wave assaults in some areas. The government collapsed in mid-April. The Khmer Rouge took over the capital on April 17. Thousands of lives were lost in the war; more than two million people were left refugees. The country as a whole faced starvation for the first time in its history. Upon taking over, the Khmer Rouge imposed a gruesome totalitarianism and began the forced relocation of much of the population.

The end in Laos was only slightly less convulsive. The Laotian settlement of 1962 had been a dead letter from the start. A flimsy coalition government nominally upheld a precarious neutrality, while outsiders waged war up and down the land. The North Vietnamese used Laotian territory for their infiltration route into South Vietnam and supported the insurgent Pathet Lao with supplies and as many as 20,000 "volunteers." While backing the neutralist government, the United States waged a secret war against North Vietnamese positions in Laos from 1962 to 1972. When the bombing of North Vietnam was stopped at the end of 1968, Laos became the primary target. By 1973 the United States had dropped more than two million tons of bombs there, leaving many areas resembling a desert. The CIA sponsored an army of Hmong tribes people, led by Gen. Vang Pao, that waged guerrilla warfare against the Ho Chi Minh Trail in Laos at a huge cost: More than 17,000 soldiers and 50,000 civilians had been killed by 1975. The U.S. withdrawal from South Vietnam left the government without any chance of survival. An agreement of February 1973 created a coalition government in which the Pathet Lao held the upper hand. With the fall of Cambodia and South Vietnam, the Pathet Lao took over, making no effort to hide its subservience to North Vietnam. In one of the great human tragedies of the Indochina wars, America's loyal allies, the Hmong, were the victims of Pathet Lao genocide. Roughly 100,000, including the legendary Vang Pao, escaped. Another 100,000 were killed in a systematic campaign of extermination that employed bombing, artillery, and possibly chemical-biological weapons. Thousands more suffered in what the Pathet Lao euphemistically called "seminar camps."[27]

[27]Jane Hamilton-Merritt, *Tragic Mountains: The Hmong, the Americans, and the Secret Wars for Laos, 1942–1962* (Bloomington, Ind., 1993), pp. 337–410.

The impact on world politics of America's failure in Vietnam was considerably less than U.S. policymakers had predicted. From Thailand to the Philippines, there was obvious nervousness, even demands for the removal of U.S. bases. Outside Indochina, however, the dominoes did not fall. On the contrary, in the years after the end of the war, the non-Communist nations of Southeast Asia prospered and attained an unprecedented level of stability. The Soviet Union continued to build up its military arsenal in the 1970s. Spurred by a hubris deriving from American failure, it intervened in civil wars in Angola, Zaire, and Ethiopia. As with the United States, however, the Soviets' reach soon exceeded their grasp, luring them into their own quagmire in Afghanistan, a "bleeding wound" that reformist Soviet premier Mikhail Gorbachev bound up in the late 1980s only at great cost.

One of the most significant and ironic effects of the end of the Vietnam War was to heighten tensions among the various Communist nations of East Asia. The brutal Pol Pot regime launched a grisly effort to rebuild Cambodia from the "Year Zero," killing millions of its own people in the process. More important from the Vietnamese standpoint, Cambodia established close ties with China. In response to Khmer Rouge cross-border raids and to preserve a "friendly" government next door, Vietnam invaded Cambodia in 1978, drove out Pol Pot, and established a puppet regime. China retaliated by invading Vietnam, provoking a short and inconclusive war. The United States, which had gone to war in Vietnam in 1965 to contain China, found itself in the ironic and morally dubious position in the mid-1980s of indirectly supporting China's efforts to contain Vietnam and sending "humanitarian" aid to an unlikely assortment of Cambodian bedfellows, including the notorious Pol Pot.

THE WAGES OF VICTORY

In Vietnam itself, the principal legacy of the war was continued human suffering. The ultimate losers, of course, were the South Vietnamese. The bloodbath predicted by some Americans did not occur, but many of those South Vietnamese who remained in Vietnam endured poverty, oppression, and forced labor. As many as 400,000 suffered the horror of "reeducation" camps, some for as long as ten years.

An estimated 1.5 million so-called boat people fled southern Vietnam in several waves between 1975 and 1989. Some perished at

Boat People
Between 1975 and 1989, as many as 1.5 million so-called "boat people" fled South Vietnam, many in small boats, in search of refuge abroad. Around one million settled in the United States. In this 1984 image, 35 refugees huddled in a small fishing boat 350 miles northeast of Cam Ranh Bay await rescue by a U.S. Navy ship after more than five weeks at sea. Many boat people did not survive the perils of escape. Some remained scattered in refugee camps throughout Southeast Asia.
Phil Eggman/Department of Defense

sea in leaky boats or at the hands of pirates; others languished in squalid refugees camps scattered across Southeast Asia. Around one million eventually settled in the United States. Many left family behind. Most had to sacrifice their wealth and all their possessions to escape. Because of the language barrier even those who had held high positions in South Vietnam had to start over in their adopted country. Arriving in the United States at a time of acute economic stress, the Vietnamese often met hostility provoked by racial

356 CHAPTER 8: The Postwar War and the Legacies of Vietnam

antagonism, nativist sentiments, and fear for the loss of jobs. For some Americans, the new arrivals provided a reminder of a painful defeat. Like other immigrant groups, the Vietnamese faced problems of adaptation to a radically different culture. Members of the South Vietnamese armed forces may have had the greatest difficulty unburdening themselves of the past. Profound tensions often developed between Vietnamese parents clinging to traditional ways and their American-born children. Some Vietnamese Americans remained unassimilated and lived near or below the poverty line. Many enjoyed remarkable success, causing Vietnamese Americans as a group to be viewed as a "model minority." In time, they began to return to their home country for visits and contributed to its economic development.[28]

In one of the most cruel ironies of a war that had more than its share of irony, the NLF, or at least most of its members, lost the war as well even though they had initiated the revolution in the late 1950s and had played a key role in the victory. In July 1976, Hanoi proclaimed the birth of the Socialist Republic of Vietnam (SRV), reunifying the country under the tight control of the Communist party. It disbanded the front organizations—including the NLF—that had been formed to fight the Saigon regime and the United States. Non-communists in the PRG were quickly purged. Some endured persecution; others, in time, fled. Some of the southerners who had led the struggle and had suffered heavily in the process were considered a threat and were kept under surveillance or even sent to reeducation camps. The NLF army was merged with the NVA in such a way that its separate identity was destroyed. Northerners came south and ran local and regional governments. To affirm its legitimacy, the new regime soon openly boasted of what it had repeatedly denied during the war—its instrumental role in creating and running the southern insurgency.[29]

Even for the ostensible winners, victory was a bittersweet prize. In the aftermath of war, the regime went to great lengths to root out bourgeois attitudes, revamping the education system along Communist lines, banning some forms of popular music, and confiscating the property of some rich people. But unification was difficult to achieve.

[28]Arnold R. Isaacs, *Vietnam Shadows: The War, Its Ghosts, and Its Legacy* (Baltimore, Md., 1997), pp. 148–161; Robert D. Schulzinger, *A Time for Peace: The Legacy of the Vietnam War* (New York, 2006), pp. 111–128.
[29]Mark Philip Bradley, *Vietnam at War* (2009), pp. 174–176.

Historic differences between north and south had been accentuated during three decades of war, and it proved impossible to force the freewheeling and resilient south into a made-in-Hanoi mold. Just as it resisted American direction in the 1960s, southern Vietnam continued to resist outside influence, complicating the task of consolidation. By the 1980s, there were even signs that, in the classic tradition of the East, the ways of the conquered had rubbed off on the conqueror. The corruption and consumer culture that epitomized Saigon during the American war carried over to the postwar Ho Chi Minh City, where the black market continued to flourish and bribery was necessary to accomplish anything.

The Hanoi regime achieved its goal of hegemony in Indochina, but only temporarily and at a cost it could not afford. In time, it became bogged down in its own quagmire in Cambodia, where, again ironically, for a decade it waged a costly and generally ineffectual counterinsurgency war against stubborn Cambodian guerrillas. The Vietnamese in 1991 happily accepted a United Nations–sponsored agreement that provided for their withdrawal from Cambodia and for the holding of elections to form a coalition government. Vietnam's occupation of Cambodia further strained already bad relations with China, the United States, and other nations of Southeast Asia, leaving it diplomatically isolated and entirely dependent on the Soviet Union.

For all Vietnamese, the most pressing and enduring legacy of the war has been economic deprivation. Thirty years of conflict, especially the destruction visited on north and south during the American war, left the entire nation a shambles. The situation was made much worse by continued high military expenditures and by a punitive U.S. embargo on trade with Vietnam. In 1978, the regime mounted an ill-conceived effort to impose communism, force industrialism, and collectivize agriculture. It banned private trade, drove out leading merchants (many of them Chinese, who took at least some of their wealth with them), and relocated people into collective zones. The results were disastrous. In the immediate postwar years, economic growth lagged at the paltry rate of 2 percent; per capita income averaged around $100. "Waging a war is easy," veteran revolutionary and premier Pham Van Dong lamented, "but running a country is difficult."[30]

---

[30]Quoted in Stanley Karnow, *Vietnam: A History* (New York, 1983), p. 9.

Responding to necessity and emulating Gorbachev's *perestroika* ("reconstruction"), in the mid-1980s a more pragmatic and reformist regime dominated by southerners launched a program of *doi moi,* ("renovation"). The new leadership hoped to stimulate growth by freeing up the economy, providing some capitalist incentives, and seeking foreign investment. Hanoi even attempted to promote economic development through tourism. Vietnamese leaders still claimed to be pursuing socialism, but they talked more and more like capitalists, proclaiming the goal of a prosperous country in which people could be rich.

Doi moi brought modest gains. Agriculture flourished under the new system, and by the end of the century Vietnam was the world's second largest exporter of rice. The parallel, or unofficial, economy also prospered for a time, especially in the cities, where there were signs of an incipient boom. Foreign investment jumped, making up for the termination of external assistance after the collapse of the Soviet Union in 1991, and the growth rate increased to around 7 percent. There were significant increases in the production of consumer goods and foreign trade.

Huge problems persisted. Despite the "tiny economic miracle" of the mid-1990s, Vietnam remained one of the world's poorest countries. The infrastructure was in horrible shape, and the economy suffered from ineffective management and a lack of capital and technology. Per capita income rose only to $376 by the end of the century; there was high unemployment. The growth rate lagged, and foreign investment declined. Although Vietnam was rich in natural resources and blessed with a high literacy rate and a people with a strong work ethic, its economic potential was nevertheless limited by rising overpopulation, a shortage of skilled labor, inadequate public services, an omnipresent and creaking government bureaucracy, and corruption reportedly as pervasive as that in South Vietnam at the end of the war.[31]

The problems at century's end raised serious doubts about the future of what was called "market Leninism." Whether real economic growth could be achieved in an oppressive political climate remained open to question. Intent on insulating itself from the changes that had destroyed communism in the Soviet Union and

---

[31]Andrew Pierre, "Vietnam's Contradictions," *Foreign Affairs,* (November/December 2000): 69–86.

Eastern Europe, the regime staunchly refused to couple economic reform with political freedom and continued to infringe on basic rights. Traditional fears of interaction with foreigners reinforced instinctive suspicions of globalization. An aging party leadership continued to stake its legitimacy on its "revolutionary heroism" in defeating the French and Americans. But its appeals increasingly fell on the deaf ears of a population 85 percent of which was younger than forty years of age and many of whom saw the old enemy, the United States, as the model of modernity. In addition, many Vietnamese, including war veterans, were increasingly disillusioned that the sacrifices made during the war had not brought rewards in terms of a better life.[32] For the nation as a whole, the promises of victory in 1975 had not been realized.

THE AGONY OF DEFEAT

For America's allies, the war had consequences that exceeded the size of their contribution. In Australia, participation in Vietnam led to sharp internal divisions and conflict. Failure to recognize the contribution of those who served left a legacy of bitterness among veterans. In New Zealand, despite the small size of the commitment, the war aroused widespread opposition and eventually provoked a major foreign policy debate that raised searching questions about the nation's role in the world and especially its relations with the United States. For South Korea, participation in Vietnam produced enormous economic benefits, helping to stimulate its rise as a major economic power. Since the end of the war, the Korean government has remained silent about its role. Only with the emergence of democracy did Vietnam become a subject for open discussion. Long-alienated veterans who bore their anger in silence now began to speak openly of the "blood money" earned at the price of those lives that "fuelled the modernization of the country."[33]

[32]Robert K. Brigham, "Revolutionary Heroism and Politics in Postwar Vietnam," in Charles E. Neu (ed.), *After Vietnam: Legacies of a Lost War* (Baltimore, Md., 2000), pp. 85–104.
[33]Jeffrey Grey and Jeff Doyle, *Vietnam: War, Myth, and Memory* (St. Leonards, Australia., 1992), especially pp. 137–150; Roberto Rabel, "The Vietnam Decision Twenty-Five Years On," *New Zealand International Review* 15 (May/June 1990): 3–11; *New York Times*, May 10, 1992.

Although the United States emerged physically unscathed, the Vietnam War was among the most debilitating in its history. The price tag has been estimated at $167 billion, a raw statistic that does not begin to measure the full economic cost. The war triggered an inflation that helped undermine, at least temporarily, America's position in the world economy. Along with Watergate, the war also had a high political cost, increasing popular suspicion of government, leaders, and institutions. It discredited and crippled the military, at least for a time, and temporarily estranged the United States from much of the rest of the world.[34]

Much like the effect of World War I on the Europeans, the Vietnam War's greatest impact was in the realm of the spirit. Like no other event in the nation's history, it challenged Americans' traditional beliefs about themselves, the notion that in their relations with other people they have generally acted with benevolence, the idea that nothing is beyond reach. It was a fundamental part of a much larger crisis of the spirit that began in the 1960s and raised searching questions about America's history and values and marked a sort of end of American innocence.

The fall of Saigon had a profound impact. Some Americans expressed hope that the nation could finally put aside a painful episode and get on with the future. Among a people accustomed to celebrating peace with ticker tape parades, however, the end of the war left a deep residue of frustration, anger, and disillusionment. Americans generally agreed that the war had been a "dark moment" in their nation's history. Some comforted themselves with the notion that the United States should never have become involved in Vietnam in the first place. For others, particularly those who had lost loved ones, this notion was not enough. "Now it's all gone down the drain and it hurts. What did he die for?" asked a Pennsylvanian whose son had been killed in Vietnam. Many Americans expressed anger that the civilians did not permit the military to win the war. Others regarded the failure to win and to support an ally as a betrayal of American ideals and a sign of national weakness that boded poorly for the future. "It was the saddest day of my life when it sank in that we had lost the war," a Virginian lamented.[35]

---

[34]The war's legacy is analyzed in Arnold R. Isaacs, *Vietnam Shadows: The War, Its Ghosts, and Its Legacy* (Baltimore, Md., 1997); Neu, *After Vietnam;* and Schulzinger, *Time for Peace.*

[35]Jules Low, "The Mood of a Nation," Associated Press Newsfeature, May 5, 1975.

The fall of Vietnam came at the very time the nation was preparing to celebrate the bicentennial of its birth, and the irony was painfully obvious. "The high hopes and wishful idealism with which the American nation had been born had not been destroyed," *Newsweek* observed, "but they had been chastened by the failure of America to work its will in Indochina."[36]

In the immediate aftermath of the war, the nation experienced a self-conscious, collective amnesia. The angry debate over who lost Vietnam, so feared by Kennedy, Johnson, and Nixon, consisted of nothing more than a few sharp exchanges between the White House and Capitol Hill over responsibility for the April 1975 debacle. Perhaps because both parties were so deeply implicated in the war, Vietnam did not become a partisan political issue; because the memories were so painful, no one cared to dredge them up. On the contrary, many public figures called for restraint. Vietnam was all but ignored by the media. It was scarcely mentioned in the presidential campaign of 1976. "Today it is almost as though the war had never happened," the columnist Joseph C. Harsch noted in late 1975. "Americans have somehow blocked it out of their consciousness. They don't talk about it. They don't talk about its consequences."[37]

Those 2.7 million men and women who served in Vietnam were the primary victims of the nation's desire to forget. Younger on the average by seven years than their World War II counterparts, having endured a war far more complex and confusing, Vietnam veterans by the miracles of the jet age were whisked home virtually overnight to a nation hostile to the war and indifferent to their plight. Some were made to feel the guilt for the nation's moral transgressions; others, responsibility for its failure. Most simply met silence. Forced to turn inward, many veterans grew profoundly distrustful of the government that had sent them to war and deeply resentful of the nation's seeming ingratitude for their sacrifices. The great majority adjusted, although sometimes with difficulty, but many veterans experienced problems with drugs and alcohol, joblessness, and broken homes. Many also suffered from posttraumatic stress disorder, the modern term for what had earlier been called shell shock or battle fatigue. In the first years after the war, veterans

---

[36]"An Irony of History," *Newsweek,* April 28, 1975, 17.
[37]Joseph C. Harsch, "Do You Recall Vietnam—And What about the Dominoes?" *Louisville Courier-Journal,* October 2, 1975.

experienced a much higher suicide rate than the general population. The popular stereotype of the Vietnam veteran in the immediate postwar years was that of a drug-crazed, gun-toting, and violence-prone individual unable to adjust to civilized society. When in 1981 America gave a lavish welcome home to a group of hostages returned from a long and much-publicized captivity in Iran, Vietnam veterans poured out their bottled-up rage. They themselves constructed a memorial in Washington to honor the memory of the more than 58,000 comrades who died in the war.[38]

Within a short time after the end of the war, Vietnam's place in the national consciousness changed dramatically. The amnesia of the immediate postwar years proved no more than a passing phenomenon. By the mid-1980s the war was being discussed to a degree and in ways that would once have seemed impossible. Vietnam produced a large and in some cases distinguished literature, much of it the work of veterans. Hollywood had all but ignored the war while it was going on, but in its aftermath filmmakers took up the subject with a vengeance, producing works ranging from the haunting *Deer Hunter,* to the surreal and spectacular *Apocalypse Now,* to Oliver Stone's antiwar epics, to a series of trashy films in the 1980s in which American superheroes returned to Vietnam to take care of unfinished business. No television leading man was worth his salt unless he had served in Vietnam. The Vietnam veteran, sometimes branded a "baby killer" in the 1960s, became a popular culture hero in the 1980s, the sturdy and self-sufficient warrior who had prevailed despite being let down by his government and nation. Not surprisingly, the design for the memorial in Washington sparked a sometimes angry dispute among veterans and sponsors reflecting still unresolved divisions over the meaning of the war. The Vietnam Veterans Memorial Fund (VVMF) dealt with the controversy by separating the warrior from the war, by deliberately refusing to take a stand on the war while celebrating the service of those who fought it. The unveiling of the memorial on November 10, 1982, evoked an outpouring of emotion from the thousands of veterans in attendance. The stark but moving

[38]For two very different perspectives, see Christian G. Appy, *Working-Class War* (Chapel Hill, N.C., 1993) and B. G. Burkett and Glenna Whitley, *Stolen Valor* (Dallas, Tex., 1998). The story of the memorial is told in Patrick Hagopian, *The Vietnam War in American Memory* (Amherst, Mass., 2009), pp. 49–79.

V-shaped monument on Washington's Mall soon became the most-visited site in the nation's capital; for many, it was a place for healing. In 1993, a memorial was added to honor the 265,000 women who served in the military during the Vietnam War. In state capitals, courthouses, and communities across the nation, Vietnam *veterans* (as opposed to *war*) memorials were constructed to honor those who served, many of them following the VVMF precedent of neutrality on the war itself.[39]

THE SEARCH FOR LESSONS

Nowhere was the impact of Vietnam greater than on the nation's foreign policy. The war shattered the Cold War consensus that had existed since the late 1940s, leaving Americans confused and deeply divided on the goals to be pursued and the methods used. Even before it had ended, the traumatic experience of Vietnam, combined with the apparent improvement of relations with the Soviet Union and China and a growing preoccupation with domestic problems, produced a drastic reordering of national priorities. From the late 1940s to the 1960s, foreign policy had consistently headed the ranking of national concerns, but by the mid-1970s it placed well down on the list. The public was "almost oblivious to foreign problems and foreign issues," opinion analyst Burns Roper remarked in late 1975.[40]

The Vietnam experience also provoked strong opposition to military intervention abroad, even in defense of America's oldest and staunchest allies. Polls taken shortly before the fall of Saigon indicated that only 36 percent of the American people felt the United States should make and keep commitments to other nations. Only 34 percent expressed a willingness to send troops should the Russians attempt to take over West Berlin. A majority of Americans endorsed military intervention only in defense of Canada! "Vietnam has left a rancid aftertaste that clings to almost every mention of direct military intervention," the columnist David Broder observed.[41]

---

[39]Hagopian, *Vietnam War,* pp. 10, 16, 110, 399–401.
[40]Quoted in Charles W. Yost, "Why Americans Seem Disillusioned by Foreign Affairs," *Louisville Courier-Journal,* October 26, 1975.
[41]David Broder, "Isolationist Sentiment Not Blind to Reality," *Washington Post,* March 22, 1975.

The indifference and tendency toward withdrawal so manifest immediately after the war also declined sharply in the next decade. Bitter memories of Vietnam combined with the anger and frustration of the 1979 Iranian hostage crisis to produce a growing assertiveness, a highly nationalistic impulse to defend perceived interests, even a yearning to restore the United States to its old position in the world. The breakdown of détente, the steady growth of Soviet military power, and the use of that power in the Horn of Africa and Afghanistan in the late 1970s produced a profound nervousness about American security. The defense budget soared to mammoth proportions in the early 1980s. Support for military intervention in defense of traditional allies increased.[42] Under the leadership of President Ronald Reagan, the nation embarked on a new global offensive against the Soviet Union and its clients.

The new nationalism was still tempered by lingering memories of Vietnam. Many Americans remained deeply skeptical of 1960s-style globalism and dubious of such internationalist mechanisms as foreign aid or even the United Nations. Fifteen years after the end of the war, a whopping majority still believed that intervention in Vietnam had been a mistake, producing strong opposition to military intervention abroad. Thus in the aftermath of Vietnam, the public mood consisted of a strange amalgam of nostalgia and realism, assertiveness and caution.

In the very different climate of the 1980s, the debate over Vietnam that had not taken place at the war's end assumed a central place in the larger and at times quite vocal debate over U.S. foreign policy. The basic issue remained the morality and wisdom of intervention in Vietnam. Concerned that in a new and even more dangerous Cold War a resurgent militance might lead to further disastrous embroilment, liberals urgently warned of the perils of another Vietnam. Fearful, on the other hand, that what they called the "Vietnam syndrome" had sapped America's will to defend legitimate interests and stand firmly against the evil of communism, some conservatives, including most notably President Reagan, spoke out anew on what they had always believed was a fundamental reality: that, as Reagan repeatedly proclaimed, Vietnam was "in truth a noble war," a selfless attempt on the part of

---

[42]Adam Clymer, "What Americans Think Now," *New York Times Magazine*, March 31, 1985, 34.

the United States to save a free nation from outside aggression. Other conservatives conceded that the United States might have erred in getting involved in Vietnam in the first place, but they went on to insist that an important interest had been established that should have been upheld for the sake of U.S. credibility throughout the world.

The second great issue on which Americans also sharply disagreed concerned the reasons for U.S. failure in Vietnam. Unwilling to concede that success had been beyond reach, many of the leading participants in the war concluded that America's failure had been essentially instrumental, a result of the improper use of available tools. Gen. Westmoreland, Adm. U.S. Grant Sharp, and others blamed the "ill-considered" policy of "graduated response" imposed on the military by civilian leaders. Had the United States employed its military power quickly, decisively, and without limit, they argued, the war could have been won. Some conservatives indeed concluded that timid civilian leaders had prevented the military from winning the war, a view that worked its way into the popular culture. "Sir, do we get to win *this* time?" the larger than life movie hero Rambo asks upon accepting the assignment to return to Vietnam and fight the second round single-handedly.[43]

Other Americans viewed the fundamental mistake as the choice of tools rather than the way they were used and blamed an unimaginative military as much as civilians. Instead of trying to fight World War II and Korea over in Vietnam, some argued, the military should have adapted to the unconventional war in which it found itself and shaped an appropriate counterinsurgency strategy. Still other commentators, including some military theorists, agreed that military leaders were as responsible for the strategic failure as civilians. Instead of mounting costly and counterproductive search-and-destroy operations against guerrillas in South Vietnam, they insisted, the United States should have used its own forces against North Vietnamese regulars along the seventeenth parallel to isolate the battlefield in South Vietnam from the northern threat.[44]

[43]William C. Westmoreland, *A Soldier Reports* (Garden City, N.Y., 1976), p. 410; U. S. Grant Sharp, *Strategy for Defeat* (San Rafael, Calif., 1978).
[44]Comments by Robert Komer in W. Scott Thompson and Donaldson Frizzell, *The Lessons of Vietnam* (New York, 1977), p. 223; Harry G. Summers Jr., *On Strategy: The Vietnam War in Context* (Carlisle Barracks, Pa., 1981).

The lessons drawn were as divergent as the arguments advanced. In the 1980s those military leaders who believed that the United States failed because it did not act decisively formulated a set of rules for intervention (or, in most cases, nonintervention) that came to be known as the Powell Doctrine, named for Gen. Colin Powell, a veteran of two Vietnam tours who served as national security adviser under Reagan and subsequently as chairman of the Joint Chiefs of Staff under Presidents George H. W. Bush and Bill Clinton. Under this doctrine, troops would be committed abroad only as a last resort and only if it was plainly in the national interest to do so. Objectives must be clearly defined and attainable. Public support must be assured, and overwhelming force must be employed to achieve certain, swift, and complete victory.[45]

Such "lessons" depended on the belief systems of those who pronounced them, of course, and those who had opposed the war in Vietnam drew quite different conclusions. To some former doves, the fundamental lesson was never again to intervene in Vietnam-like situations in the Third World. Some commentators warned policymakers to beware the sort of simplistic reasoning that had produced such dogmas as the domino theory and the Munich analogy. Others pointed to the chronic weakness of South Vietnam and admonished that even a superpower could not save allies who were unable or unwilling to save themselves. For still others, the key lessons were that American power, however great, had distinct limits and that to be effective, U.S. foreign policy had to be true to the ideals on which the nation was founded.

From the 1970s through the turn of the century, the ghost of Vietnam hovered over often bitter debates about the use of American military power abroad. Popular fears of a Vietnam-like quagmire in Central America sharply limited the Reagan administration's efforts to aid the government of El Salvador in suppressing a leftist insurgency as well as its support for a right-wing insurgency seeking to overthrow the leftist Sandinista government in Nicaragua. The First Persian Gulf War of 1991 seemed at times as much about Vietnam as about Iraqi dictator Saddam Hussein's conquest of neighboring Kuwait. Opponents of intervening to liberate Kuwait warned ominously that "Iraq is Arabic for Vietnam" and

---

[45]George C. Herring, "Preparing *Not* to Refight the Last War: The Impact of the Vietnam War on the U.S. Military," in Neu, *After Vietnam*, pp. 72–75.

predicted a quagmire in the desert. President George H. W. Bush countered that his war "would not be another Vietnam." He and his military advisers, most of whom had served in Vietnam, conducted the war largely on the basis of the Powell Doctrine, employing maximum military force to attain the quickest possible victory. When the United States and its allies thrashed Iraq and freed Kuwait in a stunningly decisive one-hundred-day war, Bush exulted, "By God, we've kicked the Vietnam syndrome once and for all."[46]

Bush's eulogy turned out to be premature. The Gulf War helped restore confidence in the nation's military institutions. Americans celebrated victory with the parades that had been so conspicuously absent after Vietnam. But these dramatic events did not expunge still painful memories of an earlier war. And when eighteen GIs were killed in bloody fighting in the streets of Mogadishu, Somalia, in October 1993, Vietnam rose up again like a storm cloud. Diplomat Richard Holbrooke called it a "Vietmalia" syndrome. President Bill Clinton immediately ceased military action in Somalia and withdrew all U.S. troops within six months. He tread carefully during the remainder of his two terms in office. Despite passionate calls for humanitarian intervention to stop brutal fighting and ethnic cleansing in the former Yugoslavia, he would do no more than send air units to Bosnia and then help broker a fragile peace. To his later regret, he refused even to consider intervention to halt horrific atrocities in Rwanda, where as many as 800,000 may have died. When he finally intervened in Kosovo in the spring of 1999 to stop Serb atrocities against Kosovars, he did so only with airpower and made clear at the outset that ground forces would not be used.[47]

Terrorist attacks on New York's World Trade Center and the Pentagon in Washington on September 11, 2001, appeared to mark the end of the Vietnam era in U.S. history. Masterminded by Osama bin Laden's al Qaeda organization, the attacks caused massive destruction and took close to 3,000 lives. Much of the intellectual and emotional baggage from Vietnam seemed swept away in a

[46]George C. Herring, "Refighting the Last War: The Persian Gulf and the 'Vietnam Syndrome,'" *New Zealand International Review* 16 (September/October 1991): 15–19.
[47]George C. Herring, "Analogies at War," in Albrecht Schnabel and Ramesh Thakur, eds., *Kosovo and the Challenge of Humanitarian Intervention* (Tokyo, 2000), pp. 347–359.

surge of grief, anger, and fear. In the anxious days after 9/11, Vietnam was conspicuous by its absence from the national discourse. Speaking with a single voice for one of the few times since the 1964 Tonkin Gulf Resolution, Congress granted President George W. Bush blank check authority to use American military forces in a new global war against international terrorism. "America is at the moment a weird inside-out image of the Vietnam era," one journalist observed.[48]

The U.S. attack on al Qaeda and the Taliban government that hosted it in Afghanistan in October 2001 seemed to sound the death knell for the Vietnam syndrome. Like Vietnam, Afghanistan had a long history of humiliating those great powers foolish enough to get involved there, most recently, of course, the Soviet Union. But U.S. actions appeared to confound historical precedents. Working with Afghan allies and employing incredibly sophisticated new high-tech weapons, the United States put the Taliban to rout and drove al Qaeda and bin Laden into the mountains. The Vietnam syndrome appeared a relic of history. A second war with Iraq in early 2003 seemed to confirm that U.S. military power had achieved an unprecedented level of invincibility. Iraqi resistance crumbled in the face of a full-fledged U.S. invasion; the capital, Baghdad, fell without real resistance; and a statue of Saddam Hussein was ceremoniously pulled down.

Once again, epitaphs for the Vietnam syndrome proved premature. After the easy *military* success of 2003, a woefully unprepared and undermanned U.S. invading force confronted the daunting and often deadly *politico-military* task of rebuilding a shattered nation and uniting a divided people. Iraqis did not welcome the Americans as "liberators," as U.S. policymakers had confidently predicted. Guerrilla-like resistance rose immediately and spread as the occupation floundered. American casualties in the "postwar" period quickly exceeded those in the invasion. By June 2003, the United States faced a full-fledged insurgency. Despite the best efforts of top Bush administration officials to suppress it, the word *quagmire* again became a part of the political vocabulary. The war dragged into Bush's second term, and the public soured on it more quickly than they had on Vietnam. The Vietnam analogy was cited more and more frequently in discussions about Iraq.

[48]Maureen Dowd, *New York Times,* September 16, 2001.

THE UNENDING WAR

One reason the impact of the Vietnam War lasted so long was that its end in 1975 did not bring peace between the United States and Vietnam. Frustrated and indeed humiliated by a small nation, the world's greatest power was in no mood for conciliation. In sharp contrast to its generous handling of Germany and Japan after World War II, the United States treated the victorious Vietnam as a defeated foe. It extended to all of Vietnam the wartime embargo imposed on North Vietnam, refused to pay the "reparations" promised by the Nixon administration in the 1973 peace settlement, demanded a full accounting of U.S. troops missing in action (MIA), and vetoed Hanoi's application for admission to the United Nations. Kissinger, the architect of America's first "normalization" strategy, insisted that Vietnam's worsening relations with China and growing dependence on the Soviet Union would force it to comply with U.S. demands. If Washington "played it cool," the "logic of events" would force Vietnam to accept U.S. terms.[49]

A serious effort at accommodation during the administration of Jimmy Carter ran afoul of the reparations issue. As part of an ambitious larger strategy of winding down the Cold War, Carter hoped to reconcile with Vietnam. His administration ceased opposing its entry into the UN, reduced travel restrictions on Vietnamese, and permitted nongovernmental organizations in the United States to send aid to Vietnam. It asked only for the most complete accounting of U.S. MIAs possible. Badly misreading apparent American generosity, the Vietnamese stuck to their position on reparations. Aware that he could never get congressional approval, Carter publicly stated that the United States owed Vietnam nothing. Hanoi reacted angrily and in the naive belief that antiwar forces in the United States would compel Washington to accede.

Normalization was also the victim of a resurgent Cold War. As the United States moved back toward confrontation with the Soviet Union and toward détente with China in the late 1970s, Vietnam turned in the opposite direction, invading Cambodia in 1978, signing a treaty with the USSR, and going to war with China. The Cold War reescalated after the Soviet invasion of Afghanistan in 1979, which ended any immediate prospect for normalization.

[49]Memorandum of Kissinger conversations with Montgomery Committee, November 14, 1975, and March 12, 1976, Kissinger/Scowcroft File, Box A1.

While normalization languished in the 1980s, the POW/MIA issue took on the power and mystique of a religion. In fact, the actual number of MIAs and the percentage of MIAs to casualties were far lower in the Vietnam War than in previous American wars. Most MIAs were air personnel who disappeared under circumstances that made their survival and the subsequent location of their remains difficult if not impossible. Each year in the rugged terrain of Indochina, it became harder to find and identify remains. The linkage of MIAs to POWs muddled an already complicated issue, suggesting that any of the missing might be prisoners. Roughly one-half of the more than 2,000 service personnel listed as POW/MIA were known to have been killed in circumstances where the body could not be recovered. Between 1975 and 1993 various congressional and executive groups studied the issue intensively and produced not a shred of evidence that a single American was being held captive in Vietnam. For the United States to demand a full accounting for MIAs from an enemy—especially a victorious enemy with whom it was still technically at war—was quite without precedent in the history of warfare.

Still, the issue would not go away. The Nixon administration had originally raised it as a means of rallying public support behind an increasingly unpopular war. In doing so, it created a monster that would turn on the government with a vengeance. Spurred by recurrent reports of sightings of live Americans behind the "bamboo curtain," the increasingly powerful POW/MIA lobby kept up a drumfire of criticism of Hanoi—and Washington. The potent National League of Families of American Prisoners and Missing in Southeast Asia created before the end of the war a stark black-and-white POW/MIA flag with the inscription "You Are Not Forgotten," which in time flew above the White House, in the Capitol Rotunda, and over state office buildings, the only flag of a political lobby group to be so honored. Sensationalist films such as *Rambo: First Blood, Part 2* and *Missing in Action* boosted popular acceptance of the myth. American suspicions were also played on, a Senate committee concluded in 1993, by "charlatans and opportunists" who built a "cottage industry out of the despair of bereaved families." Hanoi did its part by periodically doling out remains when it was expedient to do so. As late as 1993, 57 percent of those Americans polled believed that service personnel were alive and being held captive in Indochina. The myth of abandoned prisoners of war held captive by Indochinese Communists and rescued by American superheroes served urgent postwar needs for redemption, vindication, and reempowerment. It was as though Americans believed that something of themselves had been lost in the war and needed to be rescued. The myth was also used to demonize the Vietnamese.[50] It became a major obstacle to closure at home and normalization of relations with Vietnam.

Ronald Reagan brought to the MIA cause his unique brand of sentimental patriotism. He viewed resolution of the issue as a way to erase the nation's "crippling memory" of Vietnam. Responding to the surge of public interest, he assigned it the "highest national priority" and reasserted the demand for a *full* accounting. He even approved covert operations launched into Laos by private citizens and soldiers of fortune of dubious reputation searching for Americans held captive. As with the Cold War, Reagan the ideologue gave way, in time, to Reagan the pragmatist. His administration grew increasingly skeptical of the MIA lobby's claims and numbers and tired of its relentless insistence that the war could not end "until all the POWs came home." The president's shift toward détente with the Soviet Union in 1985 and Vietnam's move to *doi moi* opened possibilities for resolving long-standing issues. In 1987, Reagan sent retired army general John Vessey to Vietnam as a special emissary to discuss MIAs and related issues. The following year, 130 sets of remains were returned to the United States. Instead of appeasing the MIA lobby, the increased activity fueled suspicions among some of its leaders that more Americans were being held and shifted its anger to the U.S. government and even one-time hero Reagan. In fact, the Vessey mission marked an important turning point in postwar U.S.–Vietnam relations; an issue that had been the foremost impediment to normalization actually helped get the process moving.[51]

Progress quickened under George H. W. Bush. In his inaugural address, Bush stated as the "final lesson of Vietnam" that "no great nation can long be sundered by memory." During his first years in

---

[50]Bruce Franklin, *M.I.A., or Mythmaking in America* (New Brunswick, N.J., 1993); Isaacs, *Vietnam Shadows*, pp. 128–136.

[51]Michael J. Allen, *Until the Last Man Comes Home: POWs, MIAs, and the Unending Vietnam War* (Chapel Hill, N.C., 2009), pp. 236–258; Schulzinger, *Time for Peace*, pp. 21–41.

office, he was preoccupied with the end of the Cold War and the collapse of the USSR. In this dramatically altered international context, enmity toward Vietnam seemed increasingly outdated and even irrelevant. Leaders of both political parties agreed that it was time to move on. In 1991, the administration laid out a "road map" for normalization: When Vietnam withdrew from Cambodia, granted access to its archives dealing with MIA matters, and agreed to the establishment of an MIA office in Hanoi, the United States would end its trade embargo. As MIA issues were resolved, the two nations could proceed toward diplomatic relations. Perhaps never in the history of warfare had a loser imposed such harsh "peace terms" on the ostensible winner. The Vietnamese naturally resented the tone of the road map. But with the fall of the Soviet Union they lost their patron and they welcomed the U.S. promise of normalization. They agreed to the demands, even—remarkably—access to their archives, a step Bush hailed as a "real breakthrough" in writing the "last chapter of the history of the war." The United States in turn provided $1.3 million to help Vietnamese disabled by the war, lifted its ban on U.S. citizens' travel to Vietnam, permitted American businesses to negotiate contracts with the SRV, and allowed Vietnamese Americans to wire money to relatives in Vietnam. The two nations seemed on the verge of normalization when Bush's campaign for reelection stymied further progress.[52]

NORMALIZATION TO RAPPROCHEMENT

By the mid-1990s, conditions were ripe for normalization. Vietnam had met most of the requirements of the road map. Years of investigation, most notably by a Senate Select Committee led by Vietnam veterans John McCain (Republican and former POW) and John Kerry (Democrat and former Vietnam Veterans against the War protestor) produced no evidence that Americans were being held captive. U.S. teams assisted by Vietnamese workers dug up the countryside, interviewed villagers, and even researched Vietnam's archives in a new and grisly form of body counting. Public opinion polls indicated firm American support, if not enthusiasm, for normalization. The main effect of the continuing embargo was to

---

[52] Allen, *Last Man Comes Home,* pp. 261–276; Schulzinger, *Time for Peace,* pp. 43–50.

deny U.S. merchants access to the burgeoning Vietnamese market. American businesses increasingly lobbied for termination of the embargo.

Having publicly protested the war as a college student, Democratic President Bill Clinton moved warily. In July 1993, his administration stopped blocking international loans to Vietnam and placed diplomats in Hanoi to help Americans seeking information about missing servicemen. In early 1994, it removed the embargo. Later in the year, Vietnam returned to the United States the once proud, now crumbling, bastion that had been the U.S. embassy in South Vietnam, at one time a symbol of its powerful presence—and its humiliating departure. In July 1995, Clinton announced the establishment of full diplomatic relations. In an especially inspired choice, he named the first U.S. ambassador Douglas as "Pete" Peterson, a former Navy pilot and POW, whose first stay in Vietnam had been at the notorious prison dubbed the Hanoi Hilton. Peterson proved a highly effective agent of reconciliation.

Normalization produced limited immediate results. U.S. firms such as Pepsico, Nike, and United Airlines moved quickly into Vietnam. Nike became its largest foreign employer. But by the end of the decade, the United States was only eighth among foreign investors in Vietnam. The two nations did not conclude a trade treaty until 1999. Vietnam's lack of most-favored-nation status limited the amount it could sell to the United States and, along with its low per capita income, restricted what it could purchase.

Clinton's visit to Vietnam in November 2000 marked a major step forward. The president drew huge and enthusiastic crowds. He did not apologize for the war, as some Americans had urged, but he did highlight the theme that Vietnam was a country not a war, something many Americans never quite grasped. He visited an MIA excavation site, where he also expressed concern for the estimated 300,000 Vietnamese still missing. His stay in Vietnam also exposed the still sizable divide between the two nations. Vietnamese leaders insisted that the United States assume greater responsibility for the massive damage caused by its widespread use of dioxins and by unexploded bombs, mines, and shells. When Clinton chided the SRV for its human rights record and urged greater personal freedoms and opening up to globalization, Vietnamese leaders charged that an unrepentant and still imperialist America was still trying to impose its will on a sovereign nation.

During the first decade of the new century, economic ties expanded dramatically. The two nations concluded a bilateral trade agreement. In 2007, with full U.S. support, Vietnam joined the World Trade Organization and Congress agreed to full normal trade relations. The United States soon became Vietnam's largest market, in 2009 taking in about 20 percent of that nation's exports. Two years later, trade totaled $1.76 billion, a tenfold increase since 2001, with the balance heavily in favor of Vietnam. Trade representatives met frequently to discuss areas of contention such as American charges that Vietnam was not protecting intellectual property rights and was dumping catfish and clothing products on the U.S. market at lower prices than domestic and foreign competitors. The United States also became a major investor in Vietnam. Since 2000, that nation has become one of the largest recipients of U.S. foreign assistance, much of it going to AIDS/HIV prevention and treatment, deactivating unexploded mines, and education.

"Legacy issues" left over from the war continued to divide the two nations. Vietnam's quite extraordinary assistance in helping locate the remains of American MIAs (usually in return for substantial economic assistance) provoked some of its own people to complain that thousands of their sons were also missing "and you are looking for Americans."[53] Through technology and searches in its records, the United States has begun to help in finding Vietnamese missing in action. For years, the Vietnamese have pressed the United States to accept responsibility for and assist in cleaning up the deadly mess left from the estimated 20 million gallons of herbicides sprayed across roughly 10 percent of the South Vietnamese countryside and in treating the millions of Vietnamese victims of American dioxins. For liability reasons, the United States has refused to accept responsibility. Since 2007, it has provided substantial funds for dioxin removal and health care for victims. In 2012, fifty years after the start of Operation RANCHHAND, the United States committed itself to remove dioxin from the site of its former air base in Da Nang, an arduous, $43-million project expected to take four years. Some Vietnamese noted a big step; others complained it was too little, too late.[54]

[53]Caroline Alexander, "Across the River Styx," *New Yorker,* October 25, 2004: 44–54.
[54]*New York Times,* October 12, 2012.

Human rights issues loom large. Vietnam has changed significantly since *doi moi*. Individuals can engage in private enterprise. Vietnamese enjoy limited freedom of worship; church membership has increased. To promote tourism, the government even approved the construction of a decidedly bourgeois string of golf courses running north to south and called the Ho Chi Minh Golf Trail. To the consternation of some Americans, Vietnam remains a one-party authoritarian state. The party's strategy has been to permit some freedoms, but to crack down hard on any dissent that threatens its power. It has specifically targeted minority groups in the Central Highlands and the northwest mountain regions. Press freedoms have been restricted, and bloggers shut down. The roughly two million Vietnamese in the United States, some of them prosperous and many of them critical of the Hanoi government, have lobbied Washington to press the Vietnamese government for additional political and religious reforms. Some Americans have sought to use trade to leverage change in Vietnam. Congress and human rights groups regularly introduce legislation to punish the SRV for political repression.

In the world of diplomacy, enemies can quickly become friends, friends enemies. In the second decade of the twenty-first century, two once-implacable enemies have taken quite extraordinary steps toward a rapprochement through growing collaboration on security and military issues. The major catalyst has been the looming presence of Asia's economic giant and rising military power, China.

Vietnam's current policies mirror its historical love–hate relationship with its larger northern neighbor. It has patterned its economic reforms on those of Beijing. China is its largest trading partner. But the two countries also clash over numerous issues. Vietnam has protested China's plans to build enormous hydroelectric dams on the Upper Mekong River, a waterway vital to its economy and ecology. It fears rising Chinese influence in Laos, traditionally part of its area of influence. The most heated clashes have come over the South China Sea and its numerous islands, vital shipping lanes, and natural resources. China's claims to "indisputable sovereignty" over the entire region threaten interests Vietnam considers vital. The two nations, along with others, have asserted conflicting claims to the many islands. China has seized Vietnamese fishing boats. Although it is careful not to provoke China, Vietnam sees strategic value in a larger U.S. presence in Southeast Asia and closer ties with its former enemy.

The United States, too, has substantial trade with China, and China holds much of its soaring national debt. As a Pacific power, the United States is also uneasy about China's assertive claims and its bullying of smaller Southeast Asian nations. Some U.S. military strategists, indeed, warn of the dangers of China's growing military and especially naval power. Entangled in wars in Iraq and Afghanistan since the start of the century, the U.S. presence has diminished in areas it once dominated. In a major policy shift, President Barack Obama announced in 2010 a U.S. "pivot" back toward an area likely to be the center of world commerce in coming years. While claiming neutrality in the conflicts that roil the South China Sea, the United States has firmly defended freedom of navigation. Its position on the island disputes has been closer to that of the small nations of the region than to that of China.

U.S.–Vietnam relations have thus warmed in recent years. Hanoi speaks of a "multidirection approach" in its foreign relations. As part of its pivot, the United States has upgraded its defense ties with numerous Asia/Pacific nations including Vietnam. U.S. Navy ships regularly visit Vietnamese ports. The two navies have participated in joint nonmilitary activities. Officers from each country have exchanged visits to Hanoi and Honolulu. In 2011, the two nations signed their first defense pact, an arrangement dealing with military medicine. They have discussed forming a "strategic partnership," a somewhat vague and apparently flexible status that would allow increased cooperation without the obligations of an alliance. The slow and incremental growth of cooperation has been joined by an increase in visits by high-level officials and fulsome rhetoric about mutual friendship and cooperation. In an event rich with symbolism, in the summer of 2012 U.S. Secretary of Defense Leon Panetta visited Cam Ranh Bay, once the site of one of America's largest military bases in South Vietnam. Just as concern about China had drawn the two nations together, the importance of each nation's ties with China would appear to impose limits on how far their rapprochement can go. Both nations have been careful to stress that their budding friendship is not aimed at China. Still, the improvement of U.S.–Vietnam relations since 2010, after more than a half century of conflict, has been one of the more fascinating, if little noticed, developments in an ever-changing world.[55]

[55]James Bellacqua, "The China Factor in U.S.–Vietnam Relations," *CNA China Studies*, March 12, 2012.

A WAR THAT NEVER SEEMS TO GO AWAY

The budding accommodation between the United States and Vietnam seems unlikely to fundamentally influence this nation's continuing efforts to come to terms with one of the most divisive events in its history (most Americans are probably not even aware that relations have improved). Nearly forty years after the fall of Saigon, the war seems finally to be receding into history. It is rarely a topic of discussion and debate. It does not lurk just below the surface of popular consciousness as it did even through the 1990s. Much of the anger and bitterness have subsided. Some former hawks and doves have softened their positions. Obviously, those millions of Americans born after the mid-1960s, have no memories of it at all. Following the example of those people who established the Vietnam Veterans Memorial, the nation seems to have forged a

U.S.–Vietnam Rapprochement
U.S. Secretary of Defense Leon Panetta is shown here shaking hands with Vietnamese military officers upon departing the country after an extended summer 2012 visit. During his trip, Panetta went to Cam Ranh Bay, once an enormous U.S. military base in South Vietnam, and discussed military cooperation with various Vietnamese officials, signaling the budding rapprochement between the two former enemies.
© Jim Watson, Pool/AP Images

tenuous consensus "that the war was a tragic mistake and that . . . those who fought and died in Vietnam were brave young men who deserve this country's respect and gratitude."[56]

Still, for the Vietnam generation, the generation that fought and protested the war and still holds positions of power in government, business, and the media, that conflict continues to resonate. Most of the major issues remain unresolved; some remain unaddressed. Was it a good war or a bad war; a noble cause or essentially immoral? Was it necessary in terms of the national security or basically needless and senseless? Was it a good war waged poorly? Was it a war that could and indeed should have been won, a war lost only by the timidity of our political leaders? Or was it a war that could not have been won at a price in blood and treasure we were willing to pay? The nation was divided on these issues during the war, divided when it ended, and to a large extent, it remains divided today. The healing that has taken place is notably ethnocentric. It has given little attention to allies and enemies. It has evinced scant concern for the enormous human losses of North and South Vietnam and the damage inflicted on the landscape of that country. Moral issues concerning U.S. intervention and the way the war was fought have been swept under the rug.

Americans continue to probe the Vietnam experience for "lessons" to guide major foreign policy decisions. Even after the George W. Bush administration salvaged a tenuous stability from the debacle in Iraq, permitting Bush's successor, Barack Obama, to withdraw U.S. forces, memories of the frustration and losses suffered there appeared to reinforce the still potent Vietnam syndrome. Obama was too young to have been directly affected by Vietnam. Like George H. W. Bush, he hoped to bury its memories. But his senior military and civilian advisers were very much influenced by it. During a summer 2009 review of policy to combat a worsening situation in Afghanistan, in the words of a participant, "Vietnam walked the halls of the White House." Those strategists who pressed for a full-scale counterinsurgency effort drew from Vietnam instruction and even—surprisingly—encouragement that such an approach would work in a land as complex as Vietnam and even more inhospitable

---

[56]David W. Levy, "Closure: How the National Discussion of Vietnam Will Eventually Be Resolved," *Long-Term View* 5 (Summer 2000): 144–148; Hagopian, *Vietnam War in American Memory,* pp. 10, 16, 91–91, 110.

to foreign intrusion. In an off-the-record White House dinner, a group of historians warned Obama that Afghanistan could be for him what Vietnam was for LBJ. The president and his civilian advisers leaned heavily on Gordon Goldstein's *Lessons in Disaster*, a highly critical analysis of Vietnam decision making under Kennedy and Johnson. In a December 2009 speech at West Point announcing a major escalation of U.S. involvement in Afghanistan, Obama emphatically affirmed that comparisons of Vietnam to Afghanistan were based on a "false reading of history."[57] The subsequent failure of American escalation to achieve decisive results, combined with its enormous expense and mounting war-weariness at home, produced, borrowing from Richard Holbrooke, a "Vietiraqistan" syndrome in the form of strong popular and elite skepticism about further military intervention abroad.

Obama was right, no two historical situations are identical, and it is perilous to draw lessons from one to apply to another. Still, much can and should be learned from the American experience in Vietnam: the difficulties of intervening in a foreign civil war; the pitfalls of incrementalism; the folly of underestimating an enemy; the importance of understanding the kind of war that is being fought; the dubious morality, however noble a nation's intentions, of seeking to determine another people's destiny and of making commitments that may not be sustainable; the limits of public tolerance for questionable uses of military power abroad; a long list of dos and don'ts in the raising and handling of military forces.

Although it does not permit precise "lessons," the Vietnam War also yields cautionary principles that must be kept in mind as the United States faces a new and uncertain era. First is the centrality of local forces in international crisis situations. That the containment policy was misapplied in Vietnam seems beyond question. The United States intervened to block the apparent march of a Soviet-directed Communism across Asia, escalated its commitment to halt a presumably expansionist Communist China, and eventually made Vietnam a test case of its determination to uphold world order. By wrongly attributing the conflict to external sources, it drastically misjudged the internal dynamics. By intervening in what was at root a local struggle, it placed itself at the mercy of local forces: a

[57]Marvin Kalb and Deborah Kalb, *Haunting Legacy: Vietnam and the American Presidency from Ford to Obama* (New York, 2011), pp. 241, 271, 278, 283.

weak client and a determined and resilient adversary. What might have remained a local conflict with primarily local implications was elevated into a major international conflict with enormous human costs that are still being paid by Vietnamese and Americans today. Obviously, local forces will vary from one situation to another, but they will usually shape the contours and dictate the outcome of historical events. We ignore them at our peril!

Second is the limits of power. The task the United States took upon itself in Vietnam ultimately proved beyond its ability to achieve, a concept difficult for Americans to grasp. This nation has enjoyed an unparalleled record of success throughout its history, so much so that it has come to take success for granted. Failure comes hard, and the wages of interventionism must be relearned by each generation. Interventions will inevitably ensnare us in the complex and often incomprehensible tangle of local politics. They do not lend themselves to the quick fixes we prefer. Vietnam offers no easy instruction on how to deal with such situations. But it should stand as an enduring testament to the dangers of interventionism and the limits of power.

More than any other conflict except our own Civil War, Vietnam has lingered in the American psyche. As long as the Vietnam generation is with us and we continue to face situations that look similar, it is likely to continue to influence the way we view the world. Even as we prepare to "commemorate" its fiftieth anniversary, Vietnam remains a war that never seems to go away.

PRONUNCIATION GUIDE OF VIETNAMESE WORDS

An Loc, *battle of* [ahn-lok]
Annam [ahn-nahm]
Ap Bac, *battle of* [up-bahk]
Ban Me Thuot, *battle of* [bhan-may-twoot]
Bao Dai [bow-dye]
Bay Vien [bay-vyen]
Ben Tre [ben-tray]
Bien Hoa, *attack on* [byen-hwah]
Binh Xuyen [bin-swyen]
Bui Diem [boo-ee-zyem]
Cam Ranh Bay [kahm-rahn]
Cao Bang [kow-bahng]
Cao Dai [kow-dye]
Chieu Hoi Program [chyoo-hoy]
Cho Lon [chah-luhn]
Con Thien, *battle of* [kohn-tyen]
Dak To, *battle of* [dahk-toh]
Da Lat [dah-laht]
Da Nang [dah-nahng]
Danh va dam, *strategy of* [dahn vah dahm]
Diem, Ngo Dinh *See* **Ngo Dinh Diem**
Dien Bien Phu, *battle of* [dyen-byen-foo]
doi moi [doy-mye]
Duong Van Minh [zwahng-vahn-meen]
Giap, Vo Nguyen *See* **Vo Nguyen Giap**
Haiphong [hye-fawng]
Hanoi [hah-noy]
Hmong tribe [hmawng]
Ho Chi Minh [hoh-chee-meen]
Hoa Hao [hwah-how]
Hon Me [hahn-may]
Hue [hway]
Khanh, Nguyen *See* **Nguyen Khanh**
Khe Sanh, *battle of* [kay-shahn]
Ky, Nguyen Cao *See* **Nguyen Cao Ky**
Lao Dong [loud-awng]
Le Duan [lay-zwun]
Le Duc Tho [lay-dook-taw]
Le Loi [lay-loy]
Loc Ninh [lok-neen]
Minh Mang [meen-mahng]
Minh, Duong *See* **Duong Van Minh**

Minh, Ho Chi *See* **Ho Chi Minh**
Mu Gia Pass [moo-zah]
My Lai, *village of* [mee-lye]
Nghe An [ngay-ahn]
Ngo Dinh Diem [ngoh-deem-zyem]
Ngo Dinh Kha [ngoh-deen-kah]
Ngo Dinh Nhu [ngoh-deen-nyoo]
Nguyen Ai Quoc [ngwen-eye-kwuck]
Nguyen Cao Ky [ngwen-kow-kee]
Nguyen Chanh Thi [ngwen-chahn-tee]
Nguyen Khanh [ngwen-kahn]
Nguyen Van Thieu [ngwen-vahn-tyew]
Nha Trang [nyah-trahng]
Nhu, Madame [nyoo]
Nhu, Ngo Dinh *See* **Ngo Dinh Nhu**
Pham Van Dong [fahm-vahn-dohng]
Phan Boi Chau [fahn-boy-chow]
Phan Huy Quat [fahn-hwee-kwaht]
Phuoc Long [fook-lawng]
Pleiku [play-koo]
Quang Tri [kwang-tree]
Qui Nhon [kwee-nyahn]
Saigon [shye-gone]
Song Be [shawng-bay]
Tan Son Nhut Airport [tun-shun-nyut]
Tet Offensive [tayt]
Thich Quang Duc [teek-kwahng-dook]
Tran Hung Dao [trun-hung-dow]
Tran Van Huong [trun-vahn-hwahng]
Trieu Au [trew-oh]
Trung Sisters [trung]
Truong Dinh Dzu [trwahng-deen-zoo]
Vang Pao [vahng-pow]
Van Tien Dung [vahn-tyen-zoong]
Vietcong [vyet-kohng]
Viet Minh [vyet-meen]
Vietnam [vyet-nahm]
Vinh [veen]
Vo Nguyen Giap [vaw-ngwen-zahp]
Vung Tau [voong-tow]
Xuan Loc, *battle of* [swun-lok]
Xuan Thuy [swun-twee]
Yen Bay Revolt [ee-yen-bay]

Suggestions for Additional Reading

[This brief list is designed for students and general readers. Those interested in more detailed information on sources may consult the footnotes in this edition, the extensive and comprehensive bibliographies in the previous editions, and the updated bibliography on the *America's Longest War* Web site (www.mhhe.com/herring).]

GENERAL

Surveys of the war abound, each of them offering distinctive perspectives. Among the best are Mark Philip Bradley, *Vietnam at War (2009),* and William S. Turley, *The Second Indochina War: A Concise History* (2008), which focus on Vietnam; Mark Atwood Lawrence, *The Vietnam War: A Concise International History* (2009), which treats the war from a global perspective; and A.J. Langguth, *Our Vietnam: The War 1954–1975)* (2000), a readable and insightful account by a journalist who reported the war. Marilyn Young, *The Vietnam Wars, 1945–1990* (1991), and Robert Schulzinger, *A Time for War* (1997), are also excellent. John Prados, *Vietnam: The History of an Unwinnable War* (2009), is richly detailed and especially good on military matters.

THE FIRST INDOCHINA WAR, 1945-1954

Fredrik Logevall's splendid *Embers of War: The Fall of an Empire and the Origins of America's Vietnam* (2012) is the best introduction to this critical period in Vietnamese history and U.S. foreign policy. A good way to get at the origins of the Viet Minh revolution and the war with France is through the person of Ho Chi Minh. Two first-rate biographies are William

Duiker's magisterial *Ho Chi Minh: A Life* (2000) and the more recent Pierre Brocheux, *Ho Chi Minh: A Biography* (2007). Still useful for military operations are Bernard Fall's classics *Street Without Joy* (1972) and *Hell in a Very Small Place* (1966). A more recent study of the epic battle of Dien Bien Phu is Martin Windrow, *The Last Valley: Dien Bien Phu and the French Defeat in Vietnam* (2004). Among the best recent studies of the origins of U.S. involvement in the First Indochina War are the following: Mark Philip Bradley, *Imagining Vietnam & America: The Making of Postcolonial Vietnam, 1919–1950* (2000), an original and insightful cultural analysis, and Mark Atwood Lawrence, *Assuming the Burden: Europe and the American Commitment in Vietnam* (2005), which introduces an important new element into our understanding of early U.S. involvement. Graham Greene's classic novel *The Quiet American* (1955) is still valuable for the ambience of these years, as is Robert Shaplen's *The Lost Revolution: The U.S. in Vietnam, 1946–1966* (1966).

THE ERA OF NGO DINH DIEM, 1954–1963

Edward Miller, *Misalliance: Ngo Dinh Diem, the United States, and the Fate of South Vietnam* (2013), is a pathbreaking new study that will significantly reshape interpretations of Diem and his era. Seth Jacobs, *America's Miracle Man in Vietnam: Ngo Dinh Diem, Religion, Race, and U.S. Intervention in Southeast Asia* (2004), and *Cold War Mandarin: Ngo Dinh Diem and the Origins of America's War in Vietnam* (2006), emphasize cultural factors in the U.S.–South Vietnam relationship. David Anderson, *Trapped by Success: The Eisenhower Administration and Vietnam, 1953–1961* (1991), is important for early American involvement in South Vietnam, as is Kathryn Stadler, *Replacing France* (2007). Philip E. Catton, *Diem's Final Failure: Prelude to America's War in Vietnam* (2002); James M. Carter, *Inventing Vietnam: The United States and State Building, 1954–1968* (2008); and Mark Moyar, *Triumph Forsaken: The Vietnam War, 1954–1965* (2006), analyze early nation-building efforts in South Vietnam and draw sharply different conclusions. Two essential new studies use Vietnamese sources to explore the origins of the revolution in South Vietnam's crucial Mekong Delta: David W. P. Elliott, *The Vietnamese War: Revolution and Social Change in the Mekong Delta, 1930–1975* (2007), and David Hunt, *Vietnam's Southern Revolution: From Peasant Insurrection to Total War* (2008). Pierre Asselin, *Hanoi's Road to the Vietnam War* (2013), uses important new sources to analyze North Vietnam's major decisions.

   Robert Dallek, *An Unfinished Life: John F. Kennedy, 1917–1963* (2003), is a good place to start for JFK. Andrew Preston, *The War Council: McGeorge Bundy, the NSC, and Vietnam* (2006), analyzes personalities and the policy process in the Kennedy–Johnson years. The best book on Kennedy and Vietnam is Howard Jones, *Death of a Generation: How the Assassinations of Diem and JFK Prolonged the Vietnam War* (2003), a well-researched study that draws generally persuasive conclusions. Fredrik Logevall, *Choosing War: The Lost Chance for Peace and the Escalation of the War in Vietnam* (1999), argues that had Kennedy lived he might have resorted to diplomacy rather than gone to war. For Laos, see Seth Jacobs, *The Universe Unraveling: American Foreign Policy in Cold War Laos* (2012), and William Rust, *Before the Quagmire: American Intervention in Laos, 1954–1961* (2012).

LBJ AND ESCALATION, 1963–1968

Two well-researched, up-to-date biographies of LBJ are Robert Dallek, *Flawed Giant* (2004), and Randall Woods, *LBJ: Architect of American Ambition* (2006), the latter of which gets at the essential Johnson and interprets his Vietnam policies more favorably than most scholars. Logevall, *Choosing War*, is insightful on the 1963–1965 decisions to escalate the war, and Preston, *War Council*, stresses McGeorge Bundy's role. Johnson's phone conversations make fascinating listening and can be accessed through the Web sites of the LBJ Library and the University of Virginia's Miller Center. Edwin Moïse, *Tonkin Gulf and the Escalation of the Vietnam War* (1996), remains the authoritative account of that pivotal event. North Vietnam's decisions for war and the crucial role of Le Duan are skillfully recounted in Lien-Hang T. Nguyen, *Hanoi's War: An International History of the War for Peace in Vietnam* (2012). For the role of Hanoi's allies, see Ilya V. Gaiduk, *The Soviet Union and the Vietnam War* (1996), and Qiang Zhai, *China and the Vietnam Wars, 1950–1975* (2000). A stunningly researched and enormously useful analysis of one of the most important of the numerous peace initiatives is James Hershberg, *MARIGOLD: The Lost Chance for Peace in Vietnam* (2011).

The best analysis of the air war remains Mark Clodfelter, *The Limits of Air Power: The American Bombing of North Vietnam* (1989). An important recent study of the ground war and the frustrating efforts to measure progress is Gregory A. Daddis, *No Sure Victory: Measuring U.S. Army Effectiveness and Progress in the Vietnam War* (2011). For pacification, see Thomas L. Ahern, *Vietnam: Declassified: The CIA and Counterinsurgency* (2010). Jeffrey Record, *The Wrong War: Why We Lost in Vietnam* (1998), persuasively rebuts those who claim the United States did not use its power decisively, concluding that America's failure derived more fundamentally from its misunderstanding of the nature of the war, its underestimation of the enemy, and its overestimation of its own political staying power and military prowess.

Joseph A. Fry, *Debating Vietnam: Fulbright, Stennis, and Their Senate Hearings* (2008), and Andrew L. Johns, *Vietnam's Second Front: Domestic Politics, the*

Republican Party, and the War (2010), are important recent studies seeking to get at the role of Congress. The most astute analysis of public opinion remains John Mueller, *War, Presidents, and Public Opinion* (1976), which compares the wars in Korea and Vietnam, with interesting results. For the antiwar movement, the classic account is Charles DeBenedetti and Charles Chatfield, *An American Ordeal: The Antiwar Movement of the Vietnam Era* (1990). See also Terry H. Anderson, *The Movement and the Sixties* (1995), and Melvin Small, *Antiwarriors: The Battle for American Hearts and Minds* (2002) .

One of the biggest remaining gaps in the literature is South Vietnam. An important monograph is Robert A. Brigham, *ARVN: Life and Death in the South Vietnamese Army* (2006).

The war produced a voluminous and distinguished personal literature. Christian G. Appy, *Working Class War* (1993), and Kyle Longley, *Grunts: The American Combat Experience in Vietnam* (2007), are excellent scholarly introductions to the GI experience. Longley's *The House of the Purple Hearts: The Morenci Marines and Small Town America in the Shadows of the Vietnam War* (2013) is a compelling account of the impact of the war. Tim O'Brien, *The Things They Carried* (1990), is an insightful novel and can be instructively compared with the more "hawkish" James Webb, *Fields of Fire* (1978), and Bao Ninh, *The Horror of War* (1991), which tells of the experience of a North Vietnamese soldier. Harold G. Moore and Joseph L. Galloway, *We Were Soldiers Once . . . and Young* (1992), is a first-rate remembrance of the November 1965 battle of the Ia Drang Valley. Carol Reardon, *Launch the Intruders* (2009), provides the pilots' view of the 1972 LINEBACKER bombing campaign.

For the Tet Offensive, Don Oberdorfer's classic *Tet!* (1971) remains valuable. It can be supplemented with the more recent James H. Willbanks, *The Tet Offensive: A Concise History* (2001), and David F. Schmitz, *The Tet Offensive: Politics, War, and Public Opinion* (2005), especially good on the U.S. domestic response to Tet. William M. Hammond, *Reporting Vietnam: Media and Military at War* (1998), is a valuable analysis of that important topic. Ronald H. Spector, *After Tet: The Bloodiest Year in Vietnam* (1993), provides an excellent military history of this important period. For the horrors of My Lai, see Michael Bilton, *Four Hours at My Lai* (1992), and David L. Anderson, ed., *Facing My Lai: Moving beyond the Massacre* (1994). Nick Turse, *Kill Anything That Moves: The Real American War in Vietnam* (2013), is a searing indictment arguing that My Lai was typical, not an aberration.

NIXON, KISSINGER, AND THE END OF THE WAR

Robert Dallek, *Nixon and Kissinger: Partners in Power* (2007), is a valuable dual biography. Jeffrey Kimball, *Nixon's Vietnam War* (1998), remains the best study of that subject, although the availability of new documentation makes it a candidate for updating. Melvin Small, *The Presidency of Richard Nixon* (1999), is a fine analysis of the Nixon presidency, and William Bundy, *A Tangled Web: The Making of Foreign Policy in the Nixon Presidency* (1998), is a valuable study of the Nixon foreign policy, produced by one of Johnson's key Vietnam advisers. Monographs are few and far between. Among the best are Stephen P. Randolph, *Powerful and Brutal Weapons: Nixon, Kissinger and the Easter Offensive* (2007), and Michael J. Allen, *Until the Last Man Comes Home: POWs, MIAs, and the Unending Vietnam War* (2009). Kenton Clymer, *Troubled Relations: The United States and Cambodia Since 1870* (2007), treats that subject in broad perspective. Pierre Asselin, *A Bitter Peace: Washington, Hanoi, and the Making of the Paris Agreement* (2002), and Nguyen, *War for Peace*, are excellent on the complexities of the 1973 Paris agreements. Lewis Sorley, *A Better War: The Unexamined Victories and Final Tragedy of America's Last Years in Vietnam* (1999), overstates the military gains during General Creighton Abrams's time in Vietnam and, as Nixon and Kissinger hoped historians would do, blames Congress for America's defeat. John Prados, *Inside the Pentagon Papers* (2005), is an essential introduction to that important topic.

AFTERMATH AND LEGACIES

James H. Willbanks, *Abandoning Vietnam: How America Left and South Vietnam Lost Its War* (2004), is good on the postwar war and the fall of South Vietnam. George J. Veith, *Black April: The Fall of South Vietnam* (2012), is the most recent account. Books exploring the various legacies of the war include Arnold R. Isaacs, *Vietnam Shadows: The War, Its Ghosts, and Its Legacy* (1997); Charles E. Neu, ed., *After Vietnam: Legacies of a Lost War* (2000); and more recently Robert D. Schulzinger, *A Time for Peace: The Legacy of the Vietnam War* (2006). David Hagopian, *The Vietnam War in American Memory: Veterans, Memorials, and the Politics of Healing* (2009), is superb on how the memorialization of the war has reflected American efforts to come to terms with it.

Index